Ask for the Ancient Paths

ASK FOR THE ANCIENT PATHS

From Art to Artifice to Arisen

James Venezia

The Christian Exceptionalism in Counseling Series™

EXULTANTIS PRESS

NEW YORK

Ask for the Ancient Paths: From Art to Artifice to Arisen. Copyright TXu 1-944-558 © 2015 by James Venezia

The Christian Exceptionalism in Counseling Series™. Trademark 2015 by James Venezia

Published by EXULTANTIS PRESS, NEW YORK

All rights reserved, including the right to reproduce this book or portions thereof in any form whatsoever.

Available through the CreateSpace eStore and through Amazon.com:
ISBN 978-0-9961181-3-2

Unless otherwise noted, Scripture taken from the HOLY BIBLE, NEW INTERNATIONAL VERSION ®. Copyright © 1973, 1978, 1984 by International Bible Society. Used by permission of Zondervan. All rights reserved.

The author can be contacted at jamesvenezia@yahoo.com.

Second edition, 2016

Cover picture: *The Blind Man's Bluff Game*, Jean-Honore Fragonard, 1751

Printed in the United States of America

his is what the LORD says: 'Stand at the crossroads and look; *ask for the ancient paths*, ask where the good way is, and walk in it, and you will find rest for your souls…'" (Jeremiah 6:16, emphasis added)

THE CHRISTIAN EXCEPTIONALISM IN COUNSELING SERIES™

Welcome, dear reader, to *The Christian Exceptionalism in Counseling Series™*. This material is written to be accessible to both the neophyte as well as to the counseling aficionado. The first book in the series, *Ask for the Ancient Paths: From Art to Artifice to Arisen*, serves as a comprehensive introduction to biblical counseling. It is written as an overview of the Bible's creation-fall-redemption paradigm. The second book, *What Agreement Is There Between the Temple of God and Idols?: The Accidence of Sin and Idolatry*, explores sin and idolatry so as to eradicate it. The third book, *The Days of Reckoning Are at Hand: From Fig Leaf to Olive Branch to Laurel Wreath*, focuses on application in which one will find a more in-depth handling of diagnosis, as well as analysis of pressing topics such as suffering and loneliness.

My hope is that these books will not serve to merely inform, but rather will implement God's work of change in those he claims as his own. If you are already a Christian (one personally saved through Jesus' death upon the cross) then this series will advance God's sanctifying work in, and through, you. If you are not yet a believer then this series functions as an apologetic persuasion. The hope is that through this material you will see the unfathomable power of Christ-centered counseling, and in response find new life in him.

Wedding Procession, Gustave Brion, 1873

Ask for the Ancient Paths: From Art to Artifice to Arisen

Chapters

1. The Exordium to Biblical Counseling
2. The Counseling Ambition
3. The Centrality of Scripture in Counseling
4. The Gospel as Inception Point: From Immorality to Immortality
5. Redefining the Pygmalion Effect: Exploring the Image of God in Man
6. Man Before the Face of God: The Imperium of the Psyche
7. The Needs Imperative
8. What Has Jerusalem To Do With Vienna?: The Case Against Psychology
9. Integrationism: The Modern Day Babylonian Captivity
10. The Third-Way of Sanctification: From Abominable to Indomitable

Appendix: A Sanctification Plan

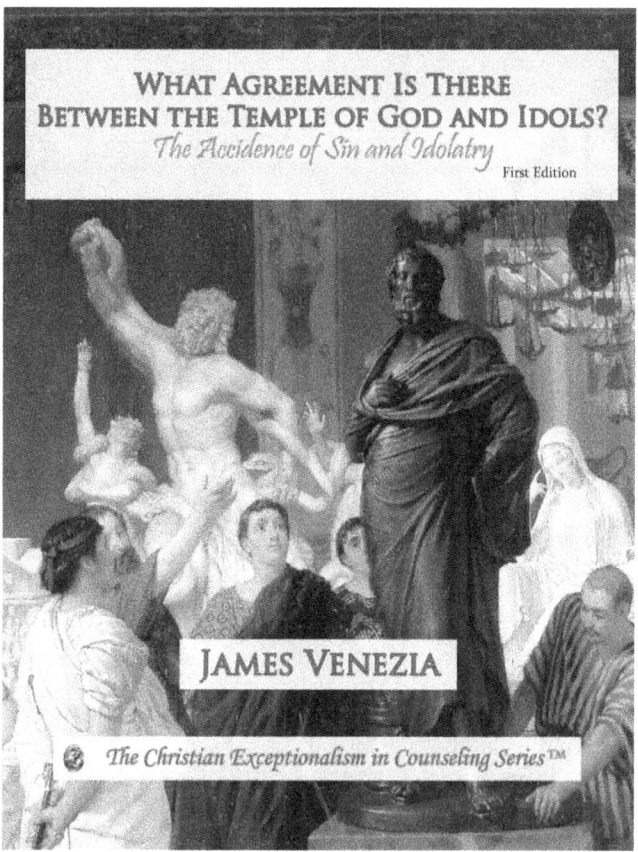

*What Agreement Is There Between the Temple of God and Idols?:
The Accidence of Sin and Idolatry*

Chapters:

1. Deliver Us from Evil

2. The World, the Flesh, and the Devil: Assessing the Threat Matrix

3. Total Depravity: This Imperiled Arcadia

4. Hamartiology: Sin in All Its Ignobility

5. Metaphors for Sin

6. Uncovering Idols of the Heart: Make Us Gods to Go Before Us

7. The Idolatry Doppler Shift

8. The Search for Eldorado Ends: Repenting of Idols of the Heart

9. Marauding Visigoths: The Autocratic Self

10. A Nouthetic Analysis of Moses

Appendix: The Demon Possession Case Study

The Days of Reckoning Are at Hand: From Fig Leaf to Olive Branch to Laurel Wreath

Chapters:

1. Memories Preserved in Amber: Adopting God's Retrospective

2. Suffering: The Kintsugi Objective

3. The Hobgoblin in the Inglenook: Assessing Loneliness

4. The Umbilicus of Personal Relationship with Christ

5. Navigating the Counseling Fjord: Preliminary Reconnaissance

6. The Basic Plotlines Which Emerge in Counseling

7. Artisanal Counseling: A Foray into Methods

8. Diagnosis: Vanishing Secrets

9. Emerging from the Chrysalis: Issues the Counselor Observes and Seeks to Change

10. Counseling and the Church: Syndicating the Vision

Also by the Author

*The Lord Kept Vigil That Night:
An Exposition of the Parable of the Lost
Son*

*Rescue Us from the Present Evil Age: Array
of Hope*

*Hurl All Our Iniquities
into the Depths of the Sea*

Contents

Preface xix

Acknowledgments xxix

Introduction 1

Section I

A Precious Cornerstone for a Sure Foundation

1. The Exordium to Biblical Counseling 9

The Currency of Counseling	9
Taking Jesus Hostage to Perceived Needs	10
The Grand Equation	13
Biblical Counseling's Core Principles	15
How Does Biblical Counseling Dovetail with the Larger Christian Message?	18
Select Truths about Biblical Counseling	20

2. The Counseling Ambition 23

Counseling in a Postmodern World	23
An Apologetic for Counseling	24
Counseling as a New Set of Lenses (as a Presuppositional Endeavor)	27
The Counseling Mission	29
Counseling as Serving the Goal of Sanctification	30
Counseling Permeates Our World	35
Counseling Statements in Everyday Life	37
The Manifest Qualities of a Counselor	40
The Question of Judgment	42

3. The Centrality of Scripture in Counseling 57

Introduction	57
The Danger of Deconstructist Reading	58
The Truth Cannot Co-exist with Human Systems of Thought	60
Presenting Truth, Refuting Error	61
Interpreting the Bible	63

The Bible Speaks to the Plenary Human Condition....................	65
Toward a Sound Doctrine of Scripture...	68
Beyond the Informative: Scripture as Formative Reading.............	69
Two Tragedies: Neglect and Misuse...	73

4. THE GOSPEL AS INCEPTION POINT:

From Immorality to Immortality **77**

"He Who Would Teach Men to Die Would Teach Them to Live"......	77
Being a Christian is NOT...	78
Jesus Would Rather Die for Us than Live Without Us....................	85
Case Study: The World's Exploitation of Jesus..............................	93
Two Aspects to Repentance...	95
Salvation: An Earthshaking Event...	96
A Personal Application of the Gospel..	98
Marks of a Christian..	100
The Transformative Power of Forgiveness......................................	102
Case Study: The Ultimate Refutation of Evolution.........................	105
Conclusion..	107

SECTION II

A LITTLE LOWER THAN THE ANGELS: *Human Design*

5. REDEFINING THE PYGMALION EFFECT:

Exploring the Image of God in Man **111**

"Is Man an Ape or an Angel?"...	111
The Fundamental Human Condition..	112
The Archimedean Point of Man's Design..	114
The Image of God: Man as Analogue...	116
The Image of God: Prophet, Priest, and King..................................	119
The Marvel of Image-Bearing...	125
Image and Likeness: Retention and Loss..	127
Mankind as Designed to Worship..	130
Mankind as Covenant Maker..	133
The Intellect as Manifestation of the Image of God........................	134
Excursus: Intelligence versus Wisdom..	137
Fixed Design Elements: Submission to God's Plan........................	139

False Humility	144
Drawing God's Design into Focus	145
"I'm a Nightmare Dressed like a Daydream": The Quest for Flawless Beauty	146
Does the Bible Distinguish Between Heart, Mind, Soul, Spirit, and Will?	148
The Center Point Theory of Design	150
The Image of God and Gender	154

6. MAN BEFORE THE FACE OF GOD:

The Imperium of the Psyche 163

The Curse upon Creation	163
Suppression of the Truth	164
The Conscience as General Revelation	169
The Contours of the Conscience	171
Life Lived With Regard to God: The *Coram Deo* Concept	173
The *Coram Deo* Concept and the Issue of Emotions	176
Case Study: Anger: Shedding Light on the Heat	178
The Image of God and the Contours of Fear	180
The Dynamics of Fear	181
Excursus: Chinese Music and the Issue of Fear	192

SECTION III

EAST OF EDEN: *The Effects of the Fall*

7. THE NEEDS IMPERATIVE 197

A Solar System of Unsynchronized Orbits	197
The Proliferation of Perceived Need	198
Need as Infinite Abyss	201
The Embattled Quest to Meet Needs	202
Case Study: Is Sexuality an Inherent Need as Part of Human Design?	204
Excursus: The Rise of Media-Generated Need	205
Excursus: Eight Perceived Human Needs and How Advertising Exploits Them	206
Excursus: Advertising Methods in the Exploitation of Needs	209
The Only Legitimate Need: Relationship with Jesus Christ	211

8. WHAT HAS JERUSALEM TO DO WITH VIENNA?: *The Case Against Psychology* 215

Setting the Stage for Secular Thought 215
The Gang of Six: Influences on the Growth
    and Development of Psychology 216
A Presuppositional Approach to Secular Thought 218
The Agenda Behind Supposed Science 220
Psychology as Purported Science 222
The Paradigm Shift: Upending Psychology's Hegemony ... 224
Should Christianity Engage Psychology in Debate? 227
Psychology as Competing Religion 230
The Religious Components of Select Philosophies 231
Psychology's Chief Purpose 235
Infiltrating the "Normal" 237
Excursus: Psychology Reads Like a Hollywood Movie Script ... 239
The Mimicry of the Kleptoparasite 240
Psychology and Evolution 242
The Art of Deception 243
Psychology's Labels 246
Select Psychology Concepts 249
Psychology's Tetrad Sophistry 253
Psychology as Intractably Balkanized 266
Psychology as Distorting Doppelganger:
    A Comparison of Psychology Terms and Bible Concepts ... 267
Insanity's Inception 274
The Hydraulic View of Emotions 277
Excursus: Psychology May Foster the Love of Money 278
Psychology Holds Forth No Hope of Cure 280
Maintaining the Hegemony 281
Case Study: Analysis of the Columbine Shooting 282
Reductionism 285
Understanding Addiction 291
Excursus: Identical Twins Studies 293
The Legalized Drug Cartel 294
Case Study: Ritalin® 299
Psychotropic Drugs and Counseling 300
The Cure of Souls: Revisiting Ockham's Razor 301

9. INTEGRATIONISM: *The Modern Day Babylonian Captivity* 305

Introduction	305
The Plunder of the Church	306
The Church's Psychology Affliction	307
The Abandoned Birthright	311
Integrationism: A Cunning Snare	313
Integrationism as Unholy Fire	316
Integrationism as Akin to Balaam's Error	317
The Call to Purgative Measures	320

SECTION IV

REDEMPTION

10. THE THIRD-WAY OF SANCTIFICATION:
From Abominable to Indomitable **325**

Echoes from Eden	325
The Creation-Fall-Redemption Model Revisited	327
Resolving the Sin Rorschach	329
Sanctification as Purification of the Firstfruits	331
The "Over-Plus" of Christ	334
The Sanctification Pentagon	335
In Sanctification Who Speaks, Who Decides?	350
Case Study: The Refusal to Rest	351
The Third-Way of Sanctification	353
Excursus: First Corinthians 13:1–12	360
Excursus: The Beatitudes	361
Sanctification Cultivates Heart Elasticity	364
The Sanctified Heart's "Patchwork"	366
The Dynamics of Sanctification: "From Menace into Muse and Muse into Wisdom"	368
The Bible's Metaphors for Sanctification	373
The Sanctification Shell-Game	381
The Allure of Caring Pragmatism: "Solutions Are Not the Answer"	383
Extracting Sanctification's Treasure	387

EPILOGUE **389**

APPENDIX: A SANCTIFICATION PLAN **391**

THE AUTHOR.. 401

PREFACE

One sunny Saturday afternoon when I was about seven years old my parents and I drove along a busy thoroughfare somewhere on the east side of Manhattan. The light ahead turned red and we came to a halt. A car pulled up next to us, a nondescript middle-aged man at the wheel. He motioned for us to lower the window, which my father promptly did. At that point the man began sharing his life-story. As our cars idled, the man spoke of his many troubles in the course of what was probably a ninety-second stoplight. My parents and I sat rapped in silent disbelief, too shocked to say a word, too intrigued to put the window back up. I can't remember the details, but I recall the man mentioning that his wife had left him and something about his life falling apart. The light turned green and, without so much as the blink of an eye, the cars bolted forward into the traffic ahead. We each let out a nervous chuckle with the frequently repeated statement, "only in New York."

New York, Winter Scene in Broadway, Hippolyte Victor Valentin Sebron, c. 1857

That motorist created an impromptu counseling session for himself at a bustling Manhattan intersection. He shared his life-story with complete strangers in the interval between green lights as if he were lying comfortably on a psychiatrist's couch. Something about that scene remains etched in my memory, something which launches this work. Occasionally I have prayed for that man. I wonder if he ever found help and hope. Did another idling motorist finally offer a word to sustain the weary, some balm for a wayward soul?[1] Did he ever find the Savior at some cross-street in Gotham's bosom?

That undistinguished New Yorker is the Everyman desperate for counsel, and willing to seek it out in the most peculiar places, among the most unsuspecting people. While that man's unction was quite unique, he is not altogether different from people everywhere who long to share their lives with someone, to know that someone hears, that a conscious sentient being records their pain and plight. Case in point, at the time of writing this text I live in a high-rise apartment building. Most days I use the elevator in which I sometimes encounter another resident. In the course of that twenty-five second trip there is occasionally an impromptu counseling session which arises. Maybe it's a caution about the impending cold weather, the drudgery of a long day at work, the inconvenience of the previous evening's power outage, or a plan to lose weight. It seems that often people have something to share even in that brief encounter, something they want healed. They seem to crave a captive audience, if even for a few moments.

This counseling series is written for any person, from any cultural background, facing any life situation, that each would find lifesaving and eternally impactful counsel. But the good news does not stop there, as those changed by Christ are equipped to in turn help others change. This work is therefore part of fulfilling the Great Commission,[2] Jesus' command that his followers would not just bring his gospel to the ends of the earth, but make disciples. This series is my contribution to that discipleship building effort.

May This Material Be a Friend to You

Yesterday I strolled through a local Barnes & Noble® bookstore simply observing people in the midst of this wonderland of word and image. A man with thick glasses crouched down, riveted to a physics textbook, a mother and her toddler sat on the floor flipping through a story book, a young woman with earbuds casually perused romance novels. As I watched these accidental explorers, I marveled at the wealth of information in one location, a veritable library of Alexandria resurrected on Route 17 South. Consider the mental exertion and eye strain that went into researching, writing, and producing each of those books, and the concomitant exertion and strain to read them. In the midst of that maelstrom of human potentiality and energy, I couldn't help but muse, "Did those readers each find a book that 'loves' them?" Will they find comforting friendship in those flimsy pages? Will they find plate-armor wisdom and blazing hope behind those glossy covers?

---

[1] Isaiah 50:4
[2] Matthew 28:19

"Write a book that loves your readers." That was the advice of dear friend and wise counselor, David Covington, when I mentioned my efforts to produce this book. I have pondered this carefully. As David and others have taught me, there could be no greater model for loving one's reader than the Bible itself. What is the nature of the Bible's love for its reader? The Bible confronts the heart with engaging story. Its storytelling takes its time (except possibly in the book of Mark) because that storytelling is an invitation to enter the presence of a holy God. It is in this sense that reading the Bible is an experience outside of time. Its story offers enough detail to allow the reader to enter into its worldview while not overwhelming him with superfluous items. It rarely presents bald abstraction, but nestles that abstraction into a comprehensive view of personhood, history, and life. The Bible is never gratuitous but remains resolute upon a singular purpose - building relationship between the reader and God himself. It is stories about God saving people, those stories themselves saving the reader.

May Morning on Magdalen Tower, William Holman Hunt, 1890

The Bible regales its readers with imbedded literary jewels; it lights up the imagination; it shocks the senses. It creates light moments of reflection and impassioned pleas to repentance. It comforts with restful swaying advice, implores with pressing confrontation, and finally effects conciliation between man and God with a salvific meta-narrative. With the Bible as my model, I have attempted, to the extent of my ability, to love my readers as the author of the Bible does.

With that in mind, this book is not read as one might read other books – to gain mere knowledge. Shadowing the Bible's own intent and approach, this book seeks to initiate or strengthen an *encounter* with the living God, to set up a rendezvous with Jesus Christ. For this reason, those who hunger and thirst for righteousness will love it;[3] while those who love the deeds of darkness will dispense with it in disgust.[4]

A Polymath's Approach

In light of the eternally impactful and masterful work produced by my former teachers Dr. David Powlison, Dr. Edward Welch, and Dr. Paul Tripp, as well as by Dr. Jay Adams (under whom I did not formally study), what more can be said which they have not already said with eloquence and persuasive conviction?

Allow me to introduce two weight training terms, "muscle memory" and "muscle confusion." Muscle memory is the way in which muscle, through repeated use, develops an autonomic response so that the mind no longer needs to actually command the muscle to act; it simply acts out of habit. Conversely, muscle confusion is the continual introduction of new motion so that muscle must be actively commanded.

While muscle memory has value for developing athletic precision, it can induce a plateauing effect in which the body no longer improves its proprioception nor builds muscle. The body grows complacent in functioning as it always has. Muscle confusion is necessary to build greater coordination and muscle mass. As muscle does not know what to expect next, it cannot fall into complacency. Thus, athletic trainers seek to build a measure of muscle memory (to perfect a particular skill) while periodically introducing muscle confusion (to keep the body in a state of kinematic progress).

I use this analogy to explain something of my approach in this book. Just as the body benefits from both muscle memory and muscle confusion, so too, any field of study benefits from a similar interplay of memory and confusion. In this context, the "memory" is tenacious adherence to sound biblical doctrine. The "confusion" is not confusion at all but merely a healthy dose of the unexpected, a certain cut across the grain to see the topic from a new slant, to set it against a striking vista.

For many years one of my dreams has been to expand biblical counseling's topical reach, to lend it a polymath's touch. I have labored to develop a full-orbed text which takes in various topics not usually covered in counseling, such as history, literature, science, art, and economics (among other topics). I have sought to sketch out a "total

---

[3] Matthew 5:6
[4] John 3:19

truth" approach to counseling, recognizing that the human experience is a highly-varied one. Additionally, the modern world impacts the psyche in myriad ways like various landscapes of media, technology, economics, politics, and science. The counselor should prepare himself with an intimate knowledge of the impact of those landscapes. Thus, in short, I have sought to offer a more panoramic view than is traditionally found in counseling texts, to eschew a parochial handling, and to avoid a kind of *deformation professionnelle* that may characterize the counseling endeavor.

It is with a spirit of humility that I seek to contribute something original, something unexpected, a varied hue, to this field. While I have labored to offer a distinctive presentation, I have tenaciously held to sound biblical doctrine. Thus, this work is simultaneously something of a distillation of, and extrapolation upon, biblical counseling. I pray that my frequent tangents and inserted artwork do not distract but rather serve as a welcomed reprieve, a moment of reflective discovery, a treat for the imagination, and an opportunity to think outside of expected channels. I have tried to have some fun with this topic, and hope you will too.

> This series does not merely shine a light; it seeks to draw out the constituents of light so that the full visible spectrum is considered.[5]

The Dedication to a Life's Work

As a teenager I traveled to Florence, Italy where I visited the Cathedral of Florence, on the Piazza del Duomo. On the eastern face of the cathedral's baptistery, one finds massive bronze doors some five meters tall. Those doors, titled the "Gates of Paradise" by Michelangelo (1475-1564), depict various Bible scenes, each panel a thrilling work of art in its own right. Our tour guide pointed out that the artist, Lorenzo Ghiberti (1378-1455), spent twenty-seven years sculpting those doors (and a total of fifty years sculpting four doors). I marveled at the dedication required to remain committed to a single task for that long. I imagined a slight sinewy man meticulously chiseling wooden molds in blazing sun and chilling snow, not daring to stop until his work was perfected. After all, these were not just any bronze doors, but those to welcome visitors into the house of God.

It took courage for Ghiberti to devote twenty-seven years to those doors. They could have been smashed in an earthquake, pillaged by marauding brigands, or melted down into swords (to protect the city against said brigands). They could have been desecrated or lost in the sands of time. Devoting one's life to casting bronze is a risky investment.

In the spirit of Lorenzo Ghiberti's dedication, this book series is likewise the

---

[5] This idea borrowed from David Powlison, Westminster Theological Seminary, Philadelphia, Pennsylvania

culmination of some twenty years of thought and study, counseling and being counseled, learning from wise teachers, and sitting at the feet of Christ in humble supplication. These books serve as a marker of, and monument to, my personal sanctification, that which Christ has willed and worked in and through me.[6] I pray that you, the reader, will benefit richly from what you encounter here. May you profoundly enjoy these books as they invite the Holy Spirit to breathe life into you. May they be a treasured counselor in the midst of life's vagary and vicissitudes. May you discover Jesus, either again or for the first time, as sovereign, as intimate ally, as first love.

Just as Ghiberti cast bronze doors for the entrance to God's house, these books serve as a kind of portal into the soul, that flesh-and-blood people would be transformed into living temples in which God himself dwells.[7] Ghiberti rendered the Bible's narrative in bronze, raised up for all to see. May that narrative serve its stated purpose, to be chiseled into hearts, that they would be recast as effulgent chambers where Christ himself reigns victorious. And while bronzes are susceptible to plundering marauders, no one may snatch God's people out of his hand;[8] his work will stand. Devoting one's life to casting hearts is an eternal investment.

A Young Girl Reading
Jean-Honore Fragonard, c. 1776

A Word of Advice

> "Some books are to be tasted, others to be swallowed, and some few to be chewed and digested." (Francis Bacon)

Birthed in Rome, Italy in 1986 to retard the proliferation of fast food, the Slow Movement not only encourages slower eating but savoring the arts, culture, and family life. My hope is that, in this frenetic technology-infused zoetrope we call modern civilization, readers will take the time to read slowly and carefully, to savor thinking, to pause for prayerful

---

[6] Philippians 2:13
[7] 1 Corinthians 3:16
[8] John 10:28, 29

consideration, to weigh in a cosmic balance the methods and motives of life, to often enjoy playful flights of fantasy, to revel in the image of God within oneself and others, to take seriously the call to daily repentance, and to ultimately let the Bible's message of salvation through Jesus Christ marinate into, percolate through, and infiltrate one's soul.

> "Men occasionally stumble over the truth, but most of them pick themselves up, dust themselves off, and hurry away as if nothing happened." (Winston Churchill)

In reading *Ask for the Ancient Paths* please keep the Bible at your side. It is crucial that this text be seen as building upon the foundation of Scripture. The better the reader knows Scripture, and the more closely he reads Scripture in conjunction with this text, the richer and more vivid this counseling model will become.

One may notice frequent sections throughout the book labeled "case study" and "excursus." What is the difference? A case study is so denoted because, following the natural trajectory of the chapter, it offers an opportunity for deeper study and reflection. An excursus is similar except that it is more tangential. It may be a cultural, historical, literary, artistic, or scientific reference which is fascinating to consider but not as directly relevant. Thus, an excursus offers a rest-stop in which to exercise the imagination.

> While I encourage the reader to study all three books in *The Christian Exceptionalism in Counseling Series*™, each book is designed as a stand-alone unit, and most of the constituent chapters are, to some degree, stand-alone. The reason is that each topic is positioned on a tripod of the Bible's creation-fall-redemption paradigm.[9]

Finally, I have included over 400 pieces of classical artwork throughout the entire series. This art is intended to more persuasively marshal the imagination, to offer the mind a reprieve from propositional truths, to extend the delight of magnificent fare. In most instances, the art is simply a creative augmentation to the topic at hand. If a painting helps expand one's grasp of the concept, then it has served this work's purpose.[10] But please don't allow style to overwhelm substance.

> "'What is the use of a book,' thought Alice, 'without pictures or conversations?'" (*Alice in Wonderland*, Lewis Carroll)

---

[9] This I describe as the fractal method of counseling in the third book in this series, *The Days of Reckoning Are at Hand: From Fig Leaf to Olive Branch to Laurel Wreath*, chapter 7: "Artisanal Counseling: A Foray into Methods."
[10] Please note that nearly all the artwork included in these books could be classified as "classical." On occasion, classical artwork contains nudity. While that nudity is never gratuitous, where it is conspicuous, it has been discretely covered so as to maintain the book's modesty. This covering is not an attempt to alter the painting, but simply to guard those readers who might otherwise be tempted to sin.

Isaac Newton (1642–1726) humbly stated, "If I have seen farther than others it is because I stand on the shoulders of giants." This presentation stands on the shoulders of the Christian Counseling and Education Foundation (CCEF) in Willow Grove, Pennsylvania. This is my contribution, and I hope, my gift to the biblical counseling movement which serves Jesus Christ so faithfully. In all essentials of the faith my thinking aligns precisely with CCEF, not out of blind compliance, but out of sincere conviction. This work, like theirs, is triumphantly gospel-centered to its core.

Spotlight on the Second Edition

The first edition of *The Christian Exceptionalism in Counseling Series*™ was officially launched on June 20, 2015. Since that time, myriad edits, updates, and additions have been applied. ("…Of writing many books there is no end…"[11]) As stated previously, reading this material is, to the extent that it accords with Scripture, an encounter with the person of Jesus Christ, not just knowledge about him, but to be confronted and searched by him. In this sense, this material is not so much informative as it is formative.

In the course of this work's advance, at crucial junctures, there have been pronounced spiritual attacks. Yet, despite the setbacks, an invisible hand presses this work forward. With each seemingly insurmountable obstacle, an unanticipated breakthrough emerges. The sense of God himself prospering this work, and seeking to bring it to fruitful completion, has invested me with a towering Christ-centered confidence, an indomitable perseverance, and an unspeakable joy in the final result.

As a side note, it has been an intriguing case study to observe reactions to this work over the past several months. It would appear that this material functions like a prism clarifying those who desire to know, and be known, by Christ. I can only surmise that with each turn of the page Jesus' own winnowing fork is at the threshing floor, an axe to the root of the heart, the disentangling of faith from apostasy. May he will and work to further his kingdom in each who encounter this series.

Please contact the author at jamesvenezia@yahoo.com with questions or comments on this series.

Like Sherlock Holmes it is time to don the deerstalker hat and insert the meerschaum pipe to investigate the psyche!

S. D. G.
January 20, 2016

---

[11] Ecclesiastes 12:12

"Commit to the Lord whatever you do, and your plans will succeed." (Proverbs 16:3)

ACKNOWLEDGMENTS

*T*hank you to my parents, Peter and Jo-Ann, for providing me with the opportunity and encouragement to write. They have read more of my writing than anyone I know and have taught me a great deal about the perseverance and discipline required to complete such a task. My father also proofread a considerable quantity of this text. I am grateful for his assistance.

Thank you to many Christ-centered teachers for their priceless mentoring and instruction. Their voices echo throughout this book series because they echo throughout my faith. They each, in distinctive ways, have continually reintroduced me to Jesus through, not just their formal instruction, but in their daily experience of knowing, and being know by, Jesus. Their collective counsel serves as a perennial corrective, encouragement, and scriptural realignment to my heart.

> "Never trust a scholar who won't tell you who his teachers were." (Aristotle)

After the Audience (Agrippa)
Lawrence Alma Tadema, 1879

This book series is a celebration of Jesus' work in and through Westminster Theological Seminary. Westminster set me on the right path early in life, a path that continues to lead me into ever richer experiences of Christ. With warm gratitude, I thank Westminster for its care for my soul and for the abundant harvest it has produced in and through so many.

INTRODUCTION

The George Washington Window, Nicola D'Ascenzo, d. 1954[1]

The Case for Christian Exceptionalism in Counseling

American Exceptionalism refers to the fact that the United States is the first nation in history in which the individual was the focus and purpose of governance, that for the first time people no longer lived under a centralized tyrannical government. This is the miracle of the American republic which has brought a cascade of liberty to the entire world. In considering this, I had an epiphany. There is a far greater form of exceptionalism which entered the world some 1,800 years before America was founded. That exceptionalism emerged with the incarnation of Jesus Christ.

Faith in Jesus Christ is the great human liberator, the renaissance of the empowered and rehabilitated human spirit. Thus, Jesus was, and still is, the belvedere of earthly emancipation from every possible aspect. It is through faith in Jesus that modern science emerged, that democracy and capitalism took shape and found fertile ground, that slaves were freed, that classic literature was penned, and that universal education was birthed. While I celebrate the towering achievement of American Exceptionalism, there would be no such thing without a vastly greater force, that of Christian Exceptionalism. This text is written as a soaring flight of triumph in a God who

---

[1] Photo by Laura Pearson, reproduced with permission of the Washington Memorial Chapel, Valley Forge, Pennsylvania

liberates captives, not just from flesh-and-blood tyrants but from the tyrant of themselves. That is the incomparable gift of Jesus on the cross.

This Christian Exceptionalism is built upon an axiomatic truth, only the Bible understands how people work, how the circuitry is routed, how the gears turn, how the levers pivot. Only the Bible understands the ghost in the machine, the psyche's esprit hidden within the somatic. The secret to the Bible's understanding is that that ghost is not a neutral phantom but an engaged spirit responding to the God who is there. The human spirit is only understood in the context of an eternal God who daily interfaces with it. Therefore, the Bible reveals that with every breath, with every thought, with every word, mankind finds himself before the face of a God with whom he is estranged, yet by whom he is lavishly courted. Only the Bible understands the psyche's intricate mechanism; only it deciphers the human spirit's hidden code.

A wise teacher once told me the Bible is fundamentally about two things, introducing Jesus as savior and changing the human heart with that truth. Thus, I might summarize this book's entire mission as making Jesus Savior and Lord within the hearts of those he claims for himself. Jesus as Savior is the promise of eternal life. Jesus as Lord is allowing him to sanctify, and have supremacy within, those belonging to him. The hope is that those who read this book will know Jesus as both Savior and Lord. Thus, as I study Scripture I ask myself, "What does this pericope teach me about Jesus as Savior, and how does it change my heart to desire him as Lord?" That is the import of biblical counseling in a nutshell.

To my surprise, many Christians harbor strong prejudice with regard to biblical counseling. They often assume that this implies a professional model requiring intense formal study, heavily based on secular psychology. They are skittish about counseling because they kowtow to a cultural expectation that only medical professionals can delve into such matters, and any attempt by laypeople to do so only opens them to potential litigation or social chastisement. Some of the criticisms I have heard of biblical counseling are:

1. Counseling is the rightful provenance of trained medical professionals.

2. Counseling is an implicit attack upon traditional theology.

3. Counseling is merely a worldly attempt to meet people's perceived needs.

4. Counseling is an accommodation to immature and childish Christians who have not yet grown up in the faith.

5. All that is needed for sanctification is to memorize and quote Scripture.

6. Counseling is nothing more than a frivolous hobby for gossiping coffee-klatch housewives.

These prejudices expose a tragic state of affairs for a church which has sold its birthright out of blind compliance to, and fear of, the world system. It is also quite regrettable that the church has been poisoned by specious forms of counseling which siphon off its vitality in the cure of souls.

While the church is often timorous vis-à-vis the term "counseling," there is absolutely nothing in the term itself which is counter-Scriptural. In fact, the Bible speaks in rich detail about the counsel which God offers his people and the counsel which they, in turn, are to extend to one another. In Isaiah 9:6, Jesus himself is prophetically described as "Wonderful Counselor" and, in John 16:7, the Holy Spirit is described as the "Advocate" (also translated "Counselor"). In effect, the entire Bible is counsel, and all of God's work in believers' lives is counsel of one form or another.

> "He is the one we proclaim, admonishing and teaching everyone with all wisdom, so that we may present everyone *fully mature in Christ*." (Colossians 1:28, emphasis added)

However, because the term "counseling" carries with it a certain distracting connotation, I often replace it with the phrase "a model and means of sanctification." That is what biblical counseling seeks to effect, sanctification. Therefore, I routinely use counseling and sanctification interchangeably (although formally, sanctification is a broader scriptural category than counseling).

While most Christians can correctly state the gospel, it is in the Christian's response to psychology that the depth and application of that gospel is exposed in his life. The issue of psychology in the church serves as a means for winnowing out those Christians who merely know the gospel from those who rightly apply it. No challenge to the gospel seems to expose the heart more quickly, or more profoundly, than psychology, since it is a thoroughly heart-directing false religion.

I would like to be clear that throughout this text there is both an explicit and implicit rejection of secular psychology. There is never any expressed, or implied, acceptance of any psychology term. However, at moments it is necessary to use the particular verbiage of psychology because it serves as a cultural shorthand, the parlance of modern society. Thus, certain terms represent a basket of symptoms and culturally-accepted descriptors. My intention in occasionally mentioning psychology terms is merely to draw attention to a concept which I always redefine in biblical categories.

> "Unlike so many, we do not peddle the word of God for profit. On the contrary, in Christ we speak before God with sincerity, as those sent from God." (2 Corinthians 2:17)

From Art to Artifice to Arisen

Section I

A Precious Cornerstone for a Sure Foundation

- 1 -

THE EXORDIUM TO BIBLICAL COUNSELING

The Currency of Counseling

How would you characterize your life? Do you long for the approval and respect of others and then rebel and isolate yourself in pride? Are you often paralyzed by fear, depression, failure, withdrawal, or escapism? What is the correct diagnosis of one's problems and what does change look like? Is lasting change even possible?

There are three central questions at the core of all human existence:

1. Who am I? (creation)

2. What is my problem? (Why do I feel emotional pain? Why is my life unfulfilled?) (fall)

3. How do I solve my problem? Where can I find help? (redemption)

Throughout history every culture has sought to answer these questions. The ancient Greeks sought answers in their philosophy. Modern man looks to psychology or reductionistic science. The Bible, however, secrets away buried treasure; for it alone holds the answers. Only the Bible knows the truth about man's design (creation), his ruin in the fall, and the means for lasting change (redemption). Unlike the Greek goddess Athena who shook her spear in the face of ignorance, the Bible does not make threats but friends of adversaries.

Biblical counseling offers both a piercing analysis of the human condition as well as permanent and abundant strategies for change based on this central truth: The only true need is for relationship with Jesus Christ. Biblical counseling does not offer principles, systems, or pragmatics; it offers Jesus, the person in whose sight one is searched, confronted, and guided to a form of change that will stand on the last day. Biblical counseling seeks to reveal the functional gods that motivate and control actions, thoughts, emotions, attitudes, and anticipations. These functional gods represent idolatrous covenants with the creation, an allegiance which began with a surrender. This allegiance is likewise broken with a greater surrender to the searcher of hearts, Jesus himself.

Exodus 19:4 states, "You yourself have seen what I did to Egypt, and how I carried

> you on eagles' wings and brought you to myself." God did not deliver the Israelites from slavery in order that they might enjoy their freedom for their own purpose. He delivered them to claim them for himself. It was for the purpose of knowing God, being with God, basking in his goodness, participating in his holiness and glory that the Israelites were set free.

Taking Jesus Hostage to Perceived Needs

Fyodor Dostoevsky's (1821-1881) *The Brothers Karamosov* (1880) contains the short story "The Grand Inquisitor" in which Jesus returns at the Second Coming and is placed on trial by the church. The church charges him with three crimes.[1]

In Matthew 4:3 the tempter came to Jesus and said, "If you are the Son of God, tell these stones to become bread." Jesus did not turn the stones into bread. Thus, the first charge against Jesus is that people are starving and need food, yet he did not provide them with food.

The Temptation of Christ
Ary Scheffer, 1854

Matthew 4:6 reads, "'If you are the Son of God,' he said, 'throw yourself down.'" The second charge is that when tempted to throw himself off the temple mount Jesus should have obliged since people need miracles and mystery.

Matthew 4:9 reads "'All this I will give you,' he said, 'if you will bow down and worship me.'" The third, and final, charge against Jesus invokes Satan's temptation to bow before him and receive "all the kingdoms of the world and their splendor." Jesus should have received these kingdoms because people need political power. Thus, on three occasions Jesus did not meet people's perceived needs. This is why, in Dostoevsky's story, the church condemns Jesus.

---

[1] Thank you to David Powlison, Westminster Theological Seminary, Philadelphia, Pennsylvania for drawing my attention to this short-story.

Yet Jesus' responses were perfectly in line with what people actually need. First, in Matthew 4:4 Jesus replied, "Man does not live on bread alone, but on every word that comes from the mouth of God."

> In Exodus 34:28, Moses fasted forty days without food or water. It is assumed that a Christophany (the presence of Jesus himself) sustained Moses. This would accord with Jesus' words that whoever drinks the water he gives him will never thirst again,[2] and Jesus' statement that he is the bread of life.[3] Whoever eats of his body will never be hungry again (meaning whoever believes that Jesus' body was crushed in payment for humanity's sin). It would appear that Moses actually experienced the sustenance of Christ himself while on Mount Sinai.

Next Jesus answered, in Matthew 4:7, "Do not put the Lord your God to the test." Lastly, in Matthew 4:10, Jesus said, "Away from me Satan! For it is written, 'Worship the Lord your God, and serve him only.'" Jesus precisely countered each accusation with an answer that cuts to the heart of man. Jesus emphasized the desperate need for his Word, uncompromised trust in God's goodness, and for the need to worship God with the entirety of one's heart.

This is an apt starting point for counseling, because each person, in his sin, believes that Jesus is not adequate to meet his deepest needs. Sinners instinctively crave that which meets here-and-now material needs while neglecting the far greater needs of the soul. Each sinner also tempts Jesus with demands in line with Satan's. The demand is, "Give me what I desire, what I feel I need, what I crave, what I worship. Give me what I lost in the fall (as I define that loss)."

However, Jesus does not answer fallen man according to his perceived needs. Jesus answers according to what he knows mankind needs - relationship with Jesus himself. Each sinner, on account of his demand, instinctively seeks the gift, not the Giver. For example, Acts 8:20 records that Simon the Sorcerer tried to *buy* the gift of the Holy Spirit. Jesus longs to give us himself – the true gift. That is the *sine qua non* of every counseling encounter.

This idea of unmet perceived needs finds fertile ground in Satan's lies. Satan's temptation of Jesus closely mirrors the Adler-Maslow pyramid of needs (hierarchy of needs).[4]

---

[2] John 4:14
[3] John 6:35
[4] Thank you to Pastor Ou Yang for pointing out the connection between Jesus' temptation in the desert and the Adler-Maslow pyramid of needs. For additional discussion of the Adler-Maslow pyramid see chapter 8: "What Has Jerusalem To Do With Vienna?: The Case Against Psychology"

The Adler-Maslow pyramid of needs:

Adler	Satan's Temptation	Maslow
	Jesus to worship Satan	Self-actualization
	...and receive the kingdoms of the world	Self-esteem
Significance	Jesus to bow to Satan...	Love and belonging needs
Security	Jesus to throw himself down and trust God to save him	Safety/security needs
Physical needs	Jesus to turn stones to bread	Physiological needs

The Adler-Maslow pyramid of needs accords closely with Satan's temptation. In the same way that Jesus was tempted, the sinner likewise is tempted to climb the pyramid, to chase perceived needs. However, while Jesus saw through Satan's deception, the sinner is easily chicaned into thinking that such needs are foundational to his existence and crucial for living a fulfilled life.

In reality, the Adler-Maslow pyramid keeps people in slavery to themselves as they chase needs which are never adequately met. Just as one, regardless of his effort, can never reach infinity, so too, one can never satisfy psychic needs that are, by design, infinite (more accurately, non-existent). Tragically, each strives with greater vigor and energy to meet illusory psychic needs, finally discovering that those needs have metamorphosed into tyrannical demands.

Second Corinthians 6:4-10 reads,

> Rather, as servants of God we commend ourselves in every way: in great endurance; in troubles, hardships and distresses; in beatings, imprisonments and riots; in hard work, sleepless nights and hunger; in purity, understanding, patience and kindness; in the Holy Spirit and in sincere love; in truthful speech and in the power of God; with weapons of righteousness in the right hand and in the left; through glory and dishonor, bad report and good report; genuine, yet regarded as impostors; known, yet regarded as unknown; dying, and yet we live on; beaten and not killed; sorrowful, yet always rejoicing; poor, yet making many rich; having nothing, and yet possessing everything.

In what way does this passage expose the falsehood endemic to the Adler-Maslow hierarchy of needs theory? Clearly, Paul did not focus on the fulfillment of inherent needs. He simply served God, in the process experiencing continual joy, regardless of his circumstance.

Likewise the book of Job offers a clear refutation of the Adler-Maslow hierarchy. Job, a righteous man,[5] suffered greatly when he lost his home, children, wealth, health, and even his wife's respect, while his friends assumed him guilty of some wrongdoing. However, in spite of his myriad losses, Job remained faithful to God refusing to succumb to selfish motives. As with Paul, Job did not evidence a basic human need for security and significance. Despite his crushing circumstance, Job rightly recognized that faithfulness to his God was his only need.

His Only Begotten Son and the Word of God, Victor Vasnetsov, c. 1896

Jesus turned the Adler-Maslow pyramid on its point and completely redefined it. Mark 12:30, 31 reads, "Love the Lord your God with all your heart and with all your soul and with all your mind and with all your strength.' The second is this: 'Love your neighbor as yourself.' There is no commandment greater than these." This is the starting point for the Christian faith. Thus, the Christian "reverse-pyramid" begins with the dual love of God and neighbor out of which flows every subsequent promise from God. Matthew 6:33 reads, "But seek first his kingdom and his righteousness, and all these things will be given to you as well." The Christian life is built upon an uncompromised seeking and serving God with the trust that God provides for every legitimate need. Thus, the Christian reverse-pyramid is predicated on a singular need, the need for relationship with God himself. God then provides for all earthly cares through his unmerited grace.[6]

The Grand Equation

> "The earth, from which food comes, is transformed below as by fire; sapphires come from its rocks, and its dust contains nuggets of gold. [Man] tunnels through the rock;

---

[5] Job 1:8
[6] Jay Adams, *The Biblical View of Self-Esteem, Self-Love, and Self-Image* (Harvest House Publishers, 1986)

> his eyes see all its treasures. He searches the sources of the rivers and brings hidden things to light. But where can wisdom be found? Where does understanding dwell? It cannot be bought with the finest gold, nor can its price be weighed in silver." (Job 28:5, 6, 10, 11, 12, 15)

Mark 10:28 reads, "Then Peter spoke up, 'We have left *everything* to follow you!'" Peter hinted at a "grand equation" governing the Christian life:

Jesus + Everything = Jesus + Nothing[7]

In Christ everything is as nothing, one's location, one's experiences, one's status, one's accomplishments. In fact, Jesus hinted at the verity of this equation when he stated in Luke 14:33, "…those of you who do not give up everything you have cannot be my disciples." Jesus did not seek to minimize the particulars of one's earthly existence, but rather to emphasize that nothing in heaven or on earth compares to the gift the Christian has been given in Jesus, and to the rewards that come with serving him.[8] The comparative separation between what the Christian has been given in Jesus and anything in the created order is as immense as can ever be conceived. Thus, by comparison with Jesus, the creation's value is reduced to a functional state of "nothingness."

Consider Paul's life, as detailed in 2 Corinthians 11:25-33,

> Three times I was beaten with rods, once I was stoned, three times I was shipwrecked, I spent a night and a day in the open sea, I have been constantly on the move. I have been in danger from rivers, in danger from bandits, in danger from my own countrymen, in danger from Gentiles; in danger in the city, in danger in the country, in danger at sea; and in danger from false brothers. I have labored and toiled and have often gone without sleep; I have known hunger and thirst and have often gone without food; I have been cold and naked. Besides everything else, I face daily the pressure of my concern for all the churches. Who is weak, and I do not feel weak? Who is led into sin, and I do not inwardly burn? If I must boast, I will boast of the things that show my weakness. The God and Father of the Lord Jesus, who is to be praised forever, knows that I am not lying. In Damascus the governor under King Aretas had the city of the Damascenes guarded in order to arrest me. But I was lowered in a basket from a window in the wall and slipped through his hands.

Paul was impervious to grief concerning his life's many hardships because he

---

[7] This equation from William Edgar, Westminster Theological Seminary, Philadelphia, Pennsylvania
[8] Mark 10:29-31

recognized the veracity of the grand equation. He continually pointed to the "glory of Christ,"[9] and the "unsearchable riches of the Christ,"[10] having a vision for that which far outshined his "light and momentary troubles."[11] The nature of this equation is a mystery to which the Christian has been made privy, but which the world utterly cannot comprehend.

Alexander the Great in the Temple of Jerusalem, Sebastiano Conca, d. 1764

Biblical Counseling's Core Principles

"In matters of style, swim with the current; in matters of principle, stand like a rock." (Thomas Jefferson)

Creation (design)[12]

1. The human heart was designed to worship.[13]

2. Each person is a covenant maker.[14] Each makes covenants with the real God or with idols.

---

[9] 2 Corinthians 4:4
[10] Ephesians 3:8
[11] 2 Corinthians 4:17
[12] For a more detailed discussion of human design see chapter 5: "Redefining the Pygmalion Effect: Exploring the Image of God in Man"
[13] Luke 4:8
[14] Romans 5:12-21

3. Each person bears the design features of a prophet, priest, and king. Each seeks to act out these stations in his world.

4. Each person lives before the face of a holy God (*coram Deo*).[15]

5. God's work is always focused on the heart, not upon circumstances.[16]

6. There is only one psychic need, relationship with God through Jesus Christ.[17]

Fall (sin)[18]

1. The sinner views God with suspicion and flees from him.[19]

2. Fallen man is totally depraved, meaning that all aspects of his being are damaged by sin. The Bible describes the human heart as "proud,"[20] "insane,"[21] "arrogant,"[22] "rebellious,"[23] "deceitful,"[24] "wicked,"[25] "weak,"[26] "foolish,"[27] and "evil."[28] Thus, as a result of sin, mankind desires and seeks that which, often unbeknownst to him, is evil (but not as fully as he might on account of God's common grace).

3. The sinner suspects that God wantonly withholds good gifts and, therefore, the sinner grabs for those gifts in his own power, and for his own purpose.[29]

4. The sinner is a covenant breaker with God.[30]

5. On account of sin each is ruled by three fears: rejection, failure, and judgment.[31]

6. Each sinner is an idol factory, continually making the creation into idols, molding these idols anew to suit any situation.

---

[15] Romans 1:18-21
[16] Ezekiel 11:19; 36:26
[17] 1 John 5:12
[18] For a comprehensive discussion of the issue of sin see the second book in this series, "*What Agreement Is There Between the Temple of God and Idols?: The Accidence of Sin and Idolatry*"
[19] Genesis 3:8
[20] Proverbs 21:4
[21] Ecclesiastes 9:3
[22] Isaiah 10:12
[23] Jeremiah 5:23
[24] Jeremiah 17:9
[25] Jeremiah 17:9
[26] Ezekiel 16:30
[27] Romans 1:21
[28] Hebrews 3:12
[29] Luke 15:12
[30] Hosea 6:7
[31] For a comprehensive discussion of the topic of fear see "The Dynamics of Fear" in chapter 6: "Man Before the Face of God: The Imperium of the Psyche"

7. Sinners institutionalize their lusts, controlling desires, loves, and wants as needs.[32]

8. The sinner's perceived psychic need is infinite and can never be satisfied.[33]

9. Unmet perceived needs become a glaring source of hatred toward God for willing the circumstance in which that which is thought to be needed is lacking.

10. The Bible uses the following terms to describe idolatry: cravings,[34] desires,[35] loves,[36] "musts," treasures,[37] and worship.[38]

11. Each sinner is a worship addict, worshipping that which is in the creation to the exclusion of the Creator.

12. The sinner focuses on the here-and-now, believing this world to be his kingdom.[39]

13. The sinner is committed to personal happiness and writing his own autobiography.[40]

14. The sinner's greatest problem is never a finiteness issue – ability, knowledge, money, or opportunity. His greatest problem is always a heart issue.

Redemption (sanctification)[41]

1. The Bible speaks to every human concern. There is no problem pertaining to the psyche that Scripture is not equipped to handle.[42]

2. The Bible presents a "from-to" model for change.[43] It does not confront the heart without presenting a viable solution to its sin problem. Thus, the Bible offers a dynamic for change; it sets the redeemed sinner in motion toward the restored likeness of God.

3. The Bible exists so that fallen man would be both brought to saving faith in Jesus Christ,[44] and made holy.

---

[32] Jeremiah 2:13
[33] Ecclesiastes 6:7
[34] Ephesians 2:3
[35] Mark 4:19; Romans 1:24
[36] Matthew 6:24
[37] Luke 12:34
[38] Acts 7:42
[39] John 18:36
[40] Philippians 1:17
[41] For a comprehensive discussion of the topic of sanctification see chapter 10: "The Third-Way of Sanctification: From Abominable to Indomitable"
[42] 2 Timothy 3:16, 17
[43] Ephesians 4:22-25
[44] John 5:39

4. Through Jesus' death on the cross he provided both justification (eternal life) and sanctification (the opportunity for growth in holiness).[45] The one who is justified (whom the Bible calls a "saint") is being progressively sanctified.

5. In sanctification, the saint is given a new focus, the eternal, to the exclusion of the temporal.[46]

6. God is more concerned with who the saint is rather than what he does, so that being is prioritized over acting.[47]

7. The saint rightly focuses on personal holiness to the neglect of personal happiness.[48]

8. In terms of the saint's growth in holiness, God is less concerned with the actual events of personal history and more concerned with one's interpretation of that history.[49]

9. The Christian is given a new set of lenses with which to see his past, present, and future. Those lenses are the way that God himself sees reality.[50]

10. God's love is not blindly unconditional (as defined by psychology) but directed toward a sanctification outcome.[51]

11. God's principle work is to change each believer into the image of Christ,[52] a change that will stand for all eternity.

How Does Biblical Counseling Dovetail with the Larger Christian Message?

The ancient Greek philosophers Plato (c. 426 – c. 346 BC) and Aristotle (384–322 BC) disagreed on how to organize knowledge. Plato assembled all knowledge into a unified system, while his student Aristotle fractured knowledge into categories or distinct disciplines such as biology, chemistry, and physics.

For millennia Aristotle's system dominated western education creating an often disjointed and confusing approach. Today, the trend is back to the Platonic system of

---

[45] John 10:10
[46] Colossians 3:2
[47] Leviticus 26:12
[48] 2 Corinthians 6:4-10
[49] 2 Corinthians 6:4-10
[50] Exodus 3-4
[51] For a comprehensive study of God's love see the third book in this series, *The Days of Reckoning Are at Hand: From Fig Leaf to Olive Branch to Laurel Wreath*, chapter 2: "Suffering: The Kintsugi Objective"
[52] Romans 8:29

integration. This is the impetus behind astrophysics, biochemistry, social-anthropology, and the like. Even university science facilities are now integrated in an effort to induce collaboration among scientific disciplines and dialogue between previously disparate studies.

The School of Athens (Plato and Aristotle)
Raphael, 1509

The reason for mentioning this is to assert that Christian thought tends to suffer from Aristotelian categorization. Biblical counseling, for example, tends to be segregated from theology proper as a subset of practical theology. This, I believe, is a false separation which does harm to Christian thought. In other words, many wrongly assume that biblical counseling is a distant theological application reserved for those who undergo special training. While biblical counseling is theological (as everything is on some level), and while wise counsel requires intense and prolonged study of God's Word, it is a travesty to see the counseling endeavor as an elite or specialized pursuit unsuitable for the common Christian. The issues biblical counseling raises are at the very heart and marrow of every Christian's relationship with Jesus.

> Biblical counseling is theology on wheels. (adapted from David Powlison)

Most populist attempts to disparage biblical counseling are largely the outgrowth of a recalcitrant anti-intellectualism which maintains a stranglehold on Christianity. This is the idea that Christians are to be pietistic or fideistic, so that they do not engage in deep intellectual understanding of their faith. The vast majority of Christians with whom I regularly interact dismiss biblical counseling as somehow imposing a certain man-centered intellectual grid upon Scripture. The truth is quite the opposite, biblical counseling seeks to plumb the depths of Scripture, to mine its hidden treasure, to uncover something more of the mysteries of the gospel so that the Christian is brought more fully into relationship with Christ, and is more fully transformed into his image.[53]

---

[53] Ephesians 6:19; 1 Peter 1:12

For this reason, in certain Christian circles I seldom use the term "biblical counseling." I simply refer to this endeavor as "growth in sanctification." My objective is to highlight a term which is more familiar and readily accepted among Christians, avoiding the ignorant and prejudicial reaction that the term "counseling" evokes in certain traditions.

> The *locus classicus* for biblical counseling is Romans 15:14, in which Paul points out that the Roman Christians are competent to instruct (counsel) one another. Colossians 3:16 also encourages Christians to teach and admonish one another.

Select Truths about Biblical Counseling

1. Biblical counseling is a subcategory of Christian evangelism. As such, it serves as an effective entrance point into the gospel, a persuasive point of contact with the unbelieving world. It casts the gospel in a light which makes it accessible to a psychologized world (while of course maintaining the gospel's full integrity). Biblical counseling is an effective tool for countering the hegemony of secular psychology but not merely for the sake of intellectual confrontation, rather for the sake of claiming souls. Evangelism, with a counseling tint, moves onto the unbeliever's ground uncovering the inner dynamics of his worldview.[54] So the counselor, like a Christian apologist, seeks to expose and highlight the tension between apostasy, on the one hand, and the knowledge of God imbedded in each image-bearer, on the other.[55]

> The ancient Greeks loved knowledge but often had trouble assessing what was true and false. Their standard was that truth is the most eloquent and beautiful argument, that truth is found in the aesthetic of logic. For this reason the ancient Greeks espoused the great debate model of education. Education should involve a debate between differing points of view, allowing various perspectives to be aired. The hope was that truth would be obvious, evident, clearly seen through its superiority to other perspectives. Thus, the spark of truth was thought to fly from vigorous debate. Biblical counseling offers a buoyant platform for debate with the secular world. It is winsome. This is less on account of its inherently elegant design, and more so because it actually works, as the regenerate are profoundly changed through faith, repentance, and growth in holiness.

Christianity has been losing its vitality and persuasiveness for generations because it has foolishly sought to accommodate itself to the world. It often seeks to be culturally relevant and "seeker-friendly," to be ecumenical and irenic, to not offend and be

---

[54] William Edgar, *Reasons of the Heart: Recovering Christian Persuasion* (Presbyterian and Reformed Publishing, 2003) 55. (applied to the counseling context)
[55] William Edgar, *Reasons of the Heart: Recovering Christian Persuasion* (Presbyterian and Reformed Publishing, 2003) 56. (applied to the counseling context)

tolerant, and finally to blindly integrate the world's perspective into its own. This is often the motive behind coupling elements of secular thought with the gospel. In so doing, Christianity has diluted itself with trends, fads, and outright falsehoods which gravely weaken its witness, sabotage its core doctrines, and threaten to capsize it in the waves of the world's cultural storms.

That being said, "How does biblical counseling establish a bulwark against deleterious cultural currents, while at the same time offering what might be thought of as a 'plausibility structure'?"[56] This is the idea that the truth is more believable when it is found in the context of institutions and social expectations which lend it credence. In other words, the question is, "What would highlight the gospel to unbelievers?" How does one couple the gospel message with that which offers the unbeliever a sense of familiarity or security?[57] Thus, offering the unbeliever the gospel positioned in a counseling stance can be effective with highly-psychologized people.

Ballerinas in Blue
Edgar Germain Hilaire Degas, d. 1917

> Augustine's (354-430) sagacious insight was faith seeks understanding, not understanding seeks faith. Human reason is fallen so that faith must realign and rebuild the reason. The Christian message calls the sinner to faith and from this flows understanding.

2. Biblical counseling is a subcategory of Christian apologetics. The Greek word *apologos* (ἀπολογος) (from which "apologetics" is derived) means literally "toward the word." So apologetics is "movement toward the Word of God." Apologetics exists to better understand, apply, explain, and live out the Word of God. Apologetics also refers to a defense of the faith. It is a way to demonstrate to the

---

[56] Term from Peter Berger, sociologist
[57] William Edgar, *Reasons of the Heart: Recovering Christian Persuasion* (Presbyterian and Reformed Publishing, 2003) 61.

world that the Christian worldview is true. Biblical counseling operates within this apologetic mission.

> The most important war is the one fought on the battlefield of ideas (those nestled within the heart). A war won with physical weapons may need to be fought again, but a victory over error shines for all of eternity.

One of the goals of Christian apologetics is to make the sinner acutely aware of his sin so as to see his desperate need for salvation. That is why the biblical counseling model is effective both for sanctification (its traditional application) and for justification (its broader application). Counseling, when correctly understood, is both a tool for refining hearts (holiness) and for winning hearts (evangelism). Counseling is rightly used to highlight the reality of sin in the unbeliever so as to point him to Christ.

3. Biblical counseling is neither art nor science; it is *sui generis* among academic studies, simultaneously three parts working in tandem. It is analytical of the heart (quasi-science), and an entering into the lives of lost and broken people for the purpose of healing (a kind of art), all suffused with a radical reliance on the work of the Holy Spirit. This is its unique third quality. Counseling is the provenance of God himself to save and sanctify whole people, to fulfill God's promise to glorify those who belong to him.[58]

4. Biblical counseling is an aspect of fulfilling God's promises to his people as it pleads with his people, accuses their accusers, and affects daily release from slavery to sin. God is already at work glorifying his people through their daily sanctification, and biblical counseling is a handmaiden to that enterprise.

> Biblical counseling might be summarized in the following way: Godly insight into lives leads to Christ-centered loving confrontation. That confrontation induces either conviction of sin (and subsequent confession of sin) or else recognition of abiding faith. The result is heart change which bears fruit as the penitent grows in ever deepening relationship with Christ himself, a relationship which, in turn, blesses the entire church.

---

[58] Romans 8:30

– 2 –

THE COUNSELING AMBITION

Counseling in the Postmodern World

Postmodernism is marked by:

1. The assumption that truth does not exist
2. The belief that there is no meaning to life
3. The idea that knowledge is no longer objective
4. The belief that ethics are not universal
5. The idea that all human interaction is only "data and language games"[1]

Ball at the Moulin De La Galette, Pierre-Auguste Renoir, 1876

Albert Camus (1913-1960), the absurdist philosopher, asserted that the greatest question facing modern mankind is, "Why should I not commit suicide?" Postmodern man has lost nearly all sense of eternal purpose. Life has been reduced to a futile chasing after meaningless possessions and experiences, the Sisyphean accumulation of mere toys and whims. The loss of a compelling social metanarrative (grand story) plays into this since, if man is merely the result of accidental evolution,

---

[1] William Edgar, *Reasons of the Heart: Recovering Christian Persuasion* (Presbyterian and Reformed Publishing, 2003) 25.

if life has no ultimate purpose, then life is a colossal cosmic waste of time. This loss of a convincing social metanarrative characterizes postmodernism, and it is in this milieu that the counselor operates. He must understand the workings of postmodernism so as to effectively counteract the forces at play to subvert the gospel.

> "When I am getting ready to reason with a man, I spend one-third of my time thinking about myself and what I am going to say and two-thirds about him and what he is going to say." (Abraham Lincoln)

In a postmodern world in which the notion of absolute truth lies shattered, one of the chief challenges facing the counselor is convincing sinners that the Bible understands them far better than they do (at least far better than psychology does). How does one convince a skeptical world that the Bible alone plumbs the dynamics of the heart, that it alone offers a roadmap to healing and change, that only relationship with Jesus Christ disentangles man's existential condition? The Bible, in effect, reverses the ravages of postmodernism by restoring a viable social metanarrative. The Bible alone offers a compelling apologetic for existence at all, that the chief end of man is to glorify God and enjoy him forever.[2] This statement alone breaks the postmodern spell by offering a brilliant singular compunction for all this human drama.

> "...we speak of God's secret wisdom, a wisdom that has been hidden and that God destined for our glory before time began." (1 Corinthians 2:7)

An Apologetic for Counseling

1. Counseling is the prerogative and rightful place of the church. The Bible's perspective is not a "professional" or "medical" model.[3] The Bible sees the church, as it remains under the auspices of Scripture, as eminently gifted by the Holy Spirit to counsel those both within and without the church. Sadly, the church has abdicated its counseling imperative, selling its birthright for worthless counsel.[4]

2. Counseling is not only for the "train-wrecks," the severely depressed, or the emotional needy. There is a tendency to narrowly think of counseling as a ministry to the suffering, aggrieved, or grieving. While these all too common human experiences are crucial junctures for wise counsel, counseling must be seen as a comprehensive approach to all life situations. Counseling is just as needed and applicable during times of celebration, victory, or general contentment. Counseling rightly occurs in these "winning" moments as a way to draw them into

---

[2] Westminster Shorter Catechism, Question 1.
[3] David Powlison, Westminster Theological Seminary, Philadelphia, Pennsylvania
[4] For further discussion of this issue see the third book in this series, *The Days of Reckoning Are at Hand: From Fig Leaf to Olive Branch to Laurel Wreath*, chapter 10: "Counseling and the Church: Syndicating the Vision"

a radically Christ-centered narrative. As counsel is neglected at the towering junctures, an opportunity is forever lost to shape the heart.

> "Speak to one another with psalms, hymns and spiritual songs. Sing and make music in your heart to the Lord, always giving thanks to God the Father for everything, in the name of our Lord Jesus Christ." (Ephesians 5:19, 20)

3. Counseling is not necessarily a formal event or a scheduled activity; it pervades each interaction every day. Counseling is nestled into every dialogue so that one must counsel and receive counsel; it is impossible not to do so. Thus, everyone counsels and receives counsel in every human interaction, whether he wants to or not. The counseling one gives, and that which he receives, is either Christ-centered or man-centered; there is no other option.

> "We wander through life in a darkness in which none of us can really see his neighbor. Only from time to time, through some experience that we have of our friend, or by some remark, he stands for a moment as though illuminated by a flash of lightning. Then we see him as he really is." (Albert Schweitzer)

There should be daily confrontations with the truth. With each interaction, Christians should either be called to repentance or encouraged in their display of faith. Thus, counseling can often be barely noticed and subtle, or conspicuous and pronounced. It can involve few words or it can be conducted through in-depth conversation. No matter how it takes place, counsel is compelled to take place. The Christian, recognizing this imperative, is careful to let no word or opportunity go to waste.[5]

> "Be very careful, then, how you live – not as unwise but as wise, making the most of every opportunity, because the days are evil." (Ephesians 5:15, 16)

How does one purposefully bend wood? One must patiently apply water, heat, and pressure so that the wood bends over time. Too much water, excessive heat, or sudden pressure will snap it. The counselor applies the water of God's salvation, the heat of his wrath, and the pressure of his Word to bend recalcitrant hearts (all the while recognizing that the final bending is solely the work of the Holy Spirit). The counselor does not seek to win the battle at the expense of losing the war. He works as God works, with a persistent and calculated focus on winning the heart.

4. The call to counsel, whether formally or informally, is a high-calling to be handled with the utmost integrity and respect for God's driving passion to justify people and know them personally.

---

[5] Colossians 4:6

Consider 2 Kings 6:6, 7, "The man of God asked, 'Where did it fall?' When he showed him the place, Elisha cut a stick and threw it there, and made the iron float. 'Lift it out,' he said. Then the man reached out his hand and took it." The Christian may read this account of Elisha's "telekinesis" with a sense of awe that he could display such unfathomable power over the physical world, that the laws of physics might bow to this righteous man.

The Matterhorn, Edward Theodore Compton, 1879

However, later, in Matthew 17:20, Jesus offered the following metaphor, "…Because you have so little faith. Truly I tell you, if you have faith as small as a mustard seed, you can say to this mountain, 'Move from here to there,' and it will move. Nothing will be impossible for you." Even greater than the ability to make iron float or to move a mountain, there is no more awesome and fearsome force on earth than the power to sanctify wayward hearts. The biblical counselor is a participant in that earth-shattering endeavor. The calling to participate in the invasion and reclamation of the heart is a vastly higher calling than any of the prophets before Christ could ever experience. The Christian has been given power, not to defy the laws of physics, but to move mountains, not physical mountains, but mountains of worship. That is the greatest miracle that any human being can experience, to see a heart once besieged by sin subsequently vanquished by God's Spirit, regenerated and renewed, so that where one was once the chief of sinners,[6] a brazen murderer of God's people, one is now a faithful exponent of that same God.

---

[6] 1 Timothy 1:15

One of the reasons that Christians frequently cannot see the issues of the heart is because, as Ephesians 4:19 warns, "Having lost all sensitivity, they have given themselves over to sensuality so as to indulge in every kind of impurity, and they are full of greed." Persistent sin causes one to lose sensitivity to the condition of the heart. The loss of sensitivity is a byproduct of a heart that is callous toward God, loves its own sin, and is blind to how to love others without regard for oneself.

Counseling as a New Set of Lenses (as a Presuppositional Endeavor[7])

Three-dimensional movies, pioneered in the 1950s, required viewers to don special glasses with a red and blue lens. (The differently-colored lenses cause each eye to see a slightly offset image so objects "jumped" off the screen.) This could serve as a metaphor for the heart; the heart is insane in that it dons differently-colored lenses to cause particular images to "jump out" for greater effect in its sinful mission. Just as moviegoers wear 3-D glasses to cause images to emerge from the screen, so too, sin causes particular "images" to emerge and dominate the psyche. The Bible corrects this aberration so that the lenses with which one views the world, are not differently colored, but resolve, disambiguate, and clarify as God sees reality. Thus, there are at least two ways of looking at any fact or set of circumstances. One set of lenses looks at the subject in a way that glorifies God; all others glorify the creation.

> "Who has understood the mind of the Lord, or instructed him as his counselor?" (Isaiah 40:13)

This leads to the next point which is, what might be termed a "presuppositional view of counseling," a view which compels examination of the counseling objectives, methods, and outcomes. When this view is brought to full focus it offers stunning contrast and clarity to see reality as God does.

> "'To whom will you compare me? Or who is my equal?' says the Holy One. 'Lift your eyes and look to the heavens; who created all these?...'" (Isaiah 40:25, 26)

Abraham Lincoln (1809-1865) said, "It takes great social skill to describe others as they see themselves." The Christian counselor seeks to describe others, not as they see themselves, but as God sees them, as revealed in his Word. Even more so, the Christian counselor does not seek to merely describe, but to be used as an instrument of change. What is in need of change? The deepest recesses of the psyche, the worship command center.

The serpent foisted upon Eve two lies, "Did God really say, 'You must now eat from

---

[7] This concept "presuppositional endeavor" borrowed from David and Sharon Covington, "Introduction to Biblical Counseling" notes, 2004

any tree in the garden'?" and, "You shall not surely die."⁸ Upon these two lies, the serpent sought to usurp God's authority in arrogantly authoring a competing and compelling false story. The setting of this story was a cruel God whose command against eating from the tree was only to wantonly keep humanity subjugated. Satan's purpose was both to persuade mankind to cease and desist from God's creative efforts, and to exalt mankind as his own god, one with as much or more potential as the true God. The serpent's prodding was to act on this presumption and to eat. The serpent chicaned Eve into believing that she herself was the hero of a new story, a hero who, with the serpent's help, could overcome the obstacles of a selfish God, and in so doing soar to become like God himself. This story replays every moment of everyday in every sinner's heart.⁹

Between Hope and Fear, Lawrence Alma-Tadema, 1876

Each person tells himself a story every moment of everyday. That story (like the one to which Eve subscribed) involves rendering himself as a tragic hero with a self-centered plot, purpose, setting, and villains. The sinner seeks to utterly remove God from his life story, hoping to become, both functionally and propositionally, an autonomous being. Those who cannot viably remove God altogether, invariably seek to shoehorn him into their plots, so that God functions as a mere handmaiden to their directives. In this objective, the Bible's story, intended to illuminate the presence and power of sin so as to eradicate it, is tyrannized by rogue human reason. God continually confronts the sinner's self-centered, self-glorifying stories, enticing him to abandon errant stories so as to adopt God's own. God longs to reclaim sinners and

---

⁸ Genesis 3:1, 4
⁹ Some ideas in this paragraph from David and Sharon Covington, "Introduction to Biblical Counseling" notes, 2004

then retrofit them as saints into his emerging story.

> Psalm 1:1-3 offers three states with regard to sin: walking, standing, and sitting:
>
> Blessed is the man who does not walk in the counsel of the wicked or stand in the way of sinners or sit in the seat of mockers. But his delight is in the law of the Lord, and on his law he meditates day and night. He is like a tree planted by streams of water, which yields its fruit in season and whose leaf does not wither. Whatever he does prospers.
>
> God acts to deter walking, standing, or sitting among the wicked so that the Christian can become like a planted tree bearing good fruit in Christ.

The Counseling Mission

Like an apple that is outwardly shiny but inwardly rotten, people often hold forth a competent and confident exterior, the carriage of a sound and stable life. The counselor peers below the surface to see the reality of the heart's condition. This is not always easy, and not always welcome. The counselor must be thoroughly trained in God's Word to see rightly, and to apply the truth in love. He must also earn the right to speak into other's lives. Only then will his message of repentance and call to faith have a meaningful effect.

The counselor's objective is never that another merely feel guilty for sin (although that may be appropriate). The mere feeling of guilt being largely unproductive and uninvited, the counselor seeks to parlay psychic guilt into restoration with God. The proper recognition of guilt before a holy God and subsequent repentance does, in fact, bear fruit which lasts for eternity. In the same way, the counselor's objective is not to cause another to simply conform to outward expectations, to adopt mere behavioral changes for the sake of appearance. That is functionally cavorting with the Pharisees.

The counselor does not regard another based on his current situation or condition, but based solely on what Scripture reveals about that person. For example, a homeless Christian enjoys a superior condition, from God's perspective, to an affluent non-Christian.[10] While certainly the counselor would do everything he could to improve the plight of the homeless, he recognizes that there is a reality operative in even the lowest Christian that transcends his current state. The point is that the counselor operates in the paradigm presented by Scripture, not the faux-paradigm offered by the world. The counselor peers behind outward appearance so as to spy an inner hidden condition. It is that inner reality which directs the wise counselor in crafting his counsel.

---

[10] For example, Job was temporarily homeless.

> "God sees not as man sees, for man looks at the outward appearance, but the Lord looks at the heart." (1 Samuel 16:7)

The Conversion of Saint Paul, Luca Giordano, c. 1690

Thus, the Christian is not regarded in any state other than as a new creation in Christ,[11] reclaimed by a holy God, regardless of his statements to the contrary and regardless of his life's outward appearance. Conversely, the unbeliever is not regarded in any state other than being a guilty, lost sinner before a holy God, regardless of his statements to the contrary, or the seeming contraindication of his life's outward appearance. The counselor recognizes the inner reality of each and charts a course based on the way God sees that person, not based on appearances, past transgressions, successes, social status, intelligence, or future prospects.

> "So from now on we regard no one from a worldly point of view. Though we once regarded Christ in this way, we do so no longer." (2 Corinthians 5:16)

Counseling as Serving the Goal of Sanctification

While creation, in general, is "good," mankind was created "very good."[12] As very good image-bearers, people are each mini-revelations of God.[13] This means that each is an eternal representation of God adapted to the temporal sphere. Mankind is

---

[11] 2 Corinthians 5:17
[12] Genesis 1:25; Genesis 1:31
[13] Genesis 1:26

essentially the nexus of the eternal and the temporal.[14] Nothing else in the creation is of this ilk as nothing else was invested with God's eternal character (not even the angels).[15] Thus, mankind is of a categorically different nature than the rest of the creation. Mankind is, as a "Day Six" creation, the highest revelation of God. Therefore, the study of mankind's inner being is far more fascinating than anything else in the creation. Nothing compares to understanding the human psyche, to uncovering its motives and reasons, to exposing its attempts at self-deity, and to helping it become a reclaimed, revived, resurrected being in God's original design. There is no greater thrill than seeing the image of God fully restored in mankind.

> Numbers 11:29 states that Moses wished that all the Lord's people were prophets. This foreshadows the church in which God's people would be not just prophets, but priests and kings, as well. In Christ the fullness of mankind's design is restored and magnified. Those in Christ are prophet (assigning meaning), priest (bringing blessing), and king (displaying power).

First Corinthians 4:9 states that Christians are a spectacle to the whole universe. The universe is the stage upon which mankind might know and glorify God ("the playground of differentiation" as theologian John Murray pointed out), and even more so, act upon that knowledge and glory. The biblical counselor participates in this grand theater, directing lost souls to find their way home to God himself. In so doing, the counselor participates in this cataclysmic cosmic spectacle; this is an incomparable honor and a high calling.

In this high calling counseling takes up the mission of effecting sanctification. It teaches the ignorant, confronts the rebellious, comforts the contrite, shapes the impressionable, and ignores the mocker. Good counseling performs all of these functions simultaneously as it exposes the contours of the human heart, often a confused and tangled web of shifting allegiances. The regenerate heart is to be exposed in all of its xenolithic sin and glorious faith. Christ-centered counseling is equipped to do this.

The most valuable gift one gives others is to invest his time into helping them to know God, to become holy like God. There is no more rewarding and fruitful work than the study of the human psyche, not merely for the purpose of uncovering sin, but for the final goal of prompting repentance and rebirth. On the flipside, there is no greater source of pain than to see slaves to sin wallow in fruitless effort and debilitating lies.[16]

> "Instead of saying that man is a product of his circumstances, it would be more accurate to say that he is the architect of his circumstances. From the same material

---

[14] 2 Corinthians 4:7
[15] 1 Peter 1:12
[16] Acts 20:31; Romans 9:3

> one man builds a palace and another a hovel." (Thomas Carlyle)

The biblical counselor does not simply seek to save souls; he longs to reclaim whole persons. He labors to transform rebellious people into the image of Christ himself. This is the greatest gift the Christian could ever offer the world, meeting the greatest need – the need to be transformed into God's likeness. While moralism, and other false attempts at change, will be burned in a consuming fire, the transformation effected by the Holy Spirit will stand on the Last Day. Christians are to seek the kind of change that will be tested by Christ and found to be of his authorship.[17]

Consider the following verses concerning the type of change that God himself seeks to effect in Christians:

1. "Therefore everyone who hears these words of mine and puts them into practice is like a wise man who built his house on rock. The rain came down, the streams rose, and the winds blew and beat against that house; yet it did not fall, because it had its foundation on the rock. But everyone who hears these words of mine and does not put them into practice is like a foolish man who built his house on sand. The rain came down, the streams rose, and the winds blew and beat against that house, and it fell with a great crash." (Matthew 7:24-27)

This building process applies to sanctification. If change for Christ is built on solid rock it will withstand the storms of life and endure for eternity; if not, one will suffer loss.

2. "The thief comes only to steal and kill and destroy; I have come that they may have life, and have it to the full." (John 10:10)

Jesus longs that each Christian would experience abundant life in himself. Jesus died that each Christian might know the kind of life that Jesus himself lived, one of vibrant fellowship with his Father.

3. "By the grace God has given me, I laid a foundation as an expert builder, and someone else is building on it. But each one should be careful how he builds. For no one can lay any foundation other than the one already laid, which is Jesus Christ. If any man builds on this foundation using gold, silver, costly stones, wood, hay or straw, his work will be shown for what it is, because the Day will bring it to light. It will be revealed with fire, and the fire will test the quality of each man's work. If what he has built survives, he will receive his reward. If it is burned up, he will suffer loss; he himself will be saved, but only as one escaping through the flames." (1 Corinthians 3:10-15)

---

[17] 1 Corinthians 3:13

Those in Christ will survive the First Judgment upon their sin since there is no condemnation for those in Christ.[18] However, what one has done for Christ will be tested. If one's works are built upon the foundation of Christ they will stand the Second Judgment, a judgment, not upon the Christian's sin, but upon his works. If those works are built upon anything other than Christ, they will be immolated in a consuming fire. Thus, the Bible warns that some will enter heaven as though naked. This issue of the Second Judgment primarily applies to sanctification. Christ-centered change will stand on the Day of Judgment, but man-centered attempts at change will be exposed as worthless and obliterated.

Roman Ruins with a Prophet, Giovanni Paolo Pannini, 1751

4. "God chose us in Him before the creation of the world to be holy and blameless in his sight." (Ephesians 1:4)

Those in Christ are blameless; that is the justification that Jesus won on the cross. Once justified God begins a process of sanctification, to make the Christian holy in his sight. Thus, the Christian is already justified (blameless), and is being sanctified (made holy).

---

[18] Romans 8:1

5. "We proclaim him, admonishing and teaching everyone with all wisdom, so that we may present everyone perfect in Christ." (Colossians 1:28)

Biblical counselors seek to facilitate this perfection in Christ, so that it would become reality in those they counsel.

6. "Do not be taken captive by hollow and deceptive philosophies which depend upon the basic principles of this world rather than on Christ." (Colossians 2:8)

One of the roles of a biblical counselor is to serve as a sentinel alerting others to both imminent and long-term dangers. As sentinel, he warns those he counsels about the "hollow and deceptive philosophies" which daily assail them.

> They (the Levites under Korah) came as a group to oppose Moses and Aaron and said to them, 'You have gone too far! The whole community is holy, everyone of them, and the Lord is with them. Why then do you set yourselves above the Lord's assembly?' (Numbers 16:3)
>
> This Korahite mentality is a profound danger within Christian circles in which the goal is to simply help others find eternal life (to be justified), while neglecting God's passion for making disciples,[19] those transformed into vessels of holiness (to be sanctified). Many Christians, like the Korah-led Levites, believe that holiness is mystically infused as a result of saving faith. While certainly there is a death-to-life change of identity through faith, holiness is progressive, requiring continual confrontation with, and resting in, the Spirit. Holiness comes through persistently living in relationship with God, being searched, torn down, and rebuilt by his Spirit.

Consider Exodus 29:38-46 which states that the Israelites were commanded to offer two lambs on the altar each day, one in the morning, the other at twilight. The lambs were to be presented with flour, olive oil, and wine. For generations to come this burnt offering was to be made regularly at the entrance to the Tent of Meeting before the Lord. There God would meet Moses and speak to him; there also he would meet with the Israelites, and the place would be consecrated to his glory.

This section of Exodus was a command to daily sacrifice. The purpose was to remind the Israelites of their ceaseless need for God, as well as to offer a continual invitation to repentance. In this way, the Israelites underwent a rudimentary form of "proto-sanctification." (The image of sacrificing a one year old lamb is an obvious reference to Jesus who, in John 1:29, is referred to as "the Lamb of God, who takes away the sin of the world!" Jesus would not only remove the penalty for sin, but is a continual sacrifice effecting daily sanctification in believers.)

---

[19] Matthew 28:19

Counseling Permeates Our World

> Paul then stood up in the meeting of the Areopagus and said: 'People of Athens! I see that in every way you are very religious. For as I walked around and looked carefully at your objects of worship, I even found an altar with this inscription: TO AN UNKNOWN GOD. So you are ignorant of the very thing you worship—and this is what I am going to proclaim to you.
>
> The God who made the world and everything in it is the Lord of heaven and earth and does not live in temples built by human hands. And he is not served by human hands, as if he needed anything. Rather, he himself gives everyone life and breath and everything else. From one man he made all the nations, that they should inhabit the whole earth; and he marked out their appointed times in history and the boundaries of their lands. God did this so that they would seek him and perhaps reach out for him and find him, though he is not far from any one of us. 'For in him we live and move and have our being.' As some of your own poets have said, 'We are his offspring.'
>
> Therefore since we are God's offspring, we should not think that the divine being is like gold or silver or stone—an image made by human design and skill. In the past God overlooked such ignorance, but now he commands all people everywhere to repent. For he has set a day when he will judge the world with justice by the man he has appointed. He has given proof of this to everyone by raising him from the dead.'
>
> When they heard about the resurrection of the dead, some of them sneered, but others said, 'We want to hear you again on this subject.' (Acts 17:22-32)

Paul's objective is to demonstrate that everything is religious. Consider for example that music is powerful counsel. It appeals to one's affections, feelings, tastes, and desires; it seeks to shape the whole person to direct and affect worship.[20] Most modern musical themes center around, "I want."[21] It is fascinating that Revelation 18:22 records:

> The music of harpists and musicians, pipers and trumpeters,
>   will never be heard in you again.
> No worker of any trade
>   will ever be found in you again.
> The sound of a millstone

---

[20] David Covington, Biblical Counselor
[21] Edward Welch, Westminster Theological Seminary, Philadelphia, Pennsylvania

will never be heard in you again.

At the destruction of Babylon it is the musicians who are the first to be sent to their doom.[22] Additionally, Ezekiel 33:32 records, "Indeed, to them you are nothing more than one who sings love songs with a beautiful voice and plays an instrument well, for they hear your words but do not put them into practice." Ezekiel's audience, entranced by musical pleasure, cared nothing for the meaning of his lyrics. They only sought sensual counsel. The point is that music offers compelling counsel.

Destiny
John William Waterhouse, 1900

Consider that the newspaper functions as a daily counselor. Ninety-percent of the newspaper is about money.[23] The way that news stories are packaged, developed, and editorialized offers an implicit religious perspective on life. Advertisements, classifieds, and even the horoscopes, tend to center around money. The evening news is counsel seeking to advance a particular worldview. The news is not an objective, unbiased look at the world. The "facts" it presents are intended to shape one's beliefs: focus on this, fear this, want this, and judge in this way.

> Advertising, clothing, entertainment, art and architecture all counsel what to live for, what to desire, and ultimately what to worship.

The point is that each person continually offers and receives counsel; it is simply

---

[22] This insight from Al Menconi, "Putting a New Song in the Heart"
[23] David Powlison, Westminster Theological Seminary, Philadelphia, Pennsylvania

impossible not to. Even the creation itself offers a kind of counsel. Every tree, mountain, and river counsels on God's character, and mankind's purpose.

> "The heavens declare the glory of God; the skies proclaim the work of his hands. Day after day they pour forth speech; night after night they display knowledge." (Psalm 19:1, 2)

Counseling Statements in Everyday Life

1. "I wish you good luck." This is a statement about ultimate reality, offering pressing counsel. It communicates that there is no personal God; only chaos and chance rule the universe. The world's sense of luck is the hope that occasionally in a chaotic universe something favorable happens. Colossians 1:16 says that all things were created by Christ and for Christ. Therefore, there is no luck, only a sovereign God who works through all events for his glory.

2. "I'm just having a bad day." This is counsel which communicates many things in just one statement. It offers an excuse for sin, that sin is not really one's fault but the fault of one's situation. If only the circumstances would change (the day were better), then the sin would also. This is also a statement about God, that God is not good for creating a bad day. Psalm 118:24 informs, "This is the day the Lord has made. Let us rejoice and be glad in it." Additionally, Isaiah 50:4b states, "He wakens me morning by morning, wakens my ear to listen like one being instructed." Thus, for the Christian there is no such thing as a bad day. Each day was carefully planned by God before the creation of the universe. Each and every day is good because it is another manifestation of God's revealed goodness, each another opportunity to repent and change. For that, the Christian is eminently grateful.

3. "I thought she was taller than me; I'm glad she is not." This is pointed counsel as it asserts the value of a person; one's value is in that which is seen. This young woman has revealed a lust of the eyes, that she sees people with eyes that crave, desire, and long for the right appearance. This is exactly the folly of the Israelites who, in 1 Samuel 9:2, chose Saul as their king because he was an "impressive young man - a head taller than any of the others." Saul, it turned out, was a disastrous king. Like the Israelites, Christians routinely invest truth into that which is pleasing to the eye, almost always with dire consequence. Those who value that which is of the eye end up in grave pain, loss, and regret. (John 7:24, thus, admonishes, "Stop judging by mere appearances, but instead judge correctly.")

> "So from now on we regard no one from a worldly point of view. Though we once regarded Christ in this way, we do so no longer." (2 Corinthians 5:16)

4. "When I go fishing, that's my time." This is a statement about what one thinks he has a right to, what he believes belongs to him. Often people operate as if their time is their own, that they can do with it as they choose. One's time is not his own and it certainly does not exist for private, self-serving purposes.

5. "I'm a Gemini so I am naturally impulsive." Astrology is a false religion, a deviant standard of evaluation, with which to augur the outcome of one's life. As such, it is an abomination before God. Astrology holds forth a surrogate gospel which promises a measure of deliverance from the vicissitudes of a precarious world. Yet it leads one astray through mock-predictions. Astrology is an idol keeping its devotees in bondage to a man-centered contrivance of the cosmos. It is for this reason that in Exodus 22:18, God commanded sorcerers and mediums to be put to death. While, of course, under the new covenant in Christ, Christians do not literally put astrologers to death, they do put their craft to death by refusing to participate in it.

6. "She doesn't mean to hurt you, she just needs more encouragement." This statement offers counseling about the nature of sin. The implication is that people have needs which must be met by others, so the source of one's sin is that others have not met one's needs. Therefore, the back-story is that others are to blame for one's sin because they withheld their debt of encouragement. This statement also implicates God, as it sees relationship with God as insufficient to meet psychic needs so that one must turn to human sources. In light of God's supposed failure, one must turn to his creation for deliverance.

Jesus rebuked the Pharisees using the strongest words imaginable; he called them a "brood of vipers," "whitewashed tombs," "evil doers," those who honor God with their lips but whose hearts are far from God.[24] Did the Pharisees need encouragement?[25] Did they need higher self-esteem or more self-confidence? No, it was the exact opposite; they needed radical repentance. In Luke 18:11, a Pharisee stood up and prayed, "God I thank you that I am not like other men – robbers, evildoers, adulterers – or even like this tax collector." But the tax collector prayed, "God have mercy on me a sinner."[26] The Pharisee, like the tax collector, needed to humble himself and in sorrow admit his guilt before God.

7. "No one likes me; I am no good at anything." Falling into the trap, the counselor reflexively contradicts such a statement with, "Of course people like you and you are good at many things." Such a response only feeds and emboldens the idols of the heart. The statement, "No one likes me; I am no good at anything," arises from the failure to meet a standard that one sets for himself. This standard is set out of pride because one wants to be the center of attention, to be highly-regarded in other's eyes.

---

[24] Matthew 23:27; Matthew 15:8
[25] This concept from David Powlison, Westminster Theological Seminary, Philadelphia, Pennsylvania
[26] Luke 18:13

When that standard fails, a deceitful self-deprecation, or even self-hatred, sets in.²⁷

A Little Nimrod, James Jacques Joseph Tissot, c. 1882

In making such a statement the motive is to camouflage one or more dysfunctional idols, such as seeking the praises of men, or other lustful desires. The idolater's mission is to revitalize those idols so that they function as he intends. When the kind counselor responds, "Of course people like you and you are good at many things," this is exactly what the idolater wants to hear. The counselor has unwittingly taken the bait, rehabilitating dysfunctional idols so that they now serve the purpose for which they were installed, to make one feel as though he can gain abundant life outside of relationship with God.

As a side note, if the counselor does not go along with the plan to rehabilitate idols, the counselee will likely up the ante. He may resort to further self-deprecation or tears to finally enlist the counselor's sympathy. The wise counselor carefully navigates this minefield. He maintains a careful balance of truth in love, the desire to free one from sin, while not being callous to real or perceived suffering. The wise counselor expresses genuine care while pursuing a truthful exposition of the heart.

> Exodus 4:31 states that the Israelites heard from Moses and Aaron that the Lord was

---

[27] For further discussion of the issue of low self-esteem see "Self-Esteem's Deception" in the second book in this series, *What Agreement Is There Between the Temple of God and Idols?: The Accidence of Sin and Idolatry*, chapter 9: "Marauding Visigoths: The Autocratic Self"

> concerned about them and had seen their misery. Then they bowed down and worshipped God. This is part of the counseling objective, that people would know the Lord's concern for them and that this would result in worship.

8. "It's my fault that my son is rebellious." There may be a measure of truth in such a statement. Proverbs 22:6 states, "Teach a child in the way he should go, and even when he is older he will not depart from it." Additionally, 1 Timothy 3:4a states, "He must manage his own family well and see that his children obey him…" The Bible places a high degree of responsibility on a parent's role. While a parent is to require his child to exhibit discipline and respect for authority, that child also makes his own choices and determines for himself what he will worship.[28] A well-considered statement of parental failing is to be commended for seeking to take warranted responsibility, yet this misses the deeper contours of the parent's heart. The wise counselor peers behind such a statement to spy something of a flourishing fear of man, or possibly brooding failed pride. Therefore, such a statement may merely be a subtle preamble to the speaker moving to rehabilitate faltering idols.

The point of this section is to demonstrate that statements are never neutral. They are theory-laden, meaning that they must be interpreted by means of a certain worship context. The world is a veritable Rube Goldberg machine of buzzing and whirling counsel. Every statement, no matter how seemingly trivial, is religious, or "theological," and therefore necessarily offers counsel about the nature of reality, mankind's identity, the purpose of life, and the discernment of right and wrong. Counsel is given in both what one focuses on and in the way that focus is communicated. Thus, every statement has built into it an implicit narratological focus concerning the person of God, and man's rightful response to that God. In fact, it is impossible not to offer counsel in everything that one does and says. One continually interprets his world either through a God-centered, or a godless, set of lenses. The question is, "Which lenses will one wear, and which will one encourage others to wear?"

The Manifest Qualities of a Counselor

The godly counselor exhibits:

1. **Compassion.**[29] The counselor is gentle and patient, yet bold, forthright, and clear. He can express anger over sin perpetrated, and injustice endured. He is also empathetically sorrowful when faced with human suffering.[30]

---

[28] For example, while King David failed to discipline his sons Amnon and Absalom, they are still to blame for their reprehensible acts.
[29] For a comprehensive handling of this topic see "The Counselor's Compassion" found in the third book in this series, *The Days of Reckoning Are at Hand: From Fig Leaf to Olive Branch to Laurel Wreath*, chapter 2: "Suffering: The Kintsugi Objective"
[30] Zechariah 7:8

> "No one will care what you know until they know that you care." (Richard Craven)

Solomon and the Queen of Sheba, Giovanni Demin, d. 1859

2. **Humility.** The counselor recognizes that he too stands before a holy God as a redeemed sinner, saved through unmerited grace.[31]

3. **Integrity.** The counselor, on account of his own struggle with sin, speaks as one who has experienced sanctification first hand, and serves as a credible witness to its veracity.[32]

4. **Persistence.** The counselor is vigorous and determined. He does not give up on a Spirit-pursued counselee as a reflection of the fact that God himself does not give up. However, the counselor is only persistent to the extent, and in the way, that God himself is. He discerns when a counselee is unwilling to receive counsel on account of a defiant heart.[33] Thus, while he pursues those who are in the grip of sin, he is careful not to become a meddler.

5. **Correct adjudication.** The counselor does not judge the heart; he points out evidence of that which resides in the heart. He draws attention to that evidence so that

---

[31] 1 Peter 3:15, 16
[32] 1 Timothy 1:15
[33] Matthew 10:14; Hebrews 13:5

the counselee can either refute it or repent, as the Holy Spirit prompts.[34]

> "So from now on we regard no one from a worldly point of view. Though we once regarded Christ in this way, we do so no longer." (2 Corinthians 5:16)

6. **Wisdom.** The counselor is given wisdom to peer through carefully arranged camouflage and diversionary tactics. He develops an instinct for spying that which resides in the heart.[35] The biblical counselor has vision to see through a relational façade, to study indicators of the heart's constituents, while not judging the heart directly. The counselor is keenly aware of how desperately wicked the heart is,[36] and so, under the Spirit's leading, develops the skill to mark out the contours and dimensions of that wickedness.

The counselor both exposes and confronts for a compelling purpose, to either invite relationship with God for the first time, or to restore broken relationship with God. Counseling is not just about uncovering idols, as an end in itself, but has the grander purpose of bringing abundant life in Christ through vibrant fellowship with him.

> "Never discourage anyone...who continually makes progress, no matter how slowly." (Plato)

The Question of Judgment[37]

Years ago I interviewed for a ministry position. In the course of the interview, I was asked to summarize my core doctrinal beliefs. In the middle of my statements concerning sin, the interviewer paused and said with a frown, "James, you sound dogmatic." In polite society this is code for sounding judgmental and intolerant. That is how the discussion of sin will always strike those who do not grasp its import and prominence in Scripture. Those who overlook God's burning hatred of sin, and his desperate desire to free his people from it, invariably soft-pedal the profundity of Jesus' death on the cross, and in so doing reduce sanctification to mere cosmetic alteration.

Without doubt the most pressing point of contention in counseling is the issue of judgment. Just the word "judgment" conjures thoughts of a Sanhedrin tribunal, the Inquisition, the Salem Witch Trials, Gestapo tactics, and McCarthyism, reckless

---

[34] 1 Corinthians 6:3
[35] 2 Corinthians 2:11
[36] Jeremiah 17:9
[37] For additional development of the topic of godly confrontation, rightly assessing evidence of the heart, and the call to repentance, see the third book of this series, *The Days of Reckoning Are at Hand: From Fig Leaf to Olive Branch to Laurel Wreath*, both chapter 7: "Artisanal Counseling: A Foray into Methods" (the section entitled, "The Judah and Tamar Syndrome") and chapter 8: "Diagnosis: Vanishing Secrets" (the section entitled, "What Christians Often Say and What They Mean")

power trampling personal rights and ravaging innocence. Modern opposition arises from the postmodern mindset that absolute truth does not exist, and that therefore subjective morality ought not to be imposed upon another. The modern world, firmly in the grip of liberalism, seeks to tolerate all things, so that the mere notion of upholding standards is itself deemed judgmental and intolerant.[38] Beguiled by the world, Christians generally see any discussion of personal sin and repentance as implicitly judgmental.

In my opinion, one of the chief drivers for the abandonment of sound judgment in modern Christianity has to do with a church that has become feminized. While some may welcome this as a supposed intenerating presence, this is actually the insidious work of Marxist-based feminism which steadily infiltrates the church with a liberationist spirit. This feminization includes, not merely the growing trend of ordaining women to pastoral ministry, but the proliferation of an often counterfeit form of love that overlooks sin and its consequence. I believe that a trenchant feminist agenda floats like a haunting scepter above church life, so that warranted judgments of many kinds are routinely neglected.

A Meeting of Doctors at the University of Paris
Chants Royaux

As God's image-bearer, each person is designed to interpret, and therefore assign meaning to, interpersonal encounter. Put another way, people are designed to make judgments about right and wrong, good and evil, intended to accord with God's own judgments. However, does one judge rightly, with God's own eyes and with his intention? To neglect a measure of sound judgment is to shirk a duty with which one has been entrusted. To judge rightly brings protection, wisdom, and prosperity to oneself and others, while not to, forfeits those blessings.

In fact, it is impossible not to judge right from wrong, good from evil. To not make judgments would be tantamount to rendering oneself functionally blind and deaf.

---

[38] This idea from Rush Limbaugh, radio commentator

Yet, many Christians do just that with regard to the sin within themselves and in those around them. The reason most Christians eschew discussion of sin and repentance is because they love their sin and work tenaciously to prevent it from being exposed. That is why any perceived judgment of sin is so vehemently opposed.

> In Numbers 16: 1, 2, and 41, consider that one man, Korah, rebelled. He drew two others, Dathan and Abiram, with him. Then 250 Israelite community leaders quickly followed. Soon the whole assembly of Israel grumbled and gathered to oppose Moses. Rebellion is poisonous to the church and, even in small measure, can have a pervasive effect. Rebellion must be uncovered and confronted before it metastasizes and capsizes lives. Judgments, therefore, need to be made concerning evidence of the heart's intentions, before those intentions impose their will. This should not incite Gestapo-like tactics within the church, but should reignite a commitment to honoring and advancing the gospel.
>
> "See to it that no one falls short of the grace of God and that no bitter root grows up to cause trouble and defile many." (Hebrews 12:15)

The word "judge" bears profoundly negative freight in light of society's celebration of the Rogerian concept of unconditional love and the tolerance it spawns. The premise behind unconditional love is non-judgmental acceptance, that somehow this is the highest form of love. Thus, Christians are afraid to even state that they are making judgments because this is immediately cast as the archenemy of love. However, this defective form of love renders interpersonal relationship feckless and fruitless. Unconditional love (as psychology construes it) poisons the waters of the Christian's soul since any perceived judgment (no matter how biblically-sound) is seen as anathema to respectful relationship.[39]

> While the Christian is called to overlook an offense,[40] to cover a multitude of sins,[41] to forgive seventy times seven times,[42] and to love others as he already loves himself,[43] none of this disqualifies the imperative to help others change. There is nothing inherently contradictory in loving others and exercising righteous judgment for the purpose of effecting sanctification. Godly judgment is love toward another, as it helps free him from enslaving sin. The wise counselor has this far-reaching vision to see past momentary concerns and into eternal ones.

While he may be timorous about assessing and assigning value to ideas, lifestyles, institutions, cultural modalities, and even cultures themselves, the Christian's greatest

---

[39] For a more complete rebuttal to unconditional love see the third book in this series, *The Days of Reckoning Are at Hand: From Fig Leaf to Olive Branch to Laurel Wreath*, chapter 2: "Suffering: The Kintsugi Objective"
[40] Proverbs 19:11
[41] 1 Peter 4:8
[42] Matthew 18:22
[43] Mark 12:31

trepidation comes in judging the relationships right before his eyes. Since Christians often will not make Scripture-based and Spirit-led judgments concerning that which they see around them, they render themselves functional co-conspirators in others' demise. Within the Bible's parameters, the wise counselor is called to make proper judgments.[44] This is the life-blood of effective counseling.

> "The spiritual man makes judgments about all things, but he himself is not subject to any man's judgments." (1 Corinthians 2:15)
>
> "My brothers and sisters, if one of you should wander from the truth and someone should bring that person back, remember this: Whoever turns a sinner from the error of their way will save them from death and cover over a multitude of sins." (James 5:19, 20)

While faithful Christians correctly label homosexuality and abortion as sin, it is often far easier to focus on such global concerns than to confront the church member gossiping at the next table. Thus, while some Christians are aware of the need to judge right from wrong, they are afraid to do so in their local setting. Judgments may be deemed appropriate for faceless causes, but when applied to one's family, friends, or associates, one is soon craven. Consider the courage John the Baptist exhibited in his willingness to directly confront sin in his midst.[45]

> "Now Herod had arrested John and bound him and put him in prison because of Herodias, his brother Philip's wife, for John had been saying to him: 'It is not lawful for you to have her.' Herod wanted to kill John, but he was afraid of the people, because they considered John a prophet." (Matthew 14:3-5)

How does one rightly view judgment from a biblical perspective? First Corinthians 5:12 states, "What business is it of mine to judge those outside the church? Are you not to judge those inside?" Paul here implies that God judges the world; Christians judge the church. Christians have an obligation to be zealous for their own family of believers, the sanctification and purity of God's people. To this end, Christians are called to make sound Scripture-based judgments on what they observe within the church.[46] How else would Paul determine, for example, that some were false believers?[47]

> In American jurisprudence there is the concept of pressing charges. In certain instances if an offended party chooses not to press charges then the defendant is free from incarceration. This is not how the Bible sees issues within the church. If one

---

[44] 1 Corinthians 2:15
[45] Consider John 20:23 in regard to the Christian's call to rightly judge sin in accordance with God's Word.
[46] 1 Corinthians 2:15
[47] 2 Corinthians 11:26

> sins against another, it does not matter if the one sinned against does not seek to "press charges." Others in the church are to rightly raise the issue for evaluation and confrontation.

Esther Denouncing Haman, Ernest Normand, c. 1915

The sinner daily cultivates a narrative in which he is a tragic hero, a mere victim of circumstance. His life, therefore, is a purported largess of graciousness in the face of cosmic opposition and oppression. Any confrontation of his sin cuts this narrative at its root. It strips the sinner of his heroic mantle, reducing him to a craven scoundrel in light of a holy God. Yet, the counselor never forgets Ephesians 2:3, "All of us also lived among them at one time, gratifying the cravings of our flesh and following its desires and thoughts. Like the rest, we were by nature deserving of wrath." Thus, the confronter, recognizing his own sinful state, never forgets that he is one deserving death, yet under God's unmerited grace.

> The question of judgment could be likened to a pinched sciatic nerve to the sinner. The more the nerve is pinched, the more it is inflamed. The more the nerve is inflamed, the more it is pinched. The more the sinner opposes godly judgment, the more lush the culture in which sin thrives. This, in turn, furthers his sense of guilt so that he more thoroughly suppresses any hope of relief through healing confrontation.

The Tendency Toward Transference (Projection)[48]

---

[48] For additional development of this topic see "Counseling Threats: Stigmas and Stereotypes, Straw Men and

I curiously watched three gold fish interact in a fishbowl. The fish behaved in often fascinating ways. They routinely chased one another, sometimes displaying odd postures such as a kind of "stotting" observed in certain land animals. Various observers offered differing interpretations of the fish's behavior, such as:

1. They love to play.
2. They display territoriality.
3. They practice survival techniques.
4. They fight.
5. They engage in mating rituals.

Which observation or observations are correct? No one really knows. Each observer interpreted the fish's behavior differently based on what he expects to see. It occurred to me that each saw in the fish that which reflects the reality in his own heart. The irenic observer interpreted them to be playing. The aggressive and competitive observer viewed the fish as territorial. One who is angry may conclude that they are fighting. One who entertains romantic ideations believes the fish to be courting. Thus, the content of one's own heart colors how he interprets his world.

A Greek proverb reads, "The one who mistrusts others the most, should be trusted the least," and another adage admonishes, "Never trust one who places no trust in others." This points to the psychology concept of transference, that of which one is himself guilty he projects onto others as a kind of unwitting self-accusation. Based in a measure of truth, the concept of transference is not firstly a psychology concept but a biblical one. From the Bible's perspective one tends to project onto others the sin which lives in his own heart. Sin haunts the guilty; it is the ambiance which shades and colors his psyche, the waters in which his psyche bathes. This sin environment directs one's gaze as he continually seeks to assuage his guilt. For example, in Esther 3:8, King Xerxes' official, Haman, accused the Jews of disobeying Xerxes' laws. In actuality, it was Haman himself who was treacherous to the crown.

While psychology coined the term "transference," only the Bible correctly presents the concept. Transference is actually *coram Deo* in action.[49] One's stance with regard to God, one's sin patterns, the state of one's conscience, and one's existential condition, are all mentally transferred to others. In other words, one's sin and guilt dominate his existential environment which becomes the set of lens through which he sees others.

Shibboleths" in the third book in this series, *The Days of Reckoning Are at Hand: From Fig Leaf to Olive Branch to Laurel Wreath*, chapter 8: "Diagnosis: Vanishing Secrets"

[49] For a comprehensive discussion of the *coram Deo* concept see chapter 6: "Man Before the Face of God: The Imperium of the Psyche"

> "We tend to judge others by their actions and ourselves by our intentions." (Albert Schlieder)

Usually the counselee will reveal what he functionally worships if the counselor listens in the right way. A key to unlock the intentions of the heart is this: whatever the counselee most criticizes in others, whatever he points out as others' failing is likely what he finds to be his own failing. This is the sin that most haunts him, that from which he most seeks relief. In this regard, people are really not that complex. They will inadvertently tell the counselor much of what he needs to know through presenting a mirror image of his own heart. The counselee will project onto others the sins for which he is most guilty, and concerning which he most wants answers, relief, and repentance.

> "For I know my transgressions, and my sin is always before me." (Psalm 51:3)

Likewise, the counselor himself could easily be charged with this same projective tendent. There is only one antidote to transference: sanctification. As one grows in sanctification, as he is continually renewed by Christ, as his own idolatry fades, he is better able to see, unclouded, the idolatry in others. It is only through sanctification that the counselor gains the ability (and social right) to help others repent of their own sin. Thus, as the counselor becomes more aware of the contours of sin and faith within himself, the tendency to transference progressively diminishes. The counselor can rightly see something of the existential condition within others as he is progressively freed from sin's distorting lenses, and dons the restoring lenses of holiness.

> The threat of transference in counseling is not just in terms of content. It also involves the counseling method, or the extent and manner in which one analyzes the heart. Thus, the means by which the counselor first analyzes himself is the means by which he invariably analyzes others. One gains a glimpse into the degree to which self-assessment takes place in the counselor himself by the manner in which that assessment occurs, and is encouraged in others.

What psychology can never understand is that transference is overcome through the sanctifying work of Christ. As one is increasingly sanctified, as he daily repents of his sin, his sin is no longer the set of lenses through which he sees others. The ambiance of guilt fades, and the bathing waters of one's psyche recede, so that one's gaze is renewed. Consider 1 Corinthians 2:16b, "…but we have the mind of Christ." In other words, one is no longer a prisoner to projective accusation since he has been forgiven, possessing a new set of eyes with which to see himself and others. Thus, the progressively sanctified Christian can help others see their sin without falling prey to the charge of transference. In this way, there is an inverse relationship between one's tendency to transference and one's sanctification.

The Trial of George Jacobs Sr., 1692, Tompkins Harrison Matheson, d. 1884

The Imperative to Rightly Judge

An automobile tire is perfectly round (within tolerance for the purposes of comfortable driving). Yet, as that tire sits on a road surface it is out-of-round, having flattened at the road interface. Nevertheless, as the car travels, the tire performs in a manner that is functionally round (while, in actuality, it assumes an imperfect shape). (Even more so, the tire conforms to the deviations in the road surface, while remaining functionally round.)

An analogy could be drawn between the dynamics of an automobile tire and the biblical counselor. Like a round tire, God's work is perfect, effecting his desired results within the heart. However, God uses counselors who are "out-of-round," imperfect instruments. Christ-centered counsel, while delivered by one who is himself sinful, functions as a perfect instrument to the extent that it adheres to God's Word and upholds the gospel. The point is that the counselor, an out-of-round instrument, can trust in a good God to effect a functionally "perfect" outcome.

Matthew 7:5 offers insight into the way that this phenomenon works. "You hypocrite, first take the plank out of your own eye, and then you will see clearly to remove the speck from your brother's eye." Removing the plank from one's own eye implies ardently renouncing sin and resolving to dwell in the Spirit. This is the prerequisite for seeing clearly so as to remove the speck from another's eye. Thus, sanctification, in fact, removes the plank from one's own eye so that he is able to remove the speck from another's eye. The repentant Christian is no longer hopelessly clouded by a sinful gaze and the phenomenon of transference no longer applies. John 7:24 reinforces this with, "Stop judging by mere appearances, but instead judge correctly."

The unspoken imperative is that the Christian is to in fact remove his blinding plank (under the guidance and power of the Holy Spirit) and to then employ his newly-minted binocular vision to remove another's speck. Jesus' words imply proximity (to see into another's eye), judgment (to discern healthy tissue from an intrusion), and the courage and care to actually perform the procedure (removing the xenolith for the good of another).

> "Do you not know that the saints will judge the world? And if you are to judge the world, are you not competent to judge trivial cases? Do you not know that we will judge angels? How much more the things of this life!" (1 Corinthians 6:2, 3)

While the Christian must make judgments concerning sin (the intrusion), he has no right to judge the heart (the wellspring).[50] He points out and assesses *evidence* (fruit, indicators) of what may inhabit the heart. Sometimes that evidence may be overwhelming, in which case he implores the counselee to repent. But while the imperative for repentance may arise from the wise counselor's vision, the sanctification which accompanies it must be God's direct work. The counselor shepherds the heart; God himself is the heart's direct change agent.

The Christian's judgment is not based on the rule of law but on the rule of love. This means that all judgment is directed toward the highest good for another, and that judgment is exclusively under the auspices of Scripture, so that nothing in the Christian's judgment is based on personal opinion or for the purpose of personal gain. Free from corruption, from beginning to end, the Christian's judgment is a love-of-God-and-love-of-others endeavor.[51]

There are really two aspects to wise and godly judgment. The first is that the counselor judges based on that which is clearly stated in Scripture. This is supported by 1 Thessalonians 5:20-22, which states, "Do not treat prophecies with contempt. *Test everything*. Hold on to what is good. Reject every kind of evil." The counselor is to test everything against Scripture: his lens, litmus test, and guide in assessing sin. The second is that he assesses evidence of heart idols. This concerns assessing the motive behind actions. The question of assessing idols is a "dark horse" in the issue of

---

[50] Proverbs 4:23
[51] Mark 12:29-31

judgment, since this may not always be easy to discern, especially for Christians not accustomed to recognizing worship patterns.

The counselor judges only to the extent that the Bible makes him privy to God's standards. Thus, where God has revealed truth the counselor rightly upholds that truth. The counselor merely applies the truth in the way that God does, so that proper judgment, far from being a liability or threat, is actually a blessing guarding the path of those who receive it.

> "For the word of God is alive and active. Sharper than any double-edged sword, it penetrates even to dividing soul and spirit, joints and marrow; it judges the thoughts and attitudes of the heart." (Hebrews 4:12)

The extent to which the counselor faithfully employs God's Word is the extent to which his words implicitly function to "judge the thoughts and attitudes of the heart." The counselor looks for patterns of the heart, evidence of the content of the heart, in strict accordance with, and to the extent that the Bible does. From the opposite perspective, who is the Christian not to judge when God has clearly stated his standards and requirements? The Christian disobeys God when he refuses to judge right and wrong, good and evil, based on God's own revelation on these matters. The Christian must judge to obey God. Consider John 9:20-22,

> 'We know he is our son,' the parents answered, 'and we know he was born blind. But how he can see now, or who opened his eyes, we don't know. Ask him. He is of age; he will speak for himself.' His parents said this because they were afraid of the Jewish leaders, who already had decided that anyone who acknowledged that Jesus was the Messiah would be put out of the synagogue.

The parents of the man born blind refused to rightly judge Jesus' identity out of fear. They, thus, cowardly transferred the burden of judgment to their son. Those who refuse to make wise judgments usually do so out of fear of man.

> In the modern milieu any aggrieved party is considered morally upright. Therefore, anytime a kerfuffle arises the first to become upset gains the upper-hand in the court of public opinion. The one who is upset is judged to be the offended party, the victim, the oppressed. However, this is often not the case. Right and wrong are not to be judged by the emotional responses of those involved, but rather based on how God's Word frames the issues. The wise counselor sees past fustian to the substance of the matter, fully recognizing that the guilty party may often put on the greatest "fireworks display."

One of the People - Gladstone in an Omnibus, Alfred Morgan, 1885

"Cassandra," a member of the church I pastor, slandered me to another member, "Pam." Pam brought the slander to my attention as which time I stated quite unequivocally how God calls Christians to treat a slanderer. First Corinthians 5:11 states,

> But now I am writing to you that you must not associate with anyone who claims to be a brother or sister but is sexually immoral or greedy, an idolater or slanderer, a drunkard or swindler. Do not even eat with such people.

I emphasized to Pam the command in Matthew 18:15 that sin is first to be handled one person to another, privately, so as to guard the matter. Pam's response was that Cassandra is a new Christian and therefore should not be expected to obey God in all matters (namely in this case, to know not to slander or to follow the directives in Matthew 18:15-17). Therefore, according to Pam, Cassandra was not culpable in the matter.

Who is Pam to sit in judgment over which commands Christians are to uphold and which they are permitted to disregard? Who is Pam to decide which Christians are "new" Christians and therefore given license to sin against others? Pam's approach follows in lockstep with liberalism which keeps Christians in a childlike state, never calling them to account for clear transgression. She has, in effect, set up a patrician form of condescension in which some are considered too weak and too ignorant to obey God.

> "I am so full of niceness I have no sense of right and wrong, no outrage, no passion." (Garrison Keillor)

God does not delimit his commands to the mature, nor exonerate the immature for clear sin. (He offers a certain accommodation in disputable matters, such as with meat sacrificed to idols in 1 Corinthians 8, in which one with a weak conscience is to be guarded from falling into sin.) However, many Christians wrongly view Christianity as a kind of linear progression in which one can justifiably disregard certain aspects of the faith under the deluded notion that one is not yet mature enough to understand or obey those aspects. This is tantamount to saying that a very young child is not culpable for rebellion. In fact, the child is culpable but one may not yet be entirely aware of the extent of his rebellion. (That being said, there is a sense in which the Christian's conscience is revived and sharpened as he studies God's Word and walks in faith. This sharpening process makes him more aware of the extent of his sin.)

In effect Pam has installed herself as God in the situation, deciding the extent and manner in which other Christians are expected to obey. She has decided which commands can be disregarded because she has judged the state of another's heart, and found that heart lacking the means to obey (which implicitly blames God).

> The counselor must understand that, with regard to sin, tolerance will never be met by tolerance. In other words, those who desire that their sin would be overlooked will not in turn overlook sin. They have simply been emboldened to endow and live out judgments of their own making. (Neville Chamberlain (1869–1940), in his appeasement policy toward Adolf Hitler (1889-1945), learned this all too well.)

The "Do Not Judge" *Coup de Grâce*

When unwilling to countenance one's own sin, the final word in the discussion is usually to quote Matthew 7:1, "Do not judge, or you too will be judged." Those who quote Matthew 7:1, more often than not, overlook the verse's context. This verse specifically addresses the issue of forgiveness. The essence of the proscribed judgment is a refusal to forgive which arises from arrogating to oneself the position of eternal cosmic judge. When one installs himself as God he falsely judges that other's sins cannot, or should not, be forgiven.

Just as the judgments the Christian rightfully makes are not about the content of another's heart but about evidence of the heart, so too, he is not to make decisive judgments about the final state of another's soul, whether destined for salvation or perdition. Rather, the wise counselor references "fruit" as evidence of another's eternal state,[52] all the while recognizing that that state is ultimately determined by God alone.

> "…hand this man over to Satan for the destruction of the flesh, so that his spirit may be saved on the day of the Lord." (1 Corinthians 5:5)

I find that those who are quick to quote Matthew 7:1 are often the most judgmental Christians. With patrician condescension, they seek to pass judgment in their own way, for their own purposes. They routinely overlook offenses that they deem to be inconsequential, while drawing attention to real or supposed offenses that they decide are condemnable. Thus, most who are quick to state, "Do not judge," have donned blinders to certain transgressions, while suddenly removing those blinders to view other offenses in minute detail.

Saint Lucy Before the Judge
Lorenzo Lotto, 1532

Today many Christians are morally rudderless, cast adrift on a sea of moral relativism. For this reason, upholding God's Word, and calling other Christians to do the same, is routinely labeled as a subjective and personal attack. Additionally, confronting idolatry is seen as a hurtful affront. For example, a Christian woman in the church I pastor slandered another church member. When calmly but firmly confronted with her transgression (clearly substantiated from Scripture), she condemned this as a subjective attack. She subsequently spread more slander that she is now a victim of church discipline. As a morally directionless person, this woman is first callous to the nature of her actions (those actions being an offense in God's eyes), and therefore obdurate concerning the purpose behind any needed confrontation. Since she is blind to God's standard, she lives in a chaotic world in which those who uphold such standards are viewed as derelict vigilantes.

The biblical counselor's judgment is never criticism of another, and thus, is never

---

[52] Matthew 7:16

rooted in personal animus. It never arises out of perceived superiority, is never motivated by control, and is never solely an isolated confrontation with sin. When done with a humble and contrite spirit, judgment bears nothing of the disheartening undertones so common in the world's criticism. Likewise, the counselor sees himself as equally subject to the judgments he propounds. In this way, patient judgment-in-love wields the sword of the Spirit, so that God can do groundbreaking work in the heart.

> "For my part, even though I am not physically present, I am with you in spirit. As one who is present with you in this way, I have already passed judgment in the name of our Lord Jesus on the one who has been doing this." (1 Corinthians 5:3)

The Christian's judgment is never an isolated confrontation with sin, but always comes in the context of a "from-to" structure for directing the sinner to deeper relationship with Christ,[53] helping to castoff hindrances to that relationship so that one can live fruitfully.[54] Bible-sanctioned judgment is the tool of the humble servant helping others press forward toward the goal of greater sanctification. But the Christian must be acutely aware that in making sound biblical judgments he will at times be excoriated and marginalized in a world (and in a church) that abhors even the hint of confronting personal sin.

> "But if we were more discerning with regard to ourselves, we would not come under such judgment. Nevertheless, when we are judged in this way by the Lord, we are being disciplined so that we will not be finally condemned with the world." (1 Corinthians 11:31, 32)

---

[53] David Powlison, Westminster Theological Seminary, Philadelphia, Pennsylvania
[54] Hebrews 12:1

- 3 -

THE CENTRALITY OF SCRIPTURE IN COUNSELING

Introduction

One morning I sat in class waiting for my students to arrive. It was rare moment of almost complete peace as I prayed. Several scripture verses entered my mind and each was like a dear friend offering comfort, encouragement, a measure of rebuke and repentance, as well as renewed commitment to press forward in my faith. Suddenly the door burst open and three girls spilled into the room, breakfast and books in hand. After greeting me, the girls proceeded to gossip and complain about various matters. They bemoaned the heat, the food, and their classes, carrying on with rumors and loud unsavory talk. I tried in vain to continue my prayer but my mind was being invaded, and I could not regain my foothold.

Still Life with Open Bible
Vincent Willem van Gogh, 1885

At that moment it occurred to me that for all of eternity God had ordained in that place, at that moment, to powerfully apply his Word to my heart. He longed to shape my day around his Word, to interpret my experiences through his Word, so that I would turn from sin, experience sanctification, and more fully conform to his image. I was made to live off of his Word and it was written to govern the interpretation of my day. However, as the three rotors on a buzzing whirligig spun out words derived from the world, a counterfeit Scripture invaded my heart. Their concoction served as a toxic assault upon my spirit, and sadly my spirit felt powerless to repel the onslaught.

Each of us was created by God, for God, and to God.[1] The Christian's spirit was

---
[1] Romans 11:36

designed to derive its sustenance from God. The heart was crafted to crave only God himself. For all of eternity, each moment of each day has been carefully orchestrated that the Christian would meditate upon God's Word, bask in his truth, and more fully glorify him. Thus, any word not of God functions as Satan's attack agent, robbing the believer of his God-given right to know and contemplate God in all situations.

Each moment taken hostage by Satan is a moment lost for all eternity; each thought not of God, furthers a derelict narrative which falsely interprets oneself and one's circumstance. Thus, when deprived of God's Word, one's circumstance and the intentions of one's heart grow discordant, confused, and contradictory. For this reason, God's Word was designed to interface with every moment of the believer's every day, so that each day would accord with an eternal plan, that the believer would be known, changed, and conformed more closely to God himself.

> It may be at the time of the Great Flood, mentioned both in Chinese literature and in the Bible, that China was first called "Shenzhou" (神州), meaning "land of God." For possibly 2,500 years the Chinese called their homeland Shenzhou, but after about 500 BC China abandoned that name. As China fell away from its Shenzhou self-reference eminent philosophers arose. From about 600 BC to about 300 BC six such philosophers were born: Laozi (born c. 604 BC), Confucius (551–479 BC), Mozi (c. 470 – c. 391 BC), Mencius (372–289 BC), Zhuangzi (369–286 BC), and Han Feizi (281–233 BC). While each philosopher differed, they all recognized the *da dao* (大道), meaning the "Word," which had been lost from Chinese life, having existed for the first 2,500 years of Chinese culture. One of the earliest Chinese classics, *The Chronicle of Zuo*, attributed to Zuo Qiu Ming (5th c. BC), summarizes the concept of *dao* as the emperor's loyalty to the people and devotion to God.
>
> As long as *dao* prevailed the kingdom was at peace. What was this *dao*? It is thought to be the same "Word" described in the Bible. The Word of God as manifest through his Son, Jesus Christ.[2]
>
> With the loss of the *dao* from Chinese culture, Confucius prophesied that the "great phoenix" would no longer come to "dance" (possibly a reference to the eternal God of heaven). After Confucius' death there arose the Warring States period (475–221 BC) during which China changed dramatically, becoming a place of debauchery, lawlessness, and war. There was rampant deception and immorality throughout society.

The Danger of Deconstructionist Reading

Sigmund Freud (1856–1939) and Karl Marx (1818–1883) together spawned a societal

---

[2] John 1:1

atmosphere, reflected in literature, in which there is no fixed meaning. They asserted that an author is *necessarily* shaped by a particular cultural bias which makes him unable to ascertain truth. He is trapped in his own social and cultural bias. The reader must therefore deconstruct the author's text to uncover the meaning "behind" the text (the pretext or subtext).

The Reader
Pierre-Auguste Renoir, c. 1876

In fact, an author is not even the authority on his own text. Rather the reader is the arbiter of truth because only the reader is "enlightened." It is not just that the author and text have no meaning, but that they are enemies to meaning. The historian, for example, stands in the way of a proper revisionist reading of history because he is trapped in a particular socio-economic, racial, or gender bias.[3]

Freud posited that an author harbors hidden motives, nestled deep within his consciousness, which the reader must decipher. Marx saw that people never think as individuals but only as members of a social class. Those in power, the bourgeoisie, have only one purpose – oppress the proletariat. So the complexity and mystery of human motive is painted monochromatically.

Using a similar approach to Marxism, feminism redefines "oppressor" and "oppressed" as men and women respectively, concocting its own distinctive form of deconstruction. So, for instance, Plato (426-346 BC) (read: dead white male oppressor) would be studied, not for his truth content, but for his subconscious oppression of women, or for his bourgeoisie sensibilities. Under deconstruction guidelines, only the reader has authority to say what Plato really meant, and not *any* reader, only the properly illuminated reader.

> It is fascinating to note that while Chinese communism draws heavily from Marxism, Chinese academe takes a highly author-centered approach to text interpretation. In China the author is "god," so that the reader is tasked with

---

[3] Tom Neven, *Do Fish Know They're Wet?: Living in the World Without Getting Hooked* (New York: Baker Books, 2005)

> disentangling authorial intent.

Understanding the dangers posed by deconstruction, the Bible must be guarded from such an interpretive grid. In defiance of deconstruction, the Bible is not trapped in a particular cultural bias, but rather finally transcends culture to be universally applied and appropriated. How does the reader properly interpret the Bible? The Bible is rightly interpreted on three horizons: authorial intent, textual content, and Holy Spirit-filled reader, each functioning in tandem to reveal truth.

Mankind's finiteness means that Scripture must function as an epistemological integration point (a starting point for knowledge). Without this integration point there would be no way for mankind to distinguish truth from error, God's wisdom from the world's folly.[4]

> "Education has produced a vast population able to read but unable to discern what is worth reading." (G.M. Trevelyan)

The Truth Cannot Co-exist with Human Systems of Thought

In *The Miracle of Language* Richard Lederer recounts the following story concerning the end of World War II. On July 26, 1945, leaders Winston Churchill (1874–1965), Harry Truman (1884–1972), and Joseph Stalin (1878–1953) issued The Potsdam Declaration which demanded Japan's unconditional surrender. The Japanese delegation issued a statement that they were giving the peace offer "*mokusatsu*."

Mokusatsu is translated either "we are considering it," or "we are ignoring it." The proper translation depends upon the context. For some reason the translator provided the second meaning, "ignore," which was quickly picked up by journalists. Actually, the Japanese diplomats intended the first meaning, "considering."[5]

The United States estimated that to end the war over one million Americans would be lost invading Japan. Inferring that the peace offer had been rejected, President Truman moved forward with his plan to drop two atomic bombs on Japan beginning August 6, 1945. Four days later Japan surrendered, and the war was over. One can only speculate that if that single word had been translated differently how the course of history could have been altered.

Just as the interpretation of a single word determined the outcome of a world war, so too, the Bible must be correctly interpreted to determine the outcome of the war within the heart. In this regard, the Bible cannot be coupled, or integrated with, any

---

[4] 1 Corinthians 2:6-16
[5] Richard Lederer, *The Miracle of Language* (New York: Pocket Books, 1991) 82, 83.

other system of thought. It cannot be harmonized with, or supplemented by, philosophy or psychology. When offered an alternate system of thought, a false "gospel," the sinful heart subsumes the Bible's message, allowing human reason to gain the upper-hand in interpretation.[6] When coupled with the Bible, a man-centered perspective always cannibalizes the Bible within the heart.

Therefore the following must be eschewed:

1. Scripture interpreted through church tradition.

2. Scripture interpreted through the lens of human experience.

3. Scripture interpreted through unaided human reason (secular thought such as scientism or psychology).

> New England pastor John Harvard (1607–1638) founded Harvard University in 1636 to train aspiring pastors. Since its inception Harvard's symbol was an open book whose pages were turned *away* from the viewer. This represented the limitations of human knowledge, that there are some things which are inscrutable. In 1911 Harvard reversed the book, showing its pages *open* to the viewer. This was to communicate that man can now know everything through unaided reason.[7]

Matthew 6:24 states: "No one can serve two masters. Either he will hate the one and love the other, or he will be devoted to the one and despise the other." While this verse refers to the enslaving quality of the love of money, it could well be applied to any subjugating tyrant. Thus, the Bible cannot peacefully exist alongside any other truth claims (namely philosophy and its offshoot psychology). The Bible is in a life-and-death struggle with any interpretation of the human condition which fundamentally derives from unsanctified reason.

Presenting Truth, Refuting Error

Christians are given a duel charge: to present the truth and to refute error. The Bible is written with both this positive and negative thrust. It unfurls the truth in all its glory, while actively opposing predatory falsehood. For example, Genesis 1 is both a statement of God's victory over the forces of evil, while at the same time a direct refutation of ancient Babylonian and Sumerian creation narratives. Thus, Genesis specifically frames itself in the terms and images common to Babylonian and Sumerian cosmogonies.

---

[6] David and Sharon Covington, "Introduction to Bible Counseling" notes, 2004
[7] William Edgar, "Introduction to Apologetics" class, Westminster Theological Seminary, Philadelphia, Pennsylvania

However, Genesis reinterprets those terms and images in light of what Yahweh has done. In like manner, the Genesis flood narrative specifically sets itself in opposition to Babylonian and Assyrian flood narratives, redefining those narratives as Yahweh's redemptive-historical work. Thus, Genesis does not cower from direct confrontation with Israel's ancient Near Eastern neighbors. It specifically targets those neighbors' myths in order to refute them. In this way, the Bible's statements never arise in a historical vacuum, but rather target man-centered truth claims. For example, consider John 1:1, "In the beginning was the Word, and the Word was with God, and the Word was God." This was an implicit attack on Greek philosophy which saw the "Word" (*logos*) as a created entity.

Leviathan
Gustave Dore, d. 1883

> Fallen man fabricates a particular image of God to serve his own needs. This is a god that the sinner casts in his own image and likeness, so that he projects that which he sees in himself upon God. That is why God's Word is so vital in order to continually correct the sinful tendency to redefine God as man desires him.

Mirroring the Bible, counseling likewise assumes this dual role. It presents the truth while undermining falsehood. Like the Bible, the wise counselor does not leave falsehood unconfronted, unchallenged, and unopposed. Second Corinthians 10:5 is clear in this regard, "We demolish arguments and every pretension that sets itself up against the knowledge of God, and we take captive every thought to make it obedient to Christ." The counselor does not allow falsehood to fester, metastasize, and poison. Instead, he wages a holy war against the institutions,[8] fallacies, and wrongly-directed worship that surround him. The objective is that as falsehood is opposed and exposed

---

[8] 1 Corinthians 10:3

it is progressively replaced by truth.

> The sun produces light. In imitation of the sun, mankind invented the light bulb to produce light for himself. Just as man uses the light bulb as a substitute for the sun, so too, man uses his own reason as a substitute for God's reason. Man's reason can never interpret God's being and work because man's reason is derivative. Man's reason only exists because God's reason first exists, and therefore defines the purpose and function of reason itself. Man's reason must first be illuminated by God's in order to function at all.[9]

A critical question is, "Which types of error could rightly be considered errors of ignorance, and which are based in rebellion?" Error with regard to the gospel is never truly ignorance, while error with regard to secondary questions is often more difficult to define. How does the biblical counselor rightly judge the severity of error in analyzing the heart? How much weight does he assign to various transgressions? Which does the counselor go after, and which does he overlook for a time? The answer to these questions may not always be clear. The counselor must ask God for wisdom to know which errors lead to death and which are of a secondary nature, to be addressed over the course of time.[10]

Interpreting the Bible[11]

A solander is a storage case made to look like a book (possibly placed in a library to hide valuables). In many ways, the Bible has become little more than a solander in the hands of many modern Christians, a case in which they store and draw out a treasured man-centered worldview, a hollow Bible used to support worldly desires. But this is a grave mistake as God's Word is not to be trifled with.

The Bible is perspicuous so that the gospel is clearly understood. The Bible is necessary for salvation, authoritative on the matters on which it speaks, and sufficient in revealing all that is needed to live by faith.[12] Thus, the Bible, read through the lens of faith, reveals its truth to those who humbly and honestly seek it, while concealing itself from those who approach it with hard hearts. Consider Deuteronomy 32:47 in this regard. "They are not just idle words for you—*they are your life*. By them you will live long in the land you are crossing the Jordan to possess."

> As a young man Abraham Lincoln's family could scarcely afford paper (at that time

---

[9] Cornelius Van Til, *Christian Apologetics* (Presbyterian and Reformed Press, 2003) 67, 68.
[10] 1 John 5:17
[11] For further discussion of the issue of Bible interpretation see "Excursus: Bible Characters" in the third book in this series, *The Days of Reckoning Are at Hand: From Fig Leaf to Olive Branch to Laurel Wreath*, chapter 6: "The Basic Plotlines Which Emerge in Counseling"
[12] William Edgar, "Introduction to Theology" class, Westminster Theological Seminary, Philadelphia, Pennsylvania

> a costly luxury) so he wrote Bible verses on wooden planks. He lashed the planks to his plow in order to memorize the verses while working in the field.[13]

Every faulty approach to Scripture revolves around a man-centered worldview, one in which each person, on account of his sin, lives in such a way so as to write his own autobiography. Fallen man continually writes a story in which he is a hero; he is good and noble; his sin is not his own fault, and God is the villain.[14] God longs to impede this effort so that the sinner enters into God's own autobiography – the gospel. Thus, the Bible, at every turn, thwarts any effort to define God on one's own terms, for one's own purposes. The Bible, in effect, unequivocally dictates who God is, how he is to be understood, and what is to be one's proper response to him. In this way, mankind can never rest in a false gospel as long as the Bible is given a hearing.

> "When tempted, no one should say, 'God is tempting me.' For God cannot be tempted by evil, nor does he tempt anyone;" (James 1:13)

The Bible reveals a story in which God never changes (aseity),[15] in which God is transcendent (utterly different than his creation), and in which he is immanent (as close to his creation as he could possibly be). "[God's] immanence makes his transcendence comforting, while his transcendence makes his immanence amazing." The gospel is the singular nexus of this awe and intimacy; the almighty holy God of the universe has become Father.[16]

> "Theology is from God, teaches about God, and leads to obedience to God." (Augustine)

God longs to rewrite the sinner's story so that Jesus is hero; only Jesus is good and noble; one's sin is his own fault propelled by his own active will; and the sinner is the villain in his own life. To this end, the counselor continually draws the counselee out of his specious autobiographic story and into the only true story, that of Jesus as savior. The counselor helps to rewrite the counselee's life story so as to invert hero and villain, and reverse a false sense of good and evil, all in a manner that highlights the counselee's need for ongoing change.

> "I know that nothing good lives in me, that is, in my sinful nature. For I have the desire to do what is good, but I cannot carry it out." (Romans 7:18)

---

[13] Doris Kearns Goodwin, *Team of Rivals: The Political Genius of Abraham Lincoln* (New York: Simon and Schuster, 2005)
[14] David and Sharon Covington, "Introduction to Biblical Counseling" notes, 2004
[15] Malachi 3:6; James 1:7
[16] Andrew Field, "Introduction to Redeemer", p. 7, Westminster Theological Seminary, Philadelphia, Pennsylvania

> While the Bible does mention the significance of certain historical dreams (such as those of Joseph and Pharaoh),[17] in the Christian's life, dreams do not hold any hidden message, nor offer any meaning to be decrypted. I have had many nightmares which have left me unsettled to my core, but they signify nothing except that I have an active imagination.[18]

Joseph Explaining Pharaohs Dream, Jean Adrien Guignet, d. 1854

The Bible Speaks to the Plenary Human Condition

The following is a common test of intelligence. Three light bulbs hang in a room and three switches operating the light bulbs are placed in another room. One must determine which switch operates which light bulb. However, one can only enter each room once. How will one determine which switch operates which bulb? The solution turns upon thinking outside of the concepts presented. The answer is to turn on two of the switches for a time, and then turn one of them off. Upon entering the room with the light bulbs, one sees one bulb lit and feels for a second warm bulb. In this way, one identifies which light bulbs correspond to which switches.

In a certain sense this serves as a fit description of the way in which the Christian

---

[17] Genesis 37:5-11; 41:1-40
[18] Edward Welch, "Human Personality" class, Westminster Theological Seminary, Philadelphia, Pennsylvania

understands and weighs life using the Bible. The Bible causes one to think outside of set channels, to assess life in dramatically different fashion from the world, to see data which operates outside of the presented elements.

The Bible communicates matters of unspeakable breadth and depth. Romans 8:6 reveals, "…but the mind set on the Spirit is life and peace." First Corinthians 2:16b also reminds, "…we have the mind of Christ." Appropriating the mind of Christ means allowing Scripture to serve as one's set of lenses. Just as lenses can be positioned in any direction, the Bible is unlimited in its viewing capabilities. It is not relegated to the specific topics which it raises, but rather addresses every conceivable topic. Therefore, the Bible focuses on the plenary human condition, making sense of mankind from every angle, whether directly addressed in Scripture or not.[19]

> The Bible offers far more prescient, profound, and piercing insights into the condition of modern man than does the daily news.

While it is true that the Bible does not reveal the age of the earth or the secrets of quantum physics, it is not silent on any matter pertaining to faith. That which is needed to lead a fulfilled life in Jesus is in fact revealed.[20] As God himself authored the Bible, there is no human condition or plight that is too complex for it to handle effectively. The Bible speaks to the human condition in its entirety, all that one needs to know God personally, oneself truly, and the life for which one was designed. Thus, there is nothing that needs to be added to the Bible's understanding of people.[21]

> "In this age of space flight, when we wield the tools of science to do what was previously unimaginable, the Bible remains in every way a relevant and needed book. Our knowledge and marshalling of the laws of nature to fly to the Moon also permit us to destroy our planet. Science cannot answer the question of the right use of our abilities. It cannot decide upon benevolent and wicked applications of our knowledge. The guidelines for this are found in the Bible." (Wernher von Braun)

Psychology is literally the "study of the soul," and as such, presents a view of mankind and his problems. Likewise, the Bible presents its own psychology,[22] a comprehensive study of people and their problems. The Bible pierces deeply into the soul revealing it as it truly is.

> "The Word of God is a double edged sword cutting through bone and marrow – dividing soul and spirit." (Hebrews 4:12)

---

[19] David and Sharon Covington, "Introduction to Biblical Counseling" notes, 2004
[20] David Covington, Biblical Counselor
[21] As will be explored in subsequent chapters, the Christian is also in personal relationship with God. The Bible makes this personal relationship come alive and, in fact, that is the Bible's sole purpose, to make relationship possible and meaningful.
[22] David Powlison, Westminster Theological Seminary, Philadelphia, Pennsylvania

The Bible speaks to every human issue, and in fact, radically redefines how one sees each issue. For example, modern labels manic-depression, schizophrenia, obsessive compulsive disorder (OCD), attention deficit and hyperactivity disorder (ADHD), anorexia, and even muscle dysmorphia (an obsession with body image) are not only addressed, but radically redefined in the Bible. The Bible may contain no discrete verse for these issues, but speaks volumes about the underlying condition using its own distinct descriptors.[23]

Emperor Qianlong Practicing Calligraphy, mid-18th century

The Bible is not content to merely offer wise principles or helpful advice. Like a guided laser, the Bible goes directly to the worshipping core, uncovering and reshaping the terms of human self-understanding. The Bible addresses its issues, not in an encyclopedic way, but through gospel-colored lenses, peering into each issue as God himself sees it. Thus, each of the terms mentioned above is actually based in a problem of relationship with God, relationship which the Bible seeks to initiate and uphold through the gospel. In this way, the Bible does not see humanity as humanity sees itself but rather as God does, recognizing that complete and radical transformation of the heart is required for the cure of souls.

> As physicists hunt for the Grand Unified Theory of matter and the forces that govern it, there is already a Grand Unified Theory with regard to the human psyche. The

---

[23] For a comprehensive discussion of this topic see chapter 8: "What Has Jerusalem To Do With Vienna?: The Case Against Psychology"

> Bible offers a comprehensive understanding of the plenary human condition and its resolution. While psychology largely lies Balkanized and internally contradictory, the gospel of Jesus Christ is eminently straightforward and clarifying. Around the hub of the gospel revolve all questions and every solution to every human dilemma.

Toward a Sound Doctrine of Scripture

The ancient work *Shijing* (诗经) (begun c. 1000 BC) is a compilation of 305 poems. In this work the term "heavenly God" occurs 421 times. Confucius noted that all 305 poems reflect a pure heart, the mark of pious devotion to the holy God. When the "Word" (*dao*, 道) is lost the heart of man becomes brutal and depraved. (The ancient Chinese seem to have recognized this to some extent.)

This leads to two central truths about interpreting Scripture. It always focuses on heart worship, and always sees relationship with Jesus as the principal encounter of the renewed heart. Thus, the Bible's entire purpose could be summarized as heart change through relationship with Jesus. Consider Matthew 20:20-22,

> Then the mother of Zebedee's sons came to Jesus with her sons and, kneeling down, asked a favor of him. 'What is it you want?' he asked. She said, 'Grant that one of these two sons of mine may sit at your right and the other at your left in your kingdom.'
>
> 'You don't know what you are asking,' Jesus said to them. 'Can you drink the cup I am going to drink?'

This mother, although appearing noble, asked Jesus for victory in her battle for greater self-confidence and self-esteem, to decisively win the praises of men. She did not seek a palladium but a panacea, a Jesus of her own making to craft life as she defined it. This mother did not want Jesus; she wanted what Jesus could give her. She did not want a transformed heart; she wanted a sheltered ego.

That is usually the posture of most who seek counseling – asking a favor of God. The counselee usually wants God to grant some treasured idol, to make existing idols function as desired. God radically upends the entire counseling premise, redefines the terms of engagement, and seeks to root out idols, not stopping until his work is done.

The Bible challenges every assumption, questions every motive. In this way, it is not just authoritative but sufficient to answer every question which involves man's worshipping center. It does not just give answers, but changes the believer's questions, compelling him to adopt revamped questions, so that he recognizes the wise answers in response to those rightly directed questions.

> "No man ever believes that the Bible means what it says; he is always convinced that it says what he means." (George Bernard Shaw)

Jesus said in John 5:39, 40, "You diligently study the Scriptures because you think that by them you possess eternal life. These are the Scriptures that testify about me; yet you refuse to come to me to have life." The Bible is not merely a compendium of sound pragmatic principles; it is the only means to right relationship with Jesus. It is crucial to note that Christians do not worship the Bible; they worship Jesus Christ. The Bible introduces and reveals the person of God so that mankind might worship him alone and be conformed to his image. In this way, the Bible is never an end in itself, but the means to a far greater end.

It is vital to note that there is a necessary tension within Scripture; it is both to be blindly accepted and, at the same time, reasoned through. In other words, the Bible presents foundational truths (the Trinity, the hypostatic union, the virgin birth, the vicarious atonement, etc.) to which it calls the reader to acquiesce with regard to his reason. However, building upon those truths, the Bible invites its reader to "reason together,"[24] not an invitation to autonomous human reason, but an invitation to the use of reason under the auspices of Scripture. Therefore, the Bible is not merely memorized and recounted but explored, interpreted, and applied. This is its towering power and majestic charm, that it breaks into human history with uncontestable truths while affording the faithful the opportunity to "work out his salvation" with a measure of latitude in disputable matters.[25]

> Unlike the Bible, which is interpreted, the *Qur'an* is a literal book, memorized, and not analyzed. The extent to which the *Qur'an* controls thinking is the extent to which it stifles critical reasoning skills and original thought. This has contributed, in part, to the dearth of scientific research and great literature in the Islamic world.[26]

Beyond the Informative: Scripture as Formative Reading

The sinner often seeks knowledge of the Bible as a weapon against God and others. He manipulates God's Word so as to make it say that which he wants it to say. To this end, the Bible is routinely misused and misapplied. The following are some examples of the misuse of Scripture.

> Half-truths are the most dangerous form of lies because they offer a form which appears plausible, and bear marks of the truth while perverting it.

---

[24] Isaiah 1:18
[25] 1 Corinthians 10:23; Philippians 2:12
[26] Thomas Friedman, *The World is Flat* (New York: Farrar, Straus, and Giroux, 2006)

1. The Bible is not an encyclopedia. The Bible contains 31,103 verses which the reader tends to wrongly atomize or fragment. One speciously thinks that if he can only find the right verse he can prove his point. The Bible is not a disjointed collection of catalogued facts. It is a single comprehensive story. In this regard, the Bible never presents facts without interpreting those facts through means of a compelling worldview.

Embarkation of the Pilgrims, Robert W. Weir, 1844

> "There are no facts, only interpretations." (Friedrich Nietzsche)

One does not merely hunt for truths within the Bible. He seeks to be confronted, indwelled, and shaped by the God of the Bible. The believer seeks God himself to raze and rebuild him in God's own image. That is what the sinner most needs, not more information, but to be dismantled and recast as a new creation, one with a new heart and new eyes to see God, himself, and the world rightly.

> "Wisdom is never on the menu, you have to own the restaurant." (Carrie Latet)

This is the difference between an informative and formative reading of Scripture. An informative reading is a man-centered approach in which one controls his own assimilation of the text. A formative reading submits to the Bible so that it might shape the reader; this is a Christ-centered handling of the text.

The Bible is not content to simply convey truths or principles. Its objective is not merely to feed the intellect. The Bible seeks to arouse emotion; it targets the imagination;[27] it lances the worshipping core of man's being. The Bible is living and active so that it actually affects justification and sanctification in those who read it by faith.[28]

The Bible is a story about God entering into man's world with knowledge - knowledge of how to initiate relationship through his Son, and of how to acquire salvation by means of his indwelling grace. It is a story of God saving people which in turn saves people.[29] It is not about simply ferreting out the right verses to be applied to a given situation. The Christian is called to apply and live out the whole story, to wholly enter into the Bible's story.

> "...His divine power has granted to us everything pertaining to life and godliness, through the true knowledge of Him who called us by His own glory and excellence. For by these He has granted to us His precious and magnificent promises, in order that by them you might become partakers of the divine nature, having escaped the corruption that is in the world by lust." (2 Peter 1:3, 4)

2. The Bible is not a moral code. The Bible does not promote trying harder in one's own strength. Its objective is not to establish a set of moral requirements that one strives to uphold. It is not a catalogue of "do's" and "don't's" that one endeavors, with ever greater effort, to live out.

The counselor's objective is not to give the counselee a "doable" law, a personal "Code of Hammurabi," that lets him bask in self-aggrandizing faux-righteousness gained through his own effort. That is the casuistry for which Jesus condemned the Pharisees. Casuistry is adding laws to God's laws so as to make it possible to keep those laws without God's personal involvement. This is the heart of hypocrisy, utterly missing the point of the law which served as a schoolmaster leading sinners to cry out for a savior, to cry out for the Christ.[30]

3. The Bible is not pragmatic principles.[31] The Bible is not focused on merely making life work as mankind defines it. It does not seek that life would only make sense, that one would solely be a "successful" person, or even that one would merely find happiness, which accumulates and dissipates like mist. While there is nothing inherently wrong with life making sense, success, or happiness, this is not God's prime objective. His objective is the Christian's justification (salvation by

---

[27] David and Sharon Covington, "Introduction to Biblical Counseling" notes, 2004
[28] Hebrews 4:12
[29] David and Sharon Covington, "Introduction to Biblical Counseling" notes, 2004
[30] Galatians 3:24
[31] For additional discussion of the issue of pragmatism see "The Allure of Caring Pragmatism: 'Solutions Are Not the Answer'" in chapter 10: "The Third-Way of Sanctification: From Abominable to Indomitable"

faith) and sanctification (growth in holiness). Unless the Christian understands that he will be disenchanted with his faith, fumbling about and confused, wholly lost as to his purpose.

The Bible is not a compendium of pithy sayings. It is a comprehensive story introducing the reader to Jesus Christ, and seeking to change that reader through faith in Jesus. Thus, the Bible is not merely trying to be "helpful." It is a means God uses in the war for souls, a war for man's worship and allegiance. God intends to win that war, and has already provided Christians with the full means in Jesus to achieve victory.

The universe is under-girded and permeated by a person, and relationship with that person brings permanent change. The Bible, therefore, is about seeing the universe through a particular lens which reveals that person, God himself. The objective of every historical event, every trial, and every joy is relational, to either initiate or further relationship with one's God.

> God communicates in two ways, through his Word, specifically (special revelation), and through his creation, generally (general revelation). Art should highlight that creation, magnify its beauty, and capture its majesty so as to obviate God's communication through the creation. Art should make the creation come alive to mankind, distill it, clarify it, so as to allow mankind to see God's hand in it, to serve as a catalyst to eyes of faith.

In light of this relational intent, the Bible reads most like a novel – a grand story of salvation, through which God saves.[32] The Bible is stories of salvation which actually save the reader.

> We also often treat the Bible as if it were the ultimate how-to book, an encyclopedia of practical wisdom and insight. But the Bible is more like a novel… The term 'biblical' needs to be redefined. It cannot mean merely 'from somewhere within the pages of Scripture.' In light of the way the Bible is written, as a single fabric or thought stretching from front to back, biblical must mean 'in keeping with what the Bible is about.' And the Bible is about God's unstoppable passion to be known, loved, and served through Jesus Christ – by those he has made.[33]

While the Bible is best thought of as a novel, it is most accurately described as an autobiographic novel. An autobiography, of course, is the written life story of the one who has experienced that story first-hand. The Bible is written by God to

---
[32] David and Sharon Covington, "Introduction to Biblical Counseling" notes, 2004
[33] David Henderson, *Culture Shift: Communicating God's Truth to Our Changing World* (New York: Baker Books, 1998)

reveal what he knows and experiences. That is why the Bible, from beginning to end, revolves around Jesus.

> "And beginning with Moses and all the Prophets, he [Jesus] explained to them what was said in all the Scriptures concerning himself." (Luke 24:27)

God revealed his autobiography to mankind so that his autobiography would become the basis for ours. His autobiography is to become the motivation for, and the sole contributor to, each person's autobiography. God's desire is that one's entire life story would be completely enveloped in the story of Jesus, his death and resurrection.[34] The writing commences when the Grand Author enters into the believer's life so that he intertwines his life story with the believer's, eventually causing the believer's self-fashioned story to fade and God's to predominate. The Bible follows a particular narratology which it seeks to reiterate, refocus, and reinforce with every turn of the page. That storyline emphasizes mankind's towering design, desperate sinfulness, and the rebirth appropriated by faith in Jesus Christ.

Two Tragedies: Neglect and Misuse

The Dentist, Gerrit van Honthorst, 1622

I am blessed with an excellent dentist. The moment he inspects my teeth he can tell exactly the manner in which, and extent to which, I brush and floss. With just a glance

---

[34] Philippians 3:10

he might say, "You're not flossing enough around that bottom right rear molar." My dentist instantly knows one's level of diligence or neglect with regard to oral hygiene. You can't fool him (nor would you want to). I believe that God gifts the wise counselor with a similar ability regarding the human soul. The counselor spies something of the contours and rhythms of the heart, something of the way in which faith is either maintained or neglected.

At the time of the writing of this book I pastor a fledgling congregation. Beside daily communication, I see my church members twice a week during which time we study Scripture, pray, and share issues of our lives and faith. Just as my dentist knows teeth, I know something of the heart condition of those in my church. I can tell almost immediately the extent to which each studies God's Word, prays, or struggles with grave sin. I can tell when someone has spent the week either growing in faith, or reveling in a man-centered story. I can tell when he has wrestled deeply with the God of Scripture, or when the Bible is merely treated as a quaint compendium of inspiring platitudes. How can I tell? There are a host of issues that clue me in.

When God's Word is neglected or misused there is woven through conversation a ribbon of anxiety, a certain accumulated calculus of pride, a subtle inclination to complaint or gossip. There is a lack of discipline about the eyes, a certain lust of the flesh that seems to attend the body's comportment, a slight tremor of desire that unsettles the face, a shadow of doubt casting itself across one's being, a self-focus driving a wedge into relationship so that one moves in and about other's lives in a self-consumed manner.

I can tell fairly accurately the extent to which fellow Christians study God's Word. I can sense if it is a rich daily feast, an occasional meal, or a guilt-ridden Sunday morning binge. I can sense if the heart is submissive to Christ, inclined to him, desiring him. When God's Word is faithfully and vigorously studied there is a peace under-girding conversation, a nondescript breeze of humility, an inclination toward gratitude, a discipline about the eyes, a basking in forgiveness and a willingness to forgive, a power, a persuasion, a desire for purity, and a ready willingness to move selflessly into other's lives. The Word lends a garland of grace to speech,[35] a softness to the spirit, the slightest slump to the shoulder, and a joy about the face.

Thus, there are two tragedies with regard to the study of Scripture. The first is neglect; few Christians faithfully read the Bible. They know little about it, fail to study it carefully, and merely use it to gain momentary inspiration rather than to encounter the person of God himself. Christians often flaunt a few verses to support their own personal opinions of God which causes them to flout Scripture's plenary teaching.

---

[35] Proverbs 1:9

> "Take up and read. Take up and read...I snatched it up, opened it, and in silence read the paragraph on which my eyes first fell: 'Not in rioting and drunkenness, not in chambering and wantonness, not in strife and envying, but put on the Lord Jesus Christ, and make no provision for the flesh to fulfill the lusts thereof.'[36] I wanted to read no further, nor did I need to. For instantly, as the sentence ended, there was infused in my heart something like the light of full certainty and all the gloom of doubt vanished away."[37]

The Roses of Heliogabalus, Lawrence Alma Tadema, 1888

The second tragedy is misuse. While Christians may read the Bible, they often do not understand nor appropriate its core teachings. They read it with idolatrous hearts, hoping to gain a weapon in their war against God and others. They read it to gain control over others and to feel self-righteous. Whether the Bible is neglected or worshipped, silent or blaring, the effect is the same: Christians become isolated from God, know little about their own sin, and soon assume the traits of false believers, or worse, false teachers.

It is not uncommon to find Christians who read the Bible daily, have memorized large sections (so as to quote it easily), and yet are ignorant concerning its most fundamental teaching. They do not understand justification, sanctification, idolatry, sin, or the worshipping quality of the heart. They read the Bible, but without Holy Spirit-directed faith. The hope is that both counselor and counselee will vociferously avoid both pitfalls, neglect and misuse, so that Scripture is well-rehearsed and rightly

---

[36] Romans 13:13
[37] Augustine of Hippo, *Confessions* (Oxford University Press, 2009)

interpreted as the reader is indwelled by the Holy Spirit.

> The one who loves his sin seeks a silent Bible that, if it were to be read, would conform to his own personal story.[38]

As a final note, it is crucial to understand that a sound doctrine of Scripture sees the Bible as the sum and substance of God's communication with mankind. This counseling paradigm does not countenance the concept of open theology, or ongoing revelation from God. This book's approach presents the Bible as sufficient to encompass all that God wants mankind to know, both corporately and individually. The Bible's canon is also closed so that there is no further direct revelation from God. Thus, throughout this text, when referring to the "Holy Spirit's leading," "God's work in one's life," or even "God tells us," these concepts are always assumed to be under the auspices of, and solely within the confines of, Scripture.

---

[38] David and Sharon Covington, "Introduction to Biblical Counseling" notes, 2004

- 4 -

THE GOSPEL AS INCEPTION POINT:
From Immorality to Immortality

"He Who Would Teach Men to Die Would Teach Them to Live"[1]

In 1961 the German capital, Berlin, was severed by the Berlin Wall (part of the Iron Curtain). The wall was built to stop East Germans from escaping to West-German-controlled West Berlin. During the wall's twenty-eight year history, East Germans devised creative ways to escape such as, digging tunnels, using hot air balloons, driving tiny cars under barricades, and even sliding on a wire suspended over the wall. (Of course, anyone caught escaping, was either shot on sight, or imprisoned for life.) On June 12, 1987, former-president Ronald Reagan (1911–2004) challenged the Soviet Union to tear down the Berlin Wall. Many believe that this bold speech proved to be the catalyst for the wall's demise on November 9, 1989.

While it is unwise to press the analogy too far, there is a connection between this anecdote and the gospel. Like attempting to traverse the Berlin Wall, mankind often seeks to traverse his separation with God. He devises clever means to span the chasm, to curry God's favor through his own creative devices. While some did succeed in surmounting the man-made Berlin Wall, with regard to God's holiness, all human attempts always prove futile. The wall separating God and man, built through mankind's own sin, had to fall through God's own agency. That was the purpose of Jesus' work on the cross; he reduced to rubble the insurmountable barrier of sin. Sadly, in defiance of the cross, mankind continues his vain attempts to overcome sin through his own means and in his own efforts.

> The tower of Babel is considered the first false religion, mankind's attempt to ascend to heaven by means of his own work.[2]

The Christian life begins and ends with the gospel, the remission of sin through the shed blood of Jesus Christ.[3] All Christian counseling is essentially a drawing out, explanation of, and confrontation with, the gospel. All that which the counselor seeks to expose and sanctify, revolves around this central message of salvation.

Do not assume that just because one comes from a Christian home, or shows a measure of Christian morality, that one is in fact a Christian. Becoming a Christian

---
[1] Michel de Montaigne (1533-1592)
[2] Genesis 11:1-9
[3] Matthew 26:28

involves a specific "worship transaction" which takes place between the penitent and God himself at the moment of saving faith. John 3:7 is clear that one must be born again, to appropriate to oneself the payment for sins which Jesus affected through his death.

> "But even if we or an angel from heaven should preach a gospel other than the one we preached to you, let them be under God's curse! As we have already said, so now I say again: If anybody is preaching to you a gospel other than what you accepted, let them be under God's curse!" (Galatians 1:8, 9)

Being a Christian is NOT:

1. Mere belief in God

> "For since the creation of the world God's invisible qualities—his eternal power and divine nature—have been clearly seen, being understood from what has been made, so that people are without excuse. For although they knew God, they neither glorified him as God nor gave thanks to him, but their thinking became futile and their foolish hearts were darkened." (Romans 1:20, 21)
>
> "You believe in one God. Good! Even the demons believe and tremble." (James 2:19)

2. Simply understanding who Jesus is

> "When Jesus came to the region of Caesarea Philippi, he asked his disciples, 'Who do people say the Son of Man is?' They replied, 'Some say John the Baptist; others say Elijah; and still others, Jeremiah or one of the prophets.' 'But what about you?' he asked. 'Who do you say I am?' Simon Peter answered, 'You are the Messiah, the Son of the living God.'" (Matthew 16:13-16)

John 6:14, 15 reads, "After the people saw the sign Jesus performed, they began to say, 'Surely this is the Prophet who is to come into the world.' Jesus, knowing that they intended to come and make him king by force, withdrew again to a mountain by himself." The people did not want a Messiah; they wanted a king. Second Corinthians 5:16 states, "So from now on we regard no one from a worldly point of view. Though we once regarded Christ in this way, we do so no longer." This indicates that each, before becoming a Christian, saw Jesus as something less than a savior.

The Jewish crowds wanted a savior of their own making, at times a king (displaying power), a prophet (bringing meaning), or a priest (bestowing blessing) but they refused to submit to a Messiah, who in their minds failed to legitimate human pride and its obstreperous devices. The people could not countenance a Messiah who did not accord with their self-serving desire, to be saved from their situation rather than from themselves. They wanted a false messiah who allowed them to remain largely untouched at their worshipping core, to define salvation in man-centered, man-glorifying terms, namely the deliverance of Israel from Roman occupation (a near obsession among many first century Jews).

The Appearance of Christ Before the People, Alexander Ivanov, 1857

> I find it fascinating that mankind seeks to reduce Jesus to less than a savior, while at the same time exalting mere men as saviors. For example, in *The Legend of King Arthur*, there are three supposed saviors, Merlin the magician, the French knight Lancelot, and King Arthur himself. Merlin, a kind of prophet figure, seeks to instill wisdom. Lancelot, the purported paragon of chivalrous virtue, seeks to lead humanity toward purity of heart (as would an anointed priest). Arthur, the enlightened king, seeks to institute a just civilization. All three are thought to function for salvific purpose. However, each fails, as in the end civil war breaks out and chaos reigns.[4]

The Bible clearly presents Jesus as exemplary, but does not present Jesus as merely an exemplar to follow. Mankind, faced with an exemplar, merely views him through the lens of idolatry. Thus, sinners only see those aspects of an exemplar that their idolatry allows them to see.

> I have taught for nearly a decade. With each of my classes, and to each of my

---

[4] T. H. White, *The Once and Future King* (United Kingdom: Collins, 1958)

> students, I offer a Christian demeanor and worldview. What is fascinating is that for most, my Christianity is almost entirely overshadowed by those aspects of my persona that they admire, emulate, or even shun. Often my students want to know about my personal habits, my earning prospects, the type of car I drive, or my travels. They see these as the "treasure" I offer. While I de-emphasize these elements, highlighting my changed heart of faith, this effort is largely overlooked. Each sinner envies those who possess what he thinks he needs to be delivered from his prison of circumstance.

3. The result of only reading the Bible or attending church[5]

Many who routinely attend church are not true Christians. They have learned to play along with the obedience game. Second Peter 2:1-20 mentions false teachers who deceive the church. They escaped the corruption of the world through knowing Christ but are again entangled in it, turning their backs on the truth. These false teachers have learned how to behave well, so that they win praise from men, but there is no living interaction with God himself. Additionally, 2 Corinthians 11:14, 15 warns that Satan masquerades as a servant of light and his servants as servants of righteousness. Thus, some with a servant's appearance may be emissaries of Satan.

> "You study the Scriptures diligently because you think that in them you have eternal life. These are the very Scriptures that testify about me, yet you refuse to come to me to have life." (John 5:39, 40)

4. Just an emotional experience

For a short time I taught with a startup Christian school, founded by a man who is Pentecostal. The first week I taught only two students. Sensing that my students had never repented of their sin and personally received Jesus by faith, I reviewed the gospel in detail.

One night the school's founder held what could be termed a "deliverance" gathering. Those in attendance spoke in tongues, blew a *shofar*, danced and ran around the room, shouted, screamed, and cried, all the while believing that this was by means of the Holy Spirit's power. That night my two students, in attendance at this meeting, cried uncontrollably. The meeting's organizer declared with a triumphal tone that that night the two had become true Christians, having receive the Holy Spirit's anointing.

At my next class the students seemed more distant than usual. They spoke to me in belligerent tones and finally walked out of class stating that my lesson lacked the

---

[5] For further discussion of the church's role in believers' lives see the third book in this series, *The Days of Reckoning Are at Hand: From Fig Leaf to Olive Branch to Laurel Wreath*, chapter 10: "Counseling and the Church: Syndicating the Vision"

power of the Spirit. I later discussed with the founder the fact that the students, based on their own words, clearly had not received Jesus' vicarious atonement upon the cross, and therefore were not Christians. He was indignant, insisting that they were indeed Christians because they had cried at the deliverance meeting and demonstrated the Spirit's power in their lives.

> Mark 11:8-10 recounts that the crowds shouted, "Blessed is he who comes in the name of the Lord!" and one week later called for Jesus' crucifixion.

Let's be very clear. The Spirit's presence and power in one's life is inextricably linked to the gospel, Jesus' death upon the cross for the salvation of sinners who receive the gift of salvation through faith. Without the gospel, the Holy Spirit is not present. Pentecostalism siphons off an experience of the Holy Spirit from the gospel, making it a prideful display of power, a flight of lust of the flesh,[6] an "unholy fire" created for show.[7] Pentecostalism makes this display of power its own false gospel with no connection to Jesus' death for the forgiveness for sins.[8]

Later the founder made a revealing statement. He said to me, "Jesus himself spoke to me and told me the truth about this. I don't know what your Jesus told you."

5. Only feeling God's love[9]

Matthew 5:45 states, "He causes his sun to rise on the evil and the good, and sends rain on the righteous and the unrighteous." This verse reveals the nature of common grace which would allow one to experience God's love even when he is not part of God's family.[10] Feeling God's love is part of how he cares even for the wicked.

6. Being a good and gracious person

Confucius (551-479 BC) lived in the region of Lu ravished by war. He conceived his five virtues (five relationships) specifically in response to the corruption, injustice, and lasciviousness surrounding him. He hoped to infuse society with a practical philosophy based on the principle of virtue (*ren*, 仁) in order to alleviate human suffering and poverty. With this in mind, Confucius and his disciples traveled throughout China searching for a ruler willing to adopt and implement his philosophy. But Confucius died disheartened and in obscurity, never having realized his goal. As Confucius discovered, moralism, in all its forms and in all times and places, always

---

[6] 2 Peter 2:14
[7] Leviticus 10:1
[8] Galatians 1:6-9
[9] For a comprehensive handling of the topic of God's love see the case study "God's *Sui Generis* Love" found in the third book in this series, *The Days of Reckoning Are at Hand: From Fig Leaf to Olive Branch to Laurel Wreath*, chapter 2: "Suffering: The Kintsugi Objective"
[10] For further discussion of the issue of common grace see the second book in this series, *What Agreement Is There Between the Temple of God and Idols?: The Accidence of Sin and Idolatry*, chapter 1: "Deliver Us From Evil"

The Emperor's Approach
Xuande, 1435

fails to change the fundamental inner condition of mankind. This is because mankind is not firstly a moral being but a worshipping one.

> "Who is wise? He that learns from everyone. Who is powerful? He that governs his passions. Who is rich? He that is content. Who is that? No one." (Benjamin Franklin)

Being a good and gracious person may be evidence of saving faith, but it is not the means of salvation. The idea that one could save himself through his own effort, or that he could change through his own strength, is moralism. Moralism fatally misconstrues mankind's constitution. Man's problem is not simply one of moral misalignment, but one of deviant worship, raising and bowing to false gods (those gods taking on varied and sophisticated forms). Understanding the nature of mankind's problem, Jesus willfully died on the cross, that worship would be construed anew.

> "No man can redeem the life of another
> or give to God a ransom for him..." (Psalm 49:7)
>
> "Since ancient times no one has heard,
>   no ear has perceived,
> no eye has seen any God besides you,
>   who acts on behalf of those who wait for him.
> You come to the help of those who gladly do right,
>   who remember your ways.
> But when we continued to sin against them,
>   you were angry.
>   How then can we be saved?

> All of us have become like one who is unclean,
>   and all our righteous acts are like filthy rags;
> we all shrivel up like a leaf,
>   and like the wind our sins sweep us away.
> No one calls on your name
>   or strives to lay hold of you;
> for you have hidden your face from us
>   and have given us over to our sins.
> Yet you, Lord, are our Father.
>   We are the clay, you are the potter;
>   we are all the work of your hand.
> Do not be angry beyond measure, Lord;
>   do not remember our sins forever.
> Oh, look on us, we pray,
>   for we are all your people." (Isaiah 64:4-9)

Mark 10:21 reads, "Jesus said to the rich young man, 'Go and sell everything and follow me and you will have treasure in heaven.'" While this may sound like moralism (doing some good in order to gain eternal life), it is far from this. Jesus, knowing the idolatry in this man's heart, sought to remove the one obstacle which stood between him and saving faith. Additionally, the parable of the sheep and goats, in Matthew 25:31-46, is often misunderstood. Those who were hungry, thirsty, strangers, naked, sick, and prisoners, the righteous fed, gave water to, invited in, clothed, cared for, and visited. Matthew 25:34 states that God speaks these words to the righteous, those who *already* possess an inheritance in his kingdom. Since God addresses those who are already saved, their acts did not save them. Their acts arose from their saving faith, so as to reveal that faith as genuine.

7. The result of being raised in a Christian home

The Jews thought they were accepted by God through family lineage. In fact, they each needed to receive God into their hearts by faith as Deuteronomy 6:5, 6 states. They each needed personal relationship with God in order to be saved. Jesus affirmed this when in Luke 3:8 he stated that God can raise rocks to be children of God.

8. Acquired through baptism

As God parted the waters, the Israelites crossed the Reed Sea. They passed through the waters as people moving from death to life, having entered the waters in a state of death (pursued by the Egyptians) and emerging from them in a state of life (the Egyptians defeated).[11] In this same way, baptism is a statement that one has already

---

[11] Exodus 14:21-31

passed from death to life. It does not affect salvation; it merely recounts or proclaims that salvation has already occurred. Baptism is principally a proclamation for those who have already repented at the foot of the cross. Therefore, baptism is an outward sign of an inward salvific reality. In Acts 8:36, 38 and again in Acts 10:47 one reads that those who first believed were baptized. While pedobaptism is a biblically valid proclamation of God's covenant faithfulness, it must be emphasized that baptism never makes one a Christian.

The Baptism, Julius LeBlanc Stewart, 1892

> "For Christ did not send me to baptize, but to preach the gospel—not with wisdom and eloquence, lest the cross of Christ be emptied of its power." (1 Corinthians 1:17)

Nothing one does can ever make him a Christian. One becomes a Christian through faith alone that Jesus' death on the cross was sufficient to pay for one's sins. First Corinthians 15:22 states, "For as in Adam all die, so in Christ all will be made alive." First John 1:9 states, "If we confess our sins he is faithful and just to forgive us our sins and purify us." Salvation is appropriated by faith alone, through God's grace alone.

> "Not because of who I am
> But because of what you've done
> Not because of what I've done
> But because of who you are" ("Who Am I?", Casting Crowns, 2007)

Christians gladly speak about heaven, but often neglect mentioning hell for fear of offending others. Such Christians want to love others into the kingdom of God. If that love is rendered innocuous through the neglect of crucial teachings about sin and death, then what passes for love is not love at all. However, in a kind of pincer movement, the Bible simultaneously presents both sides, the path of death and the way to life. Christians therefore rightly hold forth a two-pronged message. For the one who willfully persists in his sin eternal death awaits. For the one who turns to God in repentance eternal life awaits.

> As evidence of God's common grace, Greek mythology contained trail-markers of the gospel. For example, Leda, the wife of King Tyndareus of Sparta, bore twin boys, Castor and Pollux, called the Dioscuri. Castor was mortal, the son of the king of Sparta, and Pollux was immortal, the son of Zeus. After Castor was killed in a fight, Pollux begged Zeus to allow him to share Pollux's own immortality with his dead brother. Zeus relented, pronouncing that they would spend alternate days on Olympus and in Hades.[12]
>
> This story bears certain similarities to the biblical concept of vicarious atonement – the idea of one interceding on behalf of another for the sake of salvation. As with Pollux, Jesus Christ, the immortal Son of God, pleads with his Father on behalf of those he calls "brothers." While Zeus reluctantly offered a compromise (an alternating participation in heaven and hell), the Christian message is one of uncompromised jubilation as, on account of Jesus, mankind is showered with unmerited favor.

Jesus Would Rather Die for Us than Live Without Us[13]

> The gospel is the most highly-improbable story that actually happened.

A television commentator said about Christianity, "You've got to change with the times; you've got to change or you fade away." This statement drives to the heart of a modern siege upon the church as many seek a gospel that permits ever-expanding displays of depravity, a gospel that accommodates man rather than submits to God. People are often desperate to be justified before God, while at the same time affording a place for self-serving pride. Any teacher who appears to offer both (justification while maintaining human pride) is heralded as a genius and a hero (such as health-and-wealth preachers). However, Scripture repeatedly warns of false gospels peddled by false teachers.[14] The Bible presents only one path to salvation.[15] All others are Satan's deceit meant to cast men into eternal perdition. Thus, the gospel is the one message that has never, and will never, change, as Jesus is the same yesterday,

---

[12] Delle Cave Ferruccio and Marta Gotin, *Agrigento: The Valley of the Temples* (Folio Vienna, 2004)
[13] This phase from Heartlight.org, devotional for December 19th
[14] 2 Timothy 4:3
[15] Galatians 1:6-9

today, and forever.[16]

Scripture on how to become a Christian:

1. "He was oppressed and afflicted, yet he did not open his mouth; he was led like a lamb to the slaughter, and as a sheep before her shearers is silent, so he did not open his mouth. By oppression and judgment he was taken away. And who can speak of his descendants? For he was cut off from the land of the living; for the transgression of my people he was stricken." (Isaiah 53:7, 8 (Acts 8:35))

2. "'I looked for a man among them who would build up the wall and stand before me in the gap on behalf of the land so I would not destroy it, but I found none. So I will pour out my wrath on them and consume them with my fiery anger, bringing down on their own heads all they have done,' declares the Sovereign Lord." (Ezekiel 22:30-31)

> As children we were taught that when overcome by the billowing smoke of a house fire we should, "Stop, drop, and roll." Similarly, Luke 23:30 states, "Then 'they will say to the mountains, 'Fall on us!' and to the hills, 'Cover us!'" However, when faced with God's blazing wrath, his white-hot fury toward mutinous subjects, there will be no escape from the flames, no covering which proves impenetrable. That is the entire reason why Jesus died on the cross, to shield those in him from God's raging fire upon sin.

3. "Blessed is he whose transgressions are forgiven, whose sins are covered. Blessed is the man whose sin the Lord does not count against him and in whose spirit is no deceit." (Psalm 32:1-2)

> Eve looked at the forbidden fruit with a heart of desire. Deceived by the serpent, she sought salvation in the fruit, that which would give her life without God. Central to this desire was the quest for salvation as she defined it. Fallen mankind routinely desires that which he believes to be his actual salvation; this becomes his worship addiction.

4. "For God so loved the world that he gave his one and only Son, that whoever believes in him shall not perish but have eternal life. For God did not send his Son into the world to condemn the world, but to save the world through him. Whoever believes in him is not condemned, but whoever does not believe stands condemned already because he has not believed in the name of God's one and only Son." (John 3:16-18)

---

[16] Hebrews 13:8

The Gospel as Inception Point

John 3:16[17]	
For God	the greatest lover
so loved	to the greatest degree
the world	the greatest number
that He gave	the greatest act
His only begotten Son	the greatest gift
that whosoever	the greatest invitation
Believeth	the greatest simplicity
in Him	the greatest person
should not perish	the greatest deliverance
But	the greatest difference
Have	the greatest certainty
everlasting life	the greatest possession

5. "...if you do not believe that I am the one I claim to be, you will indeed die in your sins." (John 8:24)

6. "Salvation is found in no one else; for there is no other name under heaven given to men by which we must be saved." (Acts 4:12)

7. "All the prophets testify about him that everyone who believes in him receives forgiveness of sins through his name." (Acts 10:43)

The Crowning with Thorns
Titian, c. 1545

The Chinese word *da* (大), meaning "big" or "great," is composed of two characters: *yi* (一) "one" and *ren* (人) "person." The implication, which may derive from the Bible, is that there was only one man who was truly great.[18]

8. "Through him everyone who believes is justified from everything you could not

---

[17] The source of this analysis of John 3:16 is unknown.
[18] Acts 4:12; Colossians 1:16

be justified from by the law of Moses." (Acts 13:39)

> Don Henley of the Eagles sang, "I'm getting down to the heart of the matter, and I think it's about forgiveness."[19] From the Christian perspective forgiveness is, in fact, the heart of the matter. This is the most profound and pressing reality in each life, the desperate need for forgiveness before a holy eternal God.

9. "I am not ashamed of the gospel, because it is the power of God for the salvation of everyone who believes: first for the Jew, then for the Gentile. For in the gospel a righteousness from God is revealed, a righteousness that is by faith from first to last, just as it is written: 'The righteous will live by faith.'" (Romans 1:16-17)

10. "Therefore, there is now no condemnation for those who are in Christ Jesus, because through Christ Jesus the law of the Spirit of life set me free from the law of sin and death." (Romans 8:1, 2)

> "Be assured that on the Last Day there will be neither angel nor lawyer to plead your case." (Abraham Lincoln)

11. "That if you confess with your mouth, 'Jesus is Lord,' and believe in your heart that God raised him from the dead, you will be saved. For it is with your heart that you believe and are justified, and it is with your mouth that you confess and are saved." (Romans 10:9, 10)

12. "For it is by grace you have been saved, through faith—and this not from yourselves, it is the gift of God— not by works, so that no one can boast." (Ephesians 2:8, 9)

> Isaiah chapter 1 is written as a covenant lawsuit against God's people, Israel. This lawsuit involves the following:[20]
>
> 1. The witnesses, the heavens and the earth, are summoned.[21]
>
> 2. On sure testimony, the defendant is indicted.[22]
>
> 3. There would appear to be no hope for the defendant Israel because the prosecutor is also the judge.[23] However, in an unprecedented turn of events, the judge himself enters a plea on behalf of the defendant. Thus, the unthinkable happens;

---

[19] This lyric from "The Heart of the Matter" (1989) is paraphrased.
[20] Alan Groves (1952–2007), "Prophets" class, Westminster Theological Seminary, Philadelphia, Pennsylvania
[21] Isaiah 1:2-9
[22] Isaiah 1:10-17
[23] Isaiah 1:18-23

> the judge himself steps down from his judgment seat and pleads on behalf of the defendant. It turns out the judge is also the savior.
>
> 4. The judgment is finally rendered and the outcome is the people's vindication through the judge's just adjudication (a foreshadowing of Christ's vicarious atonement).[24]

The Last Judgment, Michelangelo Buonarroti, c. 1520

13. "But now he has reconciled you by Christ's physical body through death to present you holy in his sight, without blemish and free from accusation— if you continue in your faith, established and firm, not moved from the hope held out in the gospel. This is the gospel that you heard and that has been proclaimed to every creature under heaven, and of which I, Paul, have become a servant." (Colossians 1:22, 23)

14. "He saved us, not because of righteous things we had done, but because of his mercy. He saved us through the washing of rebirth and renewal by the Holy Spirit,

---
[24] Isaiah 1:24-31

whom he poured out on us generously through Jesus Christ our Savior, so that, having been justified by his grace, we might become heirs having the hope of eternal life." (Titus 3:5-7)

> Colossians 1:15 describes Jesus as the "first born over creation." Those in Christ participate in his "first born" quality.[25] This concept is tied to the redemption of the first born in Numbers 3:45-48. In Numbers, the Levites were employed in the service of the tabernacle in lieu of the first born among Israel. However, the first born in Israel numbered 22,273, while there were 22,000 Levites. This meant that Moses had to redeem the remaining 273 with five shekels of silver each.[26] It is fascinating that 1 Peter 1:18, 19 states, "For you know that it was not with perishable things such as silver or gold that you were redeemed from the empty way of life handed down to you from your forefathers, but with the precious blood of Christ, a lamb without blemish or defect."

15. "If we confess our sins, he is faithful and just and will forgive us our sins and purify us from all unrighteousness." (1 John 1:9)

To become a Christian is to be justified before God, and therefore free from the guilt of one's sin. Once that occurs, God then initiates a plan of sanctification, the objective of which is to free one from indwelling sin. This is the two-pronged purpose of God's work on earth – to justify the guilty and to sanctify the saved. If God has saved his people, then he desires to change them so that sin is eradicated and he alone can dwell within them.

One of the most difficult concepts for fallen sinners to understand is that salvation is by faith alone. Faith cannot be defined in the world's terms, and stands utterly separate from any worldly concept. Faith is not the power of positive thinking; it is not just the willingness to exercise deferred gratification; it is not merely showing humility. Faith is a deliberate and definitive worship transaction with God in which the sinner submits his will to God's, "being fully persuaded that God [has] power to do what he [has] promised."[27] Hebrews 11:1 states, "Now faith is confidence in what we hope for and assurance about what we do not see." Faith is a persuasion, confidence, and assurance in God's ability to save who put their trust in Jesus.

In defiance of faith, mankind, in his pride, desperately desires to be justified based on his good works. This is the motivation for the vast majority of good that is done – that one's good acts would serve as a bargain with God, a negotiation for his acceptance. Even the righteous, who have been justified by faith, often seek to add to their salvation through good works. Trenchant human pride refuses to believe that one is

---

[25] Romans 8:23; Hebrews 12:23; James 1:18; Revelation 14:4
[26] Numbers 3:47
[27] Romans 4:21

saved purely through the selfless act of another, Jesus Christ.[28]

> In Old English the word *bletsian* meant "to cause blood to flow." It later assumed the nuanced meaning of "to win divine favor by means of a blood sacrifice."[29] In Christianity divine favor is gained through the blood sacrifice of Jesus Christ on the cross.[30] Therefore, the word "bless" retains the idea of favor acquired through the spilled blood of Jesus.

Jesus Disputing with the Elders, Juan de Valdes Leal, 1686

The Christian counselor does not present Jesus as merely a moral teacher, or as simply a good example of how to live. He presents a savior who died to free humanity from its sin. Thus, sound biblical counseling builds upon one foundation alone, the need to be personally known by Jesus, not to merely imitate Jesus as an inspiration for enlightened conduct (the spirit behind "What would Jesus do?"). Yet, Jesus as Messiah is always the one concept which rebellious mankind refuses to accept, and to which he will not submit.

A Jesus who is merely an example is based on the assumption that humanity is

---

[28] Romans 4:24, 25
[29] Louis Heller, et al., *The Private Lives of English Words* (Tarrytown, New York: Wynwood Press, 1991) 19.
[30] Hebrews 9:22

fundamentally capable of saving itself through its own means, and simply needs the right model or encouragement to do so. This is the basis for the sinner's Faustian bargain that limitless knowledge would deliver him from the prison to himself. Under the terms of such a bargain the sinner would gladly know Jesus' teaching, if only he could sidestep being known by Jesus. The Christian faith begins and ends with one pivotal truth; mankind must be delivered from himself by a savior who seeks to raid, ravish, and raze the heart so that he can be reified in it.

Consider the following example. If one sees a person drowning, what should one do? Throwing a drowning man a book on swimming instructions is pointless. One must enter the water and save him; that is what Jesus did. He entered our world as both God and man to die on a cross to save those who could not possibly save themselves. False religions are human attempts to save mankind through moralism, man trying to save himself through his own effort. Christianity is God reaching down to save mankind through his son.

Ephesians 6:19 states, "Pray also for me, that whenever I speak, words may be given me so that I will fearlessly make known the mystery of the gospel." Counseling continually unfolds to the counselee the mystery of the gospel. The gospel is the heart and marrow, the life-blood of every interaction. While one might instinctively think that such an approach is too simplistic, it is actually the most profound counseling that could ever be offered. The gospel's impact and reach within the human psyche is inexhaustible. As the counselor applies the central truths of the gospel, there is a slow but steady shaping process which eventually takes hold. The gospel, not as mere propositional truth, but as the person of Jesus himself within his people, permeates, enlists, directs, and recasts the heart.

When confronted with the gospel, it is fascinating to witness an audience's reaction. One glimpses something of the condition of each person's soul as the gospel is preached; some appear frightened, others mildly amused, some angry, others confused, and still others joyful. The gospel strips away the façade exposing the true condition of the heart. This is its towering presence and power. As the axis around which humanity either voluntarily or involuntarily revolves, the gospel causes hearts to either soar with joy or cringe with regret. Thus, one is reminded that to Jesus Christ every knee will one day bow.[31]

> Set before the world life and death, good and evil. Tell the children of men that they are all in a state of misery and danger, condemned by their prince, and conquered and enslaved by their enemies. This is supposed in their being saved, which they would not need to be, if they were not lost. Now go and tell them that if they believe the gospel, and give up themselves to be Christ's disciples; if they renounce the

---

[31] Romans 14:11; Philippians 2:10

> devil, the world, and the flesh, and be devoted to Christ as their prophet, priest, and king, and to God in Christ as their God in covenant, and evidenced by their constant adherence to this covenant their sincerity herein, they shall be saved from the guilt and power of sin; it shall not rule them; it shall not ruin them. He that is a true Christian shall be saved through Christ.[32]

Case Study: The World's Exploitation of Jesus

The Feast of Attila, Moritz Than, 1870

In her best-selling book, *Jesus CEO: Using Ancient Wisdom for Visionary Leadership* (1995),[33] Laurie Beth Jones presents the thesis that Jesus Christ, although he lived 2000 years ago, is the "noblest" model for modern CEOs. She writes that her perspective is based on the "self-mastery, action, and relationship skills that Jesus used to train and motivate his team." She sees Jesus as "harnessing spiritual energy" to implement the "Omega management style" – one which is both authoritative (masculine), and cooperative (feminine). In this way, in just three years, Jesus trained twelve men to radically change the world.

Jones' outlines numerous crucial leadership qualities which Jesus demonstrated such as:

1. The ability to remain committed to a mission
2. Unwavering belief in oneself

---

[32] Matthew Henry Commentary; Mark 16:14-18
[33] Laurie Beth Jones, *Jesus CEO: Using Ancient Wisdom for Visionary Leadership* (New York: Hyperion, 1995)

3. The ability to ration one's energy
4. The humility to say thank you
5. Unbounded optimism
6. The ability to conquer one's fears
7. The sense that one cannot be thwarted
8. The ability to instill vision in others
9. The foresight to train one's replacements
10. The desire to love others to the end

Jones analyzes Jesus' life through the lens of how to effectively run a modern corporation. She uses Jesus as a convenient model for success in a ruthless, profit-driven world. However, what she fails to understand is that Jesus' purpose and mission was not to instill business acumen, but rather to renew the human heart.[34] His purpose was to "set captives free" so that they were no longer slaves to themselves, but children of God himself.[35] Jesus repeatedly emphasized that his kingdom was not of this world.[36]

> Jesus lived and died so that mankind would not seek the gifts, but the Giver of the gifts. When one merely desires the gifts and not the Giver, simply longs for the blessing and not the Blesser, he utterly maligns and tramples upon the meaning of Jesus' death upon the cross.[37]

With this in mind the model CEO is not one who uses Jesus as an example but one who has surrendered his life and will to Jesus, so that Jesus' spirit lives within a repentant heart. The model CEO is not one who operates based on sound principles or management techniques, but one who sees himself as first a humble servant of the God he worships. When a CEO first recognizes his servile position with regard to God, then he will treat those around him with the same beneficence that Jesus did.[38] The key concept here is that becoming the model CEO is not driven by what one does or says, but rather by who one is. The transformation is not from the outside in, but from the inside out.[39]

> The CEO who loves "praise from men more than praise from God" will easily be tempted by greed, will prove ineffective, and will experience fractured relationships.[40] But the CEO who loves praise from God more than the praises of men, will put others' best interests ahead of his own.

---

[34] Luke 10:27
[35] Ephesians 4:8
[36] John 18:36
[37] Hebrews 10:29
[38] John 10:11-13
[39] Matthew 23:25, 26
[40] John 12:43

Two Aspects to Repentance

Repentance must be seen from two sides: repentance for one's sin (transgressions against God's law) and repentance for one's self-righteousness (attempts to uphold God's law in one's own strength). Thus, there are two aspects to repentance. The first is calling the rebellious to repent of their transgressions against God's standards; the second is calling the self-righteous (those seeking obedience to God's law) to repent of their attempts at righteousness in their own strength.[41]

The pride of the first is an outward rebellion and defiance of God's standards. The pride of the second is a self-glorifying attempt at perfection without God. The first is the outwardly disobedient as a reflection of inward defiance; the second is the outwardly obedient as a cover for an inward contempt.

> In post-12th century versions of *The Legend of King Arthur*, the French knight, Lancelot, was considered the paragon of virtue, the quintessence of purity of heart. Yet, Lancelot wore his purity as a badge of superiority. Finally, his self-imposed mortification of the flesh was revealed as reckless folly as he sought an adulterous affair with Arthur's Queen Guinevere. As with Lancelot, all supposed virtue is a farce outside of regeneration in Jesus Christ.

The one who is inwardly and outwardly rebellious is a fairly straightforward study. The one who is inwardly rebellious, yet outwardly obedient is more enigmatic. (Drawing on *The Legend of King Arthur* once again, Arthur's long-lost son, Sir Mordred, might serve as an excellent example of the inwardly rebellious, yet outwardly obedient, as displayed in the beginning stages of his involvement with the Round Table.) The self-righteous person may claim to repent, but his repentance is only a sorrow for failing to meet his own moral standard. His repentance is merely a recommitment to continue to try to save himself through this own effort. This person's so called repentance could be likened to "gap insurance" (insurance to cover the gaps in other coverage). This means that repentance through Jesus is nothing more than an attempt to bridge the gap in one's own efforts to save himself. Thus, at heart, the self-righteous person's virtue is merely to avoid the need for a savior, to avoid Jesus; "[the] way to avoid Jesus was to avoid sin…"[42]

> "One must abandon every attempt to make something of oneself, even to make of oneself a righteous person." (Dietrich Bonhoeffer)

The self-righteous, therefore, in his supposed repentance, actually resists the gospel since his repentance seeks to merely gain the strength within himself to obey God

---

[41] Some ideas in this section from Andrew Field, "Introduction to Redeemer," p. 5, Westminster Theological Seminary, Philadelphia, Pennsylvania
[42] Quote from Flannery O'Connor (1925–1964)

without Jesus. The Christian, therefore, rightly recognizes that even his best attempt to keep God's law is delusional arrogance, an ill-conceived plan to become his own savior.

The Voyage of Life – Manhood, Thomas Cole, 1840

Salvation: An Earthshaking Event

A crucial issue to understand is that the gospel is a patient message. It works like flowing water to slowly, but systematically, cut through the heart's granite casing. Likewise, the gospel drills through the stone of societal evils so that all social blight is finally healed and corrected by means of the gospel. Thus, for example, the Christian rightly opposes abortion but sees the spread of the gospel, transforming hearts which in turn transform society, as the final answer to the abortion affliction. The Christian seeks to free society from substance abuse, but only sees the gospel as breaking affliction, replacing it with the worship of God. The Christian opposes homosexual marriage but works with gospel-directed focus to call the sexually-deviant to repentance so that the marriage question withers in the rising sun of regenerate hearts.

For the Christian, questions of cultural depravity and social justice are ultimately resolved by means of the gospel, a message that confronts, breaks, transforms, and finally resurrects civilizations, transcending economic, political, or educational solutions. Thus, the gospel becomes the undergirding ethos by means of which all tormenting symptoms are alleviated.[43] The gospel, saving individuals, effects a collective change, a groundswell of glorious mutation. It maintains a "calm level gaze,"[44] ever-conscious of an eternal duty to fulfill rather than a mere temporal one. The point is that direct confrontation of individual hearts effects indirect confrontation of all social institutions and practices, so that as the former are reformed the latter are

---

[43] Of course, James 2:16 admonishes the Christian to direct and immediate intervention when such intervention is direly needed.
[44] This phrase from a Newsmax documentary on Queen Elizabeth II.

transformed.

Becoming a Christian:

1. Involves honest repentance before God

> "The time has come – the kingdom of God is near. Repent and believe the good news." (Mark 1:15)

2. Is an unforgettable turning from death to life

> "Through Christ the Spirit of life set me from the law of sin and death." (Romans 8:2)

3. Is God's invitation into his family and into new life through understanding one's guilt before a holy God and asking for his forgiveness

> "Father I have sinned against heaven and against you. I am no longer worthy to be called your son." (Luke 15:21)

> The Gospel presents three central truths:
>
> 1. Justification (past). One is saved from the penalty of his sin.
> 2. Sanctification (present). One is saved from the power of his sin.
> 3. Glorification (future). One is saved from the presence of his sin.[45]
>
> This is the basis for all biblical counseling. Every aspect of counseling simultaneously draws in each of these three truths. Put another way, all counseling must contain each of these three truths in order for the counsel to in fact be truthful.

The church is filled with those who are not truly saved, yet tragically believe that they are. A glaring problem is "easy repentance" or "easy grace." Romans 16:17, 18 states,

> I urge you, brothers, to watch out for those who cause divisions and put obstacles in your way that are contrary to the teaching you have learned. Keep away from them. For such people are not serving our Lord Christ, but their own appetites. By smooth talk and flattery they deceive the minds of naïve people.

Those still in a state of death destroy the life of the church as they pretend to be ministers for Christ. Becoming a Christian is never a light matter so that one who

---

[45] Jay Adams, *A Theology of Christian Counseling* (Zondervan, 1986) 177.

becomes a Christian would unmistakably know that this transaction with God has occurred.

> "I have been constantly on the move. I have been in danger from rivers, in danger from bandits, in danger from my fellow Jews, in danger from Gentiles; in danger in the city, in danger in the country, in danger at sea; and in danger from false believers." (2 Corinthians 11:36)

When one becomes a Christian quickly, in an emotional flurry, he must question whether he has merely done so for some perceived gain. Maybe this is done to be accepted by a group, as a way to gain power and prestige over others, as a way to feel good about oneself, or as a source of pride. Philippians 1:17 refers to those who preach Christ out of selfish ambition. Thus, while some may preach out of selfish ambition, others may likewise accept that preaching out of an equally selfish ambition.

A Personal Application of the Gospel[46]

I traveled a great distance to a foreign land to share the gospel. I experienced hardship, suffering, insults, threats, persecution, and even attacks. I have been cold, lost, harassed, and in danger. If I focus on my experience then I might conclude that God is not really God. If he were omnipotent, he could have spared me from this. I could also conclude that God is not good, because if he loved me I would not have experienced these trials.

But when I consider the gospel, my life story, my autobiography, changes. In coming to that foreign country I separated myself from my culture and home. However, the distance Jesus traveled to earth was far greater. His separation from his Father in heaven was infinitely more wrenching. Philippians 2:7, 8 states, "…but made himself nothing, taking the very nature of a servant, being made in human likeness. And being found in appearance as a man, he humbled himself and became obedient to death – even death on a cross!"

I have experienced attacks and persecution. Jesus experienced far greater attacks and persecution. He was crucified though completely innocent of any wrong doing. Luke 18:32 states, "He will be handed over to the Gentiles. They will mock him, insult him, spit on him, flog him and kill him." Revelation 13:8 also reminds, "… the Lamb of God that was slain from the creation of the world."

> "By oppression and judgment he was taken away.

---

[46] For more development of this topic see "The Gospel and Suffering" in the third book in this series, *The Days of Reckoning Are at Hand: From Fig Leaf to Olive Branch to Laurel Wreath*, chapter 2: "Suffering: The Kintsugi Objective"

> Yet who of his generation protested?
> For he was cut off from the land of the living;
>   for the transgression of my people he was punished.
> He was assigned a grave with the wicked,
>   and with the rich in his death,
> though he had done no violence,
>   nor was any deceit in his mouth.
> Yet it was the Lord's will to crush him and cause him to suffer,
>   and though the Lord makes his life an offering for sin,
> he will see his offspring and prolong his days,
>   and the will of the Lord will prosper in his hand." (Isaiah 53:8-10)

Jesus warned that those who are in him will experience troubles, persecution, and hardship. Believers should expect that. Second Timothy 3:12 reminds, "In fact, everyone who wants to live a godly life in Christ Jesus will be persecuted…"

As I reinterpret my life through the lens of the gospel, I see that what I experience is a participation in Jesus' eternal glory. My life's experience has become an instrument used by Jesus to advance his story, to further his work and mission to the world. His story has become my story. Seen in this way, God is no longer distant

The Farewell of Abelard and Heloise,
Angelica Kauffman, 1780

and weak; he is no longer capricious and mendacious. He is no longer an enemy but an intimate ally who has invested something of his vision, work, and purpose into me. My life experience is not outside of his sovereign will; it is at the heart of his sovereign will. The events of my life are linked to an eternal plan, and in this way bear the imprimatur of God's own glory. "That is why, for Christ's sake, I delight in weaknesses, in insults, in hardships, in persecutions, in difficulties. For when I am weak, then I am strong."[47]

> "The apostles left the Sanhedrin, rejoicing because they had been counted worthy of suffering disgrace for the Name." (Acts 5:41)
>
> "For our light and momentary troubles are achieving for us an eternal glory that far outweighs them all." (2 Corinthians 4:17)
>
> "Remember Jesus Christ, raised from the dead, descended from David. This is my gospel, for which I am suffering even to the point of being chained like a criminal. But God's word is not chained. Therefore I endure everything for the sake of the elect, that they too may obtain the salvation that is in Christ Jesus, with eternal glory." (2 Timothy 2:8-10)

With my life-story interpreted in the right way, I see the Bible's truths emerge. I can honestly consider it pure joy to experience hardships of many kinds because I know that such hardship and suffering perfects my faith, allowing me to participate in Christ's suffering and glory.[48] The counselor performs this same reinterpretation for those he counsels. He recasts, reshapes, and reforms others' autobiographies through the lens of the gospel so that they see their life-story as a participation in the work, mission, and eternal glory of Christ himself.[49]

> Tom Robbins stated, "We're our own dragons as well as our own heroes, and we have to rescue ourselves from ourselves." In fact, Jesus is the only hero who can slay the inner dragon, rescuing mankind from himself.

Marks of a Christian

Islam cannot peacefully coexist with other religions. Its goal is geopolitical domination, and it will not rest until it achieves its objective.[50] For a different reason, a similar claim could be made about Christianity. Christianity is also utterly focused on complete domination, not of the geopolitical world, but of the human heart. Christianity cannot peacefully coexist with any other truth claims within the heart. James 4:5 states, "Or do you think Scripture says without reason that the spirit he caused to live in us envies intensely?" The Holy Spirit will not allow false gods to peacefully coexist within the Christian. Those false gods, like strychnine to the soul,

---

[47] 2 Corinthians 12:10
[48] James 1:2, 3
[49] For additional discussion of the topic of suffering see the third book in this series, *The Days of Reckoning Are at Hand: From Fig Leaf to Olive Branch to Laurel Wreath*, chapter 2: "Suffering: The Kintsugi Objective"
[50] Samuel Huntington, "The Clash of Civilizations?," *Foreign Affairs* (1993) (contains the Huntington thesis)

must either be destroyed or else gain mastery over their host.

The following are marks of a heart that has been claimed by Christ:

1. Passion for studying the Bible, longing to live by God's Word

> "But if I say, 'I will not mention his word or speak anymore in his name,' his word is in my heart like a fire, a fire shut up in my bones. I am weary of holding it in; indeed, I cannot." (Jeremiah 20:9)

2. Clear understanding of the means of salvation, by faith alone, through God's grace alone; lives in this reality and clearly explains the basis of his salvation to others

> "Now, brothers and sisters, I want to remind you of the gospel I preached to you, which you received and on which you have taken your stand." (1 Corinthians 15:1)
>
> "But even if we or an angel from heaven should preach a gospel other than the one we preached to you, let them be under God's curse!" (Galatians 1:8)

3. Progressively growing in faith, continually taking greater risks for God's glory which always involve forsaking and denying oneself (There should be diminished focus on one's own existence and ever-greater desire for, and focus on, God's.)

> "Therefore, my dear friends, flee from idolatry." (1 Corinthians 10:14)
>
> "I have been crucified with Christ and I no longer live, but Christ lives in me. The life I now live in the body, I live by faith in the Son of God, who loved me and gave himself for me." (Galatians 2:20)

4. Being sanctified so that one shows progressive growth in holiness

> "Those who belong to Christ Jesus have crucified the flesh with its passions and desires." (Galatians 5:24)

5. Increasingly hates his own sin and daily renounces sin so that God's discipline and correction are treasured with a thankful heart

> "In the same way, count yourselves dead to sin but alive to God in Christ Jesus." (Romans 6:11)

6. Abundantly displays the fruit of the Spirit (Jesus was clear that a Christian would be evidenced by his fruit.)

7. With each passing day more fully renounces the world and its ways; increasing hatred of the world's lies, deception, and enmity toward God

> "You adulterous people, don't you know that friendship with the world means enmity against God? Therefore, anyone who chooses to be a friend of the world becomes an enemy of God." (James 4:4)

8. Longs to see others also know and love God; continual call for repentance and a pleading with others to receive eternal life

Elisabeth of Thuringen
Edmund Blair Leighton, d. 1922

One of the clearest marks of a true Christian (in contrast to a false Christian) is his regard for Jesus. Those who know and love Jesus speak about him directly in their varied circumstances and settings. Those who are mere cultural Christians or nominal Christians may speak generally about "God" but rarely mention Jesus by name. This often indicates the intentions of the heart. Another indication of a false Christian is one who only speaks about Jesus in a Christian setting, such as at church or in a Bible study, but does not utter his name in any other context. As 2 Timothy 3:5 admonishes, "…having a form of godliness but denying its power. Have nothing to do with such people."

The Transformative Power of Forgiveness[51]

Consider the following excerpt from *Unbroken: A World War II Story of Survival,*

---

[51] For further discussion of the topic of forgiveness see "The Cure of Souls: Revisiting Ockham's Razor" in chapter 8: "What Has Jerusalem to Do With Vienna?: The Case Against Psychology"

Resilience, and Redemption (2010),

> The Pacific POWs who went home in 1945 were torn-down men. They had an intimate understanding of man's vast capacity to experience suffering, as well as his equally vast capacity, and hungry willingness, to inflict it. They carried unspeakable memories of torture and humiliation, and an acute sense of vulnerability that attended the knowledge of how readily they could be disarmed and dehumanized. Many felt lonely and isolated, having endured abuses that ordinary people couldn't understand. Their dignity had been obliterated, replaced with a pervasive sense of shame and worthlessness. And they had the caustic knowledge that no one had come between them and tragedy. Coming home was an experience of profound, perilous loneliness.
>
> For these men, the central struggle of postwar life was to restore their dignity and find a way to see the world as something other than a menacing blackness. There was no one right way to peace; every man had to find his own path, according to his own history. Some succeeded. For others, the war would never really end. Some retreated into brooding isolation or lost themselves in escapes. And for some men, years of swallowed rage, terror, and humiliation concentrated into what Holocaust survivor Jean Améry would call 'a seething, purifying thirst for revenge.'[52]

In *How Evil Works: Understanding and Overcoming the Destructive Forces That Are Transforming America* (2010), David Kupelian asserts that the only cure for what mankind terms "mental illness" is what God calls repentance. The entranceway into this repentance was perfectly codified in the Lord's Prayer.[53] This prayer serves as a microcosm of the entire Christian life and experience, one in which God's name is glorified, one rightly recognizes his utter dependence on God (for his daily bread), and one asks for, and in turn offers, forgiveness. Thus, the climax of the prayer is this request for God's forgiveness and the willingness to, in turn, forgive. This is the basis for Christian wholeness, peace, joy, relational unity, psychic health, as well as the soul's healing from the ravages of sin."[54]

The mirror side of this issue is that what psychology calls "mental illness" (and, in fact, all supposed aberrations of the psyche) arises from nothing more than the absence of forgiveness before God, and in the refusal to forgive.[55] Withholding forgiveness resides in the arrogance that one is his own god, sitting in judgment upon

---

[52] Laura Hillenbrand, *Unbroken: A World War II Story of Survival, Resilience, and Redemption* (New York: Random House, 2010) 349.
[53] David Kupelian, *How Evil Works: Understanding and Overcoming the Destructive Forces That Are Transforming America* (Threshold Edition, 2010) 110, 111.
[54] David Kupelian, *How Evil Works: Understanding and Overcoming the Destructive Forces That Are Transforming America* (Threshold Edition, 2010) 111.
[55] David Kupelian, *How Evil Works: Understanding and Overcoming the Destructive Forces That Are Transforming America* (Threshold Edition, 2010) 111.

mankind for one's own self-glorification. This "playing God," fed by narcissistic ideations, quickly devolves into every form of psychic deviance, such as what is termed paranoid schizophrenia, bipolar disorder, impulsive disorder, and suicidal ideations. These are nothing more than the outworking of a life lived without God's forgiveness and in defiance of God's forgiveness, all the while installing oneself as his own god in judgment over all supposed or real infractions upon his hegemonic rule.[56]

God commands the Christian to forgo revenge (in any form that it might take) for a very simple reason: God knows the human heart. He knows as one plans, seeks, and acts for revenge, he becomes like the one he hates. God knows that seeking to mete out evil for evil only causes the perpetrator to become further entrenched in evil himself.

> Jesus' teaching on forgiveness often feels like a cryptic message from a distant planet. Today, it is rare to hear Christians ask for forgiveness, and it is even rarer for them to grant forgiveness (as they perpetrate often clandestine forms of revenge). In a highly-psychologized world, the concept of forgiveness has been swept away in a torrent of blame-shifting.

Incidentally, assisting in this godless quest is anger which serves as a ready narcotic for the narcissist. Anger continually feeds the delusion that one is his own god, since it carries with it the feeling of deity.[57]

Consider Revelation 22:1, 2 which reads,

> Then the angel showed me the river of the water of life, as clear as crystal, flowing from the throne of God and of the Lamb down the middle of the great street of the city. On each side of the river stood the tree of life, bearing twelve crops of fruit, yielding its fruit every month. And the leaves of the tree are for the *healing* of the nations.

What is the cure for what is termed "mental illness"? The healing that only Jesus offers. This is the enigmatic answer to the great riddle of the Sphinx. Only forgiveness before God, only repentance at the foot of the cross untangles the human psyche. While psychology's diagnoses more deeply embed the illness since at their root they are a covering for sinful responses to one's world,[58] only Jesus frees one from the bondage to serving one's own self-deluding purposes. It is in relationship with Jesus that sinful responses to one's world slowly evaporate, that the healing takes effect as

---

[56] Matthew 18:32-35
[57] David Kupelian, *How Evil Works: Understanding and Overcoming the Destructive Forces That Are Transforming America* (Threshold Edition, 2010) 111.
[58] David Kupelian, *How Evil Works: Understanding and Overcoming the Destructive Forces That Are Transforming America* (Threshold Edition, 2010) 113.

one is incrementally freed from himself.

Prisoners Exercising (after Dore), Vincent Willem van Gogh, 1890

"Forgiveness is setting a prisoner free and then discovering the prisoner was you." (John Eldredge)

Case Study: The Ultimate Refutation of Evolution[59]

Jesus Christ claimed to be God and therefore had all power, authority, and wisdom. He freely forfeited his personal use of these qualities choosing instead to sacrifice his life. He pursued a life of humility, poverty, and selfless service. At thirty-three years of age he surrendered himself to savage torture and death in order to open the possibility of eternal life to those who were formerly his enemies.[60]

Jesus' death on the cross makes peace with his enemies so that they are now friends. Isaiah 11:6 states, "The wolf will live with the lamb, the leopard will lie down with the goat, the calf and the lion...a little child will lead them." This passage presents a vision of life free from evolutionary thinking, life lived in peace with God and

---

[59] For additional discussion of evolution see "Psychology and Evolution" in chapter 8: "What Has Jerusalem To Do With Vienna?: The Case Against Psychology"
[60] Philippians 2:5-11

therefore in peace with one another.

Luke 1:53 states, "He has filled the hungry with good things but has sent the rich away empty." Those who, according to evolution, are considered the "rich" (the strong, the competent, the proud) are left empty, while those who hunger for God, he fills. Reality works in the opposite direction of evolution. Evolution says the rich are filled with good things when, in fact, God opposes the rich. It is the strongest who are most lost, empty, and most "dead" because they rely upon themselves, and in so doing deny their desperate need for God. So as evolution says that the strongest are the most likely to survive, according to the Bible, they are least likely to survive, while the weakest, as they hunger for God, are given his salvific grace. In this way, the weakest survive for an eternity, while those who rely upon their own power end up facing eternal death.

> While David used Goliath's own sword to slay him,[61] Jesus slew Satan in utter defiance of the world's methods. Through means of an unfathomable paradox, Jesus defeated Satan by laying down his life in willful submission to his Father.

Colossians 2:15 states, "And having disarmed the powers and authorities, he made a public spectacle of them, triumphing over them by the cross." Jesus' sacrifice on the cross destroyed the powers of the strong. Through his death he achieved the final triumph. Thus, everything about Jesus' life and death is an affront to evolution. Jesus' death was the vanquishing of those who wield earthly power through their own sinful means. Thus, those "weak" in Christ have defeated those strong in the world.[62]

Christ on the Cross Formed by Clouds
Louis de Silvestre, 1734

This one life proves that the purpose of human existence is not the survival of the fittest and strongest. In the case of Jesus, he was *the* fittest and strongest, since no one in history has ever matched his power and wisdom. But Jesus forsook his own survival in order to save those who were weakest and least

---

[61] 1 Samuel 17:51
[62] Colossians 1:16-18

able to survive, people who were slaves to sin. In effect, Jesus' death on the cross inverted the entire premise of Darwinism.

Conclusion[63]

Those who are participants in the new covenant under Jesus cannot invalidate it, for it never depended upon them, but only upon him who was and is their federal head and representative before God. Of Jesus the demand was made and he met it. By Jesus man's side of the covenant was upheld and fulfilled, and now no condition remains; it is solely made up of promises which are not based upon meeting some condition. Today believers are not under the covenant of "If one does this he will live," but under that new covenant which says, "Their sins and their iniquities will I remember no more." It is not now "Do and live," but "Live and do;" we think not of merit and reward, but of free grace producing holy practice as the result of gratitude. What law could not do, grace has accomplished.

For the Christian there is a new life which is unseen, nor fed by the provisions of the earth. The Christian is conscious of having been raised to life, for he was once dead, and he knows it; but now he has passed from death into life, and he knows it quite as certainly. A new and higher motive sways him now; for he seeks not self but God. Another hand grasps the tiller and steers the ship in a new course. New desires are felt which were foreign in his former state. New fears are mighty within him,—holy fears which he once ridiculed. New hopes are in him, bright and sure, such as he did not even desire to know when he lived a mere carnal life. He is not what he was: he is new, and has begun a new career.

He is not what he should be, but assuredly he is not what we used to be. The Christian's consciousness of being a new man in Christ Jesus is often as sharp and crisp as his consciousness of existence. He knows that he is not only and solely what he was by his first birth; He feels within myself another life — a second and a higher vitality which has often to contend with his lower self, and by that very contention makes him conscious of its existence. This new Person, God himself, is, from day to day, gathering strength, and winning the victory. It has its hand upon the throat of the old sinful nature, and it shall eventually trample it like dust beneath its feet. It took the Lord himself to make, such as we are, new. None but a Savior on the throne could accomplish it; and therefore let him have the glory of it.

---

[63] This entire section adapted from Charles Spurgeon (1834–1892) sermon No. 1816, January 1, 1885

Section II

A Little Lower than the Angels: *Human Design*

- 5 -
REDEFINING THE PYGMALION EFFECT:
Exploring the Image of God in Man[1]

Pygmalion, Jean-Baptiste Regnault, 1786

"Is Man an Ape or an Angel?"[2]

The ancient Chinese recognized a common human ancestry from An Deng (安登) and Nv Wa (女娲) (many believe these to be analogues of Adam and Eve). Today, there is debate among Chinese archeologists as to whether the Chinese specifically evolved from Peking Man (discovered in Beijing in 1929) or from a more distant human ancestor.

At a college in central China there is a garden containing a statue of Peking Man. (The statue is merely an artist's rendering.) According to a plaque next to the statue, Peking Man is thought to have lived 500,000 years ago. Yet oddly, the statue depicts Peking Man holding a ping-pong paddle with the inscription "champion" ("冠军") at his feet.

---

[1] This chapter might be labeled using the traditional theological heading of *ordo salutis*.
[2] Benjamin Disraeli (1804-1881)

This inscription seems like a mockery of the supposed Peking Man. Is there a suppressed recognition that Peking Man did not live as some might imagine? Is this depiction a veiled statement that the concept of a transitional man is merely the figment of a collective imagination, just a fanciful myth – and society somehow knows it? It would appear that mankind is confused about his own origin and, at times, departs from the official evolutionist template. It is as if man occasionally tires of the lie, allowing a certain protesting mockery to surface.

The Fundamental Human Condition

> "Herein lies the tragedy of the age: not that men are poor, not that men are wicked, but that men know so little of men." (W.E.B. DuBois)

The Pygmalion effect theorizes that people act in accordance with the expectations placed upon them (those expectations being based upon supposed design qualities), so that high expectations bring glowing behavior, and vice versa. This harkens back to the ancient Greek idea of a fatal flaw within man, some component which, as part of his design, causes him to commit wrong. Such a fatal flaw, if it exists, would implicitly place blame for sin with man's Designer.

What expectations does the Bible place upon mankind? How does the Bible describe mankind? The following list offers a summary:

Dignifying Descriptions of Man	Disparaging Descriptions of Man
Image and likeness of God[3]	Body of death[4]
Powerfully and wonderfully made[5]	Wretched, pitiful, poor, blind, naked[6]
God's workmanship[7]	Child of wrath[8]
Temple of the Holy Spirit[9]	Dust and ashes[10]
Son of God[11]	Children of the devil[12]
Good and noble soil[13]	Worthless servant;[14] wretch[15]
More than a conqueror[16]	Slaves to sin[17]
Salt of the earth[18]	Worm[19]

---

[3] Genesis 1:26; 1 Corinthians 11:7
[4] Romans 7:24
[5] Psalm 139:14
[6] Revelation 3:17
[7] Ephesians 2:10
[8] Ephesians 2:3
[9] 1 Corinthians 3:16
[10] Genesis 2:7; 18:27
[11] Matthew 5:45; Romans 8:14
[12] John 8:44
[13] Luke 8:15
[14] Matthew 25:30
[15] Romans 7:24
[16] Romans 8:37
[17] John 8:34

Light of the world[20]	Whitewashed tomb[21] (beautiful on the outside, but inside are full of dead men's bones and everything unclean); brood of vipers[22]
"…Are you not much more valuable than they?"[23]	"What is man that you are mindful of him?"[24]
Sons of the kingdom[25]	Sons of the evil one[26]
Wheat[27]	Weeds[28]
Good seed[29]	Evil[30]
Sheep[31]	Goats[32]
Saint[33]	Sinner[34]

Echo and Narcissus, John William Waterhouse, c. 1903

The Bible speaks in various ways about mankind depending upon the particular context. Some descriptions are ontological (by design) and others are functional

---

[18] Matthew 5:13
[19] Psalm 22:6
[20] Matthew 5:14
[21] Matthew 23:27
[22] Matthew 12:34
[23] Matthew 6:26
[24] Psalm 8:3,4; Hebrews 2:6-8
[25] Matthew 8:12
[26] Matthew 13:38
[27] Matthew 13:25
[28] Matthew 13:25
[29] Matthew 13:38
[30] Matthew 7:11
[31] Matthew 25:33
[32] Matthew 25:33
[33] Ephesians 3:18
[34] Luke 18:13

(status with regard to God such as a sinner or a saint). Man's design is "very good." Yet, as a result of the fall, he descended into evil and became a depraved being. Finally, mankind was redeemed in Christ so that his entire being might be glorified (not just his soul, but his body as well, a revolutionary concept in the Hellenistic world).

The biblical counselor must accurately understand the Bible's teaching about design, fall, and redemption so that throughout the counseling process he can highlight which aspect is being addressed: foundational design characteristics, indwelling sin, or redeemed and glorified sonship.

In defiance of the Pygmalion effect, the Bible asserts that God placed unimaginable collaborative expectations upon mankind, but that man did not act in accordance with them. According to the Bible, man bears no fatal design flaw. His problem is more akin to an igneous intrusion, a foreign entity which invades the design space. Man's sin bears no connection to design, but rather is an intruder into God's otherwise perfect order. This intruder is one which man invites, hosts, and satiates in a desperate attempt to usurp the position of the Great Designer himself. In this way, mankind is complicit with the sin which has infiltrated, and takes up residence within, himself.

> Consider that each person desires to be considered good and strives to be optimistic with regard to his existential condition. The human psyche reveals that it is invested with the characteristics of a holy eternal God, a God who is good and whose plans are perfect. Without a good and holy Creator there would be no reason to seek to be considered good, and no basis for optimism with regard to one's life and future. In a chaotic universe ruled by chance, goodness and hope are groundless and meaningless, and would therefore hold no central position within the psyche.

The Archimedean Point of Man's Design

An Archimedean point is a vantage point from which to see the whole, to remove oneself from the object of study so as to see it in relation to its surroundings. In order to understand himself, mankind must first admit that he knows nothing about himself until God reveals the truth of who he is. Thus, only God sits at the Archimedean point because only he sees and understands mankind, both individually and corporately, as he really is. Therefore, each person, despite living through his own experiences, actually knows nothing about those experiences until God tells him what they mean. Mankind does not know how to rightly assess or weigh the meaning and purpose of his life since his sin blinds him to who he is. He is likewise deceived concerning the correct solution to his most pressing problems. In this way, mankind is utterly dependent upon God's revelation in order to rightly understand himself.

> Brain surgery has been performed in nearly every ancient culture except the Egyptian. The Egyptians were remarkably careful about altering the human body as they believed that this bore eternal consequence.

Indoor Games, Torii Kiyomitsu, 1764

An overseas counselee once said, "How dare you claim to counsel my people since you know nothing about them." My respectfully-voiced response, "The Bible knows far more about your people than your people know about themselves." Why? The Bible reveals with piercing clarity mankind's precise existential state so that people, both corporately and individually, are only truly revealed through the lens of Scripture. In fact, without this lens one knows nothing about himself.

Likewise, a young woman once scolded me, "You can say nothing about my life since you know nothing of what I have experienced in the past." My response, "You are right that I do not know the specifics of your past, but from the Bible, I know something about how you have responded to those past experiences. The reality is that you do not understand your own experiences until God tells you what they mean."

The image of God is uniform across history, cultures, and races so that it remains a tectonic constant. This means that one who correctly knows the Bible is able to not only understand, but effectively counsel, even those from a radically different culture. In fact, it is true that the student of the Bible knows people of various cultures better than they know themselves. Thus, the biblical counselor is rightly able to minister to any people, in any place, at any time in history, since the image of God and the contours of sin and idolatry are universal constants.

The point is that the Bible offers the counselor an Archimedean point both with regard to mankind generally, and with regard to individuals specifically. The depth of the counselor's understanding of people is a function of the depth of his understanding of the Bible, and not a function of being privy to specific experiences or cultural expressions (although contextualizing the gospel is important). Put another way, the counselor should be much less interested in the specifics of what has happened to a counselee, as he is to know how the counselee has responded to what has happened. The Bible reveals the tides and tumult of the heart; it exposes the psyche with formidable vigor and crystalline clarity. The counselor can place tremendous confidence in the Bible to reveal all that needs to be revealed about the heart's machinations.

The Image of God: Man as Analogue[35]

Modern western minds may have trouble fathoming just how radical is the Genesis cosmogony in the context in which it was written. In ancient Near Eastern culture only a suzerain was considered the image of the gods. The Genesis creation account is such a forward-thinking democratizing force because it asserts the unthinkable, that *every* person is in the image of God. Thus, even the lowest peasants, as image-bearers of the holy God of the universe, enjoy an equivalent cosmic status to that of a king. This was a preposterous concept in the ancient world.[36]

As image-bearer, every person reflects something of God's "very good" creation. In fact, studying people is far more thrilling than studying anything else in creation (which, by comparison, is described as merely "good").[37] Each person as God's workmanship, regardless of his ability, intelligence, or personality traits, is a unique manifestation of God himself, a representative of that God to the universe. In this way, the image of God is both ontological (existence) and economic (function).[38]

> I happened upon a mirror shattered on the ground. I searched for all the pieces to put them together, but it was impossible. So I kept only the largest piece. I played with it as a toy reflecting light into dark places where the sun could not shine. This became a metaphor for my life. I came to understand that I am not light, or the source of light. I merely reflect light which is already there. I am only the fragment of a mirror whose whole design and shape I do not know. Nevertheless, even as a shattered image-bearer, with what I have, I was born to reflect eternal light into dark places.[39]

---

[35] Genesis 1:26
[36] Harvie Conn (1933–1999), "Orientation in Ministry" class, Westminster Theological Seminary, Philadelphia, Pennsylvania
[37] Genesis 1:4, 31
[38] Clair Davis, "Doctrine of Man" class, Westminster Theological Seminary, Philadelphia, Pennsylvania
[39] Adapted from an unknown source

Man, in each of his design characteristics, is an analogue of God himself. This means that man was created to reveal God's being to the universe. Man's outer being (body) and inner being (psyche, conscience) are revelatory of the being of God, just as revelatory as the laws of physics.[40] As analogue, man thinks in analogical fashion. Thus, his acts of interpretation are merely a reinterpretation of what has already been fully interpreted by God in Scripture.[41] The fact that man is conscious of his own existence predicates itself upon the fact that God himself is self-conscious. Thus, man's entire being (mind, body, heart, soul, will) is revelatory, and man knows that he is the revelation of a holy God. In this sense, man is continually confronted with being a "creature."[42]

Archimedes Thoughtful
Domenico Fetti, 1620

Have you ever noticed that the front of an automobile looks like a human face? Is it possible that we enjoy forming that which is in our own image because we are imitating the Great Designer?

The image of God in man has historically been a misunderstood doctrine. For example, Shakespeare wrote, "What a piece of work is man, how noble in reason, how infinite in faculties; in form and moving how noteworthy and admirable, in action like an angel, in reasoning like a god: the beauty of the world, the highest of the animals."[43] Shakespeare, in keeping with the European Enlightenment, hijacked the image of God concept, deifying mankind and investing him with nobility and capability in defiance of God. Conversely, throughout history totalitarian regimes have denied the image of God in order to justify targeted genocide. When magnified, the image of God becomes distorted and grotesque, a means for hubris. When denied, the image of God becomes a means for human degradation and unrelenting eugenics. The Christian rightly understands the image of God as a truly astounding, awe-inspiring aspect of human existence while never allowing that image to be

---

[40] Cornelius Van Til, *Christian Apologetics* (Presbyterian and Reformed Press, 2003) 33.
[41] Cornelius Van Til, *Christian Apologetics* (Presbyterian and Reformed Press, 2003) 35.
[42] Cornelius Van Til, *Christian Apologetics* (Presbyterian and Reformed Press, 2003) 55.
[43] William Shakespeare, *Hamlet*, Act II, scene ii (c. 1602)

separated from the person of God.

> In his landmark work, *The Romantic Ethic and the Spirit of Modern Consumerism* (1987), Colin Campbell theorizes that modern consumerism burgeoned from the odd nexus of the aesthetically-pleasing and the morally upright. Somehow popular consciousness adopted the idea that those marked by impeccable style were more virtuous. This mentality spawns a consumer culture built upon social hierarchy and the assumption that status is linked to higher morality and inherent nobility. It was this connection which launched Western consumerism. The point is that mankind will only act if he can rationalize what he is doing as good. Without this rationalization he lacks the moral imperative to act. Consumerism took deep root in the twentieth century as it was linked to a certain redefinition of the good.

Job 28:3 states, "Mortals put an end to the darkness; they search out the farthest recesses for ore in the blackest darkness," and Job 28:11, "They search the sources of the rivers and bring hidden things to light." Mankind has been invested with towering abilities to explore, understand, and manage the earth. However, on account of sin he uses these abilities, not under God's provenance, but in defiance of God. Without God himself as the direct source of investiture, the image within man is meaningless and the exercise of mankind's abilities only leads to destruction and loss. Thus, the image of God exists to cause mankind to rightly understand his place with regard to God, the extent of his capabilities, and to ultimately spawn worship of God.

> "He has made everything beautiful in its time. He has also set eternity in the human heart; yet no one can fathom what God has done from beginning to end." (Ecclesiastes 3:11)

The image is not static like a photograph, but manifests a dynamic, living, breathing organism. In the state of sin, the image lies darkened and denuded, but as the Christian is sanctified the image intensifies, enlivens, and illuminates within him. Thus, the image is sharpened, coming into clear focus, as the Christian lives according to God's will.

> Airlines still report passengers as "souls" onboard a plane.

The sense of personhood runs far deeper than one thinks. Consider a common occurrence. Not knowing that someone is in a room, one inadvertently turns off a light as that person sits quietly in that room. There is an almost reflexive anger and sense of personal affront from the one in the room (even when that person knows that the lights were extinguished as an honest mistake). The point is that the sense of personhood is dominant in the psyche, and it is vulnerable to feeling violated. This sense of personhood causes mankind to embark on a quixotic mission to maintain a sense of dignity. Any violation upon personhood, any perceived or real indignity, is rarely, if ever, excused by the sinful heart.

Several years ago I walked into an orthodox Jewish restaurant in my neighborhood. (While I have at times been mistaken for Jewish, I don't wear a *yarmulke*, so I clearly can't be mistaken for an orthodox Jew.) I waited to be seated but waiters and waitresses buzzed by without even looking in my direction. I saw open tables but no one was seating me. I surmised that the tables must be reserved for an occasion, so I made my way to the take-out counter. I waited for someone to take my order, but again, no one said a word to me. None of the staff looked in my direction, nor made eye-contact. Other customers, approaching the counter, were greeted with, "May I take your order?" Although I waited patiently, I did not receive a greeting. I tried to get a waitress' attention, but she wheeled around and darted into the kitchen. It suddenly dawned on me; I'm not going to be served; my patronage is not welcomed here. I saw no angry faces, and received no nasty looks. I was simply and purely invisible.

In the years since, I have come to understand why I was not served. Orthodox Judaism, in observance of its dietary laws, forbids its members from eating with Gentiles. (Peter felt Paul's wrath for violating his conscience in this regard.[44]) I hold no ill-will. I recount this story merely to make a point about the issue of personhood. As an image-bearer of the God of the universe, I was designed to be noticed. I was meant to be greeted, to be counted, to be included. There is something in my design which bears a gravitas, not that I am distinguished among men, but that I am invested with an eternal soul. To be overlooked, to be excluded, to be neglected, to be rendered functionally invisible, to at times be treated as a "clinking, clanking, clattering collection of caliginous junk" by the world,[45] brings with it a justifiable measure of pain, a feeling of being violated, a sense of being stripped of an invested nobility.

As image-bearers we were each designed to bear a certain weight and significance, to carry a veiled dignity, to represent the presence of God himself. Thus, there is no sin in feeling a sting of outrage when one's personhood has been violated. However, for the Christian that sting dies quickly, because he knows who he is in Christ, a redeemed son of God. A Christian can overlook an offense to his personhood because he is now an exalted member of God's family. He can sustain injustice without retribution, and without bitterness, because his invested dignity is not besmirched by man. It is only besmirched by a sinful response.

The Image of God: Prophet, Priest, and King

---

[44] Galatians 2:11-13
[45] "The Wonderful Wizard of Oz" (1939)

Prophet:

The function of the prophet is to assign meaning, interpret, and speak truth. Mankind, as prophet, is invested with an unrelenting desire to know the truth (whether of personal matters or of the creation itself). This desire to know the truth drives mankind to plumb the universe in a quest to experience "the ultimate triumph of human reason."[46]

Isaiah's Lips Anointed with Fire
Benjamin West, 1782

> There is an odd phenomenon, the inability to tell a lie while looking into another's eyes. ("Look me in the eye and say that.") Why is the psyche tremulous with the thought of lying while looking into another's eyes? Is there something in the connection of two people's eyes which reveals the soul? Clearly, humanity is more than a material being interacting out of purely pragmatic purpose. Without question, humanity contains a preprogrammed conscience which retains a "moral memory," one which cannot be fully expunged. This conscience somehow plugs into the eyes through a hidden spiritual conduit.

Priest:

The function of the priest is relational, bringing blessing and peace, comfort, and rest to the Creation. First Peter 2:9, 10 states,

> But you are a chosen people, a royal priesthood, a holy nation, God's special possession, that you may declare the praises of him who called you out of darkness into his wonderful light. Once you were not a people, but now you are the people of God; once you had not received mercy, but now you have received mercy.

> There is this perplexing dual tendency in modern fashion: on the one hand a

---

[46] Stephen Hawking

> penchant for glitzy regal display, and on the other, a peculiar countercurrent of dirty, ripped, and poorly-fitting clothing. In dress mankind tends toward extremes, either to exalt himself in god-like splendor or to deface and denigrate himself with an impoverished "orphaned" look. Both extremes evidence man's abiding rebellion against a holy God, to with one Promethean hand grasp at God's stunning majesty, while with the other flaunting, even celebrating, man's wicked, dilapidated state.
>
> In the Bible, a priest was to wear a seamless article of clothing, a sign of his dignified station. In this same vein, in past generations to wear ripped or tattered clothing was a disgrace which all, but the most impoverished, eschewed. Today, however, there is a perplexing fashion trend, the popularity of ripped clothing. There is something in this modern trend which seems like a brash "anti-priest" statement, that people today regard themselves as in defiance of priestly character.

King:

The function of a king is to command authority, to act with power, to exercise judgment, and to display wrath. In Genesis 2:19 Adam named the animals and, in so doing, both assigned meaning and demonstrated a derivative mastery over the Creation. This mastery is brought to fruition for those in Christ, as Romans 8:37 reveals that the Christian is more than a conqueror.

> "I said, 'You are 'gods'; you are all sons of the Most High. But you will die like mere men; you will fall like every other ruler." (Psalm 82:6, 7)
>
> "Already you have all you want! Already you have become rich! You have begun to reign—and that without us! How I wish that you really had begun to reign so that we also might reign with you!" (1 Corinthians 4:8)

> According to Greek mythology, King Sisyphus was an exceptionally treacherous potentate. He frequently had his guests murdered, employed deception for personal gain, and betrayed loyalties. For his many transgressions, Sisyphus was sent to Hades where he was consigned to roll a boulder up a mountain. Just as the boulder reached the summit it rolled back down, a torturous task to be repeated each day for eternity. This story indicates a truth within men; they were designed to work and their work was meant to have some meaning, to carry significance in an eternal economy. Daily work done in futility is a source of searing personal angst, as it affronts something of man's kingly function.

The three stations, prophet, priest, and king, while damaged in the unbeliever, are resurrected in the believer so that the Christian is simultaneously prophet, priest, and king experiencing, exercising, and enjoying the fullness of these stations with a regenerate heart.

Man as Image of God			
What Man Is		**What Man Does**	
1. **Material body** – dust with divine form and function[47]	Prophet – truth, meaning (Holy Spirit)	7. **Working** – man works because God works[48]	King – commands authority (Father)
2. **Intellectual** – reasoning mind[49]	^		
3. **Moral** – heart, conscience[50]	^		
4. **Emotional** – designed to feel[51]	Priest – relationship, comfort (Jesus)		
5. **Social** – designed for vertical and horizontal relationship[52]	^		
6. **Spiritual** – designed to worship[53]	^		

General Alexei Yermolov, George Dawe, 1823

In his novel, *Thus Spoke Zarathustra* (1883), Friedrich Nietzsche (1844-1900) envisioned mankind as the sole authority unto himself, the *Ubermensch* (superman). In Nietzsche's cosmology, the *Ubermensch* represents a kind of eschatological redemption in which mankind is finally delivered from his God-delusion.[54] In Nietzsche's view, mankind can only truly soar to new heights when he is free from the concept of an eternal world. Thus, Nietzsche sought to glorify man in the here-and-now.[55]

I raise the Nietzschean *Ubermensch* to highlight something of the nature of the biblical image of God. Mankind is a profoundly *God*-centered being, one of

---

[47] Genesis 2:7
[48] Genesis 2:15
[49] Isaiah 1:18; Acts 17:17; Hebrews 11:19
[50] Psalm 51:4
[51] John 11:35; Ephesians 4:30
[52] Luke 15:20; Hebrews 10:25
[53] John 4:24
[54] Wikipedia article "Ubermensch"
[55] For a discussion of Friedrich Nietzsche's influence upon the development of modern psychology see "The Gang of Six: Influences on the Growth and Development of Psychology," in chapter 8: "What Has Jerusalem to Do With Vienna?: The Case Against Psychology"

unfathomable potential, but only to the extent that he remains an analogous and derivative creature. Nietzsche sought to strip humanity of its Godward referent so as to assign salvific capability to mankind himself. The Bible, however, in disclosing man's identity, and in realizing man's potential, maintains an adamantine coupling between God and man. Nietzsche (like all philosophers and psychologists) believed that he could revoke the truths governing the psyche, treating mankind as a malleable entity to be sculpted as he chose. In reality, mankind is subject to preset design characteristics which cannot be altered.

> Mankind was made for greatness, just not a greatness that could be achieved through anything in the creation.

> Terrorists hate the West yet use western-made airplanes, internet, mobile phones, satellites, televisions, and video recorders to conduct their attacks. They could not attack the West without the technology they acquire from the West.[56] For example, in order to attack the United States certain terror organizations effectively recruit and raise funds using the internet, an American invention. In similar fashion, mankind, in his sin-driven hatred of God, can only attack God because of God's own image invested in mankind. Mankind uses "borrowed capital" such as his reason, to launch his assaults upon God himself.[57]

God is eternally prophet, priest, and king in their quintessence. Man, as God's image-bearer, is analogous prophet, priest, and king, displaying God's own personhood to the world as nothing else in the creation can. That is why human being's exist, to exhibit God's own character and invisible qualities to his creation. In becoming "savior," God transcended himself, reaching beyond his eternal existence. God as savior, in allowing himself to be sacrificed and to die, assumed the supreme manifestation of his character. Thus, God did not remain simply prophet, priest, and king but, rather, showed himself to be capable of something far beyond. In becoming savior, God manifest a quality that had not been witnessed since the beginning of time.

> "An enigma wrapped inside a riddle enclosed in a mystery" (Winston Churchill)

However, another aspect must be considered. Since God's very first creative acts were *redemptive* acts, does this raise the prospect that God always functioned as savior with regard to his creation? He was, throughout his dealings with his people a salvific presence, standing between them and the wrath that they rightly deserved.

---

[56] William Edgar, "Introduction to Apologetics" class, Westminster Theological Seminary, Philadelphia, Pennsylvania
[57] Cornelius Van Til, *Christian Apologetics* (Presbyterian and Reformed Press, 2003)

> "They all ate the same spiritual food and drank the same spiritual drink; for they drank from the spiritual rock that accompanied them, and that rock was Christ." (1 Corinthians 10:3, 4)

Work, Ford Madox Brown, 1863

So while the salvation wrought through Jesus' death on the cross marks a new epoch, a new covenant in God's dealing with man, that death also maintains the thread of salvation that God weaves throughout the entire Bible. Thus, God, throughout history, was always already savior but, nevertheless, displayed something eminently new in Jesus' death. Jesus act of salvation, the penultimate act in human history (his second coming to be the ultimate), was a never-before-beheld disclosure of God's character.

Each Christian is redeemed, reinvigorated, revived and iridescent prophet, priest, and king. While all three functions exist within each Christian, each is called to emphasize certain aspects of those functions in particular times and places. Sometimes one is called to function as a priest, at others as a prophet, and at still others as a king. Each is called to emphasize a particular function based on the dictates of any given situation. A Christian, exercising proper wisdom, rotates between these roles as he correctly assesses the needs of those around him. But like Neptune's trident, three-pronged yet unified, one is simultaneously prophet, priest, and king, distinct yet conjoined at all times.

> It is important to emphasize that men and women are each called to the roles of

> prophet, priest, and king, but often within distinct contexts and for specific purposes. A wife is called to be a helpmate to her husband (but a woman is not a helpmate to a man, generally).[58] While a wife is called to serve her husband's vision and purposes, she is also called to exercise the roles of prophet, priest, and king within the context of being a helpmate. For example, a mother rightly exercises authority over her children (a kingly function), but she serves under her husband's authority in this, submitting to him as he, in turn, submits to Christ's authority.

> There is an old adage that it is impossible for everyone to do what they love. The Christian is often called to sacrifice what he loves for the sake of serving Christ. The great paradox is that as one serves Christ, he soon finds that he loves what Christ loves.

The Marvel of Image-Bearing

Mankind, in every facet and contour, is a tour de force of unimaginable execution, an aurora borealis of scintillating wonder. Each person, as image-bearer, was designed to be admired, to serve as a celebration of the Great Designer. God fashions each person in such a glorious manner that his life is an exhilarating exploration and cultivation of unfathomable qualities. Each is a unique blending of gifts and abilities, attributes and experiences, perfectly mated to his calling in life. Each possesses within him infinite qualities meant to be played out on a temporal stage. Invested with the infinite, each life is linked to an eternal script. More than just highly-significant, each life is a masterpiece to behold.

> "Few men during their lifetime come anywhere near exhausting the resources dwelling within them." (Richard Byrd)

However, this marvel of image-bearing must be unfurled carefully so that the truths of man's design do not overrun his anthropological condition, that of *fallen* image-bearer. Additionally, mankind's invested qualities are not to be admired in abstraction, but for the purpose of celebrating the original designer. That is why they exist, that in exploring himself, mankind might turn his gaze toward God with reverent praise.

> Recently while traveling, I befriended an elderly gentleman on a tour we took together. In the course of our conversation it surfaced that this man is a Jungian psychologist. I was eager to discuss with him many of the concepts in this book, to receive his impressions. To my delight we launched a year-long debate between psychology and biblical counseling which proved highly-edifying. This man has a truly amazing mind. With facility he quotes eminent philosophers and interjects fascinating historical anecdotes. He writes with almost poetic beauty. He grasped the

---

[58] Genesis 2:18

> crux of my arguments with lightning speed and offered piercing analysis. I was left with a sense of awe in this man's mental gifts, yet with a profound sadness that such gifts are used for the wrong purpose. This vignette captures in a nutshell the human tragedy, incomparable gifts used to defy and dethrone the Giver.

Young Woman Resting, Francisco-Masriera Manovens, 1894

Mankind possesses within himself incomparable creative power, power invested in him to glorify God in ways that the animal-world never can. One of the ways mankind glorifies God is through song. God glories in word, in language, and song is the pinnacle of language, the highest showcase of word. Mankind was designed to not just recognize, but to conceive, magnificent music, a quality invested in his being as image-bearer. Music makes God's creative acts more intense to the human consciousness.

> While mankind has developed various instruments, many with soaring artistic quality, no sound compares to the human voice. While the psalmist invites all of creation to sing to the Lord, nothing in creation can match the tonality of the human voice.

Mankind's ability to create music is just one example among many of the fact that it is exhilarating to interact with and study people, to celebrate God's qualities revealed in and through people. There is no such thing as an inherently boring person, since nothing that God has created could ever be boring, especially his own image-bearers.

Thus, when two images of God interact there is a timeless meeting of hearts and minds. Boredom in interpersonal interaction arises because of sinful covering and hiding, the shielding of one's image-bearing qualities. Sin creates boring people.

> "God designed the human machine to run on himself. He himself is the fuel our spirits were designed to burn, or the food our spirits were designed to feed on. There is no other." (C.S. Lewis)

Satan's singular focus is to destroy God's work. Often Satan's most effective means do not involve a wrecking-ball but the subtle confusion of God's created order. Satan intermingles that which God separated, and separates that which God desires to bring together. The theory of evolution is such a crafty artifice because through it Satan intermingles species, advancing the lie that hybrids once existed. But this is not a new strategy. Even in ancient Greek mythology the concept of hybrid creatures exists (such as the Centaur, half man and half horse, or the Sphinx, a lion with a woman's head). This mingling of the human and animal is Satan's attempt to confuse and vandalize God's creative effort.[59]

> Under the dictates of the world system, the fashion industry and media denigrate the image of God by reducing it to a grotesque form of beauty, a manufactured and stylized beauty.[60] Mankind's natural beauty, invested by God himself, has become a vainglorious display of man's perversion, a plundering of the image, reducing it to mere material form.

Image and Likeness: Retention and Loss

"Ozymandias" (Percy Bysshe Shelley, 1818)[61]

> I met a traveller from an antique land
> Who said: 'Two vast and trunkless legs of stone
> Stand in the desert. Near them, on the sand,
> Half sunk, a shattered visage lies, whose frown,
> And wrinkled lip, and sneer of cold command,
> Tell that its sculptor well those passions read
> Which yet survive, stamped on these lifeless things,

---

[59] In Daniel 7:8, the prophet Daniel sees a vision of four powerful beasts which attack and blaspheme God himself. These beasts perpetrate various deceptions such as the illusion that they have ultimate dominion over the earth. In Daniel 7:4 a lion beast with wings "stood on two feet like a man, and the heart of a man was given to it." This is a perversion of man, a mutilation of the human form, and thus is a direct attack on the image of God. The beast desecrates the image invested into humans.

[60] For further discussion of the world system see the second book in this series, *What Agreement Is There Between the Temple of God and Idols?: The Accidence of Sin and Idolatry*, chapter 2: "The World, the Flesh, and the Devil: Assessing the Threat Matrix."

[61] Percy Bysshe Shelley, "Ozymandias," *Miscellaneous and Posthumous Poems of Percy Bysshe Shelley* (London: W. Benbow, 1826) 100.

> The hand that mocked them and the heart that fed:
> And on the pedestal these words appear:
> 'My name is Ozymandias, king of kings:
> Look on my works, ye Mighty, and despair!'
> Nothing beside remains. Round the decay
> Of that colossal wreck, boundless and bare
> The lone and level sands stretch far away.

After the fall, the image of God was retained but the likeness was destroyed. This means that mankind still possesses the basic machinery or components of God's design, but that machinery does not operate as it was intended. The following are three metaphors for understanding man's fallen nature:

1. Mankind as "semi-ruined temple,"[62] or in Edgar Allen Poe's (1809-1849) words, "one of those piles of commingled gloom and grandeur." Mankind was created as a glorious temple, a sacred dwelling for God's own Spirit.[63] That temple was majestic in design, a reflection of God's own being. Tragically, in the fall the temple was severely damaged, but not obliterated. Mankind, bearing some semblance of the original design, still displays the rudiments of his Creator's handiwork. Fallen mankind is only partially ruined but not irretrievably so, given to evil, but not without hope of redemption. The image of God remains, so that mankind is a redeemable being. The likeness, however, has been obliterated, so that man, in thought, word, and action, fails to reflect the character of God. While still an image-bearer, a glorious temple, an analogue of God's being, man is nevertheless a dead being, devoid of God's likeness.

> "A noble wreck in ruinous perfection" (Childe Byron)

> "Some of his disciples were remarking about how the temple was adorned with beautiful stones and with gifts dedicated to God. But Jesus said, 'As for what you see here, the time will come when not one stone will be left on another; every one of them will be thrown down.'" (Luke 21:5, 6)

H.G. Wells (1866-1946) wrote, "I am a temporary enclosure for a temporary purpose; that served, and my skull and teeth, my idiosyncrasy and desire will disperse, I believe, like the timbers of a booth after a fair." Wells, I believe, missed the crux of the issue with regard to human existence. There is no temporary person, as each person is carefully and lovingly created by God to know God and have eternal relationship with him.

---

[62] Augustine of Hippo, *Confessions* (Oxford University Press, 2009)
[63] 1 Corinthians 6:19

Absolutely no life is a mistake to finally be "dispersed." In this regard, beguiled by evolutionary thinking, some are led to believe that society's problem is overpopulation. In fact, there is no such thing as too many people, no overpopulation. This is a myth foisted upon society by secular progressive humanism as an excuse for societal failings and injustices. A holy and good God surely provides for all those he creates. It is because of human sin, greed, deception, corruption, laziness, addiction, and foolishness that some are deprived, so as to lack the necessary means to live. Mankind's plight is not an overpopulation problem but a depravity problem.

2. Mankind as a car that operates, but always in reverse.[64] The engine works well but propels the car in the wrong direction.

3. Mankind as a saw that cuts well, but never in a straight line.[65]

> Mankind is a mixture of extraordinary genius and naïve incompetence, and it is often impossible to distinguish between the two. (adapted from Douglas Adams)

The Bible sees people as:

1. Of noble design, but lost and damaged

2. Individuals exercising freewill, but slaves to their hatred of God's authority

3. Made to experience pleasure, but seeking it in all the wrong places

4. Rational problem solvers, but using reason as a weapon against God

Laocoon Group:
Agesander, Athenodorus, and Polydorus of Rhodes
Late 2nd C. BC, Rome, Italy

As a word of caution, the doctrine of the image of God in man can easily degenerate

---

[64] This metaphor from Claire Davis, Westminster Theological Seminary, Philadelphia, Pennsylvania
[65] This metaphor from Cornelius Van Til (1895–1987), Westminster Theological Seminary, Philadelphia, Pennsylvania

into humanism. The danger is that as soon as the concept of human potential is separated from its basis in a holy eternal God, mankind quickly ascribes to himself the status and stature of a god. How can the Christian celebrate human potential, and look with wonderment upon human achievement, while not falling into the humanist trap?

The answer seems to lie in two directions. First, continually predicate all statements of design upon God himself who remains its archetype, its template. Second, keep design in balance with the fall. While human potential is astounding, the fall maintains a stranglehold, so that unredeemed human ability is routinely a raised dagger against God himself; it is wrongly applied, and serves mankind's ultimate destruction. However, the fall does not have the last word as mankind is redeemable, renewable, capable of radical rebirth and worship recalibration through faith in Christ. This deliverance actually improves upon mankind's original design so that, in Christ, mankind is ultimately able to achieve far more than before the fall. Thus, in describing mankind, creation, fall, and redemption must be held in proper balance.

> A Chinese visionary invented paper money in AD 806. However, it was initially rejected as worthless. In response, the inventor staged his own death, and had his friends burn paper money in his memory. He reappeared a few days later in a mock "resurrection." This convinced people that paper money had real value. The point in mentioning this is to assert that since mankind has eternity in his heart,[66] he seeks some means to procure eternal life. Knowing that he was created to live forever, man seeks any means at his disposal to secure his own resurrection without God.

Mankind as Designed to Worship

William Penn (1644-1718) wrote, "If a man is not governed by God, he will be ruled by tyrants." His words are eerily prophetic for our time. Just as nature abhors a vacuum and rushes to fill it, so too, society abhors a worship vacuum. The human heart cannot exist in a worship vacuum so that if it does not worship the true God, it turns to convenient false gods (such as statism). Larger, ever more intrusive, government is the symptom of a society that collectively worships the world and its false gods.[67] As American society progressively denies and rejects the true God, it becomes increasingly obsessed with worldly pursuits, such as money and pleasure, making it ever more susceptible to "soft tyranny."[68] (Incidentally, once government acquires an appetite for greater power it is never relinquished without a bloody revolution.) The point is simply that mankind must of necessity worship, if not the true God, then a false one of its own making.[69]

---

[66] Ecclesiastes 3:11
[67] For further discussion of statism as an aspect of the world system see the second book in this series, *What Agreement Is There Between the Temple of God and Idols?: The Accidence of Sin and Idolatry*, chapter 2: "The World, the Flesh, and the Devil: Assessing the Threat Matrix."
[68] This concept "soft-tyranny" from Mark Levin, radio host
[69] Deuteronomy 30:17

> It is fascinating that in every theory concerning the coming New World Order (in which Antichrist will rule the world) there is a provision not just for a one-world government, currency, and financial system, but also for a one-world religion. Of course, the nature of this religion is highly-speculative, but the fact that one is anticipated indicates that mankind recognizes himself to be inextricably consigned to worship.

The heart is conscribed to worship. Worship is the center of man's being; the core constituent of his design. Man must worship because he is invested with the image of his Creator. Within his spirit man knows that there is a God to whom he will give account.[70] This is the most basic, most rudimentary, reality in which every person lives moment by moment, day by day.

The heart is a hive of activity with geared cranes and whirring lathes. Although it may at times appear dormant, it never is. It continually hums with worship machinery, churning out idols like a productive factory. Incidentally, the heart is non-discriminatory with regard to worship. It will worship anything upon which it places its desire; that object of desire does not need to be overtly religious.

Additionally, the heart is the most indomitable force on earth. No man can conquer the heart. It is resilient and resistant beyond all measure. For this reason, only God can break and rebuild it. Only God can, for example, cause one who was tortured and dehumanized to forgive his tormentors. Only God can cause man to lay down the weapons of revenge and to forgive a wrong.

C.S. Lewis (1898-1963) said that every person will live forever; the question is, "Where?" Mankind is an eternal being, designed to interface with the infinite qualities of God himself. In fact, the finite "good" created order is carefully designed to never satisfy the infinitude within the heart. Invested with the infinite, man can never find refuge in the finite. Ecclesiastes 3:11 states, "He has made everything beautiful in its time. He has also set eternity in the human heart; yet no one can fathom what God has done from beginning to end."

> Every culture honors its dead with some form of ritual, often with accoutrements for the afterlife. Every civilization uses religious ritual to either appease angry gods, or bargain with the gods for some desired outcome. Thus, engrained in the psyche is the haunting specter of a terrifying spiritual world. It is as if the human soul resides in a physical world, but is attuned (often faintly) to an unseen world, which it intensely fears.

---

[70] Romans 1:18, 19

In the spirit of Zeno's dichotomy paradox (repeatedly traveling half the distance from point A to point B one would never reach B), even on the verge of feeling satisfied, human need is still infinite. Thus, one can never fill the deepest longings within himself with anything other than relationship with his Creator. Although in his sinfulness mankind tries to convince himself otherwise, the creation is not the Creator. However, man seeks to invert creation and Creator in a desperate gamble that the former will function as a suitable substitute for the latter. God, in his grace, has extended to mankind the means to correct that inversion. Jesus' death upon the cross is the final corrective to mankind's blurring of the Creator-creature distinction.[71]

The Accolade
Edmund Blair Leighton, 1901

Jesus rights the transposition so that the human heart, indeed the entire cosmos, is correctly apprehended.

> In popular culture aliens are always portrayed as far more intelligent and technologically superior to mankind. Is characterizing aliens as more intelligent and technologically sophisticated part of a human quest to worship something greater than itself? Humanity routinely projects onto aliens the qualities of gods, something it believes to be worthy of worship. (This is part of an end times delusion in which humanity is being lured into the worship of demons under the guise of omnipotent alien beings.[72])

The world loves those who put their heart into everything, but the question is, "What

---

[71] For further discussion of the Creator-creature distinction see the second book in this series, *What Agreement Is There Between the Temple of God and Idols?: The Accidence of Sin and Idolatry*, chapter 5: "Metaphors for Sin"

[72] For further discussion of this issue see the excursus: "Alien Abduction" in the third book in this series, *The Days of Reckoning Are at Hand: From Fig Leaf to Olive Branch to Laurel Wreath*, chapter 5: "Navigating the Counseling Fjord: Preliminary Reconnaissance"

is in one's heart?" Is one's heart overrun by idolatry, or fully in submission to Christ? Christians are called to distinguish themselves with every word, thought, and action, to show what they worship in each interpersonal relationship. Thus, the cross of Christ is a worship dividing-line. It separates, clarifies, and unbraids Christians from the world. Therefore, through its interaction with Christians, the world is either brought to repentance and faith, or led into more pointed rebellion.

Mankind as Covenant Maker

In nearly all ancient civilizations there is a curious social custom: revelers raise their glasses together before drinking. This is only ever done with alcoholic drinks as a display of thanks to supposed gods for their libations. The reason is that nearly all ancient peoples believed that alcohol came from the spiritual world because of its intoxicating effect on the mind and body.[73] This practice might be thought of as a kind of "proto-covenantal" ritual.

The fact that man is a worshipping being is his most fundamental, most defining, existential aspect. As a worshipping being, man is a covenant maker. He continually enters into covenants whether with the true God or with idols. Covenant-making propels his every thought, word, and action and, as such, is a crucial starting point for understanding people, for resolving the reasons and seasons of the human heart. All counseling of necessity revolves around this central truth of man as covenant maker.

Mankind has an innate sense that he was designed to exist in covenant with the holy God.[74] He was designed to know, uphold, and glory in the truth of God, to covenantally interact with God alone. However, in hatred of God, fallen mankind enters into covenants with idols, allegiances with the creation in the hope of finding meaning, blessing, and power. However, such covenants invariably result in purposelessness, cursing, and weakness. Man wants serviceable gods which allow him to maintain his own autonomy, while pretending to be a God worshipper. However, man makes covenants with these serviceable gods only to discover that they are mercurial tyrants stripping him of his invested dignity and rendering him a guilt-ridden naked sinner.[75]

Mankind continually replaces the truth with lies, forging covenants with false gods. This results in a root intellectual inconsistency and confusion within man. Through defective covenantal relationships mankind has become an intellectual nomad, desperately chasing wisps of meaning, and hunting for validation of his flawed truth claims. In seeking to justify himself, mankind shifts the terms of any argument, redefines right and wrong, and rejiggers good and evil, so that he might emerge on the

---

[73] Tom Standage, *A History of the World in 6 Glasses* (New York: Walker and Company, 2005) 20.
[74] Cornelius Van Til, *Christian Apologetics* (Presbyterian and Reformed Press, 2003) 55, 56.
[75] Cornelius Van Til, *Christian Apologetics* (Presbyterian and Reformed Press, 2003) 45.

winning side of his worship gamble, that gamble being that false gods will deliver him from the weakness, futility, and cursing which daily assails him. Thus, mankind lives out a grand idolatrous *non sequitur*.

The Four Seasons, Winter, Francois Boucher, 1735

> The following has been termed the "Feminist Father's Creed":
>
> Rules for dating my daughter:
>
> 1. I don't make the rules.
> 2. You don't make the rules.
> 3. She makes the rules.
> 4. Her body, her rules
>
> Take note of the final rule, "her body, her rules." This could not more succinctly encapsulate the heart's defiance toward God, the deluded notion that one's body belongs to oneself, and that therefore one can do with it as one pleases. Such is the mission statement of the modern world resulting in untold human degradation. In fact, the human body was created by God, for God's glory, as an eternal dwelling of his Spirit.[76]

The Intellect as Manifestation of the Image of God

---

[76] 1 Corinthians 3:16; 6:19

The created order is intrinsically theistic,[77] inexhaustibly intricate, and invites endless discovery. In being intrinsically theistic, the Creator's signature is found on every atom in every last corner of the universe. God fashioned the universe's order which man progressively uncovers with a sense of rapturous wonder. The human mind, as an aspect of image-bearing, was designed to be "receptively reconstructive."[78] This means that mankind was designed to explore, discover, and re-imagine God's work by means of a kind of recursive algorithm which distills the whole into manageable subunits, thus, retracing God's hand throughout his universe. What's more, mankind holds a burning urge to explore because his mind is perfectly suited to the task.

> The European Enlightenment of the 16th and 17th centuries brought with it heightened interest in coffee drinking. Alcohol was the drink of the Dark Ages, but the Enlightenment, as a time of rationalism, logic, and the scientific method, required alert minds. Coffee soon became the preferred drink of intellectuals who frequented coffeehouses to discuss the latest philosophies, politics, and science, necessitating a drink that stimulated and sharpened the intellect. Therefore, coffee was perfect for the "Age of Reason," inspiring passionate and perspicacious thinkers.[79]

While mankind was designed to uncover God's creative work, because of sin there is a tension between mankind's passive reception of knowledge and his creative construction of knowledge.[80] There is an inherent distortion in knowledge since sin renders such knowledge divorced from the person of Christ. Just as all of history is the record of God's promise and delivery of salvation (so that even the secular demarcation of time as B.C. and A.D. revolves around Jesus Christ), so too, all aspects of the created order are likewise, designed by God to reveal the knowledge of Jesus Christ. Thus, every quark bears witness to Christ's grand act of redemption. Mankind was specifically set apart to recognize that all of creation revels in the theater of redemption and, therefore, mankind was meant to uncover the creation as part of understanding salvation through Christ.

When the Bible refers to the "mind" it refers to a God-focused *prohairesis*. In other words, the biblical concept of mind is a subcategory of a larger concept, the *nous* (or the *nouthetic*) which is the fountain of ruling passions and worship. While science would label the mind a tangible material entity to be empirically studied and quantified, the Bible speaks about the mind as an intangible entity assuming the same semantic range as "heart" and "soul." In this regard, one of Satan's ploys is to deceive mankind into thinking that the body rightly has priority and authority over heart issues, so that the demands and limitations of the body are considered determinative and

---

[77] David Powlison, "Which Presuppositions? Secular Psychology and the Categories of Biblical Thought," *Journal of Psychology and Theology* 12.4 (Winter, 1984): 274.
[78] Cornelius Van Til (1895–1987), Westminster Theological Seminary, Philadelphia, Pennsylvania
[79] Adapted from Tom Standage, *A History of the World in 6 Glasses* (New York: Walker and Company, 2005)
[80] David Powlison, "Which Presuppositions? Secular Psychology and the Categories of Biblical Thought," *Journal of Psychology and Theology* 12.4 (Winter, 1984): 273.

controlling over the mind and heart.

The Chess Players, Joseph Clark, 1860

Verses which address the mind:

1. "Do not conform to the pattern of this world, but be transformed by the renewing of your mind. Then you will be able to test and approve what God's will is—his good, pleasing and perfect will." (Romans 12:2)

2. Ephesians 4:18 states, "They are darkened in their understanding and separated from the life of God because of the ignorance that is in them due to the hardening of their hearts." The ignorance mentioned here is not a dearth of information, but the outgrowth of defective nouthetic worship.

3. "Once you were alienated from God and were enemies in your minds because of your evil behavior." (Colossians 1:21)

> There is debate concerning the mind's function within various cultures. For example, it is often said that Westerners think linearly, while Easterners think circularly. The question then arises: Is there a single brain design, or are there fundamental differences in intellectual architecture across ethnicities? Does the Bible present an archetypical cognitive configuration, or does it countenance sundry approaches to the accumulation and application of knowledge?

> I contend that the mind's design mirrors that of the Bible's cognitive architecture. Scripture is constructed around a clear linear logic, a directed progression, but that logic and progression is conveyed by means of various literary devices more artistic than scientific. Thus, the Bible's logic operates on a swivel, adapting itself to various contexts. Nevertheless, I would reject the notion that, within certain cultures, the brain is hardwired to function by means of a circular logic.

Excursus: Intelligence versus Wisdom[81]

Mankind craves intelligence, and he can gain it to some extent through his own efforts. God in his goodness gives unimaginable abilities to mortal men so that they might walk on the moon, perform open heart surgery, and split the atom. These achievements provide some temporal benefit, but not necessarily an eternal one. Eternal blessings can only be achieved through the appropriation and correct application of wisdom.[82] However, man rarely seeks wisdom because he is already wise in his own eyes.[83] True wisdom is only gained through direct relationship with God. It is the gift of God to those who, with humble hearts, admit their need, and ask for it.[84] In summary, Jesus himself is wisdom.[85]

> For nearly 2,000 years, based on Aristotelian philosophy, Westerners believed that intelligence was found in the heart muscle.

Like the ancient Greeks, most Christians confuse intelligence with wisdom, wrongly assuming that intelligence begets wisdom, or that intelligence enjoys closer proximity to wisdom. The intelligent may be better equipped to reason through the implications of their actions and, therefore, may, at times, appear wise. However, from the Bible's perspective intelligence and wisdom are wholly distinct qualities. While the intelligent reason through consequences more efficiently, they nevertheless commit evil with equal fervor, possibly just in a more cloaked and sophisticated form.

> There are generally thought to be two types of intelligence:
>
> 1. Fluid intelligence is that displayed by young people, who adapt quickly to a new situation.
>
> 2. Crystallized intelligence is that displayed by older people, who draw heavily

---

[81] For further discussion of the topic of intelligence versus wisdom see "The Paradigm Shift: Upending Psychology's Hegemony" in chapter 8: "What Has Jerusalem To Do With Vienna?: The Case Against Psychology"; additionally, the section "Depravity Through the Lens of Proverbs" found in *What Agreement Is There Between the Temple of God and Idols?: The Accidence of Sin and Idolatry*, chapter 3: "Total Depravity: This Imperiled Arcadia" may be profitable in this discussion.
[82] 1 Corinthians 1:30
[83] Isaiah 5:21
[84] John 4:10
[85] 1 Corinthians 1:24

> upon experience in problem solving.

Wisdom is rightly assessing reality. It is knowledge of how life ought to be arranged and living accordingly. The book of Proverbs reveals that wisdom begins with the fear of God and implies that it grows through relationship with him.[86] Unintelligent people can be wise; intelligent people can be foolish. Wisdom

The New York Library
Paul Cornoyer, d. 1923

and intelligence are not causal, although often mistaken for one another. Incidentally, it would be better to be an unintelligent fool than an intelligent one. The intelligent fool has more tools at his disposal with which to further the destructive impact of his rebellion. Thus, greater unregenerate intelligence merely becomes a more potent weapon brandished against God.

It must be noted that wisdom never implies a comprehensive understanding of all of reality. Issues such as the nature of evil and God's ultimate purposes are beyond the reach of even the wisest.[87] But the wise, in relationship with God through Jesus Christ, know what can be said with absolute certainty, what should be joined, what should be separated, what rebellion and obedience look like, and how to effectively communicate the truth. A wise person rightly divides good and evil, knows when to battle evil and when to flee from it.[88]

Is wisdom acquired with age? From the Bible's perspective wisdom is never a function of age;[89] the unregenerate elderly are just as foolish as the unregenerate young (in some sense, more so). The aged often simply lack the energy to act on the full-extent

---

[86] Proverbs 9:10
[87] Job 9
[88] Genesis 39:12; Isaiah 5:20; Jude 1:9
[89] 1 Timothy 4:12

of their rebellion.[90] In this way, diminished rebellious energy masquerades as wisdom. (Additionally, the life experience which comes with age can at times hold forth mock-wisdom, more akin to technical knowledge and know-how, than God-directed wisdom.) Thus, from the Bible's perspective, age, if not sanctified in Christ, is merely a path to greater sinfulness.[91] There is something in the sinner's existence which darkens and deadens with age; this is not just a somatic event but a spiritual one.

Fixed Design Elements: Submission to God's Plan

> "You turn things upside down, as if the potter were thought to be the clay! Shall what is formed say to him who formed it, 'He did not make me?' Can the pot say to the potter, 'He knows nothing'?" (Isaiah 29:16)
>
> "To dream of the person you would like to be is to waste the person you are."[92] (Anonymous)

As part of God's eternal plan and design for each person, there are certain aspects of human design which are unchangeable. These include one's:

1. Time in history
2. Race and nationality
3. Gender
4. Parents
5. Siblings
6. Birth order
7. Physical features
8. Mental capacity
9. Aging
10. Death

> When I was a child my friends often joked that I was born 100 years too late. My personality, sense of morality, and interests seem more suited to Victorian England than to postmodern America. I have often longed to live in a different time, imagining that my life would somehow feel more at home. I assume that I would experience greater happiness in bygone eras. But this, like all sin, grows from distrust of God's plans and purposes. God brought me into existence at exactly the right moment in history to fulfill his purposes through me.[93] I was not born a moment too late nor too early. That is a source of joy and assurance as my life bears

---

[90] Genesis 19:4
[91] 1 Kings 11:4
[92] This quote is likely intended as a humanist message of self-love. Through the Christian lens, it could mean that often the sinner seeks to assume a different identity in defiance of whom he was created to be. An aspect of submission to God is to accept those elements of one's being which are by design.
[93] Romans 5:6 supports the idea of God's perfect timing in all things.

the imprimatur of a good God.

Implications:

1. God precisely designs and deeply loves what he creates, carefully crafting each person in each and every detail for a grand purpose. Psalm 139:13-16 says that God created man's innermost being, knit him together in his mother's womb, so that each is fearfully and wonderfully made. Isaiah 45:9-11 says that God's design is not to be questioned. "Do not quarrel with your maker since the Lord says, 'Do not question me about my children or give orders about the work of my hands.'" Additionally, Ephesians 2:10 states, "For we are God's workmanship, created in Christ Jesus to do good works."

Duty
Edmund Blair Leighton, 1883

At a church event, a Christian woman repeatedly mentioned how short she is. While others assured her of her attractiveness, it was clear to me that she was, like so many, inappropriately assessing herself. Second Corinthians 5:16 admonishes not to judge anyone from a worldly point of view. That admonition does not just apply to others, but to oneself as well. It is just as offensive to God to judge oneself from a worldly point of view as to judge others in that way. In other words, this woman focused on, and valued, her height at the expense of those aspects of her design that God focuses on and values. She assessed herself through a materialistic (godless) set of lenses, and while she appears to be a victim of faulty genes, she actually victimizes herself.

Thus, possibility one of the most overlooked aspects of sin is the fallacy that one's life belongs to, and is rightly evaluated by, himself. Christians, while intellectually asserting that they have been bought by Jesus at a price,[94] frequently function as though their lives still belong to themselves, that they can and should use and appraise their lives for their own good pleasure.

> "You were made by God and for God…and until you understand that, life will never make sense." (Rick Warren)

2. Outward appearance is not an indication of God's love. Once, in response to being told how talented and beautiful she is, an actress responded that she had a won the "life lottery." I found that a somewhat odd response as she sought to glorify blind chance rather than the God who created her. However, her term "life lottery" tends to encapsulate how many view their existence. One must understand that his life is not the result of chance random events, but follows the dictates of a loving God who plans all for his good purposes. One whom society deems stupid, short, ugly, or handicapped is often considered an evolutionary mistake. What if people are carefully designed so that even "imperfections" are really part of a master plan and an eternal purpose?

Conversely, what the world calls "giftedness" may not be from God's perspective. The one who possesses superlative intelligence or talent is often denied the opportunity to see what God can do with very little. Thus, in the Christian worldview the one who is gifted is the one recognizes his limitations and inabilities, so as to trust in an unseen God. Thus, for the Christian his limitations *are* his gift, as this gives him the opportunity to see what God can accomplish in, and through, him.[95]

> In 1 Samuel 16:7 the Lord said to Samuel, "Do not consider his appearance or his height…"
>
> "As he [Jesus] went along, he saw a man blind from birth. His disciples asked him, 'Rabbi, who sinned, this man or his parents, that he was born blind?' 'Neither this man nor his parents sinned,' said Jesus, 'but this happened so that the work of God might be displayed in his life.'" (John 9:1-3)

3. Comparisons are Satan's lure to lust of the eye and lust of the flesh.

> "Charm is deceptive and beauty is fleeting but the woman who fears the Lord is to

---

[94] 1 Corinthians 6:20
[95] 2 Corinthians 12:9

> be praised." (Proverbs 31:30)
>
> "But when Jesus turned and looked at his disciples, he rebuked Peter. 'Get behind me, Satan!' he said. 'You do not have in mind the concerns of God, but merely human concerns.'" (Mark 8:33)
>
> "…for, 'Who has known the mind of the Lord so as to instruct him?' But we have the mind of Christ." (1 Corinthians 2:16)
>
> "For who makes you different from anyone else? What do you have that you did not receive? And if you did receive it, why do you boast as though you did not?" (1 Corinthians 4:7)
>
> "We do not dare to classify or compare ourselves with some who commend themselves. When they measure themselves by themselves and compare themselves with themselves, they are not wise. We, however, will not boast beyond proper limits, but will confine our boasting to the sphere of service God himself has assigned to us, a sphere that also includes you." (2 Corinthians 10:12, 13)

4. God's work in his people is not yet complete.

> "The Lord will fulfill his purpose for me…do not abandon the work of your hands." (Psalm 138:8)

5. One tends to wrongly focus his attention upon seeking to overcome his finiteness, to free himself from the confines of "creaturehood." Fallen mankind, obsessed with his finiteness, wrongly believes this to be his deepest problem, and that which keeps him from the abundant life he feels he deserves. Man's finiteness is integral to God's design, and therefore never the source of his trouble.[96]

6. Scott Adams' book title, *It's Obvious You Won't Survive by Your Wits Alone* (1995) captures a truth pertaining to design. Each person has been perfectly designed so that only in relationship with Jesus, only in reliance upon him, will one's life function as God intended. One's precise combination of physical features, talents, intelligence, and limitations, are all carefully positioned so that, as they interface with one's life situation and calling, one must rely upon Jesus. For example, I am of a specified height and weight; I have a particular appearance; I enjoy a certain IQ level, and am invested with specific talents (some evident, others untapped). That comingling of traits abuts with my life circumstance, so that only through faith in Jesus, only through reliance upon him, can I emerge victorious over that

---

[96] For additional discussion of this topic see "Fallen Man Believes Finiteness Is His Problem" in the second book in this series, *What Agreement Is There Between the Temple of God and Idols?: The Accidence of Sin and Idolatry*, chapter 4: "Hamartiology: Sin in All its Ignobility"

circumstance. Thus, one of Jesus' objectives is to continually demonstrate to me that I will not prosper by my wits alone. I need his wisdom, his personal investment into my life in order to experience what it was meant to experience, to achieve what it was meant to achieve, to overcome threats, and to finally glorify God. I participate in a finely-tuned calculus which God overseas so that he might be glorified in my life.

Women Spinning in Fondi, François-Joseph Navez, 1845

Walt Disney (1901-1966) was known to challenge his "Imagineers" with daring technological feats. In each exhibition, film, or ride, Disney sought to push the envelope so that his company produced results unlike anything anyone had seen before. When Disney proposed a new idea, if his staff broke out into laughter with heads shaking, he knew he was on track. The more they told him that his plan was impossible, the more certain he was that it was the right plan. In fact, Disney worried when the response was too tepid. If the reaction was not strong enough, he knew he was not dreaming big enough, that his kingdom building was not moving at the right pace.[97]

There is something in this that captures an element of the Christian life. God has

---

[97] Pat Williams, *How To Be Like Walt: Capturing the Disney Magic Every Day of Your Life* (Deerfield Beach, Fl: Health Communications Inc., 2004)

> gifted each Christian with a certain skill set. Yet, God's plans for the Christian require more than that skill set is capable of on its own. Thus, the Christian, if he is to achieve what God plans for him, must rely upon a God who is invisible but present to give him the ability he lacks to accomplish God's kingdom building.[98] Thus, if the Christian continually operates within his comfort zone, within the confines of what he can safely accomplish on his own, he probably is not living by faith.

False Humility

As a side note, I currently pastor a fledgling congregation where I occasionally ask members to assume certain ministry responsibilities. I may ask a member to lead worship, to share a testimony, to organize a prayer meeting, to administer an event, to teach or to preach. I am frequently shocked to hear members respond that they do not have the ability to take on such a role. Typical responses include, "I don't sing well enough." "My teaching skill is inadequate," or simply, "I can't do it." My frequent response is, "You may be right, but this is an opportunity to trust the Holy Spirit to give you all that you require to meet the task."[99]

Many Christians espouse a false understanding of humility, thinking that humility means saying that one cannot do something, or that one is not good enough at something, and leaving it at that. This is failed self-pride, judging oneself through other's eyes and determining that one does not measure up to the task. At its root, such faux-humility is a hostile stance toward God, one that does not trust him to accomplish previously unlikely results given one's often limited ability. Remember, when asked to interpret Pharaoh's dream, Joseph responded, "I cannot do it, but God will give Pharaoh the answer he desires."[100] Likewise, 2 Corinthians 12:19 states, "But he said to me, 'My grace is sufficient for you, for my power is made perfect in weakness.' Therefore I will boast all the more gladly about my weaknesses, so that Christ's power may rest on me."

Humility is not saying simply that one cannot do something; that is pride's insignia. True humility recognizes that despite one's inabilities, flaws, and limitations, God can accomplish the improbable through anyone. In fact, he has ordained life in exactly this way. Thus, Jesus said, "I am the vine; you are the branches. If you remain in me and I in you, you will bear much fruit; apart from me you can do nothing."[101]

Conversely, when a Christian has been gifted with a distinguished skill or talent, denying that that talent exists is likewise dishonoring to God. There is nothing wrong

---
[98] Genesis 41:16
[99] Colossians 2:22, 23 offers some explanation of this.
[100] Genesis 41:16
[101] John 15:5

with saying that one is gifted in some way, as long as one credits God. Romans 12:3, "For by the grace given me I say to every one of you: Do not think of yourself more highly than you ought, but rather think of yourself with sober judgment, in accordance with the faith God has distributed to each of you." Paul indicates that one should think of himself in accordance with the way that God does. Thus, one with superlative ability recognizes that ability with a spirit of God-directed praise. For example, I am a good tennis player. When asked if I play tennis well, the proper response is, "Yes, I play well and I thank God for that ability." So, in summary, that which the Christian believes he cannot do, he trusts in God to accomplish in, and through, him. That which the Christian does well, he thanks God for.

Drawing God's Design into Focus

How much of human life is tragically wasted worrying about those design features over which one has no control? How much expended time, money, effort, and pain could be saved in simply accepting that which God designed? For example, consider the

Lay Thy Sweet Hand in Mine and Trust in Me
Edmund Blair Leighton, 1891

obsessive modern focus on beauty, height, intelligence, innate talents, cultural expression, avoiding aging, and finally escaping death. Matthew 6:27 reminds, "Who of you by worrying can add a single hour to his life or a single cubit to his height?" The sinner routinely cultivates his daily rebellion against God in wrongly casting his design and circumstance as his chief source of concern; this becomes his maddening obsession.

"…outwardly we are wasting away, inwardly we are being renewed day by day." (2

> Corinthians 4:16)

There are certain aspects of one's life which he cannot change, and upon which he should not focus attention. One's parents, gender, birth order, time in history, height, appearance, and aging process all distract from the most pressing issue, the renewal of one's heart in Christ. Will one live by faith in the midst of these unchangeable aspects of his being? Will one seek God and desire to know him in the midst of the scenario in which one has been placed? Will one see that that scenario is precisely weighted and calibrated to compliment the work that God desires to do in and through him? In this context, repentance is a righteous refusal to be attentive to that which is meaningless in God's sight. In repentance, the sinful focus on overcoming finiteness transforms into a desire to be indwelled by a God who seeks to raid and ravish the heart for his kingdom building efforts.

> Recently, I stumbled upon a perplexing, if not troubling, fact: adults in remission from childhood cancer rarely marry (even when declared cancer-free for many years). How does one explain this phenomenon? What is it about having experienced a devastating childhood illness which causes most to eschew marriage? Is there a feeling of possessing "damaged genes," and a reticence to pass those genes on to progeny? How would such a person be wisely counseled?

"I'm a Nightmare Dressed like a Daydream":[102] The Quest for Flawless Beauty[103]

> "The world will be saved by beauty." (Fyodor Dostoyevsky)

In Genesis 3:16 God made a pronouncement to Eve, "Your desire will be for your husband and he will rule over you." A woman's often compulsive desire for a husband is a motivating relational force. This desire introduced an asymmetry with regard to the gendered expressions of sin, such that women seem to lavish more attention on beauty than men. On account of the fall, women desire men's attention and, to this end, tempt men with beauty. This also makes women more prone to lust of the eye, evaluating the world based on what they see. (Remember, it was Eve who looked at the fruit with lustful longing.[104])

> "It is amazing how complete is the delusion that beauty is goodness." (Leo Tolstoy)

Like Pygmalion who fell in love with an ivory statue of his own making, the modern

---
[102] "Blank Space," Taylor Swift, 2014
[103] For further discussion of the issue of beauty see item twenty-two, "Sin as being people of the eye," in the second book in this series, *What Agreement Is There Between the Temple of God and Idols?: The Accidence of Sin and Idolatry*, chapter 5: "Metaphors for Sin"
[104] Genesis 3:6

world seems to be captivated by what might be termed the "pretty girl syndrome," the inordinate desire for beauty. Young women are increasingly taught that all of life should be a celebration of their beauty, leading them to believe that their purpose is to glorify themselves that, like Charles Lindbergh (1902–1974) landing at Le Bourget, every event should be a riot of self-celebration. At the same time, every perceived life crisis is often little more than the inability to receive adequate adulation. Listen carefully to most emotional crises; they usually arise from being insufficiently recognized as the god that one envisions himself to be.[105]

Lady Godiva, Edmund Blair Leighton, 1892

> You've heard the expression, "Feed a cold; starve a fever." With regard to beauty, this might become, "Feed a tender heart; starve a prima donna," the tender heart "cold" with regard to the self, and the prima donna feverish with herself.

Jesus reversed the effects of the fall and broke the Pygmalion trance. Through renewal in Christ, each person's desire can rightly be for God himself. Romans 11:36 is a source of assurance that each person comes from a holy God, through that God's will, and was created to bring him glory. A woman who knows Jesus is free from chasing after the attention of men, no longer conscribed to lust after a man. She recognizes that she belongs to Jesus, was created by him to glorify him. This frees her to love others without regard for herself, to pursue and achieve that which God

---

[105] For further discussion of this topic see "When Suffering Arises from One's Own Failing" in the third book in this series, *The Days of Reckoning Are at Hand: From Fig Leaf to Olive Branch to Laurel Wreath*, chapter 2: "Suffering: The Kintsugi Objective"

wills for her life. She is no longer under the curse of the vanity and futility of making life into a grand fashion show, a daily referendum on her beauty.

> In the West, most people want a suntan all year-round. This is considered a mark of beauty. The perception is that tan people have just returned from an exotic vacation or enjoy outdoor leisure activities (such as skiing or boating), making them appear wealthier than others. However, in the Far East, light-skinned people are considered more pulchritudinous. This may grow from the fact that laborers traditionally toiled in the blazing sun and became dark, while the wealthy remained cool indoors. Therefore, light skin is an indicator of wealth. The point is that society defines beauty based on the perception of wealth.

While the fascination with, and pursuit of, flawless beauty, a quest for power and superiority, often controls the hearts of modern people, Ephesians 5:27 reveals that Jesus plans "to present her to himself as a radiant church, without stain or wrinkle or any other blemish, but holy and blameless." For those in Christ, beauty and perfection are found in Jesus' accomplished salvation on the cross. Jesus promises, and is able, to remove each stain and blemish from his people so that their future looks bright. But for those outside of Jesus, the future is a losing proposition, one in which each day brings greater decay, ultimately culminating in eternal destruction.

> In 113 BC Prince Liu Che (刘彻) (156–87 BC) of the Han Dynasty (206 BC – AD 220) was buried in a suit of more than 2,600 wafer-thin pieces of jade because this was believed to preserve the body and increase the possibility of immortality.
>
> Alexander the Great (356–323 BC) was buried in a giant vat of honey which, because honey never spoils, was thought to preserve his body for eternity.

Despite the fact that the flesh fades and wrinkles form, the Christian can rejoice. Second Corinthians 4:16 reads: "Therefore we do not lose heart. Though outwardly we are wasting away, yet inwardly we are being renewed day by day." By this is meant, the Christian experiences an inner growth and beauty that far outweighs the loss of outward appearance.

Does the Bible Distinguish Between Heart, Mind, Soul, Spirit, and Will?

The Hebrew term *nefesh* (נֶפֶשׁ) and the Greek term *nous* (νοῦς) carry with them the same semantic range, denoting heart, mind, soul, spirit, and will. These concepts are integrated into one living being.[106] Thus, in the Bible, these are a single concept, not splintered as in psychological thinking. *Nefesh* and *nous* incorporate:

---

[106] Genesis 2:7

1. The sense of "self" (personhood), the consciousness
2. The faculties of perceiving, interpreting, judging, assessing, and understanding
3. The conscience, the ability to act decisively with regard to good and evil
4. The center of one's vitality
5. The reason
6. The will
7. The sense of purpose and desire
8. The seat of the emotions
9. The spirit of man that communes with God

> Throughout the ancient world it was generally thought that the kidneys were the reins of the human consciousness, the seat of desire and wisdom.

Verses which offer insight into *nefesh* (נֶפֶשׁ) and *nous* (νοῦς):

1. "And you, my son Solomon, acknowledge the God of your father, and serve him with wholehearted devotion (*nefesh* (נֶפֶשׁ)) and with a willing mind, for the LORD searches every heart and understands every motive behind the thoughts. If you seek him, he will be found by you; but if you forsake him, he will reject you forever." (1 Chronicles 28:9)

The Education of the Princess
Peter Paul Rubens, c. 1625

2. "Furthermore, since they did not think it worthwhile to retain the knowledge of God, he gave them over to a depraved mind (*nous* (νοῦς)), to do what ought not to be done." (Romans 1:28)[107]

3. "I appeal to you, brothers and sisters, in the name of our Lord Jesus Christ, that all of you agree with one another in what you say and that there be no divisions among you, but that you be perfectly united in mind (*nous* (νοῦς)) and thought (*nous*

---

[107] also see Romans 7:23; 7:25; 11:34; 12:2

(νοῦς)).″ (1 Corinthians 1:10)[108]

4. "So I tell you this, and insist on it in the Lord, that you must no longer live as the Gentiles do, in the futility of their thinking (*nous* (νοῦς))." (Ephesians 4:17)[109]

> Genesis 1:20 states, "And God said, 'Let the water teem with living creatures (*nefesh* (נֶפֶשׁ)), and let birds fly above the earth across the expanse of the sky.'"[110] Ecclesiastes 3:18, 19 states,
>
> > I also said to myself, 'As for humans, God tests them so that they may see that they are like the animals. Surely the fate of human beings is like that of the animals; the same fate awaits them both: As one dies, so dies the other. All have the same breath; humans have no advantage over animals. Everything is meaningless.'
>
> It is fascinating that Genesis uses the word, *nefesh* (נֶפֶשׁ), to describe all "living beings," both animals and humans. This hardly implies an evolutionary link but, rather, highlights their common identity as created beings.

Separating soul and spirit in the Bible is a common exegetical fallacy which opens the door to a false distinction between the "psychological" and the "spiritual." This is the classic dichotomist (soul and spirit as unified concept) versus trichotomist (soul and spirit as distinct concepts) debate.[111] The danger in trichotomy is that it easily leads to the fallacy of seeing the soul as the provenance of psychology, and concerns of the spirit as under the auspices of Scripture. This is not the case. The Bible makes no distinction between soul and spirit; they are the same concept. It is vital to recognize the Bible's dichotomist view of the human constitution so as to guard against the trichotomist fallacy, which easily slips into an acceptance of psychology.[112]

The Center Point Theory of Design[113]

Mankind's design dictates that he was intended to live in obedience to God, to bask in God's goodness and glory, to serve God alone. On account of man's sin, he creates for himself a delusive and artificial world in order to separate himself from his Creator. The degree to which mankind ensconces himself in a man-centered world is the

---

[108] also see 1 Corinthians 2:16; 1 Corinthians 14:14, 15, 19
[109] also see Ephesians 4:23
[110] also see Genesis 9:12; Ezekiel 47:9
[111] Dichotomist refers to two aspects of the human being, body and soul. Trichotomist refers to three aspects of the human being, body, soul, and spirit.
[112] For additional discussion of the dichotomist-trichotomist debate see "Integrationism: A Cunning Snare" in chapter 9: "Integrationism: The Modern Day Babylonian Captivity"
[113] For further discussion of this issue see "Idols in Counterbalance" in the second book in this series, *What Agreement Is There Between the Temple of God and Idols?: The Accidence of Sin and Idolatry*, chapter 6: "Uncovering Idols of the Heart: Make Us Gods to God Before Us"

degree to which he experiences emptiness and longing. As a result, there is a kind of "Minsky moment," a rebound effect which takes hold within the human soul, a longing for an eternal home in God, a quest for refuge in the God of the universe. It is as if there is an invisible pivot point around which mankind rotates. The further his deviation from God's standards, the greater the longing for a counterbalance. In other words, mankind seeks to compensate for that which he lost due to sin. The nature of that compensation is to, in some way, regain that which he knows was damaged or lost.

For example, evolution tells people that they are nothing more than accidents of nature, the collision of cold mechanical elements with no grand purpose. On account of being made in the image of God, and having the eternal invested within him, mankind instinctively knows he is not merely a highly-evolved animal, the result of chance chaotic events. Thus, he seeks to create a counterbalance to offset the known loss. I believe that counterbalance is the explosion of self-love and self-esteem. In this way, the modern obsession with self is possibly an outgrowth of pervasive evolutionary thinking. That which mankind lost due to sin, his true identity as image-bearer, he seeks to regain through an equal and opposite error. That which was degraded through man-centered means, mankind seeks to rectify through other equally man-centered means.

Put another way, the universe cries out that man is loved. Man strips away the love of a good Creator, so as to make the universe cold and impersonal. However, man cannot escape his center-point (in this case, the knowledge that he is loved), so he fashions for himself a counterbalance, a sense that he can love himself, that finding love within himself will correct the loss. However, this man-centered attempt to regain the lost center-point of man's existence ends in even greater loss and burning angst.[114]

In reading the following chart, begin at the center column ("Man's Design"). This is the original design element based in the person of God, what mankind was created to be and to experience. The left column ("Attempted Dismantling of the Design") is the way in which mankind has desecrated his design and, in so doing, has lost his center-point in God. The right column ("Reconstructive Efforts") is man's attempt to regain his design through some surrogate means. Thus, the dotted line (◀····:) denotes a futile attempt to regain the lost position, the illusory hope of retaking Eden.

---

[114] For further discussion of the issue of self-love see the second book in this series, *What Agreement Is There Between the Temple of God and Idols?: The Accidence of Sin and Idolatry*, chapter 9: "Marauding Visigoths: The Autocratic Self"

Attempted Dismantling of the Design (the stripping process)	Man's Design (Person of God as center-point)	Reconstructive Efforts (the attempted design reconstitution, a compensating counterbalance)
	1. Noble. Created august with inherent dignity; the pinnacle of creation	
Theory of evolution strips mankind of his noble design		The attempt to regain a feeling of nobility through self-esteem, even narcissistic, thinking
	2. Relational. Meant to experience vibrant and intimate personal relationship with God	
Isolation from God leads to social isolation on account of shame and fear of rejection		The use of money, power, permissiveness, or sexuality for false experiences of relationship; jumping on and off a carousel of relationships which offer momentary thrills with no need for permanence or commitment
	3. Experiential. Meant to experience a world richly-infused with God's invisible qualities	
A world increasingly arbitrated through prepackaged experiences, the artificial, and the programmed, which induce a bloated and vacuous virtual world		Longing for the tactile, the visceral, the spontaneous, and that which is unfettered; a quixotic quest to reconnect with that which is natural and physical (such as the land)

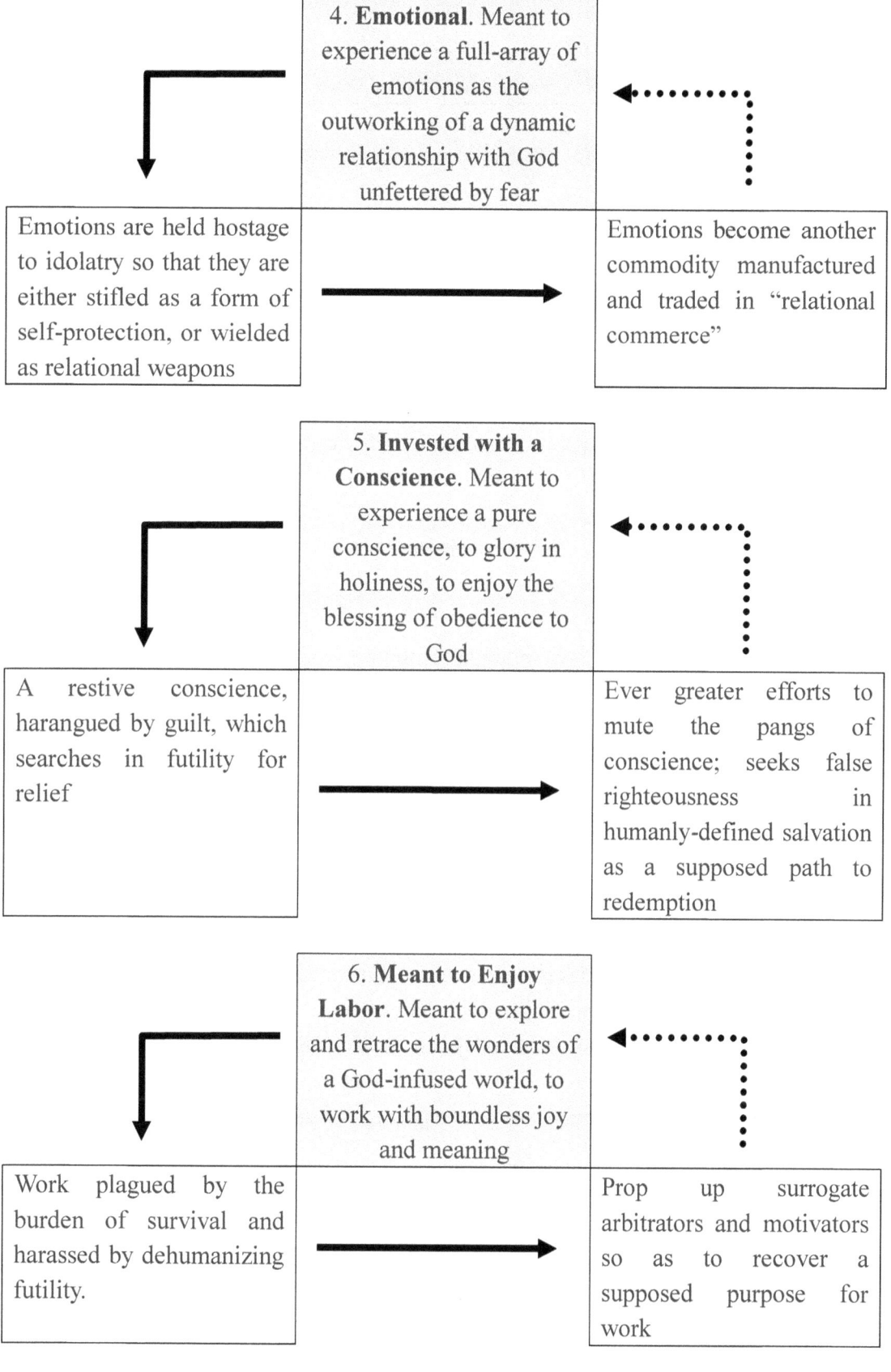

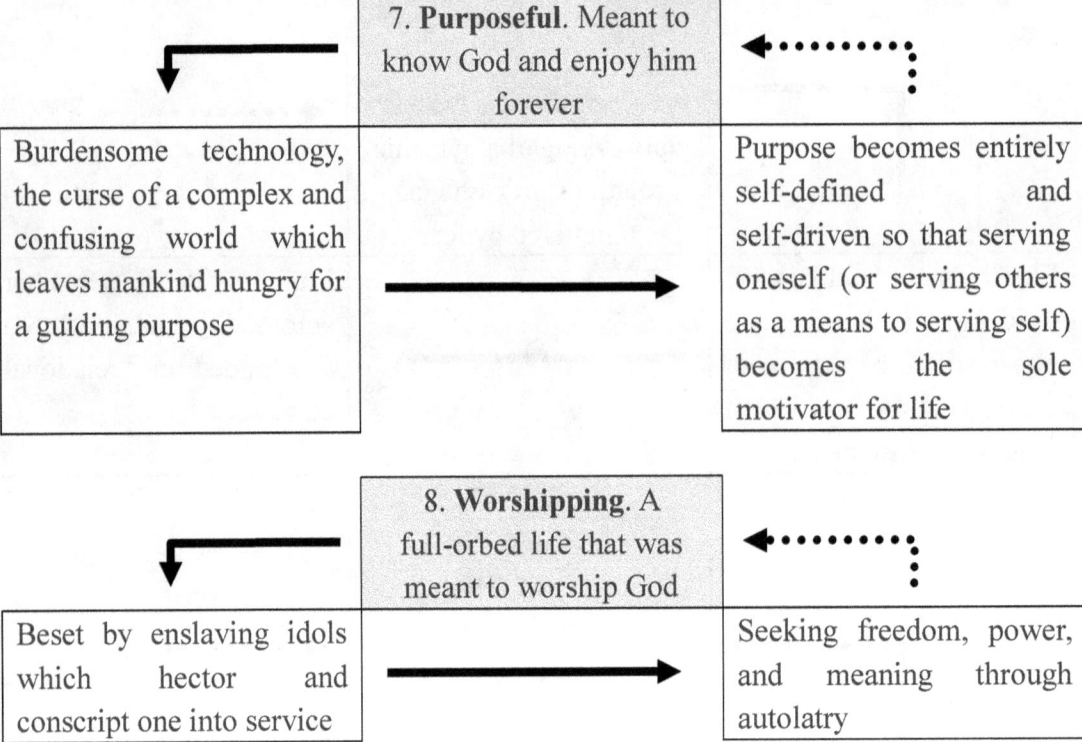

Many societal elements can be explained through this concept of center point theory. Man possesses a God-ward design; he was meant to know and serve God, to bask in God's goodness, wisdom, and wonder. As man turns from God to the supposed refuge of man-made institutions, relationships, and activities, he still possesses within himself the desire to know the truth, goodness, and wholeness of God himself; that is embedded in man's design. As human thought and institutions attempt to dismantle that design, man compensates through counterbalancing efforts, seeking to reconstitute the loss. In this way, he craves and adopts the opposite of the stripping element. This compensating counterbalance, seeking to regain the center point, never succeeds as it merely immerses man in another thicket of lies. Man soon finds himself in a labyrinth of self-delusion from which he can never extricate himself. (As a side note, the ancient Chinese expression "Míng zhēng àn dòu" (明争暗斗) describes man's heart as intricate corridors, court yards, and chambers within a palace. The idea is that the heart is highly-complex in its conspiring and scheming.)

> Man continually fashions an artificial world thinking that somehow he can either improve upon the created order, or escape what he considers to the be the limitations and drawbacks of that order. Man builds for himself a world in which he can secure his own destiny but, in the process, loses both his security and his destiny.[115]

The Image of God and Gender[116]

---

[115] Genesis 11:4
[116] For further discussion of the issue of gender see the case study, "Is There a Fundamental Gender Asymmetry With Regard to Sexuality?" in the second book in this series, *What Agreement Is There Between the Temple of God and Idols?: The Accidence of Sin and Idolatry*, chapter 5: "Metaphors for Sin"

The postmodern world is tyrannized by an obstreperous form of feminism which lashes out at the mere suggestion of gender asymmetry, when such asymmetry is perceived to connote inequality. In discussing gender, it is best to follow the Bible's three major categories: design, fall, and redemption. Such an analysis presents a certain parallax to gender roles, at once design distinctive, yet warped by sin, and finally egalitarian on an eternal stage. The Bible does something quite surprising with gender, an ingenious earthly asymmetry followed by an eternal parity, all precisely planned to glorify the Creator.

Gender by Design (Ontology)

My Next-Door Neighbour
Edmund Blair Leighton, d. 1922

Considering its ancient Near Eastern heritage, the Bible offers a stunning ontological equality with regard to men and women, while highlighting certain distinct functions. Men and women are equally image-bearers,[117] yet each assumes a unique role in God's earthly economy. For example, God fashioned Eve as a suitable helper to Adam.[118] This design dynamic is universal for marriage, maintaining itself throughout time and place. Thus, gender design heterogeneity mirrors and highlights function.

It is through gendered humanity, and its related functional asymmetry, that God deigned to glorify himself. For example, by design, husbands are rightfully in authority over their wives, and wives are to submit to their husbands.[119] That is an earthly set of roles intended to glorify Christ as husband and wife each submit to Christ. This does not mean that all women are to be

---
[117] Genesis 1:27
[118] Genesis 2:20
[119] Colossians 3:18; Ephesians 5:22; Titus 2:5; 1 Peter 3:3

in submission to all men, only a wife to her husband, and only as an earthly manifestation of a greater mutual submission to Christ.

> John Eldredge, in his book *Wild at Heart* (2011),[120] postulates that since God created Eve after Adam and since God ceased creating after Eve, that Eve was superior to Adam (an even higher form of "very goodness"), and that woman is the pinnacle of God's creative efforts. Eldredge's point is that Eve was more beautiful than Adam, representing God's highest aesthetic accomplishment. While Eldredge is generally correct that women are aesthetically more pleasing than men, women are not the pinnacle of creation, "very goodness" at its zenith. In understanding masculinity and femininity, it is vital to sort out the Bible's teaching on design, fall, and redemption. Women's focus on beauty may be less a function of design and more a function of the fall.

How Did the Fall Skew Gender Roles?

While Paul was not misogynistic, it would appear that he does present a fundamental gender bias with regard, not to the *presence* of indwelling sin, but to the inclination to *recognize* sin as such. For example, in 1 Timothy 2:14, Paul wrote, "And Adam was not the one deceived; it was the woman who was deceived and became a sinner." In line with Satan's entrapment of Eve, women seem poised to excuse sin in themselves and others. It is ironic (and tragic) that Eve looked at the fruit and, in so doing, became spiritually blind. I believe something of this spiritual blindness carries over into women's general refusal to countenance sin. (I might term this "hamartical blindness.") Women appear to have built up a formidable immunity to the recognition of sin, brandishing reflexive defense mechanisms against repentance.

Let's go back to where the problem started. While, at the moment of the fall, Adam was present with Eve,[121] the serpent specifically targeted Eve, a young woman, with temptation.[122] Why? On account of Eve's status as Adam's helper, did she present a certain vulnerability to temptation which the serpent exploited? Was Eve, on account of her role as submissive wife, more inclined to defy authority? Did Eve harbor a desire for authoritative parity with her husband? In other words, was Eve particularly susceptible to the serpent's temptation because she desired liberation from her role vis-à-vis her husband?

Genesis does not address this directly. However, gender roles were poisoned in the fall. In Genesis 3:16, God placed two curses upon the relationship between husband and wife. The first relational curse ("Your desire will be for your husband."[123]) causes

---

[120] John Eldredge, *Wild at Heart: Discovering the Secret of a Man's Soul* (Thomas Nelson Publishing, 2011)
[121] Genesis 3:6
[122] Genesis 3:1
[123] Genesis 3:16

women to inordinately desire to be loved. The second curse ("He will rule over you."[124]) changed Eve's position from that of treasured helpmate to fearful subject. (Incidentally, the gender disparity in physical design serves as a reminder of God-ordained role distinctions, and the concomitant directives for how husband and wife are to relate.)

This two-pronged relational judgment is the inception point for an anomaly between man and woman. A woman's desire forms a nidus around which certain sin patterns cluster (which then induce certain sin patterns in man). The point is that the woman's desire, introduced at the fall, injects a foreign element into relationship between women and men, and between women and God. This intrusion incites a cascade of sin in humanity so that, from this relational aberration, blossoms a litany of false worship.

Planning the Grand Tour
Emil Brack, d. 1905

> Note in Revelation 17:18 that the whore of Babylon (a woman) is the great city that "rules over" the kings (men) of the earth. Is this Satan's attempt to reverse the curse upon the relationship between husbands and wives?[125] In Satan's economy, the kings of the earth (as representatives of Adam) are to be ruled by the great city which is a woman (a descendant of Eve). In attempting to reverse the effects of the fall (to women's supposed advantage), Satan leverages human desire for a cunning deception.

Men and women share the same sinful tendencies; there is a common lust of the flesh. However, in light of the twin relational curses, a response asymmetry arises from the unique positions and pressures which face men and women. For example, as part of

---

[124] Genesis 3:16
[125] Genesis 3:16

their God-ordained design and calling, men tend to more naturally seek out, and assume, positions of authority and command. Women tend to naturally seek out, and assume, positions of nurture and comfort. For this reason, the manifestation of their heart rebellion takes on somewhat distinct textures, contours, and facets.

A woman, possibly on account of her husband's authority (if she is married), and in fear of his generally more imposing size, is tempted to harbor a pronounced liberationist bent. This tends to vitiate against the recognition of sin, and undermines the call to repentance before a God who describes himself with masculine nomenclature. The woman, as poised liberationist, sees submission to authority as a fearful vulnerability. To one filled with desire, and under what is perceived to be threatening rule, there is ample motive for covenantal treason.

> "Gossip is the opiate of the oppressed." (Erica Jong)

It goes without mention that men and women are equally sinful, each building up an immunity to recognizing sin. However, there seems to be an entrenched defensive weaponry within the heart of young women, an instinctual rejection of a call to repentance. Does 1 Peter 3:7 imply something of this in describing women as the "weaker vessel"? It would appear that Peter did not refer to inferior physical strength, but to a certain debility of spiritual constitution, possibly with regard to the recognition of sin.

> Throughout the animal kingdom, in most species the male is more beautiful than the female and attracts the female for mating. For example, the male peacock has an exquisite tail, while the female is small and unremarkable. The male lion is majestic, and the male fish is the most colorful.
>
> It is fascinating to note a pole reversal in humans. Women are generally more attractive than men (or focus more attention on appearance) since it is the female that seeks to draw the male forward. This accords with the Bible's teaching in Genesis 3:16, "Your desire will be for your husband, and he will rule over you." The reversal in male-female attention to beauty is possibly a product of the fall. A woman, in sinfully desiring a husband, may turn to beauty as a kind of weapon of relational conquest.
>
> However, because men are physically more imposing and tend to generally be more physically aggressive, society (influenced by a Marxist-derived feminism) paints men as more sexually desirous. However, this is a fallacy. In fact, the Bible tends to suggest the opposite, that women are in fact the sexual aggressors, often using subtle suggestion and cunning charm to conceal their root intent.[126]

---

[126] Proverbs 6:25

Women, in particular, seem to nurse a disdain for the admission of sin, either in themselves or in others. They seem especially skilled at deflecting guilt for sin and excusing it. Most pointedly among young women, confrontation with sin, no matter how caring, no matter how biblically-sound, is viewed as, by definition, attacking and hurtful. While, of course, such a charge may at times have warrant, in the vast majority of cases women refuse to countenance sin possibly because it is an offense against a *Father* God. Relating to a God, who describes himself in masculine terms, may cause women to seek to overcome the relational curses (inordinate desire and a husband's rule)[127] in defiance of God. Thus, women may, in particular, rebel against the concept of transgression against this *masculine* God. This may explain a certain willed blindness in women to the recognition of sin.

> "A man ought not to cover his head, since he is the image and glory of God; but woman is the glory of man." (1 Corinthians 11:7)

Additionally, as a woman's desire is for her husband, this powers a predatory desire to be loved. This may explain why women place inordinate focus on construing God's love as unconditional. The desire for a husband's love gets mangled so that there is an overreaching grab for God's love, but not as God defines it.

First Timothy 2:15 states, "But women will be saved through childbearing--if they continue in faith, love and holiness with propriety." However, the translation "saved" is not entirely accurate to the Greek word *sozo* (σῴζω); a better translation is "sanctified." Is it possible that through bearing and raising children, women experience a sanctifying corrective to their hamartical blindness? Does this verse imply that women are lent a certain sensitivity to sin in the process of raising children? Raising children might spawn a movement toward heightened awareness of sin, and the pressing need for repentance. Thus, part of God's objective in childrearing is that women (and men alike) would be sanctified.

> Incidentally, why do young women overwhelmingly support liberalism, while older women (presumably mothers) tend to skew more toward a conservative mindset?

Let's be very clear. Men and women are equally sinful, equally separated from God, and equally inclined to raise idols in defiance. While men and women both suppress the truth with equal fervor, they may not do so in a uniform manner. The point is that women, on account of the unique relational curses upon Eve, display a particular bent toward resisting the *recognition* of sin, seeking instead to redefine it in guilt-denying terms so as to avoid submission to the heavenly Father.

---

[127] Genesis 3:16

Equally Betrothed to Christ

Proverbs 31 is, on its surface, an acrostic of the idealized wife. It is also a prophetic picture of the submissive wife and self-sacrificing husband, each having experienced redemption in Christ. In the vein of Proverbs 31, Ephesians 5:22-28 is clear that wives are to submit to their husbands, and husbands are to sacrifice for their wives. In effect, Christian wives and husbands, both submissive to Christ (yet assuming distinct roles), are commanded to correct the postlapsarian relational curse that Satan exploits. While Satan promotes a secular feminist agenda as a false reversal of the fall, those in Christ are given the means to actually reverse its effects.

Signing the Register, Edmund Blair Leighton, d. 1922

While the fall apparently brought a gender asymmetry with regard to the recognition of sin, this is corrected in Christ along with an assurance of redemptive equality. Thus, from the Bible's perspective, both men and women are redemptively "androgynous." Romans 8:17 describes all believers, both men and women, as joint heirs with Christ (a concept unthinkable in the ancient Near East where women were excluded from inheritance). Each Christian, whether male or female, is equally a "son" of God and heir to his kingdom. For the Christian, gender is not functionally obliterated, but finally rendered irrelevant, in light of salvation in Christ. Galatians 3:28 states, "There is neither Jew nor Gentile, neither slave nor free, nor is there male and female, for you are all one in Christ Jesus." In the same way that, for example, ethnic Judaism is not obliterated but rendered irrelevant for attaining salvation, so too, gender is not eliminated, but subsumed in light of eternal identity in Christ.

> "Husbands, in the same way be considerate as you live with your wives, and treat them with respect as the weaker partner and as *heirs with you* of the gracious gift of life, so that nothing will hinder your prayers." (1 Peter 3:7, emphasis added)

Man Before the Face of God:
The Imperium of the Psyche

The Curse upon Creation

Genesis 1:26 and 1:30 state that man is to rule over the fish, birds, livestock (sea, air, and land) and "over all the creatures that move along the ground." This last phrase is a fascinating addition since it specifically focuses attention on the serpent. Adam was given a directive as to how he was to respond to the serpent. He was to rule over it and command it, so as to cast evil from the garden.

However, Adam failed to rule in God's place. Instead, he abdicated his authority with dire consequence. At the fall a "cascade of evil" entered the universe.[1] The result of this rebellion was first a curse upon the serpent, cursed above all animals.[2] Genesis 3:16 continues with a dictum that there would be pain in childbearing, and that a wife would desire her husband. Additionally, husbands would rule over their wives. Genesis 3:17 further stipulates that Adam's rebellion resulted in the ground being cursed and work becoming arduous. The curses were upon the serpent, birthing, marriage, and the land.

> The curse upon the creation is generally thought of in spatial terms. However, it must also be thought of as temporal. Just as there is a curse upon the ground and upon relationships (men and women, mankind and animals, and most importantly, mankind and God), so too, there is a curse upon time.
>
> Social scientist Marshall McLuhan (1911–1980) wrote, "For [early] man space was the uncontrollable mystery. For technological man it is time that occupies the same role." Mankind is desperate to overcome the curse on time and thus seeks countless methods to sequester, harness, and conquer time. Daniel 12:4 offers a hint of this. "But you, Daniel, close up and seal the words of the scroll until the time of the end. Many will go here and there to increase knowledge." This is often considered an end times prophecy in which mankind will move with ever greater speed in a futile effort to overcome the limitations of time. The result is generally disastrous as man's increased speed, his desire to control time for sinful purposes, only causes him to fumble, flounder, and finally fail.

---

[1] Douglas Green, Westminster Theological Seminary, Philadelphia, Pennsylvania
[2] Genesis 3:14

Suppression of the Truth

Albert Einstein (1879–1955) avidly studied philosophy seeking to reconcile his scientific theories with his views about the nature of reality; he rightly surmised that the two are inextricably linked. Einstein even occasionally spoke about the relationship between his theories and a concept of God. Here are a few well-known Einstein quips:

1. "God doesn't play dice."

Creation of Sun and Moon, Michelangelo Buonarroti, c. 1511

2. "God is subtle, but not malicious."
   "Who knows? Perhaps he is a little malicious."

3. "Science without religion is lame and religion without science is blind."

Throughout his life, Einstein often altered his description of God to suit his purposes, sometimes casting God as an omnipotent personal being, and at other times using "God" as a shorthand for an abstract quality of nature. While Einstein renounced the Bible as "childish," he could not deny that the universe holds profound mystery and inexplicable order.[3] This caused him to repeatedly admit his admiration for the universe's structure. But Einstein felt that the concept of a personal God was merely a euphemism for human weakness.

---

[3] Walter Isaacson, *Einstein: His Life and Universe* (New York: Simon and Schuster, 2007)

As Einstein's thought reveals, people do not, indeed cannot, live in a worship vacuum. They live with a constant knowledge of their guilt and condemnation before a holy God. Romans chapter one is clear; man's response to the knowledge of God is desperate flailing suppression, humanity constructing for itself a house of cards which seems a fortress for sheltering its rebellion, until the winds of truth sweep it away. When the wispy garment of his insurrection is removed, when the heart is vivisected, mankind is shown to be nothing more than a naked sinner.

> The heavens declare the glory of God;
> > the skies proclaim the work of his hands.
> Day after day they pour forth speech;
> > night after night they reveal knowledge.
> They have no speech, they use no words;
> > no sound is heard from them.
> Yet their voice goes out into all the earth,
> > their words to the ends of the world.
> In the heavens God has pitched a tent for the sun. (Psalm 19:1-4)

> The very fabric of the universe cries out, "You are loved."

> The wrath of God is being revealed from heaven against all the godlessness and wickedness of men who suppress the truth by their wickedness, since what may be known about God is plain to them, because God has made it plain to them. For since the creation of the world God's invisible qualities – his eternal power and divine nature – have been clearly seen, being understood from what has been made, so that men are without excuse. (Romans 1:18-21)

The concept of suppressing the truth in Romans 1:18 is literally, in the Greek, "putting the truth into prison."[4] This highlights the inherent contradiction within the sinner; he imprisons the truth while allowing lies to gallivant unrestrained. Romans 1:21 anneals a crucial concept for understanding people, *coram Deo* (before the face of God). The import of Romans 1:21 is that the unbeliever knows God (lives before the face of God, recognizes his guilt before a holy God, and is convicted by his conscience that he is a sinner) but neither worships him, nor shows gratitude toward him.

> In the ancient world, statues of a king were placed throughout his kingdom to remind subjects of his presence and their need to obey him. In effect, "statues of the king" reside both within the human psyche and in every last element of the creation. These statues serve as a moment-by-moment reminder of God's rightful authority over the

---

[4] William Edgar, *Reasons of the Heart: Recovering Christian Persuasion* (Presbyterian and Reformed Publishing, 2003) 53.

> universe, and the sinner's guilt as mutinous subject.

Don Giovanni and the Statue of the Commander
Alexandre Evariste Fragonard, c. 1835

A good illustration of Romans 1:18-21 is a ball floating on water.[5] To push the ball below the waterline requires effort and energy. Once one stops exerting this energy the ball pops back to the surface. The non-Christian must exert energy to suppress the truth. He must actively convince himself anew each day that a holy, good God does not exist and that he is not subject to that God's wrath. When he ceases to actively suppress the truth, it reasserts itself. In fact, the more forcefully one tries to hold the ball underwater the more forcefully it springs back to the surface. The more vigorously man suppresses the truth the more aggressively it re-injects itself into the psyche.

> There is a fascinating tradition throughout the world – blowing out candles on a birthday cake. This practice seems to carry with it a prophetic warning, that with each passing year one's life will one day be snuffed out like a flickering flame. The extinguishing of a small light, and the ensuing darkness on one's birthday, bears a reminder that one day the sinner's life too will be extinguished and cast into darkness.

The Pagani sports car, built near Modena, Italy, has the name "Pagani" written on every one of its parts (down to the tiniest fastener). Likewise, God's identity and character are written on every last sub-atomic particle within his creation. In this way, every moment of everyday the sinner is confronted with this holy God before whom he is called to repent. Thus, man's conscience convicts him of sin (his internal sense of divinity) as the universe around him "speaks" of a holy good God (the external sense of divinity).[6] Yet, mankind suppresses the knowledge of this God, seeking instead to run, hide, deny, discredit, and dismiss it. This is the *coram Deo* concept,

---

[5] This illustration from Scott Oliphint, Westminster Theological Seminary, Philadelphia, Pennsylvania
[6] Psalm 19:2

that the non-Christian actively suppresses the truth as he lives before a God-infused universe continually reminding him of God's personal presence.[7]

> Why are horror films so popular among young people (predominantly young women)? Here are two theories. The first, young people are bored and desire excitement. Horror films serve as an emotional anesthetic as there is something in danger which thrills. The second, because each person is a sinner, he holds an abiding fear of judgment before a holy God. Horror films offer a means to trivialize one's deepest fear, to project that fear onto a distant and definable entity such as a ghost, monster, alien, or axe-murderer. This allows the sinner to mold his fear into a recognizable face or discernable image. In this way, God is removed and the fear that should properly be directed toward him is minimized, dulled, deflected, and neutralized as it is projected onto created things.

Aristotle (384-322 BC) (and later John Locke (1632-1704)) developed the *tablia rasa* theory which sees mankind as a blank slate upon which experience writes one's character. The Bible vigorously disagrees; the non-Christian's error with regard to the nature and identity of God is not a matter of innocent ignorance. The heart is not a blank canvass waiting for paint to be applied, nor is it a silent backdrop upon which sound may emerge. The Bible sees the heart as already an unsightly portrait, already a cacophony. The heart is, from its inception,[8] inclined toward errant worship, emboldened with a galvanic current of hatred toward God and his laws, as well as committed to the love of self and its pleasures.

> A philosopher once described life as a sculptor chiseling a shapeless stone. This is not the Bible's perspective. The "sculptor" is not an abstraction, and the psyche is not a "shapeless stone." Quite the contrary, the psyche already bears the unmistakable contours and dimensions of sin. Those contours and dimensions are either reshaped and rectified by God himself, or else accentuated and sharpened by Satan.

In light of Romans 1:18-21, it is vital to note that no person is neutral with regard to God; no action, thought, or word is neutral. Each person lives before the face of God, continually responding in rebellion to actual guilt before that God. Likewise, each person actively suppresses the truth of God's identity, and his eternal qualities, so that every aspect of mankind's existence is another suppressive act vis-à-vis God's existence. Psalm 51:4 reads, "Against you, you only, have I sinned and done what is

---

[7] As a tangent, the cover of the album, *Bury the Hatchet* (1999), by the Irish band, The Cranberries, unwittingly offers a stunning portrayal of the *coram Deo* concept. A naked man, in obvious angst, crouches down on a barren desert plain as a giant eye, hovering above, stares at him. His back to the eye, the man has his head buried in his arms. This image precisely captures the idea that the sinner knows he is accountable to a holy God before whom he feels the crushing weight of his sin. Yet, the sinner, naked before God, cowers in fear, seeking to deny God's presence hovering in his midst. (Due to copyright restrictions the album cover cannot be reproduced here.)
[8] Psalm 51:5; Isaiah 48:8

evil in your sight; so you are right in your verdict and justified when you judge."

The Bible presents God's holiness as the *Zeitgeist* in which the psyche functions, so that mankind's every thought, word, and action cantillates a God-directed response. The psyche, as the stage upon which sin plays, is a God-infused and God-responsive entity. Therefore, sin is not firstly directed against the creation, generally, nor against people, specifically. All sin is firstly a with-regard-to-God mission; in fact, there is absolutely nothing in the human psyche that is not a with-regard-to-God phenomenon. One must grasp the profundity of the *coram Deo* in order to appreciate the power of this biblical counseling model.

> Consider the fact that some soldiers were born, lived, and died on the Great Wall of China. They never once left the wall as long as they lived. This is an apt description of the sinner. He is born, lives, and dies in his self-constructed isolation from God's truth, yet that truth confronts and invades his psyche at every turn.

There is an expression "to be afraid of one's own shadow," the idea being that one harbors abiding fear of every trivial or non-existent threat. This expression sheds light on the heart. Consider that one's shadow is formed as his body blocks incoming light. It is the obstruction of light which casts a shadow. Imagine that shadow to represent sin caused by mankind's suppression of the truth. Thus, as one further suppresses the truth the shadow's umbra darkens. The sinner, as his sin darkens, becomes increasingly fearful. The sin within him brings him face-to-face with evil, a highly-frightening experience. Thus, the expression "to be afraid of one's own shadow" offers some insight into the human condition, that the shadow of sin, resulting from active suppression of the truth, begets irrational fear.

> "Whom men fear they hate, and whom they hate, they wish dead." (Latin proverb)

Additionally, one might consider that a man is sometimes startled and frightened by a single leaf blowing in the wind.[9] There is something within the psyche which is easily spooked, easily unseated. This phenomenon is the direct result of the *coram Deo*. Living before the face of a holy God makes mankind perpetually fearful of judgment before that God. Man is startled by a mere leaf because he lives under the scepter of imminent perdition, a state which galvanizes man's pusillanimity.

> While a final day of judgment awaits each sinner,[10] there is a daily dose of judgment which God, in his mercy, visits upon each as a cautionary arousal from his spiritual slumber.

---

[9] I believe Martin Luther (1483–1546) offered a statement related to this concept.
[10] 2 Corinthians 5:10

The Conscience as General Revelation

In aviation the term "Jesus nut" or "Jesus pin" refers to a helicopter's main rotor retaining nut. This is the coupling locking the rotor onto the drive shaft. If this nut or pin fails, the rotor separates from the aircraft with dire consequence. Generally, the term "Jesus nut," therefore, refers to "any component which represents a single point of failure with catastrophic consequences" (failure of the whole system).[11] I find it fascinating that Jesus' name is enlisted to represent the most vulnerable and vital link in any engineering schema, almost like a desperate appeal to the holy eternal God for mercy in man's buzzing and humming whirligig life. In moments of desperation (such as the failure of a main rotor retaining nut), mankind often returns to, and calls upon, the God whom he so routinely suppresses and denies. There is some driftwood of truth within man's conscience which keeps washing up to shore.

This brings us to the next point. A palimpsest is a book whose pages have been sanded down so that each blank leaf can be used to record new content. (Palimpsests were popular in Medieval Europe when books were rare.) What is fascinating is that regardless of how well the pages are sanded they retain a faint impression of the previous writing. Modern scholars painstakingly reconstruct the sanded text beneath the current one so that two books are actually read.

This is an excellent way to understand the conscience, God's written record of his character upon each human heart. Mankind, however, through various means and for various purposes, seeks to "sand down" its conscience so that it can be written over by culture, experience, and for sinful desire. Yet, the conscience, like a palimpsest, cannot be obliterated. Its record may be faint, but it is nevertheless present, etched into the psyche.

> "Two things fill the mind with ever new and increasing admiration and awe, the more often and more enduringly reflection is occupied with them: the starry heavens above me and the moral law within me." (Immanuel Kant)

The conscience is the invested presence of God himself in mankind, like an amanuensis of God's character and qualities recorded into the psyche's black box. The conscience, as the palimpsest of the psyche, is the indelible imprint of God's character. In this regard, the conscience is God's gift, to guard mankind from himself, to engrave God's eternal virtue within man for man's own betterment.

Appallingly, mankind has come to view the conscience as a "psychic pain" to be snuffed out, an intrusive enemy.[12] Satan's objective is to cover, rationalize away, and

---

[11] Wikipedia article, "Jesus nut"
[12] David Kupelian, *How Evil Works: Understanding and Overcoming the Destructive Forces That Are Transforming America* (Threshold Edition, 2010) 110.

finally expunge guilt within the conscience, ultimately reducing it to mere subjective feelings. For example, under the Platonic system the ancient Greeks justified sexual immorality by asserting that since the body is evil, and will one day be annihilated, that which is done in the body carries no eternal consequence. Therefore, one can justifiably use his body for any purpose because his soul will one day be freed from it, at which point the soul will be pure. The Platonic system became a convenient way to overlook mankind's desperate wickedness, suppressing the truth of God in the process.

Orestes Pursued by the Furies, William Adolphe Bouguereau, 1862

> "Punishment is now unfashionable...because it creates moral distinctions among men, which, to the democratic mind, are odious. We prefer a meaningless collective guilt to a meaningful individual responsibility." (Thomas Szasz)

God reveals himself through the creation, generally, and through man's conscience, specifically, and most pointedly. In a natural environment, one is confronted with God's external general revelation, his revelation of himself through the created order. In an urban environment, one is confronted by a high-concentration of God's internal general revelation, his revelation through man's conscience (since there is a high-concentration of people). However, as God's self-revelation is suppressed in mankind's ever-gathering depravity, the city soon bears the scars of God's absence, a kind of "desert" with regard to his presence. In this way, the city represents a dearth of both external and internal general revelation. Man's active suppression of the truth (and its consequence) causes the general revelatory knowledge of God to recede.

> Consider that man-made (artificial) environments tend to spark sexual lust. There is something in cruise ships, office buildings, and cities, in general, which draws out this longing for the natural, the visceral, the emotional, for "connectedness." It seems that separation from the evidence of God in creation only heightens man's innate desire for that which seems to connect him with God. In his perversion, man often turns to the sexual, that which is tactile or sensory, as a God-substitute.

General revelation (the natural world both internal and external to mankind), when in full flourish, pushes the non-Christian to desperation, crisis, and ultimately to either greater rebellion or to repentance. Conversely, that same general revelation causes the Christian to deepen his faith, and continually repent of wanting anything other than God himself. As the non-Christian encounters special revelation (the Word of God), the process of either deepening rebellion or movement toward repentance accelerates. Thus, God's Word has a winnowing effect, causing the confirmed and resolute sinner to become more entrenched in his rebellion and, conversely, the elect to become more desirous of relationship with God.[13]

> As with all sinners, unbelieving scientists are often haunted by the notion of a Creator. For example, physicists now claim to have uncovered the "God particle." This is thought to be the "holy grail" in physical science, the explanation of all previously unexplainable phenomena. If by God particle is meant a substitute for a divine creator, then this is yet another haughty display of human arrogance wielding a scientific sword, another desperate flailing quest to tighten the screws of supposed human understanding.

The Contours of the Conscience

Medieval monks were required to stand during masses sometimes lasting several hours. In order to help the monks endure, they were given a "mercy seat" (*misericordia*), a narrow ledge along the church wall. What a tragic misunderstanding of the purpose of the mercy seat. The original mercy seat, on the Ark of the Covenant, was intended as a place upon which God himself sat in order to hear the petitions of Israel's high priest.[14] In the case of the medieval monks, however, this concept was twisted into a form of relief from the tedious traditions and rituals of men. The mercy seat became, not the mercy of God upon repentant sinners, but a refuge from

---
[13] Hebrews 4:12
[14] Exodus 25:21, 22

man-made standards and self-righteous humiliation. Thus, the conscience was blunted by a false sense of what mercy entails.

Gulliver in Brobdingnag, Richard Redgrave, d. 1888

> Romans 3:25 states, "God presented him as a sacrifice of atonement, through faith in his blood. He did this to demonstrate his justice, because in his forbearance he had left the sins committed beforehand unpunished—." The Greek term for "sacrifice of atonement" (*ilastarion*, ἱλαστήριον) is literally "propitiation" (to appease, to satisfy) which derives from the Hebrew concept of "mercy seat." (Incidentally, in Hebrews 9:5 this same Greek word is translated "mercy seat.")

The conscience, on account of man's sin, needs correction, realignment, renewal, and rebirth. Thus, in fallen man, the conscience both wrongly excuses and falsely accuses. It permissively exonerates one from his sin, at the same time erroneously redefining sin in ways that suit men's purposes. Does the conscience correctly signal that one has sinned? Yes and no. Yes, the conscience does function to convict of sin; that is its palimpsest quality. However, mankind works tirelessly to mute its conscience, to recalibrate it around false notions of sin and righteousness. For example, in the postmodern world the conscience is blunted with regard to personal morality and reprogrammed to align with issues of supposed social justice.

> Psychology's entire purpose is to suppress the knowledge of God, to keep mankind in darkness concerning the state of his psyche. Psychology offers mankind effective

> tools for suppressing the truth as it seduces him to greater immorality, self-obsession, and relational dissonance.

Carl Jung (1875-1961) wrote, "People will do anything, no matter how absurd, in order to avoid facing their own souls." There is a hidden truth in this statement as mankind either actively blunts his conscience, or makes it hyper-vigilant to false transgressions which crowd out and distract from actual sin. Thus, each sinner constructs his own "Ten Commandments" which he then obeys to exalt himself as lawgiver. In exalting himself, he sets up a diversionary tactic so as to avoid addressing actual transgression, defining sin in his own way, for his own purposes, to allow him to maintain his own pride before God. In this way, man perpetuates the myth that he is righteous through his own effort. So the conscience does bear something of its original design and function, but that function has been severely compromised and skewed, having been hijacked by mutinous subjects.

> "The fear of the Lord is the beginning of knowledge, but fools despise wisdom and discipline." (Proverbs 1:7)

Life Lived With Regard to God: The *Coram Deo* Concept

Once, as I strolled in a park, I saw two boys hurling rocks at geese floating in a pond. They giggled as the stones landed with a splash nearly capsizing their intended targets. Concealed by a thick blanket of trees, I yelled in *basso profundo*, "Stop that now!" The boys sprang up, startled. Wide-eyed, they spun around but could not see me. I heard one say, "Who said that?" They looked at each other, grabbed their books, and ran off.

Even before I spoke the boys' consciences were piqued. A still small voice within needled them, "Stop that now!" When I voiced their consciences' resident conviction there was a sudden piercing sense of impending judgment for their callous act. Even in a postmodern world swirling with moral relativism, the conscience is often nevertheless easily spooked by confrontation with its transgression, the indelible mark of God.

Transgression against authority, even in the youngest child, is never innocent; it is grounded in trenchant, albeit undeveloped, hatred of God. Is God himself in any regard culpable for this? For example, Exodus 7:13 and 9:12 reveal that the Egyptian Pharaoh's heart was hardened by God.[15] However, the Scripture's plenary teaching reveals that Pharaoh was not neutral; he desired that his heart be hardened. God simply gave him over to his own intentions.

---

[15] also see Romans 9:17

> I once saw a chic young woman sporting an oversized handbag with the statement, "I'M NOT SORRY," writ large across its front. While the bag was intended as a fashion statement, it spoke volumes of the modern piqued conscience, a conscience desperate for exoneration in its ever-growing arrogance and defiance toward God. As this fashion statement discloses, the sinner is not neutral but carries a burden of guilt.

Mankind does not live against a neutral backdrop, nor does he operate in a cosmic vacuum. He lives before a holy God, so that with each passing moment the sinner either persists in strong-armed sin or bends the knee of submissive faith. God is mankind's existential environment; he must encounter God in every thought, word, and action. Thus, mankind is never neutral with regard to the truth. The heart is always in some form of foment, either embattled or moving toward détente with his Creator.

> In 1962 a narrow manmade tunnel was discovered near the Italian island of Capri. The tunnel contained springs of boiling magma. Some believe that this was built 2,000 years ago as a replica of Hades to show what a trip to hell would look like. Likely visitors were given hallucinogenic drugs and led down the tunnel into a chamber, through which flowed an underground river.

The point is that the human heart is of necessity engaged with God, and it was deliberately designed this way, to function *coram Deo* – with regard to God. Each person lives before the face of a holy and eternal God.[16] Because the heart is a with-regard-to-God manifestation, all of life is lived as either a tacit or explicit response to God. This *coram Deo* concept is the Rosetta Stone, the linchpin, the anchor, the grounding, of all that follows in this text. This one concept deciphers the human heart and, thus, unlocks biblical counseling.

> In ancient China deities were thought to command the elements so as to bring judgment on mankind. For example, it was believed that illness was judgment for "sin" and that the offending party could only pacify aggrieved deities with animal, or even child, sacrifices. This sense of living under the scepter of divine beings (a hallmark of every known civilization), is the result of sinners living before the face of a holy God. Guilt before that God becomes twisted into an attempt to appease deities of one's own imagining, whether demons, ghosts, monsters, or ancestors. The sinner lives under the unrelenting threat of impending judgment before what he knows to be a holy cosmic judge. He therefore seeks to placate that judge and, in so doing, ameliorate the sting of his dreaded guilt.
>
> Incidentally, as a throwback to ancient sensibilities, the modern Chinese hold a

---

[16] Romans 1:21

> penchant for vertical (spiritual) dimensions. They favor a symbolic structure on the tops of buildings which represents the heavens. This indicates that a nascent sense of the eternal continues to leach into even thoroughly secular minds.

Ichabod Crane, Respectfully Dedicated to Washington Irving
William J. Wilgus, c. 1856

From Romans 1:18, 19 one understands that the non-Christian knows that there is a holy God to whom he is accountable. There is impenetrable guilt before this God, a pressing knowledge of sinfulness, a trenchant recognition of one's failing against an absolute standard. The sinner carries about in his being a continual burden of guilt which he tries, through various means, to alleviate.

For example, those who fornicate know that they have transgressed an eternal standard for which they will one day be condemned. This burden of guilt creates relational animosity as the one with whom one has fornicated becomes the embodiment of one's guilt before God. Every time one sees that person he is reminded of his transgression; there is a pang of regret, a piercing sense of loss, a sense that one has bowed to evil in complicit loyalty. This is the source of relational strife, the crippling millstone of sin, between oneself and another.

For this reason divorce readily follows those couples which engage in premarital or extramarital sex. The act of transgressing God's eternal law ever haunts the relationship so that it feels cursed. Thus, divorce is rarely due to "irreconcilable differences" (as often stated). Rather, it is as if, through divorce, the transgressors seek to flee from their sin, to escape from their evil acts, to wash away the stain of their guilt. Sexual sin blights the already troubled conscience, growing ever more imposing with time so that one's sin is always before oneself. Often the hope is that by running from the person with whom one has committed evil, one can assuage his conscience. (Of course, the conscience cannot be placated in this way.)

Fornication, like all sexual sin, carries with it severe consequence. The guilt is oppressive, the burden crushing, and this only grows with time. So one loathes the person with whom he has fornicated because that person is a continual reminder of one's guilt before a holy God, a perennial harbinger of one's coming condemnation. When the guilt and burden of sin become unbearable, divorce seems like the only way to find relief and peace, the seeming final refuge for a tortured conscience.

> "God magnifies himself to those he loves." (Winston Smith)

The *Coram Deo* Concept and the Issue of Emotions[17]

The ancient Greek gods often showed complex human characteristics. They were sometimes beneficent and magnanimous, at others jealous, deceptive, and vengeful. They routinely lied, stole, and committed adultery. Thus, the gods were capricious. When Zeus grew angry he hurled lightning bolts; when Poseidon became upset he made the sea turbulent. The Greek gods were a carnival of misplaced emotions, and mortals saw themselves as subject to their wile and whim. For this reason, people prayed to the gods, even offering animal sacrifices and money, in the hope of quenching their wrath or currying their favor.

Emotions are a fascinating aspect of man's design; they manifest the human drama in full sail, often reflecting the intensity, passion, and gravity of the human experience. Human emotion is reflective of God's emotion, a God who feels deeply. Thus, emotions are an aspect of design which not only connect mankind more deeply to his Creator, but also serve to more poignantly manifest God to the world. Emotions are designed to draw attention to God's truth, his will, and his immutable standards. They are meant to display God's interpretation of events.

> "Govern your passions, or they will govern you." (Latin proverb)

Emotions, as an aspect of the image of God in man, are not neutral. They reveal the contours of the heart, a heart living by faith or godlessness. Emotions are a window into the heart's worship, reflecting its condition with regard to God. Thus, again, the

---

[17] For further discussion of the issue of emotions see "The Hydraulic View of Emotions," in chapter 8: "What Has Jerusalem To Do With Vienna?: The Case Against Psychology"

coram Deo concept comes into play. Since man, of necessity, lives before the face of God, his emotions reflect the way in which he responds to God. Emotions are chosen based upon what one desires, loves, and longs for in any given situation, so that one may choose anger or laughter, sadness or contentment, all based on his heart commitments.

Emotions serve as a broadcasting beacon for the heart's worship condition.

Verses which connect the heart and emotions:

Self-Portrait
Arnold Bocklin, 1872

1. "But the things that come out of a person's mouth come from the heart, and these defile them. For out of the heart come evil thoughts—murder, adultery, sexual immorality, theft, false testimony, slander." (Matthew 15:18, 19)

2. "For it is from within, out of a person's heart, that evil thoughts come - sexual immorality, theft, murder, adultery, greed, malice, deceit, lewdness, envy, slander, arrogance and folly. All these evils come from inside and defile a person." (Mark 7:21-23)

3. "What causes fights and quarrels among you? Don't they come from your desires that battle within you?" (James 4:1)

The Bible does not present Stoicism, the view that emotions are to be avoided as an inherent danger or as a display of weakness. Often Christian's suppress their emotions because they think that any display of emotion is somehow inherently sinful. Emotion is a God-given gift to be celebrated, rightly developed, and used for effective communication of the truth. The Christian is never emotionally sterile; he feels life deeply, experiences piercing sorrow, exuberant joy, and burning anger.

The question is, "In what context, and for what purpose, does one feel emotion?" Does one's emotion reflect God's in that particular context? In other words, are one's emotions accurate to God's revealed will? Do one's emotions reflect reality as God sees it? Are one's expressions of emotion part of God's eternal glory, or are they geared for self-serving manipulation, wielded to draw attention to oneself? Are one's emotions merely another form of man-centered story-telling, or are they God-centered expressions of grace meant to draw attention to that which God seeks to highlight?

For example, Psalm 77 is a cry to God with the expectation that he hears his people's petitions. This psalm, in certain ways, sounds like sinful complaint but, because it is directed toward God himself, bears the expectation that God can and will act in the situation. Thus, Psalm 77 is the honest cry of the soul seeking to understand God in the context of grave circumstance. This psalm stands in contradistinction to prior instances in which the Israelites approached Moses with complaints about God. Those complaints arose from the misguided belief that God did not hear, nor care about, them. Thus, grumbling, as the Bible defines it, is the act of approaching *others* with complaints about God. Crying out to God in light of Psalm 77 is God-directed and ultimately God-honoring.[18]

Incidentally, how much of what Christians say is carefully disguised grumbling? Listen carefully. There is a cloaked theme in nearly every statement. The subtext is usually that God has in some way failed because he created a situation that is inherently "anti-mankind." Fighting against the odds, one emerges as a tragic hero through shear will and determination. Thus, one finds that most conversation tacitly presents God as the villain and the speaker as the hero.

Case Study: Anger: Shedding Light on the Heat[19]

I'm not sure if anyone else notices this, but it seems that beautiful women are often angry. (It could just be arrogance that looks like anger; often the two are indistinguishable.) What drives this beauty-anger consortium? Is it part of a manipulative game to keep men longing and chasing? Is it part of a power struggle to gain the upper-hand in relationships? Is it a means of asserting superiority over others, having the right to be angry because one is more worthy, somehow entitled to self-serving emotion? Is anger a convenient means of establishing a relational

---

[18] For further discussion of this topic see "Suffering and Complaint" in the third book in this series, *The Days of Reckoning Are at Hand: From Fig Leaf to Olive Branch to Laurel Wreath*, chapter 2: "Suffering: The Kintsugi Objective".

[19] For additional discussion of the issue of anger see "The Peril of Moralism" in chapter 10: "The Third-Way of Sanctification: From Abominable to Indominable"; also see the discussion of anger in the third book in this series, *The Days of Reckoning Are at Hand: From Fig Leaf to Olive Branch to Laurel Wreath*, chapter 3: "The Hobgoblin in the Inglenook: Assessing Loneliness"

buffer-zone out of fear of men? Beauty can be a form of warfare, and at times a way to justify anger. It would appear that beautiful people feel entitled to their emotions, regardless of their effect upon others. This may point to a deeper societal trend; as beauty proliferates, so does the incidence of anger (as well as the prevalence of insanity).

The Anger of Achilles, Jacques-Louis David, 1825

> "Once a man would spend days patiently waiting for a stagecoach to come through town. Now he explodes with rage when he must wait thirty seconds at a traffic light."

The typical psychological view on anger derives from the hydraulic theory of emotions which states that emotions are merely the result of built up pressure that must be released or vented.[20] Thus, according to psychology, emotion is values-neutral, neither inherently good nor evil. Emotions just exist and, therefore, should not be judged. In this way, anger, specifically, is never wrongly expressed; it is just the volcanic eruption of pent up feelings that must find release.

> "When a man is wrong and won't admit it, he always gets angry." (Thomas Haliburton)

The Bible, however, sees emotion as a manifestation of the worshipping core.

---

[20] For a more detailed discussion of this topic see "The Hydraulic View of Emotions" in chapter 8: "What Has Jerusalem to Do With Vienna?: The Case Against Psychology." This concept from David Powlison, Westminster Theological Seminary, Philadelphia, Pennsylvania

Therefore anger, like all emotion, reveals either idols of the heart or a heart of faith. Anger does not exist in a vacuum; it grows directly from an interpreting worshiping responsive heart. It is usually based in an overtly sinful man-centered response to the world, but it can be God-glorifying when used for his purposes.

> "Beware the anger of a patient man." (John Dryden)

Moses offers a vivid picture of this duality. In Exodus 11:8, Moses, "hot with anger," proclaimed God's final judgment on Egypt. Moses was consumed with God's burning wrath upon Israel's captors. Later, in Numbers 20:10, 11, Moses raised his staff in ungodly anger to strike rock at Meribah. As Moses shows, anger serves a purpose in tandem with one's desires, and is a direct outgrowth of often shifting heart alliances. Martin Luther (1483-1546) reflected something of this when he wrote, "I never work better than when I am inspired by anger; for when I am angry, I can write, pray, and speak well. For then my whole temperament is made alive, my understanding is sharpened, and all mundane troubles depart."

The Image of God and the Contours of Fear

According to Chinese legend, *Nian Shou* (年兽), the fearful demon, was locked in a mountain prison by the gods. At the New Year, the *Nian* was released so that he could find food. (Thus, in traditional Chinese culture the New Year (*nian*, 年) was to be feared.) The *Nian* terrorized the countryside devouring villagers, who tried in vain to appease the demon with livestock. Once, as the *Nian* entered a village, a beggar hid inside a house with red paper fluttering at the door. The *Nian*, noticing the paper, charged toward the door, but at that moment was struck by lightning. The pain was so severe that the *Nian* avoided anything red from then on. The beggar then wrapped himself in red paper, and holding a red lantern, approached the *Nian* while hurling firecrackers (which sounded like peals of thunder). The *Nian* fled in terror. Thus began the Chinese New Year traditions.[21]

The Chinese legend of the *Nian* indicates a certain endemic fear within man. How does the biblical counselor pry back the heart's veneer to uncover its tides and seasons, motives and methods with regard to fear? A good starting point is that mankind is, by design, prophet, priest, and king. However, on account of sin, these aspects of God's image have been damaged so that they do not function as intended. Each of these components has been corrupted so as to become a source of angst and anxiety, pain and loss, arrogation and devastation. Following the contours of the kingly, priestly, and prophetic offices, there are three fundamental fears that inhabit each person: fear of judgment, rejection, and failure.

---

[21] Xiuhua Ren, *Classic Legends of Traditional Chinese Culture* (2009) 7-11.

> The ten most pervasive American fears (in order from greatest to least): speaking in public, heights, insects, falling into poverty, terrorism, illness or accidents, death, flying, loneliness, and authority. How might each of these fears be understood in light of the image of God as prophet, priest and king? Which of these fears results from the more nascent fears of failure, rejection, and judgment?

The Dynamics of Fear[22]

Fear of Judgment

> "How much have we had to pay for the evils that never happen?" (Thomas Jefferson)

The purpose of the terracotta warriors found in the tomb of Emperor Qin Shi Huang (260-210 BC) was to protect the emperor in the afterlife. Whether an emperor or a peasant, each person fears death because each lives with the daily haunting knowledge that he will stand before a holy God in judgment. This is the source of mankind's obsession with conceiving Pollyanna views of the afterlife.

> "The wicked flee when no man pursues." (Proverbs 28:1)

As king each person was made to exercise authority under God and for God. Sinners have given away their status as true king, and in its

Emperor Guan
Qing Dynasty (c. 1700)

place have amassed for themselves false and delusive sources of power, such as physical aggression, dominance, the love of money, methods for manipulation, and attempts at control. The examples of how mankind effaces the image of God within himself are myriad, so that his status as king is now flaccid posturing, a hollow shell of what it was intended to be.

---

[22] The idea for these three fears from Michael Bobick, *From Slavery to Sonship: A Biblical Psychology for Pastoral Counseling* (1995) (class notes)

> "Keep your fears to yourself, but share your courage with others." (Robert Louis Stevenson)
>
> "At least half the evils of the world are caused by nothing more than the fear of boredom." (Bertrand Russell)

Having lost the status of king, mankind is plagued by the fear of judgment. He engages in a desperate search for various means to alleviate this fear,[23] such as perfectionism, self-denial, suffering, and even good works (not so much in order to serve others, but to exonerate himself). The result of this fear is often paranoia, the irrational fear that one is the intended target of clandestine malevolence. Thus, mankind harbors within itself a desperate fear of judgment, to which it affects a sinful response, the hope to be justified through its own means.

> Research finds that a person, to some extent, thinks and acts in the way that he holds his body. "Posture expansiveness" means to expand or "open" one's body space. The objective is to make oneself appear more confident and authoritative. Posture expansiveness lends one a sense of power, no matter how powerful he actually is. In fact, body posture, rather than actual title, seems to make a greater difference in how others perceive a person. This is an example of mankind seeking to regain his lost kingly function, an attempt to reverse the fall through manipulative means.

> In Chinese tradition rice is thrown at newlyweds because the rice was thought to encourage nearby evil spirits to have a "snack" instead of hectoring the happy couple. This is a manifestation of the fear of judgment within the unregenerate heart. The soul, at war with God, fears punishment for sin, continually seeking to mitigate or manage that fear through means that may seem comforting, but are wholly irrational.

Manifestations of the Fear of Judgment		
Defensive – based in self-protection	**Offensive** – based in "taking ground" from God	**Answered in Christ**
Each person knows God and suppresses the truth in ungodliness.[24] Therefore, each person, when faced with the prospect of death, is	Those who themselves fear judgment may be quick to either condemn or excuse others. Thus, those who are cognizant of their guilt before a	"There is now no condemnation for those in Christ Jesus." (Romans 8:1) "Since the children have flesh and blood, he too shared in

---

[23] 1 John 4:18
[24] Romans 1:21

paralyzed by the fearful expectation of judgment, of raging fire that will consume the enemies of God.[25] This sense of impending judgment sometimes shows up as fear of the dark, ghosts, or thunder.	holy God, and fearful of condemnation from that God, are often most active in assessing others' guilt or righteousness. Condemnation of others often serves to deflect attention from one's own guilt.[26]	their humanity so that by his death he might destroy him who holds the power of death--that is, the devil-- and free those who all their lives were held in slavery by their fear of death." (Hebrews 2:14, 15)
Self-righteousness often shows itself in self-exonerating good works. Good works can be a bargaining chip or manipulative stance toward God, an attitude that one is entitled to salvation.[27]	Good works can be used to gain control over a world which one fears. When one does good to others there is a sense that they are now beholden to one's kindness.	"For it is by grace you have been saved, through faith – and this not from yourselves, it is the gift of God – not by works so that no one can boast." (Ephesians 2:8, 9)
Paranoia arises from an innate fear of a God-infused universe, since sin causes one to instinctively distrust God's motives.[28]	There is a subtext in most conversation – a subtle blame-shifting. This is an outgrowth of the pangs of impending judgment. The heart looks for ways to transfer the blame for sin to those around it or to its situation.	"So do not fear, for I am with you; do not be dismayed, for I am your God. I will strengthen you and help you; I will uphold you with my righteous right hand." (Isaiah 41:10) Christ has supremacy in all things, and through him to reconcile to himself all things.[29]
Perfectionism can result from a desire to escape God's judgment	Perfectionism can be a way to gain power over one's world.	Christians are not yet perfected, but Christ will transform the Christians'

---

[25] Hebrews 10:27
[26] For example, in Genesis 38:24-26, Judah sought to have Tamar burned to death for prostitution, yet she held his seal, cord, and staff as proof that she was pregnant through him.
[27] Matthew 23:23
[28] In Daniel 5:1-9, King Belshazzar held a banquet in which he drank from goblets pilfered from the Temple in Jerusalem. A finger appeared writing the king's grievous transgressions on the wall behind him. This vignette captures something of the nature of paranoia, a knowledge that someone (a holy eternal God) is watching and that wrath is immanent.
[29] Colossians 1:18-20

for sin. If one can be perfect then he feels as though he does not need God's mercy and forgiveness. In a delusion of grandeur, perfectionism makes mankind think he can be his own savior, that one is all-sufficient in himself.	Perfectionists feel superior to others and therefore deserving of others' respect, admiration, obedience, and praise.	lowly bodies to glorify them.[30] "The young rich ruler asked Jesus, 'What must I do to inherit eternal life?' Jesus answered, 'If you want to be perfect, go, sell your possessions and give to the poor, and you will have treasure in heaven. Then come, follow me.' He went away sad."[31]
Self-denial, suffering, and self-mortification are often sought after means for alleviating the fear of judgment. In this way, one seeks to pay the penalty for his own sin. The gamble is that one's suffering will serve as payment and he will be adjudged righteous on account of that suffering. Self-mutilation can be an extreme means of dealing with the fear of judgment, to shed one's own blood as the propitiation for one's own sin. This, like all attempts at self-justification, arises out of unyielding pride.	The Pharisees fasted twice a week and gave a tenth of their income,[32] yet their self-denial was utterly self-serving. Their fasting only served to heighten their arrogance, sense of entitlement, and hatred of God's mercy.	"But go and learn what this means: 'I desire mercy, not sacrifice.' For I have not come to call the righteous, but sinners." (Matthew 9:13)
The New Age movement speaks of a		"The Lord is my light and my salvation – whom shall I fear?

---

[30] Philippians 3:12, 13, 21
[31] Luke 18:18-23
[32] Luke 18:12

"sense of karma," that each eventually receives exactly what he has visited upon others, whether good or evil. This sense of cosmic vengeance or blessing is man-centered, man-justifying, and man-glorifying, because it is man-defined.[33] The sense of karma is an attempt to explain and order life outside of God.		The Lord is the stronghold of my life – of whom shall I be afraid?" (Psalm 27:1) "Do not take revenge, my dear friends, but leave room for God's wrath, for it is written: 'It is mine to avenge; I will repay,' says the Lord." (Romans 12:19)

Charon Carries Souls across the River Styx, Alexander Litovchenko, d. 1890

On the first day of the annual Chinese Spring Festival, thousands visit the Taoist Dong Lung Gong Temple in Tungkang to perform a centuries-old ritual to rid themselves of bad luck. After burning incense and tossing two pieces of wood, visitors receive a

---
[33] John 9:2

ceremonial whipping and spanking administered by the temple staff operating, they believe, under the auspices of the god Wang Ye (王爺).[34]

In this ritual one sees a fascinating display of the attempt to alleviate the fear of judgment before a holy God. Worshippers submit to physical punishment and humiliation as a means of purging indwelling guilt for sin, to somehow make amends with a cosmic judge. The hope is that suffering will offer propitiation for sin which then ensures exoneration before that judge. Mankind desperately seeks to pay for his own sin, to alleviate his unshakable guilt before a holy God. However, this attempted payment is the height of arrogance, a twisted perversion leaving the idolater ever more forlorn and desperate.

Fear of Rejection

Man was made to function as a priest, to bring blessing, to comfort, and to promote relationship between God and his creation, that God would be more fully manifest in his creation. In the fall, mankind lost his status as priest, rendering him plagued by the fear of rejection. This results in the longing for acceptance in a capricious world, the desire to eschew conflict, seeking covering from others, indulging in a fantasy world, forming protective factions, hunting for refuge from hatred, striking alliances in defense of one's sin, withdrawing in self-pity, and hoping to find comfort in isolation. The desire is to experience surrogate forms of blessing which extend the supposed assurance of acceptance.

"Anxiety is a thin stream of fear trickling through the mind. If encouraged, it cuts a channel into which all other thoughts are drained." (Arthur Somers Roche)

Manifestations of the Fear of Rejection		
Defensive – based in self-protection	**Offensive** – based in "taking ground" from God	**Answered in Christ**
Each person fears that he will be seen for who he is, and will be rejected. The fear is that others will witness one's sinfulness, the ugliness of one's depravity, and the irrationality of one's idolatry. In this way, they	The fear of rejection may make one critical of others as a way to deflect attention from one's own sin.	"Even though I walk through the valley of the shadow of death, I will fear no evil, for you are with me; your rod and your staff, they comfort me." (Psalm 23:4)

Those in Christ are |

---

[34] From Wikipedia article on "spanking"

will judge that one is not worthy of love.[35]		eternally anchored to him.[36] Since the bond to Christ is unbreakable, this spawns the freedom to be rejected without meaningful consequence.
The fear of rejection can result in seeking covering. This covering keeps others at a distance through various means such as bravado, passivity, anger, eccentricity, or busyness, for example.	Seeking the center of attention, to be humorous, to be competent, or to be attractive, can be a means of ensuring that others are always attentive. The objective is to make sure that one is functionally guarded against rejection. Anything which makes oneself appear to be worthy of attention is cultivated to dispel the scepter of rejection.	The Lord has clothed the Christian in garments of salvation, ensconced him in a robe of righteousness.[37] At his wedding feast, the king observed that some guests were dressed improperly and, thus, they were thrown out of the wedding.[38] Those in Christ are "properly clothed," covered from their sin. Christ's righteous robe covers the repentant sinner so that he is no longer naked in his sin.[39]
The fear of rejection can result in seeking a social refuge or relational hiding place. This can show up in craving to only be surrounded by admirers or friends. This may drive materialism, for example, as one seeks a cocoon of supposed assured acceptance. (The opposite may also take hold, an	Cain, a restless wander of the earth, feared that whoever found him would kill him. He sought a hiding place by building a city.[41] In this way, Cain sought to "take back ground" (by means of a city) that he felt had been lost to God.	Psalm 9:9 states, "The LORD is a refuge for the oppressed, a stronghold in times of trouble." This is a prophetic picture of Jesus, the Christian's refuge. Isaiah 32:2 states, "Each man will be like a shelter from the wind and a refuge from the storm…" This is a prophecy of

---

[35] On the night Jesus was arrested, Peter feared rejection, scorn, and punishment from others. This led him to deny Christ three times. (Mark 14:66-72)
[36] Hebrews 6:19
[37] Isaiah 61:10
[38] Matthew 22:11, 12
[39] Revelation 3:18
[41] Genesis 4:14

anti-social stance which makes one a popular renegade to those who prize antiauthoritarianism.) Sarah pressured Abraham to sire a child through her servant Hagar, an Egyptian. Abraham kowtowed to Sarah's request in defiance of God's promise.[40] He sought a "hiding place" from his wife in acquiescing to her ill-conceived plans.		Christ, shelter and refuge for those who put their trust in him.
Fear of rejection can result in retreat into a fantasy world, a place in which one is loved, admired, and influential. (This may be popularly labeled "schizophrenia.")	King Nebuchadnezzar cast an image in gold and commanded his subjects to worship it.[42] In this way, he fabricated a fantasy world in which he rendered himself a god.	God sent a rock to crush Nebuchadnezzar's raised idol.[43] In his mercy to his people, God casts down idols, invading and interrupting fantasies.
The fear of rejection can drive the sinner to seek false comfort in the things of the world. This can show itself as a lust for false-peace, a feigned pacifism. Additionally, a lust for pleasure often increases due to the pain of rejection. For example, gluttony can serve as a ready pacifier when faced with fear.	At the foot of Mount Sinai, Israel grew impatient demanding that Aaron make gods for them. Upon worshipping the golden calf, the people ate, drank, and became sexually immoral.[44] (Was the desire for a cast god an outgrowth of perceived rejection from Yahweh?)	Jesus said, "Take my yoke upon you, for my yoke is easy and my burden light, and you will find rest for your souls."[45] Jesus longs to bestow genuine and meaningful peace through relationship with himself.

---

[40] Genesis 16:2
[42] Daniel 3:1
[43] Daniel 2:34, 44, 45
[44] Exodus 32:1, 6
[45] Matthew 11:29

> Astronomical observation was a sophisticated and exacting science in ancient China. Celestial events were frequently read and interpreted as either approval or disapproval from Heaven. An emperor maintained his mandate, in part, through his ability to predict cosmic events. This meant that he was in tune with Heaven's will. Thus, Chinese astronomy largely developed as a way to abrogate the emperor's fear of rejection.
>
> "If you have one more friend you have one more way. If you have one more enemy you have one more wall." (Chinese Proverb)

Fear of Failure

An Iron Forge, Joseph Wright, 1772

As prophet, man was made to assign meaning, to speak the truth, and to correctly interpret in order to assess reality as God sees it. Having lost the status of prophet, mankind is blighted by the fear of failure, a fear that manifests itself in self-esteem-propelled flights of fantasy, becoming a workaholic, being consumed with envy, succumbing to laziness (as the burden of fear results in emotional paralysis), or resorting to procrastination (a crafty means of managing failure risks). Mankind's flailing hope is to find significance and meaning through his own godless efforts.

> The history of Israel is tragically marked by rejecting, cursing, and murdering true

> prophets, while embracing and exalting false ones.[46] (The very fact that Israel craved prophetic utterances in the first place was because it feared direct revelation from God. The people sought an intermediary to shield them from God.) The notion of rejecting true prophets and honoring false ones drives straight to the heart of man's fear of failure, a flailing grabbing for any guidance that promised to make flawed human reason functional.

A recent American Psychological Association study found that the high rate of apathy among today's young people is in part attributable to the proliferation of abstract superheroes. The study concluded that because young people feel incapable of meeting their hero's image or expectations they become "slackers," anti-establishment underperformers who shirk responsibility. In other words, as one fails to measure up to his hero he abandons all aspiration. This is a way to retain some dignity in the face of perceived failure.[47] How would the Bible interpret this finding? The root desire to meet man-centered standards results from a recalcitrant pride which rejects God's only standard of acceptance and success: Jesus Christ.

Manifestations of the Fear of Failure		
Defensive – based in self-protection	**Offensive** – based in "taking ground" from God	**Answered in Christ**
There is nagging fear that one's lifework will be deemed futile, that one will never succeed in fulfilling the expectations of those around him.		"Do not be anxious about anything, but in everything by prayer and petition, with thanksgiving, present your requests to God. And the peace of God which transcends all understanding, will guard your hearts and your minds in Christ Jesus." (Philippians 4:6, 7)
Laziness often results from the fear of not measuring up to certain self-imposed standards, (whether set by others or oneself). The result is to give up trying to meet the standard, to quit the "game" altogether.	Workaholism seeks to ensure that one succeeds in the world's eyes, that one's work carries lasting significance. However, work done without Jesus is against Jesus, and	"Let us not become weary in doing good, for at the proper time we will reap a harvest if we do not give up." (Galatians 6:9) Colossians 3:23, 24 states, "...work as unto the Lord and not for men knowing that

---
[46] Luke 13:34
[47] Mike Ryan, "Study: Superheroes Might Not be Such Super Role Models," *Movie Talk* (August 17, 2010)

	thus meaningless and unsatisfying, culminating in debilitating angst.⁴⁸	your reward is from the Lord..." One is eternally judged a success as he works for Christ's glory.
Procrastination grows from fear of failure. One fears starting any task because if failure results then one is confirmed as a failure. However, if one waits until the last minute he has a ready excuse for failure and, if successful, he appears to be highly-gifted. ⁴⁹ Procrastination is essentially a risk calculus for managing perceived failure.	*Thisbe* John William Waterhouse, 1909	"If you obey the Lord he will prosper the work of your hands." (Deuteronomy 30:8, 9)

"For God did not give us a spirit of timidity [fear], but a spirit of power, of love and of self-discipline." (2 Timothy 1:7) |
| Low self-esteem is nothing more than failed self-pride. ⁵⁰ One sets a standard based on those around him. He adopts those people's values and their view of success. Then one strives to meet that standard. This is a form of self-judgment in both "quality" and "quantity." In pride, one judges himself based on criteria which he sets for himself, while neglecting those criteria based in God's holiness; this is self-judgment based on quality. Additionally, | | Jesus has met the Father's standard for inclusion in his kingdom. Thus, the believer does not need to meet an illusory standard which he sets for himself. Such standards have been eliminated so that one is eternally judged a success, not based on one's own sense of achievement, but based on the achievement of another, Jesus (whose death on the cross accomplished this).

"For you did not receive a spirit that makes you a slave again to fear, but you received the Spirit of |

---

[48] Ecclesiastes 4:8
[49] This insight from Dan Allender, The Larry Crabb Seminar, Wayne, Pennsylvania
[50] For further discussion of the issue of low self-esteem see the second book in this series, *What Agreement Is There Between the Temple of God and Idols?: The Accidence of Sin and Idolatry*, chapter 9: "Marauding Visigoths: The Autocratic Self"

self-judgment based on quantity means setting standards so high that one must fail and, thus, offers a means of remaining in control of the fear. [51] (Conversely, setting a standard too low ensures never-ending success.) Depression results from viewing oneself through the wrong standards and failing against them.		sonship." (Romans 8:15) "Fight the good fight of faith. Take hold of the eternal life to which you were called." (1 Timothy 6:12)

> Money seems to shield one from all three fears: judgment, failure, and rejection. Financial prosperity seems to deflect the fear of eternal judgment since it mutes any sense that one is under wrath. There is often a false sense of justification in wealth, that somehow one is cosmically "blessed." Likewise, money seems an adequate antidote to the fear of failure, and promises to guard one from rejection, as wealth always attracts friends.

Excursus: Chinese Music and the Issue of Fear

Chinese music, whether traditional or modern, is generally sorrowful and heartbroken. What is the reason for this? Humanity is plagued by three fears: failure, rejection, and punishment. These fears form the backdrop of all human experience outside of God. At times these fears rise and soar, casting humanity into irrational responses to the world. Chinese culture, as fundamentally atheistic, exhibits these fears with a particular intensity. There is the looming scepter of punishment (for social transgressions), failure (for non-performance), and rejection (especially from family members).

> "There is no fear in love. But perfect love drives out fear, because fear has to do with punishment. The one who fears is not made perfect in love." (1 John 4:18)

As with all displays of atheism, punishment, failure, and rejection occupy a central position in the traditional Chinese psyche, surfacing in its music. Much like the ancient Greek concept of the tragic hero, the Chinese consciousness is tormented by a sense of impending tragedy that in the final analysis love, wealth, and social standing will never be gained, or if gained, lost. Thus, life is governed by the dictates of a cold

---

[51] Michael Bobick, *From Slavery to Sonship: A Biblical Psychology for Pastoral Counseling* (1995) 35. (class notes)

and mendacious universe under the control of impersonal laws which offer no assurance, no acceptance, and no home.

In many ways, the Chinese consciousness attempts to exonerate itself from the threat of failure, rejection, and punishment through circumstance-driven excuses. Thus, one is not at fault but the victim of circumstance. This surfaces in the culture's music, a commiseration in a collective sense of tragedy. (The same pattern can be seen in Chinese literature which, more often than not, begins with joy but ends in tragedy.)

A Chinese Mandarin Being Entertained
(artist unknown)

Section III

East of Eden: *The Effects of the Fall*

- 7 -

THE NEEDS IMPERATIVE

A Solar System of Unsynchronized Orbits

𝒫lanets move in predicable elliptical orbits with steady trajectories. Drawing an analogy with human relationships, in the past most people orbited around the same "sun," as there was an invisible cohesion to society, an assumed locus of collective morality and conduct. People pursued similar goals and held common values which lent stability to society. Just as planets follow predictable patterns, so too, assumed moral and social standards offered a measure of assurance in social interaction, a certain relational syzygy within society.

Astronomer Copernicus, Conversation with God, Jan Matejko, 1872

One could think of this environment of assumed standards as modernism, the idea that life followed a certain steady orbit called "community." Upon marriage, a couple's orbits tended to synchronize reasonably well, concentric circles on a shared plane. This was one reason that marriage tended to survive and thrive.

Today, however, modernism has been replaced by postmodernism, the idea that society is disjointed and lacks cohesion. There is now no longer a shared trajectory of conduct. People today orbit a sun of their own making and, therefore, wobble and gyrate on incongruous ellipses. Since they do not orbit the same sun, they are geosynchronous with only themselves.

> Peril attends a marriage between two self-obsessed people. Such a union will, without question, result in various forms of relational combat to gain attention for oneself. Warring idols, namely the need to be continually affirmed, quickly rip a marriage to shreds.

With little social consistency, little consensus on proper conduct, and little direction for one's life, relationships follow unsynchronized and incompatible orbits (which may appear to synchronize for a time). The curse of postmodernism is orbits which bring people together for a moment only to rapidly draw them apart. For example, a man and woman may marry at a moment of synchronicity only to find that they are soon drifting apart. Their orbits begin to diverge as each is more committed to personal achievement, and meeting supposed emotional needs, than in selflessly sacrificing for another. As self-interest takes priority over marriage unity, divorce appears to be the only logical answer. All of this discussion is prelude to the issue of perceived needs, a poison leaching into every corner of society.

The Proliferation of Perceived Need

One day I smelled something burning. I couldn't quite identify the strange odor, but it seemed like burning plastic. I searched throughout the house. I checked lights, outlets, and pipes, but could not find anything awry. I went back to work, but the smell seemed so close. I removed my eyeglasses and smelled them; my nostrils filled with the pungent odor of burnt plastic. (I had just purchased the glasses (with plastic lenses) that day; they must have retained an odor from the cutting process.)

I mention this anecdote to emphasize that I thought the "burning" was in my environment when in reality it was in (on) my person. The source of my irritation and consternation, which I thought was external, was actually myself. This serves as a fitting entrée to the issue of perceived needs. Perceived needs are a nagging haranguing craving which causes one to search for relief in the world around. However, the problem is a heart worship problem, a problem answered not in seeking to satisfy needs, but in repentance for wrongly entering into the entire enterprise.

Just as Adam and Eve hid from God,[1] so too, each sinner seeks to hide from God. One of the most inventive means of hiding is to redefine rogue concepts so that they appear euphemistic. This allows them to gain broad acceptance even when the underlying act is inherently sinful. The concept of "needs" seeks to strip human desire of its God-ward referent and, as such, serves as a cloaking device for the lust of the

---
[1] Genesis 3:7

flesh.

> "I would like to be the air that inhabits you for a moment only. I would like to be that unnoticed and that necessary." (adapted from Margaret Atwood)

Much of the modern focus on the self derives from a more insidious absorption with perceived needs. While everyone has biological needs for food, water, and shelter, modern attention has shifted to psychic needs, such as the need for security, significance, self-esteem, and self-actualization (based on the Adler-Maslow pyramid of needs).[2] Assumed emotional needs are so engrained in the modern psyche that they are guarded as one would guard his last supply of food, water, or air. The one who stands sentry over his supposed needs invariably molds himself after the world's image in highhanded defiance of God. Thus, this focus on needs is part of the world's conspiracy against God, to allow the world ascendancy in the human heart. The focus on needs only serves to enslave modern people as it is axiomatic that whatever one thinks he needs will control him.[3] Maintaining control over people is the world's singular objective.[4]

Allegory of Philosophy
Giacinto Brandi, d. 1691

Tragically, most expend tremendous energy chasing their perceived emotional or psychological needs, so this question of needs is invariably a major theme and source of conflict in counseling. As the counselor takes up Christ's battle-standard against perceived needs, he finds himself on the frontline of "worship combat." The sinner does not surrender his victim-mentality (as one denied his supposed rightful emotional needs) without a long and protracted fight.

---

[2] For more discussion of the Adler-Maslow pyramid see chapter 1: "The Exordium to Biblical Counseling"
[3] Edward Welch, Westminster Theological Seminary, Philadelphia, Pennsylvania
[4] For further discussion of this topic see the second book in this series, *What Agreement Is There Between the Temple of God and Idols?: The Accidence of Sin and Idolatry*, chapter 2: "The World, the Flesh, and the Devil: Assessing the Threat Matrix."

> Mark Twain (1835-1910) wrote, "Fame is a vapor; popularity an accident; the only earthly certainty is oblivion." While Twain seems to have correctly recognized the vapid nature of seeking to meet perceived needs, he did not see a savior in the midst of "oblivion." That savior draws the sinner out of his futile quest, clothes him with a royal robe,[5] and calls him friend and brother.[6] This is the grand rescue from oblivion.

The danger in the "needs game" is that it is a ready path to worship slavery. Needs are insatiable since they are nothing more than dressed-up lusts.[7] On account of the world's guile, the quest to meet needs is made to appear plausible and, therefore, often escapes detection by unwitting counselors. Cravings for control, freedom, happiness, image, intimacy, money, popularity, and power are easily swathed as legitimate needs which serve as nothing more than a veil for the heart's lusts.

> "Wealth and fame are like seawater; the more we drink, the thirstier we become." (Arthur Schopenhauer)

Is there a fundamental need for security, significance, approval, affirmation, and to be valued or respected? No. There is only one legitimate need, for relationship with Jesus Christ.[8] That one central need radically changes every relationship, interaction, pursuit, purchase, dream, goal, desire, love, and thought. The greater one's sense of psychic need, the more one feels injured by every interaction, and when perceived need continues to go unmet there is an added insult to the original injury. However, when one sees his only need to be relationship with Jesus, the sense of injury and insult soon evaporates.

A young Christian woman, who exhibits obvious selfish behavior and often hurls hurtful words, claims that she needs encouragement (which she is not receiving). Her hidden objective is to deflect attention from a manifestly needs-obsessed heart, and cast blame upon those around her for her sin. God longs to derail her plans. His objective, through ongoing repentance, is to mold her into one who longs to selflessly give encouragement, and in so doing, soon abandons her radical self-focus. The ultimate objective is that she would, through daily self-denial, assume an unmitigated desire for Jesus himself.

> "No, I beat my body and make it my slave so that after I have preached to others, I myself will not be disqualified for the prize." (1 Corinthians 9:27)

---

[5] Revelation 6:11
[6] John 15:15
[7] Edward Welch, *When People are Big and God is Small: Overcoming Peer Pressure, Codependency, and the Fear of Man* (Presbyterian and Reformed Publishing, 1997)
[8] David Powlison, "Dynamics of Biblical Change" class, Westminster Theological Seminary, Philadelphia, Pennsylvania

Need as Infinite Abyss

Matthew 18:12-14 records the parable of the lost sheep in which a shepherd abandoned ninety-nine sheep to go after one lost sheep. This parable highlights God's unimaginable and "irrational" love, to risk that which is assured to go after that which is lost. The parable defies all human logic and sensibility, which was exactly Jesus' point. Human reason relies on erroneous assessments and fallacious calculi.

Our English Coasts, William Holman Hunt, 1852

This question of needs offers a mirror image of the parable of the lost sheep. In his quest to be God, the sinner adopts the exact same pursuit tactic with regard to needs. Ninety-nine people may offer praise, but the one who did not stands out as an unmet need. Ninety-nine times one may be judged a success, but the one failure is labeled an unrequited need. Ninety-nine times a parent may lovingly serve his child, but the one perceived or real neglect is remembered as a source of scarring.

While God focused on the one out of an inexplicable love that would sacrifice all he had, the sinner focuses on the one out of an insatiable craving. Because the sinner is a bottomless pit of need, he is never satisfied with the ninety-nine but grabs for just one more. The heart readily forgets the ninety-nine and focuses on the one, when that focus suits its egoistic purpose.

Trying to meet one's perceived need, in one's own way, is at its root a muted display of hatred toward God, a vain effort to make oneself into god. Consider Jeremiah 2:13,

> My people have committed two sins:
> They have forsaken me,
>   the spring of living water,
> and have dug their own cisterns,
>   broken cisterns that cannot hold water.

This idea of digging one's own cistern is an attempt to live outside of God's gracious provision of living water. What's more, man's cisterns are broken so that they do not even hold water. This is a vivid metaphor for mankind's attempt to meet perceived needs in its own way, for its own purpose. Such attempts are futile as the heart is a leaking cistern of need.

The more one tries to function as his own god the more empty and hopeless he becomes. For example, when one's driving obsession is respect from people, there will never be enough praise and honor, never enough recognition of one's gifts, never enough admirers to remember one's name, never the assurance that one will be included, and never enough power over one's destiny.

Sinful desire makes one a bottomless pit of need (a leaking cistern). No matter what one has or achieves, no matter how much attention he is given, he always wants more. Nothing will ever satisfy the desire to be in the position of God himself, to be infinite, to be fully-independent of God.

The Embattled Quest to Meet Needs

Cephalopods (octopus, squid) possess a fascinating nervous system called a "neural net." On account of the way the neural net functions, a cephalopod cannot discern where on its body stimulation occurs. It only knows that something has made contact with it, and therefore contracts its entire body in response. Just as a cephalopod cannot discern the somatic location of stimuli, so too, those who focus upon themselves act in terms of a neural net approach to others. This is the inability to think outside of one's own emotional experience, blinded to the source and meaning of interactions. Thus, the sinner often responds to relational stimuli reflexively and without discernment. In this way, focus on oneself creates what I have termed the "neural net of relational response," a consumption with self which results in a blindness toward others. Such a response only considers that stimulus has occurred, but not why or from whom. The psyche is so consumed with meeting its own perceived needs that it simply responds without discernment, without consideration, without vision.[9]

The neural net of relational response may result in:

1. Becoming argumentative
2. Being quick to hurl insults
3. Brooding and planning revenge
4. Becoming depressed
5. Remaining detached and aloof
6. Surrounding oneself with friends who offer unquestioned acceptance
7. Turning to food to cover insecurity
8. Shopping to escape
9. Working or studying harder to gain an advantage over others
10. Becoming deceptively charming and winsome
11. Cultivating an impressive image

The Octopus Attacking the Nautilus from 20,000 Leagues Under the Sea
Alphonse Marie Adolphe de Neuville, d. 1885

If one feels he must be respected, he will find a way to ensure that others consider him competent and worthy of praise. He ensconces himself in a cocoon of self-confidence and self-exoneration to shield himself from any challenge or doubt, that he would always be deemed worthy of commendation from his target audience. If in an academic setting, he is sure to be the most articulate in the room. He seeks to put himself in a position of power, and at the center of attention. If he finds himself in a church setting, he quotes Scripture with skill. Much of way passes for piety is nothing more than another means of meeting perceived needs.

However, the sinner's perceived need is infinite, so the harder he tries to meet that need in his own way, with his own glory in mind, the greater his relational insecurity and emotional pain. The more he struggles to gain what he feels he must have, the more his struggle becomes an exercise in futility. This sense of futility produces the

---

[9] Isaiah 6:10; Ephesians 4:19a

neutral net of relational response as he flails and lashes out to gain what he feels he must have. In this way, his response to others is undiscriminating so that anyone in his path is subject to his rampaging ego.

> "Thus says the LORD, 'Cursed is the man who trusts in mankind and makes flesh his strength, and whose heart turns away from the LORD. For he will be like a bush in the desert and will not see when prosperity comes, but will live in stony wastes in the wilderness, a land of salt without inhabitant. Blessed is the man who trusts in the LORD and whose trust is the LORD. For he will be like a tree planted by the water, that extends its roots by a stream and will not fear when the heat comes; but its leaves will be green, and it will not be anxious in a year of drought nor cease to yield fruit...'" (Jeremiah 17:5-8)

Case Study: Is Sexuality an Inherent Need as Part of Human Design?[10]

A Christian woman sought counseling after her recent divorce. She claimed that subsequent to her divorce her sexual needs were going unmet and that she had no choice but to search for a boyfriend. This woman's assertion raises the question, "Is sexuality a God-infused or God-designed need within mankind?"

While this issue is hotly debated, consider the fact that Adam was designed before Eve existed. Therefore, Adam was not primarily created as a sexual being. Sexuality is a secondary relational characteristic instituted by God at the establishment of marriage. Since man is not fundamentally a sexual being, God has invested within him the imperative for self-denial with regard to sexual expression. Thus, the entire premise of sexual need is a fallacy created by psychology to excuse rampant immorality.

First Corinthians 9:27 states, "No, I strike a blow to my body and make it my slave so that after I have preached to others, I myself will not be disqualified for the prize." Additionally, 1 Thessalonians 4:3-5 states,

> It is God's will that you should be sanctified: that you should avoid sexual immorality; that each of you should learn to control your own body in a way that is holy and honorable, not in passionate lust like the pagans, who do not know God;

Even 2 Corinthians 4:10 states, "We always carry around in our body the death of Jesus, so that the life of Jesus may also be revealed in our body."

While sexuality may feel like a non-negotiable need, it is not. There is a higher

---

[10] For further discussion of the issue of sexuality see the case study, "Is There a Fundamental Gender Asymmetry With Regard to Sexuality" in the second book in this series, *What Agreement Is There Between the Temple of God and Idols?: The Accidence of Sin and Idolatry*, chapter 5: "Metaphors for Sin"

precept that one honor Christ with his body. In the context of marriage, sexuality is a gift to display mutually-honoring love, but that sexuality still falls under the command to honor Christ. Even as it reclines within the marriage suite, Christ-directed self-control must rule over the body.

Excursus: The Rise of Media-Generated Need[11]

Philo Farnsworth (1906–1971) invented television in 1927 as an educational tool, but it quickly became a venue for introducing new products to the public. TV rapidly developed into a vehicle for advertising so that it is the exalted spokesman of capitalism, an evangelist for consumerism. TV became a ready means to dominate the mind, breaking down resistance to its images. In fact, TV programming was created to fill the space between advertising (not the other way around), and that programming is carefully crafted to assail the viewer with constantly changing images which incite emotional needs, needs which previously did not exist. Television content is very deliberately engineered to spawn anxiety, fear, and longing. The television world entices one to want more than what he currently has.[12] TV

Le Chahut
George Seurat, 1890

preaches a message of "want more" and "have more," all part of a master plan to tempt the viewer to buy more.

Edward Bernays (1891–1995) is credited with coining the term "public relations" to describe the practice of conceiving and manipulating public opinion. Bernays heavily based his theories on those of his uncle, Sigmund Freud (1856–1939), who postulated subconscious components to the psyche as well as sexual triggers to human behavior. Bernays built upon Freudian psychology with his ingenious work *Crystallizing Public Opinion* (1923), a blueprint for controlling the masses for political and economic

---

[11] The following excursi develop the theme of the world as found in the second book in this series, *What Agreement Is There Between the Temple of God and Idols?: The Accidence of Sin and Idolatry,* chapter 2: "The World, the Flesh, and the Devil: Assessing the Threat Matrix."
[12] Jerry Mander, *Four Arguments for the Elimination of Television* (Prentice Hall, 1980)

purposes.

Bernays thought that people are essentially irrationally given to base desires. He believed that the public must be persuaded concerning what to think or society would descend into brutality and chaos. The masses, therefore, need a proffered "enlightened" understanding in order for society to function. Beginning in the 1920s, Bernays implemented what he termed, the "engineering of consent," a way to persuade the general public to espouse certain beliefs, and shape itself around particular goals. Bernays was adept at molding consumer habits, engineering tastes in entertainment, and swinging political views. His methods were even used by former-president Woodrow Wilson (1856–1924) to direct the American public's perception of World War I.

However, Bernays did more than merely develop clever advertising campaigns; he masterminded the growth of consumer "needs." He saw himself as an influencer and dramatizer, a genius at harnessing media and image to implant ideas and redirect tastes. Corporations clamored for Bernays' help, not just in selling particular products, but in birthing entire industries. For example, working for the American Tobacco Company in the 1920s, Bernays termed cigarettes "torches of freedom" in a ploy to entice young women to smoke. He convinced media networks to label women who smoked "advocates for women's rights." In megalomaniacal terms, Bernays described himself as an "invisible government" with control over the masses.[13]

> "The pie keeps growing because things that look like wants today are needs tomorrow…If you believe that human wants and needs are infinite, then there are infinite industries to be created, infinite businesses to be started, and infinite jobs to be done…" (Marc Andreessen, Netscape co-founder)[14]

In 1933 Bernays, a Jew, was shocked to discover that the Nazis had scrutinized his work, *Crystallizing Public Opinion*. They subsequently marshaled Bernays' work to direct public sentiment in the eventual persecution of the Jews.

Excursus: Eight Perceived Human Needs and How Advertising Exploits Them[15]

"Today the tyrant rules not by club or fist, but disguised as an advertiser; he shepherds his flocks in the ways of utility and comfort."[16] In the past armies conquered nations. Today advertising conquers cultures with far greater effectiveness because the

---

[13] Edward Bernays, *Propaganda* (New York: Horace Liveright, 1928)
[14] Thomas Friedman, *The World is Flat: A Brief History of the Twenty-First Century* (New York: Farrar, Straus, and Giroux, 2006) 267.
[15] Some ideas in this section adapted from Vance Packard, *The Hidden Persuaders* (Miller Publishing, 1957); for further discussion of this issue see item twenty-two, "Sin as being people of the eye," in the second book in this series, *What Agreement Is There Between the Temple of God and Idols?: The Accidence of Sin and Idolatry*, chapter 5: "Metaphors for Sin"
[16] adapted from Marshall McLuhan (1911-1980)

conquered thinks he is the victor. The consumer imagines that in spending he has vanquished his perceived needs. Thus, through advertising's legerdemain the subject delusively regards himself as the master. The following are eight perceived needs routinely exploited through advertising:

1. Creative outlets

In a highly-mechanized homogeneous world, human experiences have become somewhat sterilized. Even modern employment is largely devoid of human creativity. Consequently, people crave personally creative expression and the development of their hidden talents. Advertisers manipulate this desire by dangling the promise that each purchase represents an opportunity to express one's latent creativity.

2. Ego gratification

Related to the human desire for inherent worth, ego gratification is the quest to feel significant and successful. People want their egos built-up with heroic stories of their personal achievements, noble character, and victories. People continually seek to be congratulated and praised, essentially spending every moment of everyday with this in mind.

Product advertisements often play to this desire for self-congratulation such as the assertion that a luxury purchase is a well-deserved trophy after one's conquests. The product functions as a kind of praise of the purchaser, a celebration of the self. Even celebrity endorsements confer the feeling that if one purchases the product one shares in the stature of a star.

3. Emotional security

In a world of broken relationships and fractured community, psychic fragility is a pervasive problem. Most people today crave emotional security, and advertisements play upon this with the promise of comfort in a consumer-driven safe harbor. Many advertisements falsely promise permanence, the illusion of safety, and a sense of "arriving home" through consumption.

4. Historical Anchors[17]

In a highly-mobile society plagued by divorce and social upheaval, people hunger for historical connection and roots. They long to know who they are, where they came from, and to whom they are related. This is a central thrust of the human experience,

---

[17] For further discussion of the issue of personal history see the third book in this series, *The Days of Reckoning Are at Hand: From Fig Leaf to Olive Branch to Laurel Wreath*, chapter 1: "Memories Preserved in Amber: Adopting God's Retrospective"

to know and understand one's history. Some crave a national identity, others an association with an ethnic heritage, and still others, the warmth of family. A few even crave a connection with school, hometown, employer, or church. They seek out any historical anchor, especially in turbulent times.

The curse on modern life is that as one daily seeks to satisfy his needs he continually renders himself "rootless." Advertisers, as cunning manipulators of this modern longing for roots, link their products to nostalgic images of nation, ethnicity, "team," or family. They seek, through their products, to provide the consumer with a surrogate social anchor.

5. Love objects

People feel this throbbing need to be both loved and to express love. If one cannot feel love from, and express love to, a person he will often turn to pets or objects. As odd as it sounds,

A Daughter of the Revolution
John George Brown, d. 1913

people frequently buy something to love such as an automobile, home, clothing, or jewelry. They form an emotional attachment to these items in the hope of deriving love from them. Advertising exploits this desire to love, and be loved, by offering products that appear worthy of our love and able to, in return, love us. Advertisers are, in fact, desperate to sell us something to love, or at least something through which we can express love to others.

6. Reassurance of worth

People instinctively want to feel that they are valuable contributors to society. They want assurance that their achievements are meaningful, that they have earned the right to social acceptance and respect.

7. Sense of power

People crave power because it holds out the perception of sovereignty to makes one's own choices. With a sense of power, there is a built in assumption of safety because one can direct others as it suits his perceived needs. There is also a sense of being higher in the social order and, therefore, above the plight of the huddled masses. Advertisers leverage this desire for power in marketing certain automobiles, bank services, clothing, or even education. There is a sense in which the purchase will make one more in control, immune from social perils, and master of one's own destiny. Advertisers even want the purchaser to feel in complete control during the purchasing experience, a crucial component in the implantation of a sense of power.

8. Immortality

Each person has nestled within him an abiding fear of death, and this fear only grows with age. In order to alleviate this fear, people often turn to some form of consumption which promises to either "cheat" death or at least take one's mind off of it. Advertising tries, through a number of techniques, to offer the sense of a lasting legacy, the delusion that one can achieve a type of immortality. This may be through something acquired, experienced, or bequeathed. There is an insidious implication that certain purchases will allow one to live beyond death, that the purchase holds nascent victory over death.

> "We are all just prisoners here of our own device."[18]

Excursus: Advertising Methods in the Exploitation of Needs[19]

Based on advertisers' understanding of the eight perceived human needs listed above, there are ten specific methods they use to induce consumer spending:

> "Advertising helps raise the standard of living by raising the standard of longing."

1. Celebrity endorsements

This is the use of well-known stars to endorse and promote products. Consumers associate the purchase with somehow getting closer to the star, or taking on the star's privileged status.

2. Early indoctrination

Advertisers target children at an alarmingly early age for the simple reason that children fall easy prey to deceptive advertising. Additionally, children are highly-persuasive with their parents. Some studies show that when children request a

---

[18] "Hotel California," Eagles, 1977
[19] Some ideas in this section adapted from Martin Lindstrom, *Brandwashed: Tricks Companies Use to Manipulate Our Minds and Persuade Us to Buy* (Crown Business, 2011)

product, parents purchase it more than 40% of the time. Often parents are made to feel morally inferior for not meeting their children's demands.

3. Fear amplification

Advertising preys on public fears of crime, disaster, disease, and economic turmoil. Advertising often amplifies public fear and then promises its alleviation through critical purchases.

4. Gratuitous sexuality

Sexuality is often the most deadly weapon in an advertiser's arsenal. Sexually charged advertising generates almost irresistibly pleasurable associations. Those associations, once embedded in the psyche, exert a kind of hypnotic effect.

5. Habit exploitation

Advertisers leverage consumers' habits, whether healthy or deleterious, against them. Habits are couched as a rightful expression of individuality, or in some way virtuous, and then channeled into consumption.

6. The incorporation of the five senses

The more senses advertisers can bring into their craft the more likely they are to be effective. Advertising which incorporates not just sight and sound but smell or taste is highly-compelling.

7. The implication of moral superiority

Advertisers know that everyone wants to believe that he is morally "good." To exploit this desire advertisers make certain purchases appear to be morally superior to others, such as purchasing a "green" product or making a purchase from which the company donates a portion to charity. This is sometimes called "consumer altruism." In this way, people feel noble as they are consuming.

8. Inciting peer envy

Advertisers create the perception that one must maintain the lifestyle of his peers. The message is that if one falls behind his peers materially, or experientially, one has failed.

9. The revival of nostalgia

Nostalgia is a longing for the past under the often misguided notion that the past is preferable to the present. Advertisers often prey on this longing by linking products to the "good old days."

George Washington at Valley Forge, Thompkins H. Matteson, 1854

10. The use of story-telling

In the postmodern world, people are drawn to stories (probably because they are story-starved by cold and dehumanizing technology). Through attaching a compelling story to a product, that product likely comes to life in the consumer's mind.

The point of this excursus is to show the breadth and depth of perceived need. Need so thoroughly permeates the psyche that it becomes compulsive drives. Through studying the world's manipulation of this sense of need, the Christian is equipped to more fully recognize the extent of his sin, and thus seek repentance. The wise counselor is alert to the themes mentioned here, so as to clearly identify them in the counselee.

The Only Legitimate Need: Relationship with Jesus Christ

Rejection is a tragic outcome of the fall, and for this reason it often brings stinging pain. People, as God's image-bearers, were never designed to experience rejection.

However, for one renewed in Christ, experiencing ever-deepening relationship with him, the pain of rejection is modulated by an unshakeable joy. Hebrews 6:19 states, "We have this hope as an anchor for the soul, firm and secure." The Christian is anchored to an unshakable eternal acceptance, so that earthly rejection loses much of its sting, and all of its terror.

The Old Stagecoach, Jonathan Eastman-Johnson, 1871

> Whatever one thinks he needs will control him. If one's only need is for relationship with God then that is his guide, light, and goal in all things. This makes a dramatic difference in how one lives, as being filled with one's God is the touchstone of abiding freedom - the ability to serve others without regard for oneself.

While there may be an initial shock in rejection, for those deeply connected to Christ there is little aftershock. In other words, those in Christ bounce back quickly to regain their joy. The Christian invests deeply in relationships, while at the same time holding lightly to them, as one who recognizes that Jesus himself is the sole reason for his existence.

> Second Chronicles 1:11, 12 states,
>
> God said to Solomon, 'Since this is your heart's desire and you have not asked for wealth, possessions or honor, nor for the death of your enemies, and since you have not asked for a long life but for wisdom and knowledge to govern my people over whom I have made you king, therefore wisdom and knowledge will be given you. And I will also give you wealth, possessions and honor, such as no king who was before you ever had and none after you

> will have.'
>
> Early in his reign, Solomon exhibited an uncommon immunity from the need for honor among people. At that point in his life, he offered a picture of what it means to be filled with God alone. (However, tragically, Solomon would soon abandon his faith in seeking the pleasure of foreign wives and their gods.[20])

If Jesus is one's only God, all one needs is relationship with him. One only needs to sit at his feet, listen to him, learn from him, and obey him. One can let another hurl insults without responding in kind. One may feel pain from rejection and loss, but does not dwell upon, nor act upon, that pain. One's goal is not to gain others' respect, but simply to glorify God. One can walk away from indignity and remain steady, at peace, filled with joy, needing nothing from people. One can rest that even if forsaken by people, he will never be alone. One can be at peace that even if others do not recognize his gifts, God sees and plans for those he loves. One can trust that God has one's future firmly in hand, and nothing that others think, say, or do can ever take one out of his will.

> "I pray that the eyes of your heart may be enlightened in order that you may know the hope to which he has called you, the riches of his glorious inheritance in his holy people," (Ephesians 1:18)

---

[20] 1 Kings 11:4

WHAT HAS JERUSALEM TO DO WITH VIENNA?:
The Case Against Psychology

> "It appears that psychology has become your '*bete noir*,' the Satan of your position, the appropriator, perverter, and opponent of values [to which] you are committed." (Bruce Johnson)

Setting the Stage for Secular Thought

"Philosophy began on May 28, 585 BC, at 6:13 in the evening."[1] On that date a solar eclipse occurred, temporarily casting Greece into darkness. While there had been numerous eclipses before, this was the first one successfully predicted. The Greek philosopher Thales of Miletus (c. 624 – c. 546 BC) was the first in history to accurately forecast a natural phenomenon. He did it by discerning regularity in nature and formulating a postulate.

Homer and His Guide
William-Adolphe Bouguereau, 1874

It is this prediction which is widely considered the birth of philosophy and science (a single discipline at that time), and Thales of Miletus, the first philosopher-scientist. Before Thales the natural world was explained using myths which personified the universe, giving it anthropopathic attributes. Thales ushered in a tension with ancient Greek myths because for the first time the focus was on empirical evidence. It was no longer solely a theory's narrative qualities, logical coherence, or linguistic beauty which mattered. Now it must possess a measure of predictive power.

---

[1] Gordon Clark, *Thales to Dewey: A History of Philosophy* (The Trinity Foundation, 2000) 19.

> The ancient Greeks extolled the elegance of rhetoric and logic. They found truth in the beauty of well-crafted argument. Yet, they did not countenance a knowable reality, and therefore made truth into a distant abstraction. Truth was only that which was logically persuasive.

While Thales pioneered the use of empiricism and predictive theories he failed to recognize that such investigation never occurs in a vacuum. In this way, science cannot exist alone; it must be coupled with a narrative which gives it framework and meaning. (It would take another 1,800 years for theologians at the Sorbonne in Paris to link empirical investigation with Christianity, so that the correct narrative might finally launch modern science.[2])

When human reason is not grounded in the correct story of the universe it does not function properly. On its own, therefore, it is never a reliable arbiter of truth. If unaided reason were the arbiter of truth, and if reality could be correctly apprehended through the five senses, then mankind must claim omniscience, perfect and complete knowledge of all things. Thus, if the senses rightly assess truth, then man has placed himself in the position of God.

> Yuri Gagarin (1934-1968), Russian cosmonaut, and the first person to reach space, is thought to have said, upon returning to earth on April 14, 1961, "I looked and looked and looked but I didn't see God." (However, most historians believe that Nikita Khrushchev (1894-1971) later fabricated this quote and attributed it to Gagarin.)

Since mankind unaided cannot correctly assess truth, truth must be grounded in a starting point outside of human reason. This is why the Bible is so vital. The Bible provides the correct set of lenses (worldview) to draw into focus reality, mankind, purpose, the acquisition of knowledge, and ethics. Without the Bible, human thought wallows in futile and misguided speculation, oscillating between presuming to know everything and presuming to know nothing.[3] This is the blight of postmodernism, the assertion that there is no authority, no discernable truth, that all knowledge is relative. In summary, truth needs an integration point, or starting point, which only the Bible can provide. Without an authority outside of human reason, mankind is relegated to an endless cycle of futile thinking.

The Gang of Six:[4] Influences on the Growth and Development of Psychology

The growth and development of psychology has been highly influenced by:

1. **Immanuel Kant** (1724-1804). Kant falsely bifurcated knowledge into the "sacred"

---
[2] Stanley Jaki, *The Savior of Science* (Wm. B. Eerdmanns Publishing Co., 2000)
[3] This is called the "rational-irrational dialectic."
[4] The term "gang of six" from Max Stackhouse, Princeton Theological Seminary, Princeton, New Jersey

and the "secular." This formulates an assumed disconnect between the private and the public, the rational and irrational, the objective and subjective, the religious and the scientific. Kant, while believing he was helping to advance the Christian faith, actually did irreparable harm to its inclusion in the public forum. Kant's separation of religious and scientific knowledge is artificial as it fails to understand the religious assumptions upon which science is built.

2. **Charles Darwin** (1809-1882). Darwinism reduced humanity to a mere animal. This often causes people to think and act as animals would. It also causes them to see their existence as meaningless and competition as a life-and-death struggle for survival. Darwinism also brought the unforeseen consequence of spurring on the self-esteem movement as people sought an ennobling counterbalance to their presumed meaningless existence.[5]

The Abduction of Psyche
William-Adolphe Bouguereau,
1895

3. **Karl Marx** (1818-1883). Marx posited that truth should be objective and not subjective. This captures his vision for collectivism which denies validity to the individual. (Incidentally, this has become the model for textbooks. They should contain cold, rational knowledge with nothing of the heart or passions.)

> As one peruses dozens of textbooks, the words that usually come to mind are "tedium" and "monotony." Students almost always describe their textbooks as boring. Textbooks generally do not connect with reality as they present idealized knowledge. They seem to function in a mythical sanitized world devoid of authentic human experience. The textbook is, more often than not, a modern myth – a fanciful fiction of secular humanism.

4. **Friedrich Nietzsche** (1844-1900).[6] Nietzsche infamously wrote that "God is dead." By this he meant that the concept of God is irrelevant to the workings of modern life. This is the posture of modern psychology. The concept of God, while a quaint vestige of primitive mythology, holds no place in the modern understanding of

---

[5] For further exploration of this topic see "The Center Point Theory of Design" in chapter 5: "Redefining the Pygmalion Effect: Exploring the Image of God in Man"

[6] For additional discussion of Friedrich Nietzsche see "The Image of God: Prophet, Priest, and King" in chapter 5: "Redefining the Pygmalion Effect: Exploring the Image of God in Man"

people and the cure of souls.

5. **Sigmund Freud** (1856-1939). Freud destroyed absolute morality by making every moral question into a mere social construct. In fact, Freud's stated purpose was to destroy faith in the Judeo-Christian God, whom he openly despised. With this objective in mind, Freud routinely altered and reinterpreted data to suit his theories.

6. **Thomas Dewey** (1859-1952). Dewey spearheaded pragmatism which does not see the need for broad-based knowledge, but rather focuses on mere practical solutions. This has become the functional posture of modern psychology. It traffics in the pragmatic. But pragmatism always fails because it does not recognize that society is driven by ethos, not utilitarianism.

In summary, Kant falsely separated science and religion. Darwin reduced man to an animal. Marx depersonalized knowledge. Nietzsche explicitly removed the concept of God. Freud destroyed absolute morality and Dewey reduced all matters to pragmatics. Thus, the table was set for modern psychology to arise and flourish.

A Presuppositional Approach to Secular Thought[7]

The Kantian fact-value split sought to separate fact from the theory for understanding that fact. This split wrongly suggests that facts are neutral, existing on their own. However, a correct understanding recognizes that facts can never exist as neutral entities; they must be coupled with a theory. Therefore, facts are always linked to a religious perspective.

Thomas Kuhn's (1922–1996) *The Structure of Scientific Revolutions* (1962) reversed Kant's split by asserting that science and fact arise out of a philosophical or religious view of the universe. Therefore, science is, of necessity, built upon philosophical or religious assumptions. Thus, a particular religious prism refracts both the questions by which science approaches its investigation, and the outcomes which are countenanced. This is a crucial starting point for assessing all human thought (whether scientific or otherwise), the notion that it must of necessity be built upon some religious perspective, a man-centered or God-centered approach.

Crucial Assumptions[8]

1. Only God knows and interprets facts correctly.

---

[7] Adapted from Cornelius Van Til, *Christian Apologetics* (Presbyterian and Reformed Press, 2003)
[8] This entire section from Cornelius Van Til, *Christian Apologetics* (Presbyterian and Reformed Publishing, 2003)

2. The Creation (general revelation), which includes the external (the universe) and internal (the conscience), are wrongly spoken of in abstraction. Any statement about the Creation must be grounded in God's self-revelation to make sense.

3. True information about any subject must be based on the Bible's presentation of creation, fall, and redemption, since this is the nature of reality. Satan's grand deception was to separate situation, reality, and fact from the being of God. Without their Creator, facts become fractured shards with no relationship to one another.

> A student once asked me for counseling. I invited her to study the Bible in order to search for answers. She responded, "I do not deal in fantasy; I live in reality." She has it exactly reversed. Without knowledge of the God of the Bible all is merely delusional fantasy. Conversely, when one is rightly connected to, and reverential toward God, that is reality.

4. Following Satan's lead, mankind relies upon his own flawed sense of logic. He is determined to define reality based upon his own assessment of what is possible or impossible. At the fall, man became a law unto himself; his own will became the ultimate arbiter of all things. In failing to believe that human reason is depraved, man falls easy prey to the trap of thinking that truth lies outside of God's revelation.

5. Mankind is incapable of correctly assessing or defining morality without saving faith in Christ.

At the Rifle Range
James Jacques Joseph Tissot, 1869

> "Do not let them live in the land, or they may cause you to sin again me, because the

worship of their gods will certainly be a snare to you." (Exodus 23:33)

6. Every statement, whether consciously so or not, is a theological statement, because every statement assumes the presence or absence of a holy God. Thus, all secular thought is a clever mask for an errant form of theology. Philosophy, psychology, and even science, must make theological statements at every turn. Even the non-Christian, in his rebellion against God, makes statements with regard to God, revealing his functional position vis-à-vis God.[9] In this way, the sinner attempts to come to terms with his rebellion through his own means. (Remember, Pharaoh's feigned admittance of sin, false repentance, and requested prayer.[10]) Thus, every statement of fact is a profoundly theological statement, whether consciously so or not. It is impossible to be otherwise.

7. Man assumes that his conscience exists to serve himself.

8. Man believes that his understanding of himself, and all of reality, is intelligible without reference to God. This is because mankind makes himself the ultimate reference point. He further thinks that his work of interpretation is original and non-derivative. This is the basis for philosophy, and its next of kin, psychology.

9. There is never neutrality with regard to the truth. Every man-centered method to arrive at the truth presupposes the falsehood of the Christian worldview and functionally makes God into a liar. Thus, to espouse psychology (or philosophy) is to tacitly call God a liar.

10. Any statement of reality is only fact when viewed through the lens of Scripture, since only Scripture can create "facts."

The Agenda Behind Supposed Science

Mentioned previously, Thomas Kuhn's (1922-1996) landmark work, *The Structure of Scientific Revolutions* (1962),[11] paints a vivid picture of the way that science is actually conducted, and in so doing, eventually changed the public perception of science. Kuhn demonstrated that science is not an objective, neutral, or even dispassionate study, but rather is fraught with political, cultural, and worldview distortions.

Kuhn described science as developing throughout history, not through incremental and steady change, but through "revolutions," paradigm shifts. Like all revolutions, scientific revolutions are never ordered or civilized. There is acrimony, threat,

---

[9] For additional discussion of this topic see chapter 6: "Man Before the Face of God: The Imperium of the Psyche"
[10] Exodus 8:8; Exodus 9:27
[11] Thomas Kuhn, *The Structure of Scientific Revolutions* (University of Chicago Press, 1962)

deception, and betrayal as one scientific cabal, invested in the status quo, resists the change sought by a competing group. In the ensuing power struggle one group finally prevails, either maintaining the existing paradigm or adopting a new one. Every paradigm shift from the Copernican, to the Newtonian, to the Einsteinian, involved this power struggle.

What drives a scientific revolution? Data. Scientists gather data, and when that data no longer accords with the prevailing paradigm two possibilities exist. The first is to discard the data as clearly fallacious. The second is to embrace the newly acquired data and build an argument for a new paradigm. This shows that data is never objective or neutral but rather theory-laden. Likewise, its use is subject to the dictates of capricious forces.

In the early 1930s, American oil tycoon John Rockefeller (1839–1937) opposed the New Deal secular progressive welfare system established under then-president Franklin Roosevelt (1882–1945). Rockefeller believed that the government had wantonly imposed a progressive tax structure, one which redistributes wealth from the rich to the poor.

Abandoned
Luigi Nono, 1903

Rockefeller devised an ingenious, if not devious, plan. He launched a new field of study at New York's Rockefeller University called "molecular biology." This field was specifically developed to probe human genetics. Molecular biology sought to peer into the mysterious world of organic life, to uncover its secrets. But Rockefeller was interested in the science only to the extent that it advanced his agenda. He sought to prove the genetic inferiority of criminals, alcoholics, and idiots so as to roll back Roosevelt's progressive socialism. If Rockefeller could prove that certain members of society were genetically inferior, and that for them poverty was inevitable, this would siphon off popular support for the burgeoning socialist wealth redistribution plan.

At about the same time that Rockefeller pioneered microbiology, in Germany Albert Einstein (1879-1955) had risen to international fame for his theories on relativity. His views, considered a cornerstone of physics, gained ascendancy throughout the science world. However, Einstein's philosophical views were at odds with those of another eminent physicist, Niels Bohr (1885-1962) of Denmark. The two bitterly opposed one another. The behind-the-scenes wrangling was not over pure science but over philosophical questions, as Einstein's theories had embedded within them certain presuppositions about determinism and chance. Both Einstein and Bohr understood well that science is never neutral and unbiased, but invariably wedded to worldview.

For a time, Bohr had gained ascendancy, not because his arguments were more persuasive, but because of an invidious political threat. In the 1930s, with the burgeoning influence of Nazism, Germany became perilous for Einstein, a Jew. Einstein's theories were thus attacked, not on their scientific, or even philosophical, merit, but for their supposed "Jewishness." His theories were labeled "Jew science," banned from textbooks, and any scientist who taught them was professionally discredited.[12] Possibly in light of this milieu, Einstein wrote, "Great spirits have always encountered violent opposition from mediocre minds."

Psychology as Purported Science

This discussion of the nature of science has profound impact upon the study of psychology, a pseudoscience which routinely foists its defective wares upon an unwitting populace. For example, study a psychology textbook carefully and one sees the following three-part pattern.[13] The book opens with a supposed scientific discussion on brain chemistry, neurotransmitters, synapses, and the assumed biological machinery behind cognition and perception. This initial discussion hoodwinks the reader into believing that all that follows in the book is based on irrefutable science. Yet, this is its grand charade.

In actuality, the book's assumption that the psyche is reducible to biological mechanisms is itself a religious perspective, reductionism or, more pointedly, scientism. In reality, nothing in the textbook is scientifically arbitrated. The book, from cover-to-cover, is religion camouflaged as science. The book's authors would like the reader to believe that what is presented is neutral and factual, above the fray of philosophical debate. While the text may accurately describe certain biological mechanisms, their supposed connection to the psyche is highly-speculative and eminently biased conjecture, far from irrefutable science.

> The hippocampus is thought to control spatial navigation, memory, and behavioral inhibition. Is behavioral inhibition truly under the control of a brain region? Is what is labeled as "hardwiring," that which is given a supposed chemical signature, in

---

[12] Walter Isaacson, *Einstein: His Life and Universe* (New York: Simon and Schuster, 2007)
[13] David Powlison, Westminster Theological Seminary, Philadelphia, Pennsylvania

actuality a heart worship issue?

Hanging of the Sigismund Bell at the Cathedral Tower in 1521 in Krakow
Jan Matejko, 1874

After its initial chapters such as "A Science of Many Faces," "The Organism as Machine," "Interaction among Nerve Cells," and "The Cerebral Cortex," the textbook explores secondary psychological issues such as "Classical Conditioning," "Behavior Theory and Human Disorders," "The Biological Sources of Aggression," "Social Cognition and Social Reality," and "Unconscious Conflict." The text ends with tertiary issues such as "Childhood Socialization," "The Development of Morality," "Anxiety Disorders," and "Psychotherapy."[14] Thus, the book began with supposed science in order to draw the reader into its camouflaged worship commitments.

Psychology theories, while they purport to be scientific, are not built upon valid science. For an empirical study to be valid science, it must fulfill one criterion: it must be falsifiable.[15] In other words, in order to be true science it must be possible to disprove an assertion. Since psychology theory cannot be proven false, it is not science. For example, Freud's Oedipal complex is not falsifiable and, therefore, is not scientific.

Science is limited to that which is empirically falsifiable, so that only that which can be observed can be verified. In the conflict between psychology and a biblical paradigm, psychology, purporting to be based on science, concocts what it considers to be observable data to suit is paradigm, ignoring data which might corroborate a biblical view. This is a grand conspiracy, if you will, so that the Bible's understanding is abrogated and plundered.

---

[14] These chapter titles from Henry Gleitman, *Basic Psychology*, 2nd ed. (New York: W. W. Norton & Co. 1987)
[15] This is Karl Popper's (1902–1994) "falsificationism" epistemology.

> "The wise will be put to shame; they will be dismayed and trapped. Since they have rejected the word of the LORD, what kind of wisdom do they have? Therefore I will give their wives to other men and their fields to new owners. From the least to the greatest, all are greedy for gain; prophets and priests alike, all practice deceit." (Jeremiah 8:9, 10)

As image-bearer, man often makes empirical observations and conducts experiments. To be correctly understood and applied, those observations and experiments must operate under the auspices of Scripture, so that Scripture dictates the overall understanding, as well as the methods, interpretations, and conclusions that are permitted. In this way, human reason is realigned, reinvigorated, and reformed, as it is shaped by the Bible's understanding of reality. Without the Bible's direction, unaided reason wrongly dictates the methods, interpretation, and conclusions, with dire consequence.

> It has been said that religion is the poor man's psychotherapy; in reality psychotherapy impoverishes the man.

The Christian must arm himself with the truth so as to avoid being deceived by a psychology study's assumptions, assertions of fact, conclusions, and prescriptions for mental health. The wise Christian is aware of exactly what is being foisted upon him, so that he is equipped to expose the study's root assumptions. Likewise, the Christian may, where feasible, reinterpret that study in biblical terms. He lances the deception with the sword of the Spirit so as to draw out the truth.

The Paradigm Shift: Upending Psychology's Hegemony

Kelly Monroe's anthology, *Finding God at Harvard* (1993), contains an essay written by eminent Harvard psychologist, Robert Cole, the story of Cole's conversion.[16] Ruby Bridges, a six year-old black girl living in Louisiana, attended the first grade in 1960. At that time, southern schools were newly desegregated, and Ruby was one of the first students integrated into a predominantly white elementary school.

For the entire school year, Ruby was the only black student in attendance. Each morning as she went to school, and each afternoon as she returned home, Ruby was subject to racial epithets and threats. She was taunted and scorned by a churlish mob. The situation grew so threatening that federal marshals were called in to escort Ruby each day. (Some readers may be familiar with the Norman Rockwell (1894–1978) painting, *The Problem We All Have* (1964), which depicts marshals escorting Ruby to

---
[16] Kelly Monroe, *Finding God at Harvard: Spiritual Journeys of Thinking Christians* (Zondervan Publishing, 1993)

school.)

Hearing about her story, Robert Coles, a world-renowned child psychologist, traveled to Louisiana to study Ruby. Coles interviewed Ruby, asking her questions about her eating and sleeping, her social interaction, study habits, and perspective on life. He expected to see signs of trauma, paralyzing anxiety, difficulty with social adjustment, and emotional scarring. Yet, he was shocked to find her remarkably well-adjusted. She functioned as a quite normal six-year old. She enjoyed play and study time, meaningful interaction with her family and church, and generally showed no adverse effects of the turmoil surrounding her.

Coles was befuddled. Ruby did not fit his paradigm. That which he had expected to see was absent, and that which he did not expect was present. Ruby's parents were committed Christians who, while illiterate, had memorized large sections of the Bible through attentive church attendance. They helped Ruby to pray daily for her tormentors, and instructed her on loving her enemies.[17] She showed an abiding faith in Jesus, one who watched over and protected her. Faith in Christ lent her otherworldly joy and wisdom.

Coles was so flummoxed that he ended up abandoning his psychological models and himself found faith in Christ. Through Ruby, Coles came to recognize that his psychological theories were bankrupt, that they held no power to truly explain people. He was also confronted with the living Jesus who invades hearts, rebuilds lives, and offers a perspective on situations that defies human understanding. In witnessing a life transformed by Jesus, Coles saw his worldview for what it was, a lie.

> "For the message of the cross is foolishness to those who are perishing, but to us who are being saved it is the power of God. For it is written:
>
> 'I will destroy the wisdom of the wise; the intelligence of the intelligent I will frustrate.' Where is the wise person? Where is the teacher of the law? Where is the philosopher of this age? Has not God made foolish the wisdom of the world? For since in the wisdom of God the world through its wisdom did not know him, God was pleased through the foolishness of what was preached to save those who believe. Jews demand signs and Greeks look for wisdom, but we preach Christ crucified: a stumbling block to Jews and foolishness to Gentiles, but to those whom God has called, both Jews and Greeks, Christ the power of God and the wisdom of God. For the foolishness of God is wiser than human wisdom, and the weakness of God is stronger than human strength.
>
> Brothers and sisters, think of what you were when you were called. Not many of you

---

[17] Matthew 5:44

> were wise by human standards; not many were influential; not many were of noble birth. But God chose the foolish things of the world to shame the wise; God chose the weak things of the world to shame the strong. God chose the lowly things of this world and the despised things—and the things that are not—to nullify the things that are, so that no one may boast before him. It is because of him that you are in Christ Jesus, who has become for us wisdom from God—that is, our righteousness, holiness and redemption. Therefore, as it is written: 'Let the one who boasts, boast in the Lord.'" (1 Corinthians 1:18-32)

King Lear and the Fool in the Storm, William Dyce, d. 1864

From God's perspective there are essentially four types of people:

1. Intelligent and wise (fear of God, correctly assessing reality, righteous)
2. Unintelligent and wise
3. Intelligent and foolish (darkened, depraved, holding to a man-centered view of reality)
4. Unintelligent and foolish

The point is that intelligence and wisdom are not synonymous. Christians, like the world, often confuse intelligence with wisdom or, even worse, make intelligence superior to wisdom. Wisdom is of a different ilk, of an otherworldly character, with regard to intelligence.[18]

Robert Coles could best be described as an intelligent fool, one who though ingenious, used his gifts as a weapon against God. He thought himself to possess an unassailable means of diagnosis, a lock on the psyche, but his diagnosis was exposed as a fraud. From God's perspective there could be no détente between the God living within Ruby Bridges and that within Robert Coles, so that while Coles thought that he was in command of his study of Ruby, in fact, it was Ruby, as instrument of Christ, who was dissecting him. Coles was not diagnosing Ruby; Jesus was, through her, diagnosing and confronting him.

> "...tear down arguments and every high barrier that is raised against the knowledge of God to take every thought captive and bring it into obedience to Christ." (2 Corinthians 10:5)

Ruby possessed something far greater than Coles; she understood something of good and evil, right and wrong, and the proper value of life. She was invested with something of the mind of her Creator, so that her assessment of her situation accorded with his. Ruby embodied Luke 21:15, "I will give you words and wisdom that none of your adversaries will be able to resist or contradict."

Should Christianity Engage Psychology in Debate?

A few years ago, I was asked to present biblical counseling to an assembly of pastors and Bible teachers. In outlining the Bible's teaching on creation, fall, and redemption, the group and I were in unanimous agreement. But I knew sparks were about to fly as I opened my polemic against psychology. In presenting this chapter, the group was soon abuzz like a swarm of aggrieved hornets. At the break, one well-intentioned participant advised me to "just stick to the gospel," and not to speak against psychology directly. She felt it was best to let others "put two-and-two together."

Echoing this sentiment, Lyman Beecher (1775-1863) wrote, "Never chase a lie. Leave it alone, and it will run itself to death." Some argue that the church should not directly oppose psychology, but rather state the truth as the Bible does and let listeners arrive at their own conclusions. Truth, when given a proper forum and an honest hearing, will eventually vanquish falsehood and prevail.[19] While there is a measure of truth in

---

[18] For further discussion of the topic of intelligence and wisdom see the excursus "Intelligence versus Wisdom" in chapter 5: "Redefining the Pygmalion Effect: Exploring the Image of God in Man"

[19] While Augustine wrote, "The truth is like a lion. You don't have to defend it. Let it loose. It will defend itself.", I believe that God does call his people, when faced with direct falsehood, to defend truth, to make a case for the truth. For example, Acts 19:26 mentions that Paul, by directly refuting false gods, convinced many in Ephesus. Second Corinthians 10:5 states, "We demolish arguments and every pretension that sets itself up against the knowledge of God..." First Peter 3:15 admonishes believers to "always be prepared to give an answer to everyone who asks..." (Incidentally, this verse is the *locus classicus* for apologetics, the defense of the faith.) The Christian is to defend the faith with direct rebuttal to opposition.

this, and there is certainly wisdom in knowing when to speak and when to be silent. The Bible's overall import is to oppose falsehood directly, not to leave it alone, not to let it rest, lest it multiply and infect. Remember, for example, that God directed plagues toward very specific Egyptian gods.[20] In fact, each plague's form mirrored that of the targeted god so that, to onlookers, the message was undeniable.

Although my advisor meant well, Christians rarely work out the implications of the gospel, so that it remains a compartmentalized abstraction recessed from daily concerns. I am compelled to "connect the dots" since, without direct confrontation, psychology continues to run rampant in the church.

The Bible calls God's people to deal decisively with false gods in their midst. For example, Deuteronomy 7:5, 6 reads,

> This is what you are to do to them: Break down their altars, smash their sacred stones, cut down their Asherah poles and burn their idols in the fire. For you are a people holy to the LORD your God. The LORD your God has chosen you out of all the peoples on the face of the earth to be his people, his treasured possession.

Symbol	Function	Application to Modern Psychology	God's Command
1. Altar	The place where sacrifices were offered	Institutions which maintain psychology's hegemony (media, entertainment, education and government systems)	Break down
2. Sacred stone	Amulets against evil	Popular platitudes and cultural sayings which promise guidance ("believe in yourself"; "God helps those who help themselves"; "seek unconditional love"; "think happy thoughts")	Smash
3. Asherah pole	Carving of a fertility goddess raised on a hill to induce lust	Seductive teaching, the promise of deliverance from guilt (needs theory, self-esteem teaching, theories on human design, the inherent goodness of mankind)	Cut down

---

[20] Exodus 7:14-11:10

| 4. Idol | False gods promising prosperity and protection | Worshipping psychology's "gods" will lead to peace, prosperity, and protection | Burn |

The Deluge, Michelangelo Buonarroti, c. 1512

Certainly Jesus was often silent in the face of hardhearted opposition,[21] and the book of Proverbs never addresses a mocker, but the Bible is generally outspoken in the face of lies. For example, the Genesis creation account was a direct refutation of its contemporary Ugaritic and Akkadian cosmogonies. Thus, the Genesis cosmogony directly targeted opposing worldviews. Additionally, the Genesis flood narrative was directed at the competing Babylonian flood narrative in order to set the record straight. Thus, the Bible, at every turn, meddles in man's thoughts, directly subverting lies and calling believers to do the same. The Christian seeks to expose errant views so as to guard and deliver others from marauding falsehood, which easily nests itself into the heart.

Many Christians, who would otherwise present sound doctrine and a fundamentally accurate understanding of the Bible, fall into grave error with regard to psychology. Christians often accept psychology because they unwittingly acquiesce to the Kantian fact-value split. Additionally, they may fall into error on account of an unwillingness to be sanctified. Thus, those who love sin (to one degree or another) make themselves vulnerable to error.[22]

> "The Spirit clearly says that in later times some will abandon the faith and follow deceiving spirits and things taught by demons." (1 Timothy 4:1)

---

[21] John 19:10
[22] For additional discussion of this topic see chapter 9: "Integrationism: The Modern Day Babylonian Captivity"

The Christian's stated theology and his functional theology are often wildly discordant,[23] and it is in the context of psychology that that error most vigorously draws itself out. In other words, it is in the interface with psychology that the Christian's functional theology is revealed, that worship commitments are brought to light.

Daniel 1:18-20 records,

> At the end of the time set by the king to bring them in, the chief official presented them to Nebuchadnezzar. The king talked with them, and he found none equal to Daniel, Hananiah, Mishael and Azariah; so they entered the king's service. In every matter of wisdom and understanding about which the king questioned them, he found them ten times better than all the magicians and enchanters in his whole kingdom.

As with Daniel and his friends, Christians must demonstrate that the Bible is far more effective than psychology in understanding the human plight, and in effecting deliverance from that plight. If Christianity offers a cogent and compelling form of counsel it will, in theory, win the world to faith in Christ. (Of course, the Holy Spirit must do this work.)

Psychology as Competing Religion

The Vienna Circle, formed in 1922 in Vienna, Austria, was based on Ludwig Wittgenstein's (1889-1951) concept of logical positivism. Logical positivism was an attempt to present science completely free from an orienting philosophy or theology. The Vienna Circle eventually dissolved, haunted by the scepter that it is impossible for any study to be free from an under-girding philosophy or theology.

While psychology seeks to cloak itself with logical positivism, it is clearly not a pure science, nor even loosely based on science. Rather it is a religious perspective, a set of fundamental beliefs about God and man which is engaged in a life and death struggle with Christianity.[24] It is crucial to understand that nothing is neutral, regardless of how it presents itself. Every fact necessarily brings with it a religious perspective so that nothing is merely objective observation. Just as the eyes and heart are inextricably linked, so too, fact and worldview are inextricably linked.

Any perspective on people, their problems and solutions, necessarily answers

---

[23] For further discussion of the distinction between stated and functional theology see "The Herod Effect" in the second book in this series, *What Agreement Is There Between the Temple of God and Idols?: The Accidence of Sin and Idolatry*, chapter 8: "The Search for Eldorado Ends: Repenting of Idols of the Heart"
[24] David Powlison, Westminster Theological Seminary, Philadelphia, Pennsylvania

profoundly religious questions:

1. Who is man?
2. What is normal?
3. What is abnormal?
4. Who is God?
5. What is good and evil?
6. What is man's deepest problem?
7. What is the solution to that problem?

Psychology, at every turn, must answer these questions in every last corner of every theory; it is hopelessly conscribed to these questions. For this reason, psychology does not just describe people, it seeks to shape them. It has an agenda to cause people to dutifully consent to certain false views about themselves and their surroundings. Its purpose is not just descriptive but prescriptive. It is in this regard, that psychology promulgates a certain Luciferian agenda, offering supposed illumination for the masses.

Panorama with the Abduction of Helen Amidst the Wonders of the Ancient World
Maerten van Heemskerck, 1535

The Religious Components of Select Philosophies

Category	Christianity	Buddhism	Marxism
1. **History** – the grounding for the religion; a comprehensive story	Creation, Fall, Redemption	Non-existence	Evolution; brutal struggle for survival; upward surge through conflict
2. **Sacred text** – an authoritative text	Bible	*Tripitaka, Sutras*	*The Communist Manifesto* (1848)
3. **Savior** – the	Jesus Christ	Guatama Buddha	Karl Marx

enlightened founder		(c. 6th C. BC)	(1818-1883)
4. **Evil** – the enemy of the enlightened founder	Satan	Desire	Capitalism; democracy
5. **Sin** – what is forbidden or considered complicit with evil	Rebellion against a holy God	Committing wrong actions	Ownership (to be among the bourgeoisie)
6. **Good news** – the central message of salvation	Freedom from sin through repentance	Nihilism as the desired end of man	Utopia through man's inherent goodness
7. **Prophets** – those who speak the truth and provide meaning	Those who call for repentance	Those who deny God's existence	Revolutionaries of class warfare
8. **Priests** – those who comfort and make the religion attractive	Those who show mercy with rich displays of charity and grace	Temple monks	A social welfare system
9. **Evangelists/ missionaries** – those who bring the Good news to distant people			A propaganda machine
10. **Conversion** – what it means to receive the good news	Receive Jesus into one's heart as personal savior	Enlightenment through freedom from desire	Renouncing ownership

Category	Evolution	Psychology	Corporations
1. History	Nothingness produced unimaginable complexity	**Evolution; mankind as temporal, material being with no eternal referent**	The corporation's struggle to succeed; great "military" victories; the altruism of its intent and mission
2. Sacred text	Fossils interpreted in accordance with Darwin's *On the Origin of Species* (1859); scientific journals	**Greek philosophy; psychology journals, *DSM IV***	The corporation's creed or purpose statement
3. Savior	Chaos over time can produce almost miraculous results	**Sigmund Freud (1856-1939) and others**	The corporation's founder lionized as a beneficent provider to his

			employees
4. Evil	The idea of purposed or created design	**The Christian God and his moral absolutes**	Government regulation on free markets; media scrutiny
5. Sin	Asserting a superior position to mankind; that mankind was given stewardship or responsibility for the creation	**Espousing moral absolutes or making guilt an actuality with regard to a holy God; presenting the need for repentance and faith in Jesus Christ**	Not sacrificing for the company's mission
6. Good news	There is no Creator, no design, and no moral absolutes. Mankind is merely an animal and therefore free from enslaving religious dogma.	**One can manage his "demons" through self-help, psychotropic medication, or psychotherapy**	One can be financially secure, achieve lasting happiness and freedom, if one devotes all to the corporation
7. Prophets	Charles Darwin (1809-1882), biologists	**Psychology researchers, psychiatrists**	Dale Carnegie (1888-1955); Anthony Robins or any motivational speaker (often co-opting biblical salvation language)
8. Priests	Psychologists, sociologists	**Psychotherapists**	The Human Resources department which cares for employee needs, blindly accepts, and imposes no moral standard
9. Evangelists/ missionaries	Educators, media	**Educators, media**	Salesmen, advertising
10. Conversion	The realization that one is an accident of	**The realization that one is not**	Belief in the company's mission

| | closed cold natural phenomena | **morally responsible, that one is essentially a victim** | and entirely devoting oneself to it. |

The Religious Components of Psychology

Each psychology:[25]

1. Has its own clergy, luminaries who are its credentialed practitioners

2. Holds forth a false gospel, a means for attaining its definition of salvation

> Psychologist B.F. Skinner's (1904–1990) novel, *Walden II* (1948), offers a utopian vision in which the hero is a Christ-like figure whose "gospel" message is salvation through behavioral engineering. Skinner's objective was to sketch out a kind of heaven on earth.

3. Has its prophets (meaning-makers, and truth-tellers), priests (the consoling and inviting face of the discipline, its comforters), and kings (those who wield cultural and legal authority)

4. Offers a liturgy (a form of corporate worship), saints (heroes), and testimonies (those who have been converted)

5. Exalts its own theologians, those who serve as architects and visionaries for the discipline

The word "doctor" derives from the Latin word *doctorus*, meaning "teacher." In ancient times a doctor educated patients concerning health issues and offered advice on remedies. This is the posture of the psychologist, not merely as a practitioner or "technician" of the psyche, but as a worldview indoctrinator. Psychologists have in effect become secular priests and pastors who seek to cure souls, secular prophets and theologians defining what is true and right in man-centered terms, as well as secular kings ruling through institutions and governing bodies maintaining hegemonic control over society.[26]

> Analytic psychologist Carl Jung (1875-1961) wrote, "Show me a sane man and I will cure him for you." Son of a Swiss Reformed pastor, Jung spoke about the place of myth and religious ritual in the self-understanding, and eventual healing, of the

---

[25] The idea for this section from Edward Welch, Westminster Theological Seminary, Philadelphia, Pennsylvania
[26] This general idea from David Powlison, Westminster Theological Seminary, Philadelphia, Pennsylvania

> counselee. Jung saw religious expression as a shared unconsciousness or collective unconsciousness. Religion, thus, functions as a kind of socially-derived persona or social mask. Jung postulated that people need this religious meaning, a soul-directed purpose, and therefore psychotherapists offer their own brand of religion as priests preaching a theology.

In essence psychology has taken over the function of the church community (relationship for the purpose of growth in holiness), pastor (visionary, teacher), and theologian (academician, researcher). Psychology has usurped the church's authority in analyzing and counseling people. Tragically, the church has peacefully acquiesced, relinquishing the cure of souls to psychology under a misguided capitulation to supposed science and the mystery of chemical-based psychotropic medicine.

The Four Philosophers
Peter Paul Rubens, 1612

> "Woe to those who draw sin along with cords of deceit, and wickedness as with cart ropes..." (Isaiah 5:18)

Psychology's Chief Purpose

Mankind is held captive to one all-consuming obsession, to be free from his guilt before a holy God. This has been man's intent subsequent to the first rebellion.[27] As each desperately seeks to quell the guilt of sin, psychology is a convenient means to falsely exonerate the conscience, affording mankind a shield (a means of deflecting blame) and sword (a means of installing oneself as his own god) in his war against God. From the Bible's perspective, therefore, psychology is nothing more than a deliberate man-made attempt to shift blame for sin and deify mankind. While the

---

[27] Genesis 3:7

various branches of psychology finds unique ways to effect this goal, each shares a singular focus in its intent to both exonerate and glorify the sinner.

> "The wrath of God is being revealed from heaven against all the godlessness and wickedness of men who suppress the truth by their wickedness, since what may be known about God is plain to them, because God has made it plain to them. For since the creation of the world God's invisible qualities—his eternal power and divine nature—have been clearly seen, being understood from what has been made, so that men are without excuse. For although they knew God, they neither glorified him as God nor gave thanks to him, but their thinking became futile and their foolish hearts were darkened." (Romans 1:18-21)

Since through psychology's means and efforts the sinner tries in vain to solve a profoundly God-centered problem with worthless man-centered answers, psychology ultimately renders its patients far worse off. Additionally, psychology ultimately hardens its adherents against the gospel so that they are blinded to the reality of sin and their desperate need for salvation. Psychology always fails in the long-term because there can be no freedom from guilt except through the vicarious atonement of Jesus Christ upon the cross.

> "The god of this age has blinded the minds of unbelievers, so that they cannot see the light of the gospel that displays the glory of Christ, who is the image of God." (2 Corinthians 4:4)

One of psychology's core assumptions is that to understand the psyche one must begin with the individual's experience, an experience which deterministically defines him. Thus, for psychology personal experience is the starting point for all discussion of meaning, truth, reasonability, and purpose. In exalting personal experience, psychology defines that experience in any way that it desires, emphasizing certain facets and dignifying those aspects which it deems noble. However, human experience is an open book fervently in need of meaning, impoverished except through tools of interpretation which only God can provide. In glorifying human experience, psychology becomes little more than a quest without a terminus, an ill-defined process with little sense of meaningful resolution. Thus, psychology does not know when it has arrived, or even to what it is arriving. In the absence of absolute truth, it can assume any stance, take on any cause, and assign any meaning, with no sense of having really accomplished anything (except to oppose the gospel – the one premise it vies against and refuses to tolerate).

> "All the counsel you have received has only worn you out! Let your astrologers come forward, those stargazers who make predictions month by month, let them save you from what is coming upon you." (Isaiah 47:13)

The Death of Hippolytus, Lawrence Alma Tadema, 1860

Infiltrating the "Normal"

According to *The New York Times* article, "Valium's Contribution to Our New Normal,"[28] psychotropic drugs are increasingly used on what might typically be termed "normal people" to induce particular moods or emotions, or to hedge against potential anxieties. What is particularly alarming is that psychotropic drugs are now being used on well-adjusted *children* with alarming frequency for the same reasons. According to sociologist Peter Kramer, modern America has now entered an era of "cosmetic psychopharmacology," the assumption that every undesirable behavior can be medicated away. Understanding the behavior itself has become meaningless.[29]

> "Woe to those who call evil good and good evil, who put darkness for light…Woe to those who are wise in their own eyes and clever in their own sight." (Isaiah 5:20a, 21)

The terms "normal" and "abnormal" are not merely descriptive; they are prescriptive. They not only describe what is, but prescribe what should be. It is fascinating that at its advent, psychology was devised to treat the clinically insane, but today it is applied

---

[28] Robin Marantz Henig, "Valium's Contribution to Our New Normal," *The New York Times*, September 29, 2012. This article offers a brilliant discussion of the way in which psychotropic drugs are increasingly used on "normal" people to forge a new normal of human experience and behavior.
[29] Paul Wender and Donald Klein, "The Promise of Biological Psychiatry," *Psychology Today* (August, 1978): 55.

to those considered normal. Psychology has expanded its reach from the most psychologically troubled to those who generally function well in society.[30] Psychology, as fundamentally predatory, seeks to dominate evermore aspects of society and, in so doing, functions as a de facto arbiter, evaluator, and visionary for human experience.

> Psychology has installed itself as the arbitrator of normal and abnormal, and in so doing has deified itself over creation, defining for itself that which is rightly defined by God alone.

The Bible defines normal and abnormal in drastically different terms than the psychologist would. For this reason, the Bible's definition of "cure" (repentance and faith) is completely antithetical to that offered by psychology. In fact, what the Bible calls cure the psychologist might label as "psychosis." Conversely, what the psychologist might label as normal, the Bible would label as abnormal (operating contrary to God's design and will).

Is it normal to wear a tattoo? Is it normal to engage in premarital sex? Is it normal to tell a white lie? Is it normal to be anxious while speaking in front of an audience? Is it normal to gossip? Is it normal to return insult for insult? What psychology might label as normal (proper human function) the Bible might label as abnormal (deviant human function), the mark of a sinful response to one's world, defiance of God and his standards.

Psychology bases normalcy upon a humanly-derived understanding of reality, not upon God's absolute immutable standard. The logical fallacy in psychology is that that which it calls normal (commonly accepted) becomes equivalent to *normative* (morally acceptable).[31] If society as a whole condones certain activity, likewise, psychology views that activity as acceptable (such as cohabitation, a tattoo, social drunkenness, an extramarital affair, etc.). Thus, psychology tracks along in lockstep with society.

For example, if most young men view pornography then it is a common activity, but certainly not normative from God's perspective. However, psychology conflates the common with the normative or permissible, labeling that which is abhorrent and destructive as tolerable or even healthy. From the Bible's perspective normal (what is common) is not coterminous with normative (what should be). However, since psychology shows low viscosity (maybe non-viscosity) with regard to moral categories, it simply defines normal morality in term of societal trends and popular opinion. With no moral pith, psychology ends up as an amorphous sludge.

---

[30] Robin Marantz Henig, "Valium's Contribution to Our New Normal," *The New York Times*, September 29, 2012.
[31] Jay Adams, *Competent to Counsel: Introduction to Nouthetic Counseling* (Zondervan Publishing, 1970)

> Proverbs 6:6-8 reads, "Go to the ant, you sluggard; consider its ways and be wise! It has no commander, no overseer or ruler, yet it stores its provisions in summer and gathers its food at harvest." The Bible would label laziness as sin, the wanton presumption of provision from a holy God. An evolutionary psychologist might explain laziness as an instinctual survival tactic devised to conserve energy. In this way, a human vice is excused as nothing more than natural instinct. This is a classic example of the way in which psychology normalizes that which God calls abnormal.

Excursus: Psychology Reads Like a Hollywood Movie Script[32]

I contend that psychology and Hollywood (the media and entertainment industries) are cut from the same cloth, pursuing the same ends. Their worldviews track precisely, as each wields an agenda to foist upon society a preset narrative of what humanity ought to be. In the case of psychology, that narrative has absolutely nothing to do with objective study or empirical evidence. It is entirely the product of a false religious system or political agenda, whose singular purpose is to oppose Christianity.

Consider the fact that Hollywood movies have built into their story-telling device a particular prepackaged bias. That bias follows in lockstep with a liberal secular progressive agenda. The agenda is this: disparage traditional Christianity, mock absolute morality, and shame supposed imperialist aggressors (of whom the chief is Jesus Christ). In its storytelling, Hollywood presents children, women, minorities, and homosexuals (those outside of traditional power structures), as wise, beneficent, and enlightened.[33] This bias shows up time and again, either directly or indirectly, propositionally or tacitly. In fact, the secular progressive bias is so pervasive that most do not even notice it; it has simply become background noise, the expected outworking of plotlines.

Hollywood makes human rebellion appear justified, and ultimately victorious, as it showcases a liberal secular progressive agenda in all its flaunt and flourish. Psychology and Hollywood support and embolden one another, most pointedly in their unsparing assault upon a Christian worldview, and its absolute morality. Hollywood advances and celebrates psychology's agenda, to deflect guilt before a holy God and to install oneself as his own god. In this way, psychology and Hollywood read from the same script.

> A recent online psychology article speculated on why wives commit adultery. In

---

[32] For further discussion of this topic see "The World's Handmaiden: Hollywood" in the second book in this series, *What Agreement Is There Between the Temple of God and Idols?: The Accidence of Sin and Idolatry*, chapter 2: "The World, the Flesh, and the Devil: Assessing the Threat Matrix"

[33] Michael Medved, *Hollywood vs. America: Popular Culture and the War on Traditional Values* (New York: Harper Collins, 1992)

every instance, the direct or indirect reason given was a failing on the part of the husband to meet perceived needs within his wife (whether relational, emotional, or sexual). Without fail, the wife was presented as a helpless victim, justified in pursuing an adulterous affair that met her supposed needs. Invariably, the husband was the presumed party at fault, the one who, through wayward neglect or pernicious intent, brought about a tacitly abusive situation.

The Mimicry of the Kleptoparasite

Birds of America - Virginian Partridge (plate 76), John Audubon, 1825

The Botswana forked-tailed drongo, a bird of the Kalahari Desert, is the "pathological liar" of the animal kingdom, brazenly deceiving other animals by mimicking the alarm calls of numerous species which act as sentries. The objective is to falsely warn of a supposed approaching predator in a ruse to steal abandoned food. In an elaborate scheme, the drongos mimic the alarm sounds made by as many as fifty different species that inhabit the Kalahari, sometimes signaling danger when it genuinely exists, and at other times when it does not.

The reason the ruse works is that the drongos do at times provide reliable alarms. This maintains host responsiveness since animals can never know if the drongo is deceiving or not. Drongos have adapted masterfully in knowing which signals bamboozle which hosts most effectively. What's more, they continually vary their technique to keep their targeted victims guessing.[34]

---

[34] Will Dunham, "Liar! Liar! African Bird Uses Elaborate Ruse to Steal Food," *Reuters,* May 1, 2014

The drongo's tactics bear remarkable similarity to those of secular psychology. Like the drongo, psychology could be thought of as mimicking the truths of God, sometimes sounding "alarms" which have some merit, but often warning of phantom predators. Like the drongo, psychology also assumes various "voices," tailored to the particular host, assuming whichever voice will effectively capture the attention of a cultural milieu or socio-economic group.

This leads us to three principle descriptors for psychology:

1. **Predatory**.[35] Just as a predator actively seeks out and kills prey, psychology seeks to attack and destroy God's truth for the purpose of placing people into bondage to falsehood. In a cunning maneuver, psychology borrows God's own "intellectual capital" to assail his created order.

2. **Parasitic**. The purpose of a parasite is to siphon life from a vector, to feed at the expense of the host, to rob life. Psychology's observations and truth claims feed off of the truth.

3. **Poisonous**. Poison is often injected subcutaneously or ingested under the guise of life-giving medicine. As poison, psychology is essentially a grand deception which promises life, but brings death. Incidentally, this metaphor could be made more specific; psychology could be compared to hydrocyanic acid, a compound so dangerous because its poisonous effect is largely undetectable to the victim. (In a case of Shakespearean irony, hydrocyanic acid is a precursor to compounds found in most common pharmaceuticals.[36])

> One idea proposed to combat cancer is to engineer synthetic viruses which would target and attack cancer cells. The plan is to program viruses, using human genome mapping, to avoid healthy tissue and eradicate cancerous ones. This type of science, while it in theory seems ingenious and beneficent, is actually a catastrophe in the making. A similar analogy could be drawn with psychology, seemingly ingenious remedies, but a psychic calamity crouching in wait.

Thus, psychology is best thought of as all three metaphors acting simultaneously – predator (rapacious and contentious toward the truth), parasite (siphoning off life), and poison (inducing and exacerbating what it terms "mental illness" through its own calumny).

> "…in order that Satan might not outwit us. For we are not unaware of his schemes." (2 Corinthians 2:11)

---

[35] The term "predatory" borrowed from Sharon Covington, Biblical Counselor
[36] Wikipedia article "Hydrogen Cyanide"; see the discussion below on the dangers of pharmaceuticals

Psychology and Evolution[37]

The following chart explains two theological concepts, general revelation and special revelation:

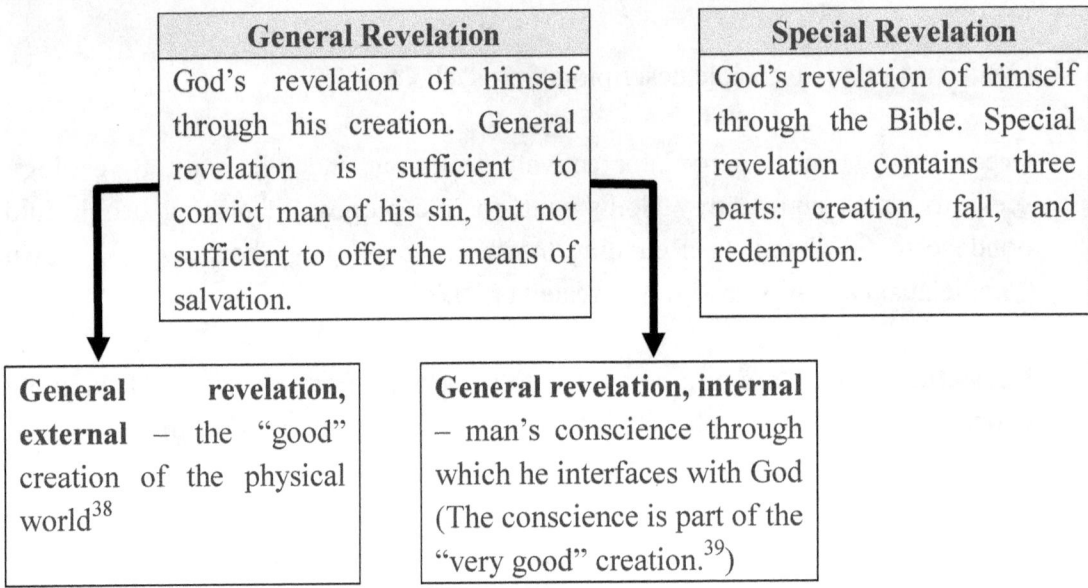

General Revelation	Special Revelation
God's revelation of himself through his creation. General revelation is sufficient to convict man of his sin, but not sufficient to offer the means of salvation.	God's revelation of himself through the Bible. Special revelation contains three parts: creation, fall, and redemption.

General revelation, external – the "good" creation of the physical world[38]	**General revelation, internal** – man's conscience through which he interfaces with God (The conscience is part of the "very good" creation.[39])

One might think of general revelation as the backdrop against which man's character could be displayed. General revelation is carefully designed to serve as a clear statement of God's goodness to man, and it offers the raw materials by which man might show his appreciation to God. However, in sin, mankind looks upon general revelation as a godless theater, and likewise, uses the general revelation as a weapon against God.

The theory of evolution principally attacks the knowledge of God through his external general revelation (the physical creation). Psychology principally attacks the knowledge of God through his internal general revelation (the conscience). In this way, the theory of evolution and psychology work in tandem. If evolution can convince mankind to deny the evidence of God around him, and psychology can convince him to deny the evidence of God within him, then sin can flourish unopposed.

However, evolution and psychology do not stop with just an attack on general revelation. They both attack the Bible, God's special revelation. Evolution's assault upon special revelation is largely limited to the creation account. Psychology then pinpoints the two remaining aspects of the Bible's teaching, the fall and redemption. Psychology indirectly, but forcefully, assails the Bible's teaching on sin and salvation

---

[37] For additional discussion of evolution see the case study: "The Ultimate Refutation of Evolution" in chapter 4: "The Gospel as Inception Point: From Immorality to Immortality"
[38] Genesis 1
[39] Genesis 1:31

so that psychology falsely assuages the guilty conscience (internal general revelation) and undermines the gospel with a false message of salvation.

Evolution perpetrates more macro-destruction to the belief in a holy Creator and his absolute morality. (In this way, evolution functions like a broad spectrum "antibiotic" of scientific materialism.) Psychology perpetrates more micro-destruction to the revelation of God through humanity's internal condition. (In this way, psychology functions like a "surgical" technique, or a personalized scientific materialism.) While evolution targets humanity's cosmic position and identity, psychology targets the human condition and psyche. Operating as complements, evolution and psychology offer a formidable front in Satan's battle offensive.

Attack upon:	The Theory of Evolution	Psychology
General Revelation	Attacks the knowledge of God in the external general revelation	Attacks the knowledge of God in the internal general revelation (the conscience)
Special Revelation	Targets special revelation's creation account (man's identity as image-bearer)	Targets special revelation's teaching on the fall (sin) and redemption (salvation)

The Art of Deception

Matthew 13:24-30 recounts the Parable of the Weeds,

> The kingdom of heaven is like a man who sowed good seed in his field. But while everyone was sleeping, his enemy came and sowed weeds among the wheat, and went away. When the wheat sprouted and formed heads, then the weeds also appeared.
>
> The owner's servants came to him and said, 'Sir, didn't you sow good seed in your field? Where then did the weeds come from?'

The Harvester
William Adolphe Bouguereau, 1868

'An enemy did this,' he replied.

> The servants asked him, 'Do you want us to go and pull them up?'
>
> 'No,' he answered, 'because while you are pulling the weeds, you may root up the wheat with them. Let both grow together until the harvest. At that time I will tell the harvesters: First collect the weeds and tie them in bundles to be burned; then gather the wheat and bring it into my barn.'

The weeds spoken of are the bearded darnel (a variety of rye grass), a plant that looks remarkably like wheat. In fact, it is almost indistinguishable from wheat until the fruit appears (the seed pod). (Remember, Jesus admonished that one would know a person by his fruit.[40]) The bearded darnel's seed is actually poisonous. Additionally, the darnel intertwines its roots with those of the wheat making it parasitic to the wheat.[41] Thus, the directive was given to let both grow together until the harvest.

Matthew 13:36-43 continues,

> Then he left the crowd and went into the house. His disciples came to him and said, 'Explain to us the parable of the weeds in the field.'
>
> He answered, 'The one who sowed the good seed is the Son of Man. The field is the world, and the good seed stands for the people of the kingdom. The weeds are the people of the evil one, and the enemy who sows them is the devil. The harvest is the end of the age, and the harvesters are angels.
>
> As the weeds are pulled up and burned in the fire, so it will be at the end of the age. The Son of Man will send out his angels, and they will weed out of his kingdom everything that causes sin and all who do evil. They will throw them into the blazing furnace, where there will be weeping and gnashing of teeth. Then the righteous will shine like the sun in the kingdom of their Father. Whoever has ears, let them hear.'

While this parable is intended as a warning concerning those who are "people of the evil one," it could also apply to Satan's works. Like the darnel, Satan's works, "everything that causes sin and all who do evil," masquerade as good fruit, when in reality seeking to destroy the good fruit. Also notice that the darnel intertwines its roots with the wheat so that it is impossible to pull up the darnel without damaging the wheat. Only at harvest time can the two be distinguished. Thus, psychology, as parasite, intertwines its root system with that of the truth, taking on the appearance of truth, so that the undiscerning are easily beguiled. The wise counselor, thus, seeks to

---

[40] Matthew 7:16
[41] Matthew 13:29

unbraid these root systems that a harvest might ensue.

Jason Carrying the Golden Fleece, Erasmus Quellinus II, d. 1678

"Half the truth is often the greatest lie."

On account of sin, no one naturally thinks about himself in a God-centered way.[42] Thus, it is easy for man-centered approaches, under the cloak of psychology, to deceive because the heart desperately craves such approaches. Under the tyranny of indwelling sin, unaided human reason always bends data to support faulty diagnoses, the assertion of false norms, and invalid conclusions. Likewise, it prescribes a course of action in line with its sinful distortions of the truth.[43] Human reason, under psychology's influence, often mimics good fruit but, in reality, feasts upon and, in turn, cultivates, fatal fruit. In this way, psychology mints functional atheists, those who may culturally ascent to sound Christian doctrine, but daily live out a godless view of themselves and others.

"Turn my heart toward your statutes and not toward selfish gain. Turn my eyes away

---

[42] David Powlison, "Which Presuppositions? Secular Psychology and the Categories of Biblical Thought," *Journal of Psychology and Theology* 12.4 (Winter, 1984): 278.
[43] David Powlison, "Which Presuppositions? Secular Psychology and the Categories of Biblical Thought," *Journal of Psychology and Theology* 12.4 (Winter, 1984): 276.

from worthless things; preserve my life according to your word." (Psalm 119:36, 37)

Psychology's Labels

There is a dark secret nestled within all secular institutions and disciplines. Keep as many as possible on the outside of the discipline's discussion so that it can be controlled by an elite intellectual oligarchy which has mastered, and continually shapes, the desired terms and arguments. This oligarchy makes simple concepts as complex as possible, since intellectual intimidation and confusion maintains control.

One of psychology's most effective tactics (indeed, that of any secular academic study) is to use confusion as a principle means of inculcation. An inner cabal of the discipline's architects keeps trade terminology as esoteric and as incomprehensible as possible. If the public is always somewhat lost as to the meaning of key concepts, it cannot argue against them and, thus, it tends to passively acquiesce to the terms of discussion imposed upon it. Thus, a bourgeois intellectual mentality keeps counseling under the direction of an elite few who have positioned themselves as recognized scientific practitioners.

One of psychology's principle tools for inculcation is its labels for the psyche. Those labels are contrived and fluid, offering the appearance of careful scientific investigation, when in reality they are false labels.[44] It is worth noting that those labels continue to multiply so that more and more of the human experience comes under a psychological label. This allows psychology to maintain ever broadened and tightened control over society, further muscling out competing worldviews (such as Christianity).

Psychology's labels for the psyche's plights:

1. **Addiction** – a chemical imbalance which leads to extreme and uncontrollable behavior

Increasingly the term "addiction" is used to describe just about any compulsive behavior, so that even behaviors which are not driven by physiology are labeled as addiction.[45]

2. **Condition** – deviant behavior which arises on account of circumstances

3. **Disease** – supposed mental illness that one presumably "catches"

---

[44] David Powlison, Westminster Theological Seminary, Philadelphia, Pennsylvania
[45] Michael Bobick, *From Slavery to Sonship: A Biblical Psychology for Pastoral Counseling* (1995) 41. (class notes)

> Psychiatry's principle text, the *DSM IV-R*, continually adds to and alters the diagnoses and labels of human behavior and conditions.

The term "disease" is well marked-out territory in the healthcare industry. As soon as a health condition is labeled a disease it comes under the auspices of the medical profession, and it becomes illegal for anyone outside of that profession to claim to cure it. In the same way that FDA approval is a weapon of economic war in the pharmaceutical industry, so too, the term disease could be thought of as a weapon of intellectual and economic war used to control public perception and ultimately the marketplace.[46]

4. **Disorder** – a genetic deviation within one's DNA

> I predict that cell phone use (namely texting) will soon be officially labeled a "disorder" or "syndrome" in which the afflicted craves constant affirmation as well as a means for the alleviation of fear. (The cell phone has become a ready escape-hatch from the fear of one's immediate company.) Such an example shows the growing trend toward "boutique" afflictions, those which promise to excuse everyday moral failings.

5. **Syndrome** – a disease or abnormal condition that develops through repeated behavior

These labels are heavily invested in a reductionistic worldview, and yet they are highly-charged worship markers. As such, these categories directly contradict biblical descriptions.

Psychology holds forth the illusion that simply labeling or identifying aspects of the psyche somehow represents a viable cure. While psychology may identify isolated aspects of the human personality (sometimes with a measure of accuracy), that mere identification does not adequately explain, diagnose, or reverse the underlying drivers. Psychology's labels set up baskets of symptoms which then masquerade as diagnosis when in reality none has been offered. For example, simply identifying low self-esteem (itself a false category) does not offer a corrective analysis. Thus, psychology plays a masterful shell-game in which mere *identification* is given the appearance of *cure*.

Additionally, psychology's descriptions and labels are concocted based on its own flawed understanding of people. What is the basis for labels such as "schizophrenic," "bipolar," or simply "mentally ill"? Would a person be labeled in the same way from

---

[46] Kevin Trudeau, *Natural Cures They Don't Want You to Know About* (Alliance Publishing Group, 2006)

one culture to another, or from one period in history to another?[47] Psychology's labels, driven by societal expectations and values, continually shift to meet society's perceived needs. Such diagnoses are not universally applicable and, therefore, are not absolutely true of the human condition. Further, through erroneous labels, psychology can actually fabricate phantom symptoms that may not have surfaced otherwise.

Ruling Passion, John Everett Millais, 1885

> Revealed truth has been exchanged for humanistic philosophy with a resulting loss of rationality. Psychology has exchanged God and his holiness for a false god and a deviant morality with a subsequent loss of guilt. Likewise, it has exchanged "creaturehood" (image-bearer) for autonomy with a subsequent loss of meaning.

Psychological ailments might have been viewed very differently in Victorian Europe as opposed to early 20th century America. The Victorians might have attributed depression to anhedonia, the inability to experience pleasure from an activity that might otherwise be considered pleasurable. (The reason is that the Victorians were expected to exercise control over their emotions; one was to display self-discipline above all else.) In early 20th century America, that same depression might be linked to hysteria, the tendency to let emotions gain full expression.[48]

---

[47] Philip Cushman, *Constructing the Self, Constructing America: A Cultural History of Psychotherapy* (New York: Addison-Wesley Publishing Co., 1995) 134–138.
[48] Philip Cushman, *Constructing the Self, Constructing America: A Cultural History of Psychotherapy* (New York: Addison-Wesley Publishing Co., 1995) 134–138.

Just as, historically, psychology's descriptions varied based on time in history and cultural milieu, so too, psychological labels can vary considerably based on situation. The issue of situational drivers for labels reveals that such labels are highly-subjective and blind to deeper heart issues. For example, in certain situations one might be labeled an introvert and, in others, an extrovert. It all depends upon what one worships at that moment.

Select Psychology Concepts

Christians are largely unaware of which terms and concepts come from psychology and which are genuinely biblical. The following select list of psychology terms is offered to alert Christians to concepts which they unwittingly adopt and then assimilate into their faith.

Concept	The Biblical Response
1. Hierarchy of needs[49]	The concept of inherent needs is a ready path to slavery, disillusionment, manipulation, and depression as one finds himself controlled by what he thinks he needs.
2. Self-esteem[50]	Self-esteem is a euphemism for self-pride.
3. Self-actualization[51]	The quest for self-actualization is essentially the relentless pursuit of one's perceived needs. This is the recipe for psychic pain and depression.
4. Self-love[52]	No one ever needed to be instructed in how to love himself.[53] This is natural to all sinners and a major source of interpersonal strife.
5. Unconditional love[54]	Unconditional love foists upon humanity a weak and pale form of love that blindly tolerates that which should be condemned, forsaking a God-centered form of love in the process.
6. The hydraulic view of emotions	This theory arises from the error that emotions are neutral and cannot be controlled. In reality, emotions arise from worship commitments.

---

[49] Alfred Adler (1870–1937), Abraham Maslow (1908–1970); for further discussion of the hierarchy of needs see chapter 1: "The Exordium to Biblical Counseling"
[50] Alfred Adler, Abraham Maslow; for further discussion of the topic of self-esteem see the second book in this series, *What Agreement Is There Between the Temple of God and Idols?: The Accidence of Sin and Idolatry*, chapter 9: "Marauding Visigoths: The Autocratic Self"
[51] Alfred Adler, Abraham Maslow
[52] Alfred Adler, Abraham Maslow; for further discussion of the topic of self-love see the second book in this series, *What Agreement Is There Between the Temple of God and Idols?: The Accidence of Sin and Idolatry*, chapter 9: "Marauding Visigoths: The Autocratic Self"
[53] Ephesians 5:29
[54] Carl Rogers (1902–1987); for further discussion of the topic of unconditional love see the case study "God's *Sui Generis* Love" in the third book in this series, *The Days of Reckoning Are at Hand: From Fig Leaf to Olive Branch to Laurel Wreath*, chapter 2: "Suffering: The Kintsugi Objective"

7. Childhood experiences as determinative[55]	The view that childhood experiences are determinative makes one nothing more than a slave to his own history, continually trolling his past for the source of his psychic pain.
8. A father's love as essential to a fulfilled life[56]	This view sets up an impossible criterion for psychic wholeness, a subjective determination that one has adequately received his father's love. One's view of his father is imperiled by a revisionist scrutiny which sees what one wants to see, and by a bottomless pit of need (so that even a mother's love would not match the sinner's requirements for a fulfilled life).
9. Stages of childhood development[57]	This theory holds that children's development should dictate discipline strategies which are often directly in conflict with the Bible's understanding of children.
10. Birth order as determinative	Birth order offers no meaningful information about one's personality or future choices. This theory fails to see the heart's response to its situation, so that situation is never determinative.
11. The unconscious[58]	The unconscious is the idea that human behavior arises out of a world of suppressed experiences. One may at times not be fully aware of his worship commitments, but there is no mysterious unconscious that controls the psyche.[59]
12. Id, ego, superego[60]	These three concepts partition the psyche in an artificial manner, essentially excusing behavior as the mere outworking of cold impersonal mechanism.
13. Psychotherapy[61]	Psychotherapy is a man-centered form of counseling which seeks some catharsis. This objective runs counter to the Bible's therapy which begins with the gospel, the catharsis of forgiveness through Jesus' death on the cross.
14. Sexuality as a chief driver[62]	Sexual desire is part of the larger biblical concept of the lust of the flesh. Sexuality is not a compulsive and uncontrollable force, as Sigmund Freud (1856–1939) construed it. Rather, sexuality comes under the auspices of far greater worship commitments.
15. "The pleasure principle" - seeking to	Invented by Freud, this concept comes under the umbrella biblical concept of lust of the flesh, a lust that seeks

---

[55] Sigmund Freud (1856–1939)
[56] Sigmund Freud
[57] Erik Erickson (1902–1994)
[58] Sigmund Freud
[59] David Powlison, Westminster Theological Seminary, Philadelphia, Pennsylvania
[60] Sigmund Freud
[61] Sigmund Freud
[62] Sigmund Freud; for further discussion of the topic of sexuality as a need see the case study "Is Sexuality an Inherent Need as Part of Human Design?" in chapter 7: "The Needs Imperative"

maximize pleasure and avoid pain	personal pleasure over obedience to God. Broader worship motives than merely the pursuit of pleasure and the avoidance of pain control the heart.  *The Love Letter* Jean-Honore Fragonard, d. 1806
16. A false dichotomy with regard to gender[63]	While there is a nuanced biblical asymmetry with regard to gender,[64] men are not from Mars and women are not from Venus.[65] Psychology formulates a false gender asymmetry to suit a certain social agenda.
17. The power of positive thinking[66]	This view sees the psyche as driven by the cognitive, that merely thinking the right thoughts changes the psychic condition. Mankind is not firstly a cognitive being but a worship being so that thoughts arise from worship commitments.
18. Cognitive therapies	Cognitive therapies wrongly assume that simply implanting the right thoughts will change one's underlying psychic condition.

---

[63] Karen Horney (1885–1952)
[64] For further discussion of the biblical asymmetry with regard to gender see "The Image of God and Gender" in chapter 5: "Redefining the Pygmalion Effect: Exploring the Image of God in Man"
[65] John Gray, *Men Are from Mars, Women Are from Venus* (New York: HarperCollins, 1993)
[66] Norman Vincent Peale (1898-1993)

19. Behavioral health	This view makes mankind into merely a behavioral being, like a computer which must function according to the dictates of its software. Mankind is not firstly a behavioral being but a worshipping being so that behavior arises from worship commitments.
20. Type A, type B personalities	These labels tend to function as euphemisms for heart idolatry. Presumed aggressive or passive behavior is not a programmed personality trait, but arises from sinful responses to one's world.
21. Alpha male	This label is a euphemism for bellicose behavior and, like all false labels, functions as a shield for idols.
22. A "hardwired" personality	The concept of being "hardwired" arises from a deterministic view of people which sees them as victims of their physiology. They are, thus, consigned to function as they are wired and, therefore, excused for deviant behavior.
23. Addictive personality	This view sees people as victims of their physiology, that they are not culpable for behavioral extremes or moral choices. While the Bible presents each person as subject to a "worship addiction," this is never an exculpatory concept.
24. Impulsive disorder (explosive disorder)	This view sees rage as essentially arising from a disease within the psyche; the objective is to excuse explosive anger. In reality, anger arises from the choices of a worshipping heart.
25. Physiology as determinative of behavior	The trend in psychology is toward reductionism, to make physiology (namely the brain) into a moral scapegoat. Thus, one is given a ready excuse for his behavior since he is presumed to be held captive to a design flaw.

Not only is the concept of an eternal holy God completely absent from these psychology terms, but the idea that each lives and responds to that holy God moment-by-moment is an even more deviant concept. Thus, psychology could be thought of as a "spiritual aphasia" – an inability to recognize the ultimate reality upon which the human being operates. The psychologist places man in a cosmic vacuum so that he functions only with regard to himself and his surroundings. In reality, man functions with regard to another person, God himself, ever confronting the psyche. God himself is the environment in which the psyche operates.[67] However, man denies, suppresses, dismisses, and destroys the knowledge of God at every turn, continually reducing the human experience to an isolated existential drama.

> "Those who cling to worthless idols forfeit the grace that could be theirs." (Jonah

---

[67] For further discussion of this topic see chapter 6: "Man Before the Face of God: The Imperium of the Pscyhe"

2:8)

One who, in a particular context, seeks attention may assume certain psychotic traits. He may, in other situations, soon "snap out" of such behavior to suit his purposes. In this sense, psychotic behavior often dissipates as it is "disciplined" out of a person. For example, around family members one may display psychotic behavior, but in a business meeting or job interview, where fortune and reputation are on the line, one may suddenly be lucid and winsome. For this reason, supposed psychoses can be confronted and subject to discipline. Just as rebellion in children must be disciplined, so too, psychotic behavior must be exposed and brought before the living Christ. Presumed psychosis must be labeled as it is, deliberate and willful insurrection directed specifically at God himself. As one's selfishness and man-centered story are confronted, and brought to light in Christ, they soon evaporate, opening the way for genuine and lasting change through faith in, and subsequent submission to, Christ.

Psychology can only offer a godless (rebellious, God-hating, man-glorifying) approach to each problem, since it holds no concept of sin before a holy God. Since psychology cannot see the deepest aspect of the human existence, it ends up as a co-conspirator in man's defiance toward God. As a tool in mankind's hand, psychology rehabilitates the dysfunctional idols which man hoists in his worship of the creation.[68] Thus, psychology, at its best offers wrongly-directed pragmatic advice,[69] and at its worst, in partnership with Satan, seeks out and destroys the remnants of God's image within man.

> The irony of the American interstate highway system is that it was intended to ease traffic congestion and speed the flow of travel. However, quite ironically, according to Braess' paradox the more highways that are built the *more* traffic that is generated, spawning a vicious cycle of construction and increased traffic, followed by more construction. This sounds similar to the nature of psychology, the more people turn to psychology the emptier and more lost they become, so that their psychoses and perceived needs multiply. Thus, a certain "Braess' paradox" takes hold in which the proliferation of psychology spawns greater incidence of psychotic behavior, which in turn increases the supposed need for psychology.

Psychology's Tetrad Sophistry

At the 1939 New York World's Fair, General Motors revealed a groundbreaking exhibit, "Futurama." It was a vision for the modern American city with superhighways running through and around it, like an endless ribbon of progress. The cities of the future had raised walkways high above the traffic below. The goal was a

---
[68] David Powlison, Westminster Theological Seminary, Philadelphia, Pennsylvania
[69] David Powlison, Westminster Theological Seminary, Philadelphia, Pennsylvania

city fully accessible by car and free from congestion. Futurama seemed like an ingenious idea, but once many of its guiding principles were implemented, it proved to be the death of the modern American city.

Pont Boieldieu in Rouen, Rainy Weather, Camille Pissarro, 1896

This anecdote reminds one of psychology's similar promises and subsequent perils. Just as humanism envisions futuristic cities while blinded to the reality of the sinful heart, so too, psychology foists upon society the delusion that one can manage his psychic condition through man-centered means. The glaring omission is that, just as a city and its technology must be understood in light of human sin, so too, the health of the psyche is a profoundly with-regard-to-God phenomenon. Thus, psychology exhibits four crucial errors in its analysis of the psyche: blindness, fabrication, magnification, and twisting.[70]

A Brief Review of the Bible's Description of the Psychic Condition[71]

Romans 1:21 states, "For although they knew God, they neither glorified him as God nor gave thanks to him, but their foolish hearts were darkened." Thus, each person lives with regard to God so that every thought, behavior, and motive is a

---
[70] David Powlison, Westminster Theological Seminary, Philadelphia, Pennsylvania
[71] For a more comprehensive summary of the Bible's description of the psyche see chapter 1: "The Exordium to Biblical Counseling"

with-regard-to-God event (the *coram Deo* concept). Mankind lives in a personal vertical dimension which he actively suppresses.[72]

On account of this fundamental human condition, psychotic behavior arises from a desire to regard the self as exculpated or even praiseworthy.[73] This points to the psyche's God-ward referent; man lives with regard to the moral absolutes implanted within him as image-bearer. He is an inextricably worshipping being, invested with a moral conscience which both accuses and excuses him. Therefore, as one invested with a conscience, he at every turn seeks to assign moral meaning to himself and his world. Thus, man, of necessity, operates with-regard-to-God (*coram Deo*);[74] it is impossible for him not to. The following are additional truths based on the Bible's understanding of the psyche:

1. The universe is personal. Thus, mankind is, at every turn, confronted with evidence of a personal God.

> "In his hand is the life of every creature and the breath of all mankind." (Job 12:10)
>
> "'For in him we live and move and have our being.' As some of your own poets have said, 'We are his offspring.'" (Acts 17:28)
>
> "Nothing in all creation is hidden from God's sight. Everything is uncovered and laid bare before the eyes of him to whom we must give account." (Hebrews 4:13)

2. God personally entered his universe to engage and overcome the human plight. Thus, not only is the universe personal, but the answer to man's psychic condition is also with regard to a person (effected by means of the person of God).

> "How long, LORD? Will you forget me forever? How long will you hide your face from me?" (Psalm 13:1)
>
> "In him was life, and that life was the light of all mankind." (John 1:4)

3. Each person simultaneously operates in a vertical (with regard to God) and horizontal (with regard to others) dimension. The vertical drives the horizontal, so that the horizontal is merely a reflection of the vertical.

> "Jesus replied, 'Love the Lord your God with all your heart and with all your soul

---

[72] For additional discussion of the suppression of the truth and the *coram Deo* concept see chapter 6: "Man Before the Face of God: The Imperium of the Psyche"
[73] Jerome Kagan, "Three Pleasing Ideas," *American Psychologist* 51.9 (September, 1996) 907.
[74] For additional discussion of the *coram Deo* concept see chapter 6: "Man Before the Face of God: The Imperium of the Psyche"

> and with all your mind.' This is the first and greatest commandment. And the second is like it: 'Love your neighbor as yourself.' All the Law and the Prophets hang on these two commandments.'" (Matthew 22:37-40)

4. The Bible, as God's Word, speaks to the plenary psychic condition. Nothing with regard to man's state is outside of its purview.

> "The unfolding of your words gives light; it gives understanding to the simple." (Psalm 119:130)

5. Humanity lives immersed in the reality of personal sin, with the individual and corporate suffering which results.

> "Look on my affliction and my distress and take away all my sins." (Psalm 25:18)
>
> "This is the evil in everything that happens under the sun: The same destiny overtakes all. The hearts of people, moreover, are full of evil and there is madness in their hearts while they live, and afterward they join the dead." (Ecclesiastes 9:3)

6. Fruitful change is a lifelong process of movement toward deeper faith in Jesus, firstly a vertical change (with regard to God) from which flows a horizontal change (with regard to others).

> "The goal of this command is love, which comes from a pure heart and a good conscience and a sincere faith." (1 Timothy 1:5)
>
> "Dear friends, now we are children of God, and what we will be has not yet been made known. But we know that when Christ appears, we shall be like him, for we shall see him as he is. All who have this hope in him purify themselves, just as he is pure." (1 John 3:2-3)

Psychology's Blindness to Data

Each fact is necessarily interpreted so that it is inextricably coupled with a theory. For this reason, there is no such thing as neutral fact. This means that one is conscribed to look at people through a religious set of lenses, a belief system which seeks to make sense of them. Psychology sees what it wants to see, and thus dons a worshipping set of lenses that reveal the world in the way that it desires. For example, when one believes that emotional problems arise from childhood trauma then he will find that trauma in his past.[75] It is easy to uncover supposed evidence that simply fits one's theories.

---

[75] David Powlison, Westminster Theological Seminary, Philadelphia, Pennsylvania

Of course, the same argument could be leveled against biblical counseling - that it sees what it wants to see. However, biblical counseling bases its understanding and prescription solidly upon the Word of God. It says not more nor less than what God has said. The counselor thus sees people as God sees them (sinners in need of salvation) and offers the only solution that God offers (salvation through Jesus). God's Word lends the counselor eyes to see people as they actually are.

King Cophetua and the Beggarmaid, Daniel Maclise, d. 1870

Proverbs 9:10 states, "The fear of the LORD is the beginning of wisdom, and knowledge of the Holy One is understanding." Any system of thought that suppresses the knowledge of God is necessarily blind to the most fundamental aspects of the human experience.[76]

Psychology is blind to this inner reality because it cannot see the God-ward orientation and concealed God-calibrated mechanics of the conscience. Psychology is blind to the vertical dimension of the human experience, that all people know God, yet suppress and deny that knowledge.

Further examples of psychology's blindness:

1. Carl Rogers (1902-1987) was a pastor who left the ministry to promote a new school of humanistic psychology based on "unconditional positive regard."[77] This

---

[76] David Powlison, 2011 Christian Counseling and Education Foundation conference

[77] For additional analysis of the Rogerian concept of "unconditional positive regard" see the case study "God's *Sui Generis* Love" in the third book in this series, *The Days of Reckoning Are at Hand: From Fig Leaf to Olive Branch*

approach purports to offer no moral judgments so that the objective is to make the counselee feel affirmed and understood. The guiding principle is that if one accepts himself then he can be fulfilled. Quite ironically, unconditional positive regard is itself an agenda with a highly-opinionated directive denying the counselee's need for repentance before God.

2. Norman Vincent Peal (1898-1993), a practicing pastor during his dissemination of cognitive psychology, birthed "the power of positive thinking." This approach reduces the psyche to a series of cognitive events, so that when the psyche is implanted with the right thoughts it achieves mental health. However, like all psychological theories, Peale's is blind to the psyche's worshipping drive. Thus, according to the Bible, "mental health" derives from rightly placed worship, not from the realignment of thought. Humans are worshipping beings continually placing their covenant trust either in false gods or in the true God.

3. Sigmund Freud's (1856–1939) "pleasure-pain principle" posits that pleasure draws and pain repels. This principle may hold some descriptive qualities, but it is not determinative, so that it does not control the psyche. Human motivation is of a completely different ilk than Freud imagined. Freud focused on sexuality as a driving motivator for human behavior, but he was blind to sexuality's Godward-referent, that it is specifically committed either in honor of, or in defiance of, God. (When strictly within the confines of marriage, sexuality is a glorious display of God's covenant relationship. When used as a weapon against God, sexuality is an ugly manifestation of mankind's self-worship.) Thus, Freud denied a holy eternal God who stands behind human behavior.

In this way, psychology is blind to sexual deviance as a manifestation of a core lust of the flesh, an implicit attack upon the person of God. Lust is broader, deeper, and more pernicious than psychology could ever imagine because it is a direct assault upon God. Thus, psychology does not see the root sexual perversion in homosexuality, fornication, and adultery because it does not know how to rightly define and delimit sexuality. It does not see the organic connection between deviant sexuality and other manifestations of the lust of the flesh such as gluttony, greed, envy, prevarication, and a host of other perversions. There is a single root which links all sinful behavior; that root is a with-regard-to-God rebellion. That is the hidden motivator for the psyche, which Freud (and others) refused to see because he was using the wrong template.

Psychology's Fabrication of Data

The Earth's climate is determined by the Sun. The northern hemisphere is warmer from March through September than from September through March. Therefore, it

---

to Laurel Wreath, chapter 2: "Suffering: The Kintsugi Objective"

only seems logical that the Earth is closer to the Sun from March through September. But this, of course, is a *non sequitur*, as any grade school student can you tell you that the Earth is farther from the sun from March through September. If the Earth is farther, how does one explain the increase in solar radiation? One must understand something more about the Earth-Sun relationship.[78]

Allegory of Astronomy, Laurent de la Hyre, 1649

The point is that human logic may often sound highly-convincing. But when that logic is not directed by the Bible, it is always in error with regard to man's nouthetic condition. One must know more about human existence than that which humanity can empirically observe or explain. Without God's own intervention, description, and assessment, human logic is relegated to fine-sounding, yet specious, arguments.

The following are some examples of psychology's fabrication:

1. Often psychology fabricates a supposed solution to the wrong problem. For example, certain schools of psychology advance the notion that childhood trauma is deterministic of future behavior. If one's past is the source of one's problem then, according to psychology, one must re-imagine or come to terms with that past. But this is enslaving because in actuality one can never alter his past, so he is forever constrained by it.[79] The Bible does not ask one to study his past in order to come to terms with events or assign blame; it asks one to repent of one's foolish response, in

---

[78] The Earth, tilted on a twenty-three and a half degree axis, angles its northern hemisphere toward the Sun from March through September. This tilt explains the elevated temperature as the incoming solar radiation is more direct during those months.

[79] For further discussion of the topic of personal history see the third book in this series, *The Days of Reckoning Are at Hand: From Fig Leaf to Olive Branch to Laurel Wreath*, chapter 1: "Memories Preserved in Amber: Adopting God's Retrospective"

the midst of, and with regard to, that past.[80]

> "Psychology makes one believe that he can correct his faults by confessing his parents' sins." (Laurence Peter)

2. Psychology advances the idea that if one can just meet his emotional needs he can experience liberation, become an actualized person. But when are one's supposed needs ever satiated? The quest to meet emotional needs places one on a treadmill of futility. The Bible, therefore, presents one's core psychic need to be entirely satisfied through relationship with one's God through Jesus Christ.[81]

The point is that psychology fabricates fictitious drivers for psychic trauma, and then posits solutions which further enslave to that trauma. Psychology, working off of the wrong template, draws upon the wrong narrative, tightening the shackles of relational and emotional slavery.

3. The Freudian schema (in the chart below) for the psyche is a complete fabrication.

The Psyche	Meaning	Function
1. Id	Pleasure	Animal
2. Ego	Reality	Conscience
3. Superego	A structure imposed on the conscience as moral guide	Latent parental restrictions forced on the individual by society, often under the guise of a projected "God"

The Freudian schema is nothing more than a fanciful story of the psyche's function. Even more so, Freud saw himself as advancing a new religion which would progressively replace the Judeo-Christian faith. Thus, Freudian psychoanalysis is a "pastoral" approach directing humanity in what, and how, to worship. In fact, in his work, *The Future of an Illusion* (1927), Freud stated that all religion is an illusion, arguing, instead, for trust in the god of reason which would one day liberate mankind from its limitations.

> There are certainly things of which one is not aware, but there is not a subconscious or hidden world deep within the psyche that must be explored and healed. The psyche is more active and deliberate than a subconscious would suggest.[82]

Freud saw the subconscious as marked by incestuous fantasies such as the Oedipal complex (boys want to kill their fathers and possess their mothers) and the Electra

---

[80] Paul David Tripp, *Instruments in the Redeemer's Hands: People in Need of Change Helping People in Need of Change* (Presbyterian and Reformed Publishing, 2002)
[81] For further discussion of the topic of needs see chapter 7: "The Needs Imperative"
[82] David Powlison, Westminster Theological Seminary, Philadelphia, Pennsylvania

complex (girls want to kill their mothers and possess their fathers). The superego or conscience is thought to be the father's commands restraining the son's actions. This conscience originates extrinsic to the boy, but at a certain point transitions to a voice intrinsic to him; the "you must not" becomes the "I must not." Freud posited that society projects this father-directive onto an otherworldly eternal God, so that God becomes the ultimate manifestation of the father's law. For Freud, therefore, the concept of God was merely a societal projection of the earthly father.[83]

> "I don't know who my grandfather was; I am much more concerned to know who his grandson will be." (Abraham Lincoln)

4. Freud's dream interpretation is a fanciful storytelling device used to implant his theories into the psyche. While dreams throughout the Bible were often direct revelation from God,[84] today they serve little purpose outside of offering the mind a creative outlet. There is little meaningful data to be derived from dreams.

5. Dissociative Identity Disorder (DID) (or more commonly, Multiple Personality Disorder) is thought to indicate the presence of distinct personalities within one person. The Bible sees each

The Dream
Michelangelo Buonarroti, c. 1533

as possessing only one personality but cultivating a highly-fragmented fantasy world. (Even many psychologists doubt that multiple personalities inhabit one body.)

6. An additional example of fabrication is Pavlov-Skinner behaviorism which, based

---

[83] For additional discussion of this topic see "The Freudian Fatherhood Fable" in the third book in this series, *The Days of Reckoning Are at Hand: From Fig Leaf to Olive Branch to Laurel Wreath*, chapter 1: "Memories Preserved in Amber: Adopting God's Retrospective"

[84] Numerous Bible characters received direct revelation in dreams such as Abimelech (Genesis 20:3-5), Jacob (Genesis 28:11-19), Joseph (Genesis 37:5-11), Solomon (1 Kings 3:5-15), Jesus' father, Joseph (Matthew 1:20; 2:13), and the Magi from the East (Matthew 2:12). However, such communication is not revelatory today as Christians discern God's will through the study of Scripture.

on the concept of operant conditioning, is a learned pattern of behavior that becomes a form of addiction. According to this view, one must be "reprogrammed" like a computer. Thus, mankind is viewed as a mechanical device without the ability to make responsible choices. Building upon the Pavlov-Skinner foundation, the radical reductionism of neuropsychology is a highly-materialistic view of the psyche, one which promises to find, in the somatic, hidden triggers for psychological abnormality.

> Recently, an eighty year-old celebrity was publicly excoriated for incendiary and hurtful statements. His wife excused his comments as arising from the onset of dementia. The implication is that the dementia controls this man's psyche and its moral choices. This way of thinking arises from a fiendish prevarication that immorality derives from a breakdown of the body or mind. This man's encroaching dementia did not cause him to speak as he did. His words arose from his heart, but the usual mechanism for stifling hurtful speech did not function so that he shared his thoughts without regard for the consequence.

Psychology's Magnification of Data

Portrait of Dr. Simarro at the Microscope, Joaquin Sorolla y Bastida, 1897

> "Some invent stories then others enlarge them."

1. One who was abused as a child suffered a grave injustice, having been sinned against. However, psychology makes that abuse into the defining event of one's life, continually conjuring that memory as an excuse for one's present failings. In this, psychology purports to understand the victim's pain and honor it, but it does neither.

In propping up an excuse for present failings, psychology magnifies the previous transgression so that it would overshadow and strip away moral responsibility for one's subsequent transgressions.

The Bible recognizes that while one was sinned against, one responds to that sin as a sinner. This means that one responds to sin with sin (namely various shades and hues of revenge), so that it is not the original event, but one's sinful response which is actually the defining event. It is one's godless response to godlessness which induces one's emotional scars. Thus, psychology magnifies childhood trauma, propping it up as the determinative life event, while blind to the ongoing sinful response which is actually determinative. In this way, psychology leaves its adherents twice cursed – continually burdened with the original transgression, while allowing that burden to foment further transgression.

> "Not the power to remember, but the power to forget, is the most important for our mental health." (Sholem Asch)

2. Humanistic psychology, advanced by Alfred Adler (1870-1937) and Abraham Maslow (1908-1970), is thought to be a purely empirical approach to the psyche, but in fact, it is far from that.[85] Like all psychological investigation, it is theory driven, and therefore shaped by a particular religious view of people. For example, Adler and Maslow saw people as prone to a needs-based inferiority complex, which can easily become controlling and thus dominate life choices. This view sees the person as "product" rather than "perpetrator," passive rather than active agent. In other words, this form of humanistic psychology casts mankind as dependent upon having needs met, and thus emotionally vulnerable when those needs are not met. However, the Bible sees mankind as willful architect of his own perceived needs, resorting to various forms of relational extortion to assuage his desire.

> "What causes fights and quarrels among you? Don't they come from your desires that battle within you? You desire but do not have, so you kill. You covet but you cannot get what you want, so you quarrel and fight. You do not have because you do not ask God. When you ask, you do not receive, because you ask with wrong motives, that you may spend what you get on your pleasures." (James 4:1-3)

3. Freud pioneered the concept of talking therapy, catharsis through speaking, the idea that repressed memories could be conjured to effect healing. While there is certainly value in God-directed verbal confession, in counseling and being counseled,[86] there is no mystical healing in merely rehearsing past experiences. The Bible is never concerned with merely recounting the past; it concerns itself with how one interprets

---

[85] For additional discussion of the Adler-Maslow model see chapter 1: "The Exordium to Biblical Counseling"
[86] James 5:16; 1 John 1:9

his past.[87] How do one's experiences serve to highlight one's desperate foolishness in the midst of those experiences? How do one's experiences reveal God leading him to the knowledge of himself? Incidentally, the concept of talking cure is a fallacy when such talk merely reacquaints one with his idolatrous heart. Speaking about one's idolatry in an unrepentant manner only dredges it up so that it further pollutes the wellspring of the heart, finally making that idolatry more resistant to removal. Often it is far better to be silent than to speak, if so doing, increases one's investment in foolishness.

> "If you then, though you are evil, know how to give good gifts to your children, how much more will your Father in heaven give the Holy Spirit to those who ask him!" (Luke 11:13)

4. The Neo-Freudian psychologist, Karen Horny's (1885–1952), most well-known work may be her analysis of neurotic trends with regard to moving toward, against, or away from people. She also spoke of the necessary rejection of the masculine bias in psychotherapy so as to develop a uniquely feminine psychology. Here, Horny set out to elevate and liberate women from repressive masculine structures and to, in some way, depreciate masculine achievement. Horny magnified some aspect of gender, but in a fictitious manner which ultimately rendered the sexes at odds, much as Marxist-based feminism seeks to. Horny, in effect, dignified a feminine rebellion against God-ordained authority structures.

Psychology's Twisting of Data

1. Freud's assumptions were proven for him with every client he met. If one believes, for example, that all psychoses are the result of sexual abuse, he will find that sexual abuse. In those cases where a clear history of abuse is not forthcoming, Freud's explanation was that the patient had repressed the memory. This creates a double-bind in which naysayers are demurred as merely being in denial.

> The lie is attractive because the truth is dangerous.[88] People instinctively run from the truth, finding the lie safer for maintaining one's sinful stance toward God.

2. Psychology speaks of guilt feelings but does not acknowledge that guilt may be real because there is actually something worthy of guilt. Psychology describes mankind as a victim of his own conscience, that that conscience is merely a repressive construct of society, a vestige of coercive Byzantine beliefs. Psychology will not acknowledge that mankind actually violates his own conscience, that he is literally guilty. Thus, for

---

[87] For additional discussion of the topic of personal history visit the third book in this series, *The Days of Reckoning Are at Hand: From Fig Leaf to Olive Branch to Laurel Wreath*, chapter 1: "Memories Preserved in Amber: Adopting God's Retrospective"

[88] David Powlison, Westminster Theological Seminary, Philadelphia, Pennsylvania

psychology emotions are redefined as constructed response mechanisms, not to be rationalized, but to be managed. The idea is to simply remove unwanted guilt. However, this misses the point that guilt is linked to a larger God-implanted mechanism for alerting the sinner to his sin. Additionally, it is impossible to fully suppress the sinner's guilt before God. Therefore, psychology's suppression mechanisms foment greater inner conflict and existential angst as the knowledge of God keeps resurfacing.

The Tournament, Pierre-Henri Revoil, 1812

Incidentally, while many biblical counselors may not use psychology directly, there is often an undetected, yet insidious, problem. Psychology's methods and approaches permeate the counseling endeavor, even while its propositional statements are excluded. Thus, while a counselor voices Scripture and states Christ-centered truths, his unstated objective may be to exonerate the sinner from his guilt through man-centered means. The counselor, in avoiding that which God seeks to confront, takes on the devil's errand.

> **What is the Difference Between Shame and Guilt?**
>
> Modern culture experiences a diminished sense of guilt because absolute standards have been reduced to pale shadows. Today, guilt is assumed to be "a psychological problem that requires therapy, not…true moral guilt that requires forgiveness."[89]

---

[89] Nancy Pearcey, *Total Truth: Liberating Christianity from Its Cultural Captivity* (Crossway Books, 2008) 119.

> While guilt is measured against an assumed standard of morality, shame is experienced with regard to other's expectations. Therefore, one experiences shame as he judges that he has failed in others' eyes. Despite the societal diminishment of guilt, there is still some muted cultural awareness of shame because each feels that he stands under others' critical gaze for not measuring up to their standards.[90] While guilt is progressively stifled as the knowledge of God is further suppressed, shame remains a formidable social force to the extent of desire for men's praise.

Psychology as Intractably Balkanized

Possibly the greatest evidence to refute psychology is the fact that it is far from unified. It is a deeply fractured mosaic of theories, Balkanized into fiefdoms struggling for authority over the correct interpretation of the psyche. Therefore, one must always speak of "psychologies," warring factions that offer diametrically opposed views of people, problems, and solutions.[91] Of course, psychologists counter that psychology functions like a symphony, each perspective playing a part which together offer a rich, varied, layered, and ultimately compelling analysis. However, this is rarely how psychologists actually view their various fields. They are more apt to view a competing theory as a threatening rival than as a complementary addition to their own.

Further, psychology offers no "grand unified theory" of human behavior and personality.[92] In this sense, psychology essentially functions as a kind of Rube Goldberg machine of evermore convoluted and confusing theories which vitiate against one another. Only the Bible offers a grand unified theory that describes, explains, and predicts with piercing accuracy.

Psychology, like all pagan thought, is inherently atomistic because in the non-Christian's mind truth and reality are intractably separated. This is exactly what Eve did in the garden; she separated truth from reality, concocting her own false sense of reality, a supposed reality in which she could be her own god. This is the basis for the modern concept of irrationalism – the inherent separation of truth and reality, the idea that there is no purpose for truth because it has no basis in reality.[93]

Thus, each branch of psychology offers its own "word of truth" or ideal image. Each operates in its own world of symbol and meaning. Like an elephant described by blind men, each describing a part but blind to the whole, so too, psychology may present

---

[90] For further discussion of this topic of meeting others' standards see "Self-Esteem's Deception" in the second book in this series, *What Agreement Is There Between the Temple of God and Idols?: The Accidence of Sin and Idolatry*, chapter 9: "Marauding Visigoths: The Autocratic Self"
[91] David Powlison, Westminster Theological Seminary, Philadelphia, Pennsylvania
[92] David Powlison, Westminster Theological Seminary, Philadelphia, Pennsylvania
[93] Cornelius Van Til, *Christian Apologetics* (Presbyterian and Reformed Press, 2003) 75.

some limited description of the psyche, but it cannot understand the whole.[94] Even that limited description is flawed because the psychologist does not know the psyche's design, meaning, and purpose. Only the Bible offers the correct micro and macro-perspective.

A further reason that psychology is splintered is that, in its various manifestations, it simply never effects permanent and meaningful change. For this reason, it continually reinvents itself around cultural norms, taking on various faces to appease socio-cultural and temporal expectations. Thus, psychology's many faces end up pocked with internal contradiction, irrationality, and speculative extrapolation. The panoply of psychologies merely serve as inventive ways to rehabilitate idolatrous rebellion against a holy God through, for a time, making the sinful condition appear to function as one had hoped. However, psychology's counsel, dominated by warring factions, soon devolves into a tangled knot of theories that confuse and destabilize the already enfeebled psyche.[95]

Autumn on the Thames
James Jacques Joseph Tissot, c. 1875

Psychology as Distorting Doppelganger: A Comparison of Psychology Terms and Bible Concepts

A Chinese proverb states, "The beginning of wisdom is to call things by their right names." Only the Bible correctly describes the plenary human condition, calling each element by its rightful name so as to uncover humanity's actual psychological state.

---
[94] David Powlison, Westminster Theological Seminary, Philadelphia, Pennsylvania
[95] David Powlison, "Which Presuppositions? Secular Psychology and the Categories of Biblical Thought," *Journal of Psychology and Theology* 12.4 (Winter, 1984): 273.

Yet, the Bible's description contrasts with that of psychology, not just in nomenclature, but in concept. First Corinthians 2:13 states, "This is what we speak, not in words taught us by human wisdom but in words taught by the Spirit, explaining spiritual realities with Spirit-taught words." Based on this verse, it is imperative for Christians to reject secular terms so as to more thoroughly employ the Bible's descriptors.

> "Whatever exists has already been named, and what man is has been known..." (Ecclesiastes 6:10a)

The conceptual competition between Scripture and psychology is nearly absolute because both are committed to the exploration, analysis, and cure of souls. Both traffic exclusively in the human condition, its motivation, goals, consequences, cognition, relationships, and finally in the solution to human depravity.[96] Thus, the degree to which scriptural truth overlaps with any secular study increases the necessity for Scripture to maintain functional control of the terms, evidence, analysis, and interpretation.[97]

> "The limits of my language mean the limits of my world." (Ludwig Wittgenstein)

The following chart contrasts psychology terms with biblical ones, so as to highlight their conceptual difference.

Psychology's Description		What Psychology Says This Problem Reveals	The Bible's Description	What the Bible Says This Problem Reveals
Normal	Abnormal			
1. Healthy desire for improvement; being confident or having a type-A personality	Addictive personality	One is genetically predisposed to addiction.	Heart worship[98]	One willfully enters into treasonous covenants with false gods in order to gain power, meaning, and blessing.
2. An active imagination; day-dreaming; harmless	Fixations	Repressed feelings or childhood	Rulers of the mind[99]	Inordinate desire which controls one's thoughts,

---

[96] David Powlison, "Which Presuppositions? Secular Psychology and the Categories of Biblical Thought," *Journal of Psychology and Theology* 12.4 (Winter, 1984): 276.
[97] J.R. McQuilkin, "The Behavioral Sciences under the Authority of Scripture," *CAPS Bulletin* 20: 31-43.
[98] Exodus 20:3
[99] 1 Corinthians 2:16, Romans 12:2

fantasies; preoccupations		traumas which must be uncovered; the need for catharsis		causing one to become obsessed
3. Ambition; alpha male; naturally competitive		Having a healthy sense of confidence; being a "go-getter"	Cravings,[100] stiff-necked[101]	Inordinate desire for that which slakes one's lusts
4. Anxieties; feelings of inadequacy (generalized anxiety disorder)[102]	Obsessive	The need for security or significance	Anxiety[103] (a single root anxiety)	Profound distrust of God's goodness
5. Asserting oneself; self-expression	Aggression as a disorder	Each person is inherently good, therefore self-expression should be tolerated, even encouraged	Denying/ suppressing[104]	Trying to convince oneself that he is not subject to a God-designed universe
6. Curiosity; inquisitiveness; seeking equality		The need for greater self-esteem; the importance of self-confidence or believing in oneself	Covetousness/ envy[105]	Looking with haughty eyes which crave the creation
7. Dynamic and energetic; the quest to be legitimized	Impulsive disorder	Healthy self-pride; the "indomitable" human spirit	Demands[106]	"Playing God" by trying to draw all of creation into the service of oneself
8. Enthusiasm,	Explosive	To be driven,	Loves[107]	Anything raised as

---

[100] 1 John 2:16
[101] Exodus 32:9
[102] David Kupelian, *How Evil Works: Understanding and Overcoming the Destructive Forces That Are Transforming America* (Threshold Edition, 2010) 105.
[103] Psalm 127:2; Matthew 6:32; Philippians 4:6-7
[104] Romans 1:18
[105] Titus 3:3
[106] Matthew 18:28-35; Luke 7:47
[107] Hosea 2:12-17

passions	personality	focused, committed, and wanting the best		an idol of the heart; anything given a higher priority than God himself
9. Fears	Phobias	The need for security and significance in a precarious world	Fears[108]	The fear of judgment, rejection, and failure as a result of living apart from God[109]
10. Guilt feelings	Morbid introspection	A socially-derived concept of guilt; no true guilt, only guilt "feelings" which should be expunged; the answer is higher self-esteem.	Actual guilt[110]	Transgression against God's moral absolutes
11. "Hard-wired" to be a loner; naturally introverted; needing time alone	Anti-social behavior		Seeking covering/ refuge; running[111]	A desire to shield one's sin, to conceal one's guilt before a holy God and avoid shame before people
12. Being "healthy and warm-blooded"; normal sexual self-expression	Sexually impulsive (nympho-maniac)	Humans are sexual beings with a right to fulfill intimacy needs. This should not be controlled or suppressed but explored and celebrated.	Lusts of the flesh[112]	Burning with desire for pleasure,[113] or any experience of sensuality which numbs the pain of separation from God

---

[108] Luke 12:4-5
[109] For further discussion of the issue of fear see "The Dynamics of Fear" in chapter 6: "Man Before the Face of God: The Imperium of the Psyche"
[110] Romans 7:9, 10; James 2:10
[111] Genesis 3:7
[112] 1 John 2:16
[113] Romans 1:27; 1 Thessalonians 4:5

13. The innate goodness of man		Left to his own devices, mankind brings forth good results from his innate sense of right and wrong.	Displaying false fruit[114]	Bringing forth godless results while making them appear noble or altruistic
14. The need for manageable goals		Finding ways to make one's life work; set manageable goals which make one content and complete	Warring idols[115]	"Mini-gods" which control, demand allegiance, and beat one into submission
15. Unmet harmless longings	Obsessive longing	The desire to improve, succeed, or to be thought highly of	Longings of the heart[116]	Wrongly wanting the gifts over the Giver; rejecting the Blesser in favor of the blessing
16. An unmet hierarchy of needs		Fundamental needs which must be met in order for one to be self-actualized	Controlling needs[117]	Seeking to meet perceived needs as an act of defiance toward God
17. Birth order		Birth order determines personality and relational dynamics.	Birth order holds no significance in shaping the psyche.	

While all of psychology could be summarized as identifying psychoses, the Bible identifies the worship of false gods or the true God. In other words, what psychology would label as deviance from a subjective norm, the Bible would label as misplaced worship. Further, what psychology would call the management of psychoses, the Bible would call suppression of God's immutable standards.[118] This is the nexus of the clash between psychology and the Bible. However, this divergence is far from

---

[114] Romans 7:5
[115] Isaiah 44:9-20
[116] Ephesians 2:3-7
[117] 1 Peter 1:13, 14
[118] Romans 1:18-21

mere semantics as there is slippage between the categories. Thus, the Bible's concepts and those of psychology do not overlap, even when they use the same word.

A cornerstone of biblical counseling is holding tenaciously to Scripture's own concepts and language. The biblical counselor may at times rightly use psychology's parlance in order to interface with culture (descriptions like schizophrenic, anorexic, obsessive compulsive, bipolar, etc.). However, the counselor considers these as merely a set of observations, descriptive language, or a basket of symptoms. He never lets such terms stand unopposed, but redefines them with biblical concepts and language. The counselor must be well-trained in recasting and reinterpreting psychological concepts in biblical terms.

Young Lady in a Boat, James Jacques Joseph Tissot, 1870

> "This is what we speak, not in words taught us by human wisdom but in words taught by the Spirit, explaining spiritual realities with Spirit-taught words." (1 Corinthians 2:13)

One theory for why Christians readily integrate psychology terms with biblical ones may have to do with the nature of language. There has been a certain democratization of language in the modern world. Languages tend to cross-fertilize with words lent and borrowed across previously rigid boundaries, English being a prime example as "the most hospitable and democratic language that ever existed."[119] While most view this phenomenon as valuable for cross-cultural communication, it is perilous when

---

[119] Richard Lederer, *The Miracle of Language* (Gallery Books, 1999)

seeking to integrate competing philosophies with the Bible. Despite the conceptual broadening which might seem to accrue, psychology's terms and concepts simply cannot be integrated with those of the Bible.[120] Such interbreeding, when applied by the sinful heart, would be lethal because secular concepts effortlessly mongrelize and cannibalize biblical ones.

> "English is a lagoon of nations because in it there are hundreds of miscellaneous words floating like ships from foreign ports freighting messages to us." (Joseph Bellafiore)

For example, seemingly innocuous secular terms such as "introvert" and "extrovert" miss the deeper contours of the heart. One may be an introvert when fearful of impending threats or desirous of that which he cannot attain. Introversion may be a symptom of failed self-pride or shame. On the other hand, one may suddenly become an extrovert when, his idols rehabilitated, he feels reaffirmed in the deepest alliances of his heart. One may become an extrovert when accepted or dominant in a particular situation. Everyone in certain scenarios is an introvert, and in others, an extrovert. The issue is which idols are rehabilitated, and which are recessed. Thus, the categories introvert and extrovert, like all psychology-derived categories, are artificial, missing the heart's deeper demands and loves. Thus, in its machinations, there is an opaque quality to the heart which psychology can never pierce.

Consider another issue. Every false view of mankind casts aspersions upon God himself, as man is portrayed as either a noble but tragic hero, or as a victim of his physicality. In line with the broken window theory,[121] small assaults upon God's character have a magnified effect upon human rebellion. Thus, with each falsehood the glaring contrast between man's likeness and God's likeness is diluted, diminishing the need for a savior. That is why false descriptions, labels, and concepts are so deadly to the Christian message, because they distract from, and erode, the Bible's teaching on man, God, and salvation. So the question stands, "What has Jerusalem to do with Vienna?"

> America is locked in a culture war between secular thought (spearheaded by the evolution-psychology tandem) and biblical wisdom. The side that is most persuasive will win over hearts and minds. To gain cultural relevance, Christianity must convince society that the Bible has surpassing power to describe, diagnose, and cure the full range of ailments of the soul.

---

[120] For further discussion of the dangers of integrationism see chapter 9: "Integrationism: The Modern Day Babylonian Captivity"

[121] For additional discussion of this topic see "The Broken Window Theory on Sin" in the second book in this series, *What Agreement Is There Between the Temple of God and Idols?: The Accidence of Sin and Idolatry*, chapter 4: "Hamartiology: Sin in All its Ignobility"

Insanity's Inception[122]

Jeroboam Offering Sacrifice for the Idol, Jean-Honore Fragonard, d. 1806

First Samuel 18:6-12 offers a glimpse into how insanity germinates within the heart.

> When the men were returning home after David had killed the Philistine, the women came out from all the towns of Israel to meet King Saul with singing and dancing, with joyful songs and with timbrels and lyres. As they danced, they sang:
>
> 'Saul has slain his thousands,
> and David his tens of thousands.'
>
> Saul was very angry; this refrain displeased him greatly. 'They have credited David with tens of thousands,' he thought, 'but me with only thousands. What more can he get but the kingdom?' And from that time on Saul kept a close eye on David. The next day an evil spirit from God came forcefully on Saul. He was prophesying in his house, while David was playing the lyre, as he usually did. Saul had a spear in his hand and he hurled it, saying to himself,

---

[122] For additional discussion of this topic see "Sin's Great Ravishment: Insanity" in the second book in this series, *What Agreement Is There Between the Temple of God and Idols?: The Accidence of Sin and Idolatry*, chapter 4: "Hamartiology: Sin in All its Ignobility"

'I'll pin David to the wall.' But David eluded him twice. Saul was afraid of David, because the Lord was with David but had departed from Saul.

From the Bible's perspective insanity is not a physiological illness (although there are clearly psychosomatic symptoms, as mentioned in the book of Psalms), but rather is born of envy, mercurial desire, misplaced passions, seeking the praises of men, cravings, rulers of the mind, controlling needs, lusts of the flesh, warring idols, and ultimately rebellious worship of the creation over the Creator. The heart, in its God-hatred, carves out for itself idols which give form to its insanity – lusts, anxieties, obsessions, desires, controlling needs, demands. So insanity, from a biblical perspective, is not an illness but a worship disorder.

Incidentally, it is worth noting that insanity is, in popular parlance, simply called being "mad." ("He has gone stark raving mad.") Past generations recognized that insanity finds fertile soil in unresolved anger. This is why Ephesians 4:26 admonishes, "In your anger do not sin: Do not let the sun go down while you are still angry." The Bible recognizes that godless anger is a caustic secretion within the heart, a vessel never designed to house corrosive anger. Thus, self-serving anger scorches the heart, rendering it a burned out shell. Anger breeds desire for revenge, and revenge in its various forms, some overt and openly hostile, others simmering and cunning, ravishes the heart. Thus, insanity has nothing to do with physiology and everything to do with a sinful response to one's world, a tightfisted defiance of God himself.

> "This is the evil in everything that happens under the sun: The same destiny overtakes all. The hearts of people, moreover, are full of evil and there is madness in their hearts while they live, and afterward they join the dead." (Ecclesiastes 9:3)

From whence does anger arise? Pride. Daniel 4:28-34 explores the link between pride and insanity.

> All this happened to King Nebuchadnezzar. Twelve months later, as the king was walking on the roof of the royal palace of Babylon, he said, 'Is not this the great Babylon I have built as the royal residence, by my mighty power and for the glory of my majesty?' Even as the words were on his lips, a voice came from heaven, 'This is what is decreed for you, King Nebuchadnezzar: Your royal authority has been taken from you. You will be driven away from people and will live with the wild animals; you will eat grass like the ox. Seven times will pass by for you until you acknowledge that the Most High is sovereign over all kingdoms on earth and gives them to anyone he wishes.'

> Immediately what had been said about Nebuchadnezzar was fulfilled. He was driven away from people and ate grass like the ox. His body was drenched

with the dew of heaven until his hair grew like the feathers of an eagle and his nails like the claws of a bird. At the end of that time, I, Nebuchadnezzar, raised my eyes toward heaven, and my sanity was restored. Then I praised the Most High; I honored and glorified him who lives forever.

Nebuchadnezzar grew insane through his unbridled hubris, as one year prior he refused to heed Daniel's stern warning to repent in renouncing his sin and wickedness.[123] Nebuchadnezzar was thus given over to his sin, becoming insane and animal-like. It was only through repentance that his sanity was restored, a renouncing of his megalomania, a surrendering of desire for supremacy over his world.

> "Words from the mouth of the wise are gracious, but fools are consumed by their own lips. At the beginning their words are folly; at the end they are wicked madness…" (Ecclesiastes 10:12, 13)
>
> "The heart is deceitful above all things and beyond cure. Who can understand it?" (Jeremiah 17:9)

The Bible is profoundly cognizant of the heart's desperate insanity, an insanity that affects each and every person, some with more demonstrable effect than others. Nevertheless, each is subject to this insanity, to one degree or another, an insanity bred in pride, cultivated through selfishness, and brought to full flower through envy and desire. Each chooses his own poison and each is a prison to himself, not a hapless victim but a willful co-conspirator in his own slavery to sin. This explains insanity in all of it various shades and textures.

Psychology is blind to the true nature of insanity. It searches for insanity's source in the wrong places and is, thus, deceived concerning its solution. Additionally, what psychology might label as "insanity" (the psychotic, paranoid delusional, neurotic, manic, or mentally ill) is a subjective standard based on a patient's perceived ability to function as society dictates. Thus, psychology labels one insane based solely on arbitrary standards of a purely pragmatic nature (while others are labeled "eccentric," "passionate," or even "gifted.")

From God's perspective insanity germinates through pride and anger, through "playing God" and seeking revenge. That insanity steadily metastasizes until it overtakes one's life in dissipation and relational loss. However, psychology is blind to insanity's inception and progression, only identifying insanity when it has crossed an imaginary line making it a liability to society.

---

[123] Daniel 4:27

The Hydraulic View of Emotions[124]

Some claim that high-impact sports such as football are necessary to help young men get out aggression, that sport can be a valuable outlet for anger, pent-up frustration, and low self-esteem. The idea of venting emotions arises from what is termed the hydraulic theory of emotions.[125] This theory states that emotions, like a hydraulic fluid, buildup under pressure that must be released, that emotions are not controlled but arise without one's consent. The idea is that emotions cannot be explained or rationalized, and therefore cannot be stopped. Emotions just exist as a neutral physiological force arising in response to outside stimuli. The humanistic view is that one is a victim of his physiology, so that emotions should not be evaluated or rationalized, since one is not responsible for them.

Corrupt Legislation, Elihu Vedder, c. 1898

The hydraulic theory contradicts the Bible's view that emotions are chosen moment by moment. Emotions arise from, and reflect, the heart's deepest worship, the product of interpreting one's world either from a God-centered or man-centered perspective. In other words, each person continually interprets how to feel about his life experiences and how to express those feelings. He either interprets life through God's Word or through fallen human reason. Emotions, like the worship they expose, are chosen, not the result of uncontrollable forces within the psyche.

Tragically, the hydraulic theory has been used to justify football's popularity. Thus, the logic goes that football serves as an outlet for anger and aggression which would

---
[124] For further discussion of this topic see "The *Coram Deo* Concept and the Issue of Emotions" in chapter 6: "Man Before the Face of God: The Imperium of the Psyche"
[125] David Powlison, Westminster Theological Seminary, Philadelphia, Pennsylvania

otherwise be visited upon society in the form of crime. However, this is an egregious error robbing generations of young men of an accurate understanding of their depraved nature, of the worshipping quality of their emotion.

Emotion, aggression, or even sexual desire, are not neutral aspects of the psyche which must be afforded an outlet. Mankind's emotional and moral decisions are chosen, cultivated, embraced, and driven moment by moment. Young men, with each life decision, either fuel or forsake the sinful tendencies within themselves. They either aggravate their sinful desire, giving it full flourish, or seek to conquer that desire. Football, often thought to quell aggression, has in fact had the opposite effect. It incites aggression, making it acceptable even commendable, effectual, and expeditious, yet another outgrowth of a psychology-infused society.

> In 1 Corinthians 7:9 Paul wrote, "But if [the widows] cannot control themselves, they should marry, for it is better to marry than to burn with passion." With such a statement did Paul tacitly support a hydraulic view of emotions? The implication seems to be that if one cannot control his libido, if he is consumed with carnal desire, then he should marry so as to afford himself a sexual outlet. While this verse would seem to support a hydraulic view of emotions (that emotions simply build up like a pressure that must be released), such an interpretation would prove problematic given Paul's clear understanding of the nature of the psyche. The biblical view is that the psyche is never sated through giving expression to its lusts. Rather, those lusts are merely exacerbated and intensified, so that acting upon lusts throws fuel upon them.

Excursus: Psychology May Foster the Love of Money

Consider this logic. Psychology is blind to the true distinctions between people. It views the human existence as fundamentally homogeneous (especially reductionistic forms of psychology which view mankind as prisoner to his genetic software). Thus, because psychology sees no fundamental distinction between people, this lends the impression that there is no way to truly distinguish oneself except through external, superficial means. From psychology's perspective, there is no discernable character development, no distinguishing sense of morality (since there is no moral standard), and no changed person. In light of psychology's views, all that is left to differentiate people is outward appearance, and other superficial means.

Thus, because modern man has been deluded into thinking that all people are fundamentally the same (even that all cultures are fundamentally the same, called "multiculturalism") there is nothing left to set people apart except appearance, political power, or wealth. For most, physical appearance is essentially genetically determined, so there is not much that can be done. One's talents and abilities generally do not develop much past their level as a young adult, and political power is limited to an elite few. The one remaining means to individuate oneself, the one means that seems attainable to all, is the acquisition of money. It would appear that anyone, whether handsome or not, talented or not, can work his way to a certain measure of wealth.

Consider 2 Timothy 3:1-5 carefully.

> But mark this: There will be terrible times in the last days. People will be lovers of themselves, lovers of money, boastful, proud, abusive, disobedient to their parents, ungrateful, unholy, without love, unforgiving, slanderous, without self-control, brutal, not lovers of the good, treacherous, rash, conceited, lovers of pleasure rather than lovers of God— having a form of godliness but denying its power. Have nothing to do with such people.

This warning sounds like a blueprint for psychology's influence in society. Psychology has unwittingly crafted people who love themselves and subsequently love money. Such people are inherently proud, disobedient to their parents, unforgiving, and without self-control. It would seem that the love of money is nestled within a broader master plan of intensifying rebellion.

Ophelia, Alexandre Cabanel, 1883

Psychology fosters a toxic atmosphere, an ethos, in which the love of money flourishes under the perception that growth in inner character does not exist, indeed, cannot exist. If man's inner life is essentially a wasteland of fruitless pursuits, then all that is left to offer some semblance of meaning is the external, the visible, the tangible. That is why the love of money (and even the love of beauty) flourishes in a psychologized world because it promises a measure of salvation from futility, mediocrity, and commonality. However, money's promises are both vacuous and destructive since mankind's purpose is to explore his inner being, one designed by God, invested with meaning by God, and ultimately meant to be renewed by God.

Psychology Holds Forth No Hope of Cure

Consider that mankind can place a man on the moon, split the atom, and clone a sheep, but it cannot solve the most fundamental problems of human relationships. It cannot solve the most rudimentary ailments of the psyche. In fact, it would appear that as the world becomes more deeply psychologized, the psyche becomes more tortured, fractured, dysfunctional, and isolated. Psychological problems seem to metastasize with each passing generation.

Possibly the most searing indictment of psychology is the fact that no one has ever truly changed through it. (Even psychology understands this, as there exists no concept of being conclusively cured.) Patients are taught to cope, to manage symptoms, to negotiate life's disappointments.[126] In this way, psychology affects a certain faulty worship within those to whom it ministers. It holds up pragmatism as the ultimate objective rather than rebirth and regeneration in Christ.

In the psychology paradigm the only way to judge improvement is if the psychologist declares that one has improved. This usually means being happier or functioning better in society. However, happiness and function do not necessarily mean improvement from God's perspective; this may only indicate rehabilitated idols, or more effectively muffled guilt for sin. Therefore, for psychology, improvement is defined as having successfully applied exonerating veneers to the psyche in order to progressively shield it from a holy God before whom it knows itself to be culpable.

Psychology shapes the heart, solidifies false worship commitments, and standardizes a godless orientation. Thus, while a patient may feel better, in reality heart idols have been resuscitated so that they function as the patient hopes. However, such idols never produce the desired outcome for long, so that the idolater is finally left weak, cursed, and faced with life's meaninglessness as he fruitlessly seeks to restore a dilapidated ego.

> Western medicine is said to be in the Hippocratic tradition (based on the Greek physician Hippocrates (460–380 BC)) or evidence-based. In the United States physicians take the Hippocratic oath, a sworn pledge to do everything possible to

---

[126] David Powlison, Westminster Theological Seminary, Philadelphia, Pennsylvania

> guard human life and to avoid harming a patient. While on the surface this pledge seems to offer a palladium, is this fraud perpetrated by those medical professionals who purport to treat the psyche? Based on what standard are physicians presumed to have avoided harm to a patient?

Maintaining the Hegemony

Riding on postmodernism's coattails, psychologists, in general, no longer believe that what they present is actually true (since absolute truth is thought to not exist). Psychology now operates to maintain power structures and cultural relevance, to keep itself firmly embedded in society's institutions (church, economics, education, government, healthcare, media, science, etc.). This power structure keeps psychology ascendant in society, dominant among other worldviews.[127]

The Lady of Shalott, Arthur Hughes, 1873

The United States federal government tacitly upholds psychology's hegemony through tightly-controlled licensure which safeguards its ability to collect health insurance fees.[128] Those excluded from licensure are denied access to the money stream, all but ensuring that they will be functionally, if not professionally, marginalized. Additionally, psychology is an ever expanding world empire, continually labeling more and more of human activity as "disease." As this labeling expands, psychology muscles out competing worldviews through the cultural and

---
[127] David Powlison, "Apologetics and Counseling" class, Westminster Theological Seminary, Philadelphia, Pennsylvania
[128] For additional discussion of this topic see "The World System: Intrusive Government" in the second book in this series, *What Agreement Is There Between the Temple of God and Idols?: The Accidence of Sin and Idolatry*, chapter 2: "The World, the Flesh, and the Devil: Assessing the Threat Matrix"

legal right to sole jurisdiction over supposed diseases.

> For proponents of liberalism, psychology is a facile tool of mass inculcation and manipulation. Psychology, in the hands of overreaching government, is a ready means of advancing a socialist agenda because it continually seeks to convince people that they are subjugated victims. This makes them ripe for exploitation by a supposed governmental savior.

In lockstep with the federal government's licensure system, modern America upholds a certain tacit social contract which asserts that those outside of a recognized mental health profession are prohibited from speaking on supposed psychological issues. Those offering advice may preface their comments with "I'm not a psychologist, but…" or "I am not trained in mental health, but…" There is an unspoken sense that those untrained in recognized mental health professions are unqualified to speak on the psyche. It is even considered unethical, legally treacherous, or psychologically damaging for the uninitiated to speak on an issue which has been claimed by a licensed profession. Those outside of recognized licensure, who speak on such issues, are routinely shamed for presumably overstepping their social bounds.

> Ironically, those psychology practitioners who *least* understand their field's theories are most likely to provide a measure of meaningful help to counselees. Those who simply operate out of a basic sense of assumed common humanity, or general concepts about life, tend to do the least damage. Conversely, those practitioners most heavily invested in their theories are often severed from a shared sense of humanity.

Psychology's social hegemony is one of the great tragedies of modern American life, an atmosphere in which family members, friends, coworkers, acquaintances or even strangers are tacitly denied the social right to speak into life situations or make moral judgments unless properly trained. This atmosphere infiltrates the church where the same social contract predominates. Church members are often silent in the face of needed counsel under the misguided notion that such matters are properly left to licensed medical professionals (or even the proper pastoral staff).

> "Everyone has heard about your obedience, so I am full of joy over you; but I want you to be wise about what is good, and innocent about what is evil." (Romans 16:19)

Case Study: Analysis of the Columbine Shooting[129]

In the years following the Columbine attacks a host of books have been written on the profile of serial killers. School administrators, psychologists, and law enforcement

---

[129] Some ideas from Greg Toppo, "Ten Years Later, The Real Story Behind Columbine," *USA Today* (April 14, 2009)

officials study these profiles in order to pinpoint and diffuse potential threats. However, these studies fail to see the true psyche of their subjects.

The prevailing myth was that the Columbine shooters, Eric Harris (1981–1999) and Dylan Klebold (1981–1999), were essentially good young men pushed to psychopathic behavior by a culture of bullying and rejection. There was speculation that they had been abused at home, that they were badly in need of anti-depressant medication, or that they were struggling with low self-esteem as a result of being demeaned in a cruel social environment. Every scenario paints Eric and Dylan as hapless victims; that is psychology's expertise.

In fact, as the truth has revealed, Eric and Dylan were delusional paranoid killers who feasted on a daily diet of hatred, relishing the chance to kill in cold-blood. Both young men, at some point, referred to themselves as "gods." In line with autolatry, Eric harbored trenchant resentment for supposed social slights and sought to exact revenge, the obvious mark of a narcissist. He frequently sketched swastikas in sympathy with Hitler's (1889–1945) genocidal ideations. Like Hitler, Eric cultivated a superiority complex and exhibited an "excruciating need for control."

> Dylan was known to listen to German industrial band "KMFDM" an acronym which translates to "no pity for the masses." This group glorifies mass violence.

It is fascinating that Eric wore the persona of a model citizen. He was amiable and courteous with peers and teachers. When he asserted himself, he was an excellent student and a gifted writer. But the mask he wore was part of a sinister plan to keep people unaware of his true intent. In order to maintain his deception, Eric skillfully played the part that others expected him to play.

Dylan, on the other hand, was deeply forlorn, longing for love and acceptance. He frequently drew hearts in his diary and entertained suicidal ideations. As Dylan's desire for love went unrequited his anger burned. On the day of the attacks he wore a shirt which read "wrath."

Eric and Dylan have often been painted as social rejects who were humiliated and bullied. However, their diaries reveal that, in fact, they often reveled in bulling others. Additionally, they showed callous disregard for the feelings of those they taunted and maligned. They daily entertained self-aggrandizing fantasies of harrowing revenge.

Their actions were carefully calculated to achieve their egocentric goal of infamy, eternal glory of a sick variation. In the words of one author, in these boys' minds "getting attention by becoming notorious was better than being a failure." Delusions of grandeur escalate until they take on a world of their own. So that those bragging about planned criminal acts, find themselves bound to them as a matter of "saving face" with peers.

Some have described the Columbine shooting as a giant Rorschach for American culture, a lens through which to analyze parenting, pedagogy, gun laws, psychotropic drugs, bullying, violent video games, alternative music, and even the proliferation of the internet.[130] However, each analysis fails to satisfy because each misses the truth of the human heart, each is blinded to the reality nestled within the killers themselves, and within a society which bares similar characteristics to such killers.

The goal of most psychological analysis is to shift blame to factors for which the subject is not responsible, to cause perpetrators to be painted as victims of oppressive family structure, peer pressure, or guilt-inducing moral absolutes. Psychology cannot see the heart's inner workings because it is blind, deceived, and insane itself. It cannot comprehend the psyche because it knows nothing of its designer.

> Psychology's insane perspective easily gains ascendancy in a culture which has rejected the true God. As faith in God wanes, errant faith commitments, such as psychology, rush in to fill worship vacuum.

The School of Athens (Pythagoras detail)
Raphael, 1509

As the Bible explains, the heart is insane, deceived, and duplicitous; it twists and rationalizes sin at every turn in order to justify the sinner before a holy God. Eric and Dylan responded to that God in hatred, rebellion, anger, deception, and self-justification. They sought to escape from that God, suppress the knowledge of his goodness, and assert themselves as gods worthy of worship. They were active perpetrators of their fantasy worlds, delusions of grandeur, and obsessive sense of

---

[130] Peter Langman, *Why Kids Kill: Inside the Minds of School Shooters* (Palgrave Macmillan, 2010)

superiority. They willfully pursued false gods in an attempt to make themselves gods. It has been said that the Bible is more relevant to current events than the evening news. In the case of the Columbine massacre, the Bible offers far more perspicuity than the media ever could.

> Consider the recent case of a wealthy Texas teenager who committed vehicular homicide while intoxicated.[131] Under the testimony of a psychologist, the defense asserted that the young man suffered from a newly-minted psychological illness called "affluenza." Affluenza is the inability for wealthy young people to discern right from wrong because their parents never imposed consequences upon them. Thus, the argument goes that a wealthy child, because he was never held accountable and always received his way, cannot be held responsible for criminal behavior.
>
> Ironically, this has traditionally been the argument used to exculpate the impoverished, especially those from inner city environments with absent fathers. The defense is usually that poverty and family upheaval spawned an inability for a young person to discern right from wrong. Thus, such a youngster, with no sense of accountability, is to be excused for crime.
>
> Psychology offers a Morton's Fork, a double-edged sword in the hands of the criminal justice system so as to exonerate both the disenfranchised and the enfranchised with the exact same defense. The implication is that the only ones truly culpable are the middling middleclass. (It is fascinating to note that in order to bring down any society Karl Marx (1818-1883) advocated specifically targeting the middleclass. If the will of the middleclass could be broken, society would implode.)

Reductionism

The former president of Harvard University, Lawrence Summers, intimated that the reason that women do not excel in math and science is partly due to genetic gender differences. (Summers was later chastised and fired for this comment.) It is strangely ironic that psychology relishes the opportunity to herald genetic differences as the excuse for nearly every human ailment, but takes umbrage with such an argument when it is deemed wrongly slanted. Psychology only allows reductionist arguments on its terms, to uphold its agenda.

For example, I find it quite remarkable that homosexuality is universally regarded as a genetic condition, written into DNA. The prevailing paradigm presents homosexuals as having been born in such a state, and therefore, as simply living out a blind evolutionary code. Homosexuals are thus cast as prisoners to their biology. I would

---

[131] Madison Gray, "The Affluenza Defense: Judge Rules Rich Kid's Rich Kid-ness Makes Him Not Liable for Deadly Drunk Driving Accident," *Time* (December 12, 2013)

think that the homosexual agenda would take the exact opposite tact, posturing homosexuality as a full-fledged lifestyle *choice*. This would seem to lend its practitioners more dignity as they would be living out their desires, in defiance of tradition. Could it be that subsumed guilt before a holy God drives homosexuals to hide behind a genetic scapegoat?[132]

> The world accepts the truth only to the extent that it accords with its lies.

Dualism is the belief that the human being is both material and spiritual, body and *nous* (heart/mind/soul/spirit).[133] Monism, on the other hand, states that the human being is only material with no spiritual component. While a host of ancient religions (such as Buddhism) subscribe to monism, psychology is a modern secular manifestation of this view, reducing the human drama to the mere interplay of physiological mechanisms, namely brain chemicals. In the philosophy of science, this view of humanity is labeled "reductionism."

A Soul in Heaven, William-Adolphe Bouguereau, d. 1905

As a dualistic approach, the Bible offers the most comprehensive and in-depth understanding of humanity because it sees the God-ward dimension of the psyche. It is that continuous interface with God which directs all else, whether for the purpose of

---

[132] For further analysis of homosexuality see the case study "Homosexuality and the Issue of Personal History" in the third book in this series, *The Days of Reckoning Are at Hand: From Fig Leaf to Olive Branch to Laurel Wreath*, chapter 1: "Memories Preserved in Amber: Adopting God's Retrospective"
[133] 2 Corinthians 4:16

suppression and denial, or for faith and obedience.[134] While certain world religions propositionally espouse to a form of dualism (such as Islam), anything other than the Bible's understanding is functionally a masked variation of reductionism.

Psychology, largely under the control of reductionism,[135] creates an environment in which instead of saying that *I* did something, one says that his body or brain did something.[136] Reductionism treats physiology as a cold machine slavishly complying with the dictates of its various mechanical components.

> The receptors and neural transmitters that mediate tastes and textures are well-known. Those that mediate pride or guilt remain mysterious.[137]

At issue in this discussion is the definition of a human being. Is a human merely the interplay of brain and body chemicals strictly dictating behavior, cognition, and emotional state? Is the human firstly a spiritual being, interacting with, and responding to a holy God? In other words, who or what arbitrates human action? Is the locus of authority the somatic or the spiritual? While certainly there is a physiological component to behavior, cognition, and emotion, the question comes down to the prime mover, the driver, the authority.

> The body is the hardware; the *nous* (heart/mind/spirit/will) is the software.[138]

With regard to psychosis and the somatic, one strikes up against the question of causation, or the "chicken and egg" question. Is the somatic the perpetrator of psychological illness, or is psychological illness the perpetrator of somatic responses? (The very use of the term "psychological illness" begs a reductionistic worldview.) Modern psychiatry presumes to conclusively know that the somatic induces psychosis. The Bible offers the opposite perspective, that worship commitments drive particular bodily reactions (While, clearly, not every somatic problem is driven by worship.).

The Bible presents a nuanced form of psychosomatics (in which the psyche is thought to influence the somatic), which might more accurately be labeled the "heart-somatic." Thus, man's worshipping core influences the somatic. For example, there is something in a godly peace, built upon forgiveness in Christ, which strengthens and reinvigorates the body. Likewise, there is something in guilt before a holy God which, like a leach, siphons off vitality.

---

[134] David Powlison, "Which Presuppositions? Secular Psychology and the Categories of Biblical Thought," *Journal of Psychology and Theology* 12.4 (Winter, 1984): 270.
[135] Jungian psychology purports a certain spiritual dimension to mankind but that dimension is abstract and mysterious.
[136] Edward Welch, *Blame It on the Brain: Distinguishing Chemical Imbalances, Brain Disorders, and Disobedience* (Presbyterian and Reformed Publishing, 1998)
[137] Jerome Kagan, "Three Pleasing Ideas," *American Psychologist* 51.9 (September, 1996): 905, 906.
[138] Edward Welch, "Counseling and Physiology" class, Westminster Theological Seminary, Philadelphia, Pennsylvania

The following sections of Scripture offer a picture of the "heart-somatic":

1. "When I kept silent,
   my bones wasted away
   through my groaning all day long.
For day and night
   your hand was heavy on me;
my strength was sapped
   as in the heat of summer.
Then I acknowledged my sin to you
   and did not cover up my iniquity.
I said, 'I will confess
   my transgressions to the Lord.'
And you forgave
   the guilt of my sin." (Psalm 32:3-5)

Phaedra, Alexandre Cabanel, 1880

2. "Because of your wrath there is no health in my body;
   there is no soundness in my bones because of my sin.
My guilt has overwhelmed me
   like a burden too heavy to bear.
My wounds fester and are loathsome
   because of my sinful folly.

I am bowed down and brought very low;
   all day long I go about mourning.
My back is filled with searing pain;
   there is no health in my body.
I am feeble and utterly crushed;
   I groan in anguish of heart.
All my longings lie open before you, Lord;
   my sighing is not hidden from you.
My heart pounds, my strength fails me;
   even the light has gone from my eyes." (Psalm 38:3-10)

3. "My son, pay attention to what I say;
   turn your ear to my words.
Do not let them out of your sight,
   keep them within your heart;
for they are life to those who find them
   and health to one's whole body.
Above all else, guard your heart,
   for everything you do flows from it." (Proverbs 4:20-23)

4. "A heart at peace gives life to the body, but envy rots the bones." (Proverbs 14:30)

While the Bible paints a picture of heart-somatics, a question remains as to how to discern between a true worship disorder, and mere behavior deviation arising from a physiological breakdown. For example, hypothyroidism can drive depression-like symptoms. However, the texture of this depression is more akin to lethargy and sloth than to existential angst. Thus, physiologically-derived depression bears a wholly different dynamic, is of a different ilk, than worship-derived depression. In other words, the body's breakdown and the heart's idolatry bear a different somatic signature. Through carefully-directed questions, and astute observation, the counselor should gain decisive hints in discerning between the two. Additionally, it is important that a biblical counselor refer a counselee for a medical evaluation (internal medicine, not psychiatry) if there is any hint of a physiological matter in need of treatment.

When behavior displays an obvious sin component, it cannot possibly be dictated by physiology. For example, outbursts of uncontrolled anger, a clear lack of self-discipline, or deviant eating habits such as anorexia, bulimia, or gluttony, are not the result of chemical imbalances. They arise from overt choices to seek that which is not God, to worship the creation over the Creator, to rest in idolatry over submission to the true God. Sinful behavior, that which bears a tacit denial of Christ, begins with a surrender to idols, and likewise must end with surrender to Christ.

Additional Examples for Analysis

1. Those who suffer from grand mal epileptic seizures tend to display uncontrollable anger. Is this anger the result of rogue electrical impulses in the limbic system? Such anger is a heart issue, a clenched fist against God, which ignites into rage possibly on account of not having control of one's mind or with the humiliation that accompanies seizures. Those who suffer from epileptic seizures tend toward depression and suicidal ideations,[139] which would further indicate that the heart is actively engaged in the response to the seizures.

2. Those who suffer a stroke (CVA, cerebral vascular accident) may use vulgar speech and exhibit erratic emotion. Such speech can offer an unprecedented window into the heart. The stroke does not cause sinful content in speech, but exposes the heart's commitments, revealing either faith or idolatry.

3. Brain tumors can affect various cognitive functions resulting in aphasias, impairments, and perceptive disorders. This impaired brain function may uncover worship issues within the heart.

4. Head trauma exacerbates preexisting personality patterns and, in this way, offers increased temptation for sin, while not directly causing sin.[140]

5. New mothers often suffer from postpartum depression. In these depressive episodes a woman may contemplate murdering her newborn. Is there a physiological driver to this depression, or is this a heart issue? The wise counselor recognizes that, while the body offers opportunity to sin, sinful thoughts always derive from a degenerate heart. Thus, postpartum depression is not firstly a physiological problem (although it may be correlated to physiology).

6. A child who strikes another may be labeled as having an impulsive disorder. However, striking another is clearly a moral decision driven by the heart. The heart knows that this is an offense against the image of God. However, the child who shouts out of turn in class, while still labeled as having an impulsive disorder, may not necessarily be sinning. He may be somewhat unaware of his transgression (unless it has been clearly identified to him as such) because there is not an obvious compromise of the conscience. Is the child acting out of rebellion, or is he merely unaware of the rules, in which case he needs teaching and direction? Issues not clearly spelled out in the Bible are not written in the conscience; thus teaching is required to

---

[139] For additional discussion of this topic see the case study "Suicide: Idols in Death Throws" in the third book in this series, *The Days of Reckoning Are at Hand: From Fig Leaf to Olive Branch to Laurel Wreath*, chapter 2: "Suffering: The Kintsugi Objective"

[140] Edward Welch, *Counselor's Guide to the Brain and Its Disorders: Knowing the Difference Between Disease and Sin* (Zondervan, 1991) 136.

delineate sin from obedience.

7. A man who displays mania succumbs to sexual sin during his maniacal episodes. The mania is a wild sense of euphoria, and as such, functions as a tempter to the desires of the heart. A heart that craves power, emotional thrills, and attention, drives the mania. This then serves as a conduit for desires and, in so doing, makes lusts seem attainable. Therefore, the mania is a somatic manifestation of heart idols.

Understanding Addiction[141]

> For much of its history, science was content to *describe* the universe's workings. Today science has shifted to manipulating and altering those workings.

Nymphs and Satyr
William-Adolphe Bouguereau, 1873

Just as the story of evolution stirs the imagination, stoking the ember of rebellion, so too, psychology is an ingenious collection of stories concocted to embolden sin. Possibly the best kept secret in psychiatry is that cause-and-effect with regard to physiology and mental illness has never been established. While pseudoscientific studies clamor to prove brain-behavior causation, this can never be proven. This is why psychiatry and psychology will always remain a collection of unsubstantiated theories, a semi-fiction that offers little more than a compelling story. The crucial question then is,

---

[141] For a comprehensive study of addiction see Edward Welch, *Addictions: A Banquet in the Grave: Finding Hope in the Power of the Gospel* (Presbyterian and Reformed Publishing, 2001)

"Does brain chemical imbalance induce psychosis, or does psychosis result in brain chemical imbalance?" Is the somatic the driver and source of psychosis, or is the *nous* (heart/soul/mind/will) the driver?

A flashpoint in the discussion of physiology and behavior is the issue of alcoholism. From time immemorial, alcohol has been the quintessential anti-depressant. In small doses it is benignly therapeutic. (First Timothy 5:23 states, "Stop drinking only water, and use a little wine because of your stomach and your frequent illnesses.") In larger doses it is debilitating and lethal. Is alcoholism a disease or a moral choice? The psychiatrist would label it a disease, even saddling it with a genetic driver. However, from the Bible's perspective, brain chemistry, whether functioning properly or failing, is never the locus for sin, and the Bible clearly labels drunkenness as sin.

Galatians 5:21 states, "…and envy; drunkenness, orgies, and the like. I warn you, as I did before, that those who live like this will not inherit the kingdom of God." The temptation to drunkenness, when acted upon, is sin. This is not a physiological problem, but one of misplaced worship. For this reason, the Bible views alcoholism as arising from sinful choices outside of desiring God. Alcoholism, like all addiction, grows from actively seeking a refuge other than God, and in this way has its root in rebellion and revenge. While psychology defines alcoholism as a disease to which one is slavishly conscribed, the Bible sees alcoholism as a willful choice from which one can be free (as with all choices) through faith in Jesus.

Alcoholism, as with all addiction, clearly draws in a broad range of physical experiences. It feels like disease because powerful physiological responses come into play. However, all addiction is firstly a relationship with God dysfunction. Addiction is driven by militant heart worship, a desperate flailing battle against the God of the universe. That is why it feels like an internal war, because it is, a war of competing worship.

The point is that physiology may tempt one to sin, but never forces one to sin. Each is always culpable for sinful behavior regardless of his somatic condition.[142] Thus, the heart initiates the human drama and the body merely mediates the heart's intent.[143] Second Corinthians 5:10 reminds, "For we must all appear before the judgment seat of Christ, so that each of us may receive what is due us for the things done while in the body, whether good or bad."

Psychology frequently uses the label "addictive personality" to exonerate the addict under the misguided assumption that something in his genetic makeup drives his

---

[142] All of that said, the wise counselor is sensitive to the body's suffering in the midst of alcohol withdrawal. Of course, the onset of delirium tremens should be treated by a physician of internal medicine.

[143] Edward Welch, "Counseling and Physiology" class, Westminster Theological Seminary, Philadelphia, Pennsylvania

behavior. This is a close cousin to the "tyranny of low expectations," endemic to liberalism,[144] which takes a patrician stance of enlightened superiority with regard to others' failing (the idea that one is not responsible, a helpless victim of his biology). Psychology's labels keep the addict in a state of dependence through crafty blame-shifting, functioning only to strengthen the root cause. In this way, misplaced labels function as a shield keeping the sinner blind to his need for repentance.

Never underestimate the power of repentance before the cross of Jesus. Repentance invites God himself into the heart to ravish, raze, and rebuild it in his likeness. Each is a sin addict, and the power of that sin is only broken with God's personal intervention, an intervention that one must ask for, submit to, and receive.

At the end of the day, the addictive personality label demeans humanity as it is a fatalistic look at the human condition. It hopelessly supposes that, as with all diseases, one is merely at the capricious whim of forces outside of his control with no known cure. The *mirabile dictu* is that God's plans and purposes are vastly greater than that. God heals the heart so that it can break the spell of its rebellion addiction.

A Double Portrait of the Fullerton Sisters, Seated Full Length in White Dresses
Thomas Lawrence, d. 1830

In this way, a repentant addict finds new life and lasting freedom, so that what once enslaved does so no more. There may always be temptation to revisit the addiction, but for those in Christ the heart can (and will) be buttressed to resist and ultimately triumph. That is Jesus' promise.[145]

Excursus: Identical Twins Studies

---

[144] This phrase from Daniel Patrick Moynihan (1927-2003), former New York State senator
[145] John 14:12, Romans 6:14

Two terms are bandied about in psychology circles, "nature" and "nurture." The classic question is from whence do mankind's psychic problems arise, from his nature (the state into which he is born) or from his nurture (the environment in which he is raised). From the Bible's perspective, nature refers to a source, driver, or propulsion for sin. Nurture refers to learned methods for how to express that sin, so that one's cultural environment teaches him new ways to live out his rebellion toward, denial of, and hatred for God. (That is part of the purpose of non-Christian culture, to offer a plausible means for living without God.) From the Bible's perspective, nature is primary and formative; one is born into sin so that it is a reflexive response to God.[146] Nurture could either be thought of as nature's enabler (co-conspirator in sin), or else as a rebuke and confrontation of the sin nature.

In drawing out the issues of nature and nurture, consider that identical twins share the exact same genetic makeup. Thus, any genetic condition must show up in each.

Findings:[147]

	The Incidence of Alcoholism
1. The general population	6%
2. The sibling of an alcoholic	12%
3. One raised together with his alcoholic identical twin	58%
4. One biological parent is an alcoholic; the child was adopted into a non-alcoholic home.	16%[148]
5. Neither of the biological parents is an alcoholic; the child was adopted into an alcoholic home.	6%

If genetics were the exclusive driver for alcoholism, then one would expect 100% of alcoholic identical twins to be alcoholics. However, identical twins share alcoholism in only 58% of the cases. Thus, lurking in the genetics is a "dark horse," as there are constitutional issues or personality tendencies (rebellion) which make one more or less prone to sinful behavior. The Bible never presents a biological trigger for sin. It recognizes a worship addiction which could manifest itself in myriad ways, such as alcoholism. While the body may tempt in a particular direction, it is ultimately the heart which decides its own course.

The Legalized Drug Cartel

---

[146] Psalm 51:5; Isaiah 48:8
[147] Edward Welch, "Counseling and Physiology" class, Westminster Theological Seminary, Philadelphia, Pennsylvania
[148] This percentage is an estimate.

Narcotics and hallucinogens existed in the ancient Near East. For instance, the ancient Greek oracles of Delphi apparently used *datura* (Jimson weed, a powerful narcotic) during their quests for visions. Likewise, the opium poppy and chamomile are natural sedatives. While naturally-occurring drugs are not evil in themselves, much drug use today, as in ancient times, is a quest for either self-absorbed pleasure or numbing escape. The evil emerges from unredeemed hearts and minds as they commit spiritual adultery in using drugs for some purpose without, or against, God.

A Café in Istambul, Amedeo Preziosi, c. 1882

Pharmakeia (φαρμακεία) (the basis for the word "pharmaceutical") is Greek for "witchcraft" or "sorcery." According to *Strong's Bible Concordance*, *pharmakeia* means:

1. Using or administering drugs
2. Poisoning
3. Sorcery, magical arts, often found in connection with idolatry
4. Metaphorically, the deceptions and seductions of idolatry

The word is used three times in the New Testament, once as "witchcraft" in Galatians 5:20, and twice as "sorcery" in Revelation 9:21 and 18:23. *Pharmakeia* is therefore considered one of the "works of the flesh," so that there appears to be a connection between the Bible's understanding of the abuse of mind-altering drugs and the works of Satan.

Psychiatry developed, and was licensed, to essentially run a legalized drug cartel, allowing otherwise dangerous chemicals to be standardized, controlled, and distributed in an orderly fashion. Psychiatrists prescribe approved drugs that chemically are not substantively different from illegal drugs such as cocaine, heroine, and methamphetamines. The only difference is that the manufacturing process is standardized, the distribution is documented and controlled, and the FDA approves their sale. Other than government oversight, there is little to distinguish a legal drug from an illegal one. The purpose of labeling certain drugs as illegal is largely to protect pharmaceutical companies' profits. For example, while barbiturates are generally illegal street drugs, their brand name version, Xanax®, is legally prescribed.

What constitutes drug abuse varies along cultural and historical lines. In the United States, banned drugs were often associated with particular subcultures which mainstream society sought to control or suppress. For example, cocaine and Ritalin® are functionally the same drug. (The latter is standardized and prescribed, while the former is not.) It is fascinating that cocaine was an ingredient in the original Coca-Cola® formula (along with alcohol and caffeine), as it was considered a healthful stimulant. However, as cocaine increasingly became associated with inner-city blight, it was criminalized. Condemning cocaine became a convenient way to incarcerate a subculture. Ritalin®, however, the choice of middleclass suburban communities, is touted as responsible therapy. In similar fashion, Valium®, often associated with suburban family life, was trivialized as "mama's little helper."

> Psychopharmacology for adolescents is lucrative as six million American children between six and eighteen years-old are currently on psychotropic drug therapies. In June, 2012, pharmaceutical giant GlaxoSmithKline was assessed a $3 billion fine for illegally marketing adult psychotropic drugs to children. Such pharmaceutical companies are not naïve. Through a carefully-derived calculus they are well aware of the risk-benefit of their illegal activities. (Corporations routinely and deliberately engage in illegal activity when their risk analysis tells them it is profitable to do so.) If Galaxo was penalized $3 billion it likely garnered profits far in excess of this before being caught.
>
> The modern practice of prescribing psychotropic drugs to children is functionally similar to sacrificing the nation's children to Molech, the ancient Near Eastern god,[149] a practice that God condemned. Additionally, Satan, routinely through means of a drug culture, targets youth since they are highly-impressionable and easily led astray.

Opium was traditionally popular in Chinatowns so criminalizing it became a convenient way to maintain a police presence within the Chinese community (often

---
[149] Leviticus 18:21; 20:2-5

viewed as unpatriotic and subversive). However, over-the-counter painkillers and prescribed drugs Vicodin® and Codeine® are opiates.

This being said, some well-intentioned biblical counselors believe in multimodal treatment plans, those which employ limited drug therapy in tandem with counseling. The idea is that certain psychotropic drugs may be necessary to temporarily stabilize a dangerously psychotic or severely catatonic person. While I disagree with this approach, if such drug intervention is used as only a very brief means to a greater end (not an end in itself), it may be within the pale of reason.[150] (I personally believe that all synthetic drug use is dangerous, even for matters of temporary stability, since any highly-controlling drug opens one to demonic influence, and increased psychosis, especially when in the throes of seething rage.)

In a medical model, pain and suffering have no redeeming value, no positive function. What psychiatry, therefore, will not countenance is that a certain degree of pain and suffering are often vital to the Christian's growth in holiness.[151] The Christian recognizes that a measure of struggle (in proportion to one's faith) is efficacious for producing a harvest of righteousness in those who believe.[152] Therefore, the Christian does not seek to reflexively eradicate measured suffering until God's work in and through it is accomplished.[153]

Drug therapies are a perilous game of Russian roulette. No one really knows the ramifications of widespread chemical-based psychopharmacology currently sweeping the world. Such drugs could bear side-effects far in excess of what anyone knows or understands and, while they may claim otherwise, the pharmaceutical industry and the FDA are wholly unaware of psychopharmacology's long-terms effects. As with all of science's supposed advances, one day society may look back with a sense of horror and incredulity at the mistakes currently being perpetrated in the name of scientific progress. The pharmaceutical industry "plays God" as it peddles FDA-approved drugs as chemical saviors, and the consequences may be severe and permanent. For example, the medical community is just now drawing a connection between psychopharmacology and the explosion of dementia (specifically Alzheimer's disease).

Let's be very clear; no chemical-based drug has ever cured any disease. On the contrary, chemicals routinely cause disease, or maintain a disease's presence. In fact, that is often their intention. Chemical-based drugs are used to merely mask symptoms,

---

[150] Edward Welch, Westminster Theological Seminary, Philadelphia, Pennsylvania
[151] David Kupelian, *How Evil Works: Understanding and Overcoming the Destructive Forces That Are Transforming America* (Threshold Edition, 2010) 108, 109.
[152] 2 Corinthians 4:17
[153] For a more complete handling of this issue see "God's Objective in Suffering" in the third book in this series, *The Days of Reckoning Are at Hand: From Fig Leaf to Olive Branch to Laurel Wreath*, chapter 2: "Suffering: The Kintsugi Objective"

while maintaining those symptoms' underlying threats.

In his book, *How Evil Works: Understanding and Overcoming the Destructive Forces That Are Transforming America* (2010), David Kupelian comes to a chilling realization, the fact that psychotropic drugs blunt the conscience so that one is no longer aware of his own sinfulness.[154] Those taking such drugs feel euphoric and at peace because their sense of guilt before God has been placated.[155] The turbulent conscience has been assuaged, and social insecurities have been mediated and ameliorated. The entire premise of psychopharmacology is to convince one that he is a victim of his body chemistry, so that moral failings and idolatrous worship are not one's fault but rather the fault of one's designer. When every sin issue is reduced to a physiological locus then the call to repentance becomes an intolerable offense, a judgmental intruder in medicine's supposed deliverance.

The Spoiled Child
Jean-Baptiste Greuze, 1765

The Christian should never seek to assuage his guilt, but to eradicate it through repentance before the cross of Jesus Christ. The Christian should never suppress his conscience (nor that of anyone else), but should seek to sharpen (make accurate) and enliven (make active) the conscience, that it might function as God intended.

As psychopharmacology expands its global reach this becomes a principle means for

---

[154] David Kupelian, *How Evil Works: Understanding and Overcoming the Destructive Forces That Are Transforming America* (Threshold Edition, 2010) 105.
[155] David Kupelian, *How Evil Works: Understanding and Overcoming the Destructive Forces That Are Transforming America* (Threshold Edition, 2010) 108, 109.

> the world's enslavement to a coming antichrist. As long as Satan can keep people psychically numb and conscience despondent, he can deaden their sense of morality and easily foist upon them deviant choices.

Case Study: Ritalin®

Psychiatry clusters a set of symptoms and labels them ADHD (attention deficit and hyperactivity disorder). Those with ADHD exhibit the following behaviors:

1. Failure to pay attention
2. Inability to listen when spoken to
3. Inability to follow directions
4. Easily losing belongings
5. Being easily distracted and forgetful
6. Fidgeting with hands or feet
7. Talking excessively
8. Blurting out answers, or refusal to await one's turn

Under psychology's mismanagement, what God would call a lack of discipline, has been labeled a disorder. Ritalin® is routinely prescribed for ADHD,[156] yet it can have profound effects upon childhood development, such as stunting the hippocampus' growth which, when damaged, is thought to lead to adult depression.

> Pedagogical theory holds that visual learners have trouble following spoken instruction, and auditory learners need instructions read or spoken in order to understand them. More recently, educators have identified a new learning style called the "kinesthetic." Those labeled kinesthetic learners are thought to require movement in order to learn. Like the ADHD label, the kinesthetic learning style has become just another convenient blame-shifting device for failure to pay attention, yet another creative excuse for a lack of discipline. Administrators and educators, exhibiting what might be the fear of man, have simply invented a means to circumvent confronting the heart, one which sidesteps the imperative for expected discipline. These supposed learning styles simply advance the tyranny of low expectations, a hallmark of secular progressive education.

Common side-effects of Ritalin® include: addiction, nervousness, agitation, anxiety, irritability, insomnia, decreased appetite, headaches, stomach aches, nausea, dizziness, heart palpitations, mania, hallucinations, hyperactivity, impulsivity, and inattention. Less common side-effects include: high blood pressure, rapid pulse rate (and other heart problems), tolerance (constant need to raise the dose), feelings of suspicion and paranoia, visual hallucinations, depression, carvings for cocaine, dermatoses (infected

---
[156] Ritalin® is methylphenidate, an amphetamine

or diseased skin), viral infection, and elevated ALT enzyme levels in the blood (signaling liver damage). It is obvious that this drug (along with all synthetic substances) wreaks havoc on the body and mind. Is this not a direct assault upon the image of God in man? It is never God's intention that the body would be imperiled or damaged through poisons in order to effect the change that he desires. It is my contention, therefore, that psychopharmacological drugs never effect the type of change that God desires.

Additionally, once on Ritalin®, it is hard to stop. The removal of any drug stimulant can lead to suicidal ideations. As with all chemical drugs, a physical dependence can take hold so that the use of prescribed drugs is often a gateway to later drug abuse. Trying to achieve a short-term benefit through a pragmatic approach always results in grave loss. (Incidentally, research has found no long-term benefit, whether physiological or social, from Ritalin®.)

> Prozac® was designed as a "personality cosmetic" to merely iron out anxiety wrinkles.[157] For this reason it is called the "self-esteem drug" because it is used to induce temporary euphoria, a way to feel confident. Prozac® is popular with those who desire to "boutique" their feelings, to induce customized emotions at will. Prozac's® known side-effects include mania, bouts of irritability, aggression, and hostility. Yet, inexplicably some pediatricians routinely prescribe it to children. This is a derelict practice robbing society of its future.

Psychotropic Drugs and Counseling

It is vital to understand that psychotropic medications can never cure the psyche's ailments. These medications cannot offer existential meaning, alleviate the root problem of guilt, or renew relationships. While they promise to deaden the most severe symptoms of the psyche's ailments, they invariably leave that psyche as a hollow shell.[158] This is why biblical counseling, which confronts the heart and offers the opportunity for repentance, is the only hope in a culture riddled with a psychotropic scourge.

> "In you, O Lord, I have taken refuge; let me never be put to shame; deliver me in your righteousness. Turn your ear to me, come quickly to my rescue; be my rock of refuge, a strong fortress to save me. Since you are my rock and my fortress, for the sake of your name lead and guide me. Free me from the trap that is set for me, for you are my refuge. Into your hands I commit my spirit; redeem me, O Lord, the God of truth. I hate those who cling to worthless idols; I trust in the Lord. I will be glad and rejoice in your love, for you saw my affliction and knew the anguish of my soul.

---

[157] Paul Wender and Donald Klein, "The Promise of Biological Psychiatry," *Psychology Today* (August, 1978): 64.
[158] David Powlison, Westminster Theological Seminary. Philadelphia, Pennsylvania

> You have not handed me over to the enemy but have set my feet in a spacious place."
> (Psalm 31:1-8)

The Cure of Souls: Revisiting Ockham's Razor

The ancient Greeks avidly mapped the constellations because they believed that the stars augured mankind's future. However, the Greeks struck up against a vexing conundrum. They encountered "wandering stars" in the night sky, exceptionally bright points which suddenly exhibited retrograde motion. The Greeks understood these wanderers to be the planets orbiting the Sun. (Planet, literally in the Greek (*planetes,* πλανήτης), is "wanderer.") Studying planetary motion was crucial for predicting the actions of their capricious gods (each planet the provenance of a particular deity). Yet, the Greeks, much to their consternation, could not predict planetary motion.

Harmonia Macrocosmica
Andreas Cellarius, 1660

The Greeks devised an elaborate model of the solar system, with ring upon circular ring. While they labored over this model for centuries, continually adding to its complexity, it never worked. In the end, the Greeks failed to predict planetary motion, and in this, failed to predict their gods' behavior. It was not until Nicolaus Copernicus (1473-1543) devised the heliocentric model that planetary motion was finally mapped. In this model, planets are placed, not on circles, but on ellipses with the Sun as one locus. With this breakthrough the universe was coming into focus. Copernicus had sagaciously implemented "Ockham's razor," a theorem which would continue to unlock the cosmic vault to scientific investigation.

Prescient fourteenth century philosopher, William of Ockham (c. 1288 – c. 1348), posited Ockham's razor which states that, all things being equal, simple theories are to be favored over more complex ones. His supposition is that the universe is designed in such a way that the simplest explanations, those which rely upon the fewest assumptions, are the most "elegant" or intellectually appealing.

Jesus Christ offered an alarmingly elegant antidote to what psychology calls "mental illness"; that antidote is forgiveness. In Matthew 6:9-15, Jesus suggested a model for daily prayer, "The Lord's Prayer," which concludes with a confession of guilt before God. This confession first seeks God's forgiveness and, in turn, voices a commitment to forgive others. This is the Christian's daily bread, to be reminded of God's forgiveness and to, in turn, forgive others. This is the way to maintain what the secular world terms "mental health."[159]

> "An act of heroism is always a breakthrough into the Great Unknown." (Valentina Malmy)

Thus, based on Jesus' words, mankind's well-being is forged from three core elements:

1. Being forgiven by God (being justified)

2. Forgiving others (surrendering a perceived right)

3. Asking for other's forgiveness (assuming a posture of humility)

This three-pronged forgiveness ensures the health of the psyche as it maintains a vibrant and growing relationship with Jesus Christ. This is the key to reversing all deviant psychosocial behavior, God's forgiveness transforming, invigorating, and electrifying the heart to in turn forgive and seek forgiveness.

The Merciful Knight
Edward Burne-Jones, 1863

> "Once you were alienated from God and were enemies in your minds because of your evil behavior. But now he has reconciled you by Christ's physical body through

---

[159] For additional discussion of the issue of forgiveness see chapter 4: "The Gospel as Inception Point: From Immorality to Immortality"

> death to present you holy in his sight, without blemish and free from accusation—" (Colossians 1:21, 22)
>
> "If we confess our sins, he is faithful and just and will forgive us our sins and purify us from all unrighteousness." (1 John 1:9)

Could the antidote to mental illness be that simple? In concept it is that simple. However, in actuality this posture of seeking God's forgiveness, and in turn forgiving, requires special grace. This entails receiving Jesus' death on the cross as the sole basis for one's declared forgiveness, and for one's ability to in turn forgive.

In *The Legend of King Arthur* the virtuous French knight, Lancelot (in post-12th Century versions), sought Arthur's forgiveness. This request was not in a spirit of repentance but for the sake of increased self-mortification, that in his guilt, Lancelot might suffer more. Thus, the unregenerate heart often harbors an insidious desire for forgiveness, one intended only to intensify the pride in suffering for one's transgressions, a supposed faux-salvation by means of galling guilt.

Consider another example. I was taken aback by a recent news article which spoke about "appropriate" ways to exact revenge. God is clear in Romans 12:19-21,

> Do not take revenge, my dear friends, but leave room for God's wrath, for it is written: 'It is mine to avenge; I will repay,' says the Lord. On the contrary: 'If your enemy is hungry, feed him; if he is thirsty, give him something to drink. In doing this, you will heap burning coals on his head.' Do not be overcome by evil, but overcome evil with good.

From God's perspective there is no such thing as appropriate revenge. The very notion of revenge is itself the poisoned fruit of a man-centered approach to life, one which makes such an act appear warranted, even noble, when conducted responsibly. Only God's Word offers otherworldly wisdom to see past the dictates of a man-centered sense of justice, a presumed justice that only exacerbates, not alleviates, what is termed mental illness.

> "The greatest revenge is the one not taken."

The command to relinquish plans for revenge dovetails with Jesus' teaching to daily seek God's forgiveness. As the Christian daily renounces his desire for revenge, he is more fully reminded of God's warranted revenge deflected from him by means of the cross.

> "My dear children, I write this to you so that you will not sin. But if anybody does

> sin, we have an advocate with the Father—Jesus Christ, the Righteous One. He is the atoning sacrifice for our sins, and not only for ours but also for the sins of the whole world." (1 John 2:1, 2)

In considering this issue one catches a glimpse of a cosmic clash of civilizations, man-centered reason versus God-centered truth. To psychology revenge is a normal and often cathartic activity when handled responsibly. However, God knows that the heart was never designed for such an activity, as what looks "sweet" is actually caustic acid, imperiling the avenger with the threat of lifelong debilitating psychosis. Psychology can never understand the healing properties of forgiveness before the cross, because to psychology the cross is little more than a trite historic novelty. In the same way, psychology can never value the towering strength of forgiveness, because it can never countenance the reason for Jesus' death. Blind to the psyche's with-regard-to-God constitution, psychology can never understand how forgiveness sets a prisoner free.

Harmonia Macrocosmica
Andreas Cellarius, 1661

In summary, psychology could be likened to the ancient Greek form of astronomy. It compounds elaborate theory upon elaborate theory, hoping to unlock the psyche's mechanics. However, that motion is beyond its reach because it holds to the wrong model. Only the right model opens the vault, that being a "heliocentric" paradigm, one with the "Son" as the psyche's locus.

> The Roman centurion understood something of the concept of Ockham's razor when, in Matthew 8:8, he said to Jesus, "...But just say the word, and my servant will be healed." One could safely extend this to read, "But only say the word, and my *soul* will be healed."[160] That is the Bible's Ockham's razor.

---

[160] John 15:3

… - 9 -

Integrationism:
The Modern Day Babylonian Captivity

Introduction

A pure diamond is essentially indestructible. One could subject it to nearly any treatment and it would neither scratch nor break. One could smash it with a hammer, place it in a white hot flame, or squeeze it in a heavy-duty vice and that diamond would remain as structurally sound, and as radiant, as ever. However, introduce just one flaw, and that same diamond becomes as brittle a glass. A flaw makes the previously indestructible, highly-vulnerable.

Madame de Pompadour, Francois Boucher, 1750

This analogy could be applied to the truth. Purely construed, the truth is indomitable. However, as flaws, of one type or another, are introduced, the truth is quickly subsumed. The more flaws the more breakage. This is a fitting introduction to the issue of integrationism, an adulteration of the truth so that the gospel is made brittle through the introduction of secular thought, namely psychology. As secular thought infiltrates the interpretation of the Bible, there is more breakage. This chapter's objective, therefore, is to produce pure diamond.

The Plunder of the Church

Exodus 12:35, 36 states,

> The Israelites did as Moses instructed and asked the Egyptians for articles of silver and gold and for clothing. The LORD had made the Egyptians favorably disposed toward the people, and they gave them what they asked for; so they plundered the Egyptians.

Plundering the Egyptians involved appropriating the riches of the world for later use in building God's temple. In a modern context, this plundering is often thought of as borrowing the world's supposed wisdom in order to build the modern temple, God's people.[1] As Israel plundered physical gold to build a material temple, are Christians called to plunder intellectual "gold" (such as psychology) in order to build the temple of the Holy Spirit, the human psyche?

The Procession of the Trojan Horse in Troy
Giovanni Domenico Tiepolo, 1773

While the invitation is enticing, psychology is not an area of plunder for the Christian's benefit, as it is not "an article of silver and gold" or an "article of clothing."[2] While Egypt's precious metals were eventually used to build the tabernacle, and its clothing served the Israelites during their journey,[3] psychology is not the material God chooses to build the temple of the human heart. Nor is it a means to clothe God's people with truth. Psychology vitiates against the Bible's understanding of people and, thus, offers only a wasteland on which God's people routinely founder and die. Psychology is a Trojan horse to the church, an apparent gift welcomed only to the peril of one's own soul.

---

[1] 1 Corinthians 3:16
[2] Exodus 12:35
[3] Deuteronomy 8:4

The New Testament epistles, each in various ways, admonished the early church against being taken hostage by Greek philosophy,[4] the ancient ancestor to modern psychology. Philosophy and psychology bear an organic connection so that, according to historian Martha Nussbaum, modern psychology draws its history and development directly from Greek philosophy.[5] For example, Sigmund Freud (1856–1939) postulated that the absence of a father's love invariably hobbles its supposed victim, an idea derived directly from the Greek philosopher Plato (c. 428 – c. 348 BC). So the New Testament's warnings against philosophy rightly apply to psychology as well.

> The stoic philosopher Epictetus (55–135) wrote,
>
> > Philosophy does not promise to secure anything external for man, otherwise it would be admitting something that lies beyond its proper subject-matter. For as the material of the carpenter is wood, and that of statuary bronze, so the subject-matter of the art of living is each person's own life.
>
> This captures the philosophy's atheistic posture, one which it transfers to its progeny, psychology.

Psychology is artificial knowledge used to manipulate mankind into self-serving action, to blunt the conscience, and dull the knowledge of God. It is a crafty tool in the hands of the wicked to tear down and destroy the church, stripping it of its birthright as restored image-bearers in Christ. There can be no détente between psychology and Christianity, no *modus vivendi*. The one must ascend and prosper, the other fade and founder. Truth and falsehood cannot peacefully coexist.

Psychology operates as a modern Babylonian captivity for Christianity, a captivity that, just as with the judgment upon ancient Israel, the church has brought upon itself often through hardness of heart and a refusal to plumb the riches of Scripture in the cure of souls. The church's exile from scriptural truth is driven by the "work of the flesh,"[6] a love of the world and a root distrust of God, resulting in an exile with which it has, in large part, become willfully complicit.

> "See to it that no one takes you captive through hollow and deceptive philosophy, which depends on human tradition and the basic principles of this world rather than on Christ." (Colossians 2:8)

The Church's Psychology Affliction

---

[4] Colossians 2:8
[5] Martha Nussbaum, *The Therapy of Desire* (Princeton University Press, 1996)
[6] Galatians 5:20

Upon boarding my flight, I took a seat next to an attractive young woman. As the plane lifted off, I noticed that she was reading *Through My Eyes* (2011), Tim Tebow's autobiography. We struck up a conversation and, to my delight, it turns out she is a Christian. We spoke with enthusiasm about our shared faith. This woman hails from a small Texan town where the "Bible and football" are held in high esteem.

Saint Martin and Saint Christopher
Pordenone, 1529

In the course of conversation, I raised the topic of psychology, its poisons and perils for Christian faith. A dark cloud soon loomed over our discourse. With a flash of annoyance, the woman said, "I guess we have a difference of opinion," donned her headphones and turned on the television in front of her. I sat in silence for the next couple of hours wondering how Christianity had come to the point of esteeming football (which glorifies violence), turning to television for escape, and defending psychology (a false religion). (What a corrosive combination to the Christian's soul.) I wish I could say that this woman's response was startling and rare, but the opposite is true. Her response is strikingly consistent with that from hundreds of other Christians with whom I have interacted on this topic. As this anecdote bears out, Christianity is now littered with psychology which daily poisons its ground water, the living water of Christ.[7] In fact, I would describe Christianity as a glowing superfund site of toxic theology, most of that theology unwittingly built upon humanistic psychology.

A Tripartite Church Culture

Tragically, with each generation psychology increasingly becomes the heart and marrow of the Christian life, as traditional biblically-sound doctrine is progressively displaced. The following chart shows how this happens. The first column (the left column) lists the church's "anemic externalities" (moralism, dead doctrine, and empty ritual). The third column (the right column) highlights the resulting "pseudo-spiritual internalities" (pietism, spiritism, and blindness to depravity). Psychology appears to offer a pivot or fulcrum that allows both to gain ascendancy in the church, which

---

[7] John 7:37-39

allows both poles to flourish. Psychology seems to offer the spiritual nourishment that each pole lacks, or the answers that prop up each pole's error.

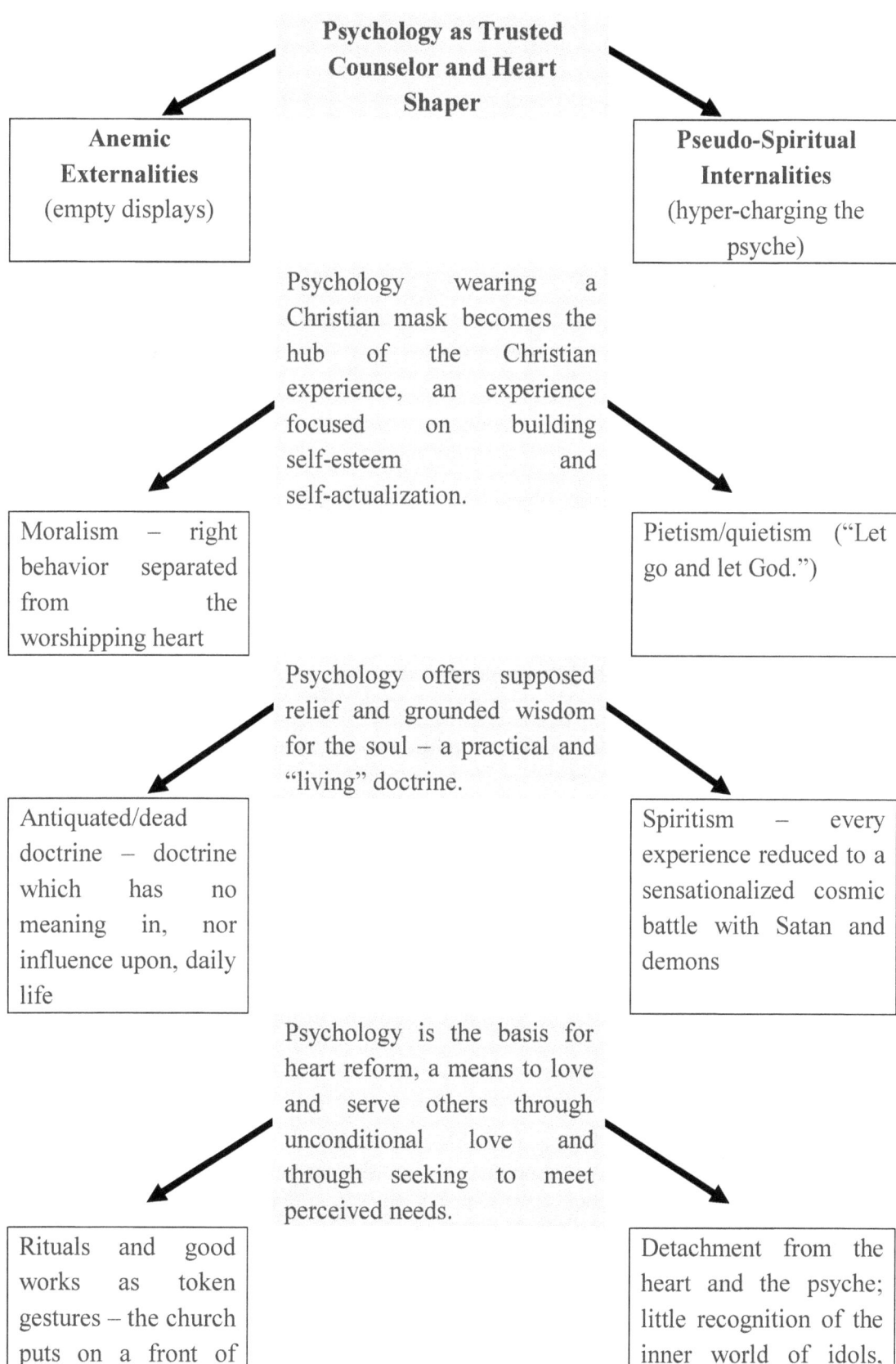

| involvement and engages in superficial mercy ministry, while neglecting heart issues |

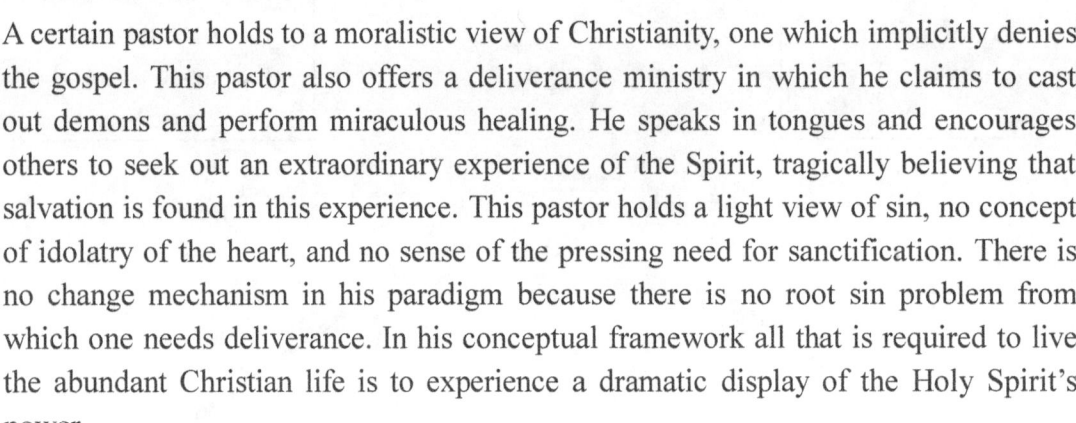

A certain pastor holds to a moralistic view of Christianity, one which implicitly denies the gospel. This pastor also offers a deliverance ministry in which he claims to cast out demons and perform miraculous healing. He speaks in tongues and encourages others to seek out an extraordinary experience of the Spirit, tragically believing that salvation is found in this experience. This pastor holds a light view of sin, no concept of idolatry of the heart, and no sense of the pressing need for sanctification. There is no change mechanism in his paradigm because there is no root sin problem from which one needs deliverance. In his conceptual framework all that is required to live the abundant Christian life is to experience a dramatic display of the Holy Spirit's power.

This pastor takes up residence in the dual world of anemic externality (moralism) and pseudo-spiritual internality (supposed deliverance through manifestations of the Spirit). Quite oddly, he also holds a high view of psychology. In fact, psychology dovetails quite nicely with his moralistic doctrine and poses no threat to his hyper-spiritual displays. He carves out a comfortable place for psychology at the center of his belief system since it props up his "bipolar theology."

In fact, psychology, moralism, and hyper-spiritualism align along an invisible axis, as each offers the other two a safe harbor to persist unchallenged. For example, hyper-spiritualism easily positions psychology as a welcomed scientific counterbalance, which does not impinge upon, nor compete with, its deliverance ministry. In light of the church's growing anemic externalities (moralistic and often irrelevant doctrine) and pseudo-spirituality (false manifestations of the Holy Spirit), psychology can enter through the "backdoor," promising some refuge from the burden of both.

Psychology offers the appearance of a sagacious look at the human condition (the antidote to the anemia) and a supposed "scientific" grounding (the antidote to the flights of hyper-spirituality). Since the church has largely abandoned hamartiology (a taking seriously of sin and idolatry) and the need for sanctification, psychology not only enters unopposed, but takes center-stage as a welcomed stabilizer between defective Christian experiences.

| I believe that integrationism is part of a carefully laid sinister plan to weaken |

> Christianity. This weakening paves the way for an eschatological one world religion which will draw heavily from psychology. It is likely that psychology is one of the chief means Satan will use to control the world population in the coming New World Order, the basis for a world religion, government, and economy. The more thoroughly psychology is "kneaded into the dough" of Christianity now, the more readily Christians will accept an outright perversion of their faith. Thus, certain aspects of this coming false religion will not seem so foreign and, in fact, will feel quite familiar. That is exactly the purpose integrationism unwittingly serves.

The Abandoned Birthright

To be charitable, one of the many reasons psychology is so popular throughout Christendom is that it is a way for the church to connect with the world on what is perceived to be common ground. It is a way to achieve a kind of détente with the world, a perceived neutral ground, or sense of camaraderie. It may also be part of an idolatrous desire to be accepted by the world, to avoid being vilified, ostracized, or persecuted. In this way the church can soften its stance through a false point of contact, a supposed basis for dialogue, and an artificial means of inclusion in the secular community.

A Widow
James Jacques Joseph Tissot, 1868

While these may seem like noble pursuits, in actuality they deaden the church to the Bible's solitary and piercing intent to bring sinners into submission to the gospel. Additionally, psychology short-circuits the sanctification process in believers. While psychology's terms may at times be employed to describe a basket of symptoms, those terms must always be reinterpreted from a biblical perspective.

The church has already been beguiled by Satan into a tacit acceptance of psychology as part of a master plan to "deceive the elect."[8] Satan is setting the stage for the gospel to be progressively undermined and rejected because of the church's submission to secular teaching. As a universally accepted means for understanding people, psychology has already been co-opted by the antichrist to control public sentiment.

In the eyes of psychology, Christianity is little more than sundry Byzantine doctrine coupled with quaint morality. Sadly, Laodicean Christians have fallen into this same mentality.[9] Such Christians often reduce their faith to a few abstract theological principles (God is love; all is by grace; no one is perfect; trust God) intended to make one into a functionally "nice" person. Thus, Christianity's *raison d'etre* has been reduced to simply raising affable harmless Christians, who find ready acceptance by the world. The church has been rendered inert as it has retreated into a life of little more than sharing an inspiring verse, ensuring that everyone is encouraged, and overlooking rebellion in the name of supposed grace. This is part of the reason the modern church lies in shambles, splintered, and confused.[10] In light of its unholy alliance with psychology, the church, as a social force, has been rendered sterile and diffident. This has allowed society's exploits and degradations to flourish largely unopposed.[11]

> Radio host Michael Savage said that the reason America has, in recent years, been ravished by socialism is because Americans do not believe in Jesus anymore. In spite of himself, Savage has struck upon the central issue. In the American theater, as faith in Jesus wanes, the state progressively rises to fill the worship void.[12]

Possibly the greatest reason for the church's loss of social clout, and its inability to experience meaningful internal change, is that the church follows psychology's lead, adopting, emphasizing, imitating, emboldening, and "baptizing" psychology's claims. The church has relinquished the concept of sin, relegating it to momentary lapses in judgment or iterative behavioral failings ("I'm-just-having-a-bad-day syndrome").[13] Secular psychology has beguiled the church through a pseudoscientific supposed medical model which perpetrates giving a voice to human struggle. Psychology promises relief in the here and now,[14] but it never makes good on this promise.

---
[8] Matthew 24:24
[9] Revelation 3:14-20
[10] For additional discussion of the state of the church see the third book in this series, *The Days of Reckoning Are at Hand: From Fig Leaf to Olive Branch to Laurel Wreath*, chapter 10: "Counseling and the Church: Syndicating the Vision"
[11] Luke 14:34
[12] For additional discussion of this topic see "The World System: Intrusive Government" in the second book in this series, *What Agreement Is There Between the Temple of God and Idols?: The Accidence of Sin and Idolatry*, chapter 2: "The World, the Flesh, and the Devil: Assessing the Threat Matrix"
[13] For further discussion of the topic of sin see the second book in this series, *What Agreement Is There Between the Temple of God and Idols?: The Accidence of Sin and Idolatry*, chapter 4: "Hamartiology: Sin in All its Ignobility"
[14] Edward Welch, Westminster Theological Seminary, Philadelphia, Pennsylvania

The church, seduced by scientism, generally promotes the view that moral failing is actually a medical issue, that the human will is subject to the dictates of rogue biology. Labeling any failing as sin is seen as hurtful and judgmental, placing a burden upon the soul that God's supposed unconditional love would relinquish. The church has generally depreciated its role to offering remedial spiritual comfort, a kind of "convalescence for the soul," while aiding and abetting secular professionals' self-proclaimed authority over the psyche. The church has been functionally reduced to offering innocuous moral platitudes, and non-threatening theological generalities, that keep people, not just morally bankrupt, but blind to their desperate need for daily repentance at Jesus' feet.

> "It is not so much the wrong answers that are the problem, but the wrong questions that really vex us."

As a personal note, I have taught on the evils of psychology in dozens of churches over the course of more than a decade. With trenchant consistency, I have been strongly criticized for this stance. I have rarely seen churchgoers so angry as when psychology is deconstructed and exposed. There are myriad reasons for this.

Firstly, in exposing psychology's error the sinful heart's principal advocate is laid bare with no exculpatory refuge. The sinner, standing alone on a barren wasteland of defunct teaching, must either repent before the cross or languish in hypocrisy. Thus, removing the psychology sanctuary leaves one in a spiritual hinterland exposed to the buffeting winds of the confronting Spirit.

Secondly, Christians, in alarming numbers, study and advocate psychology under the guise of altruism. Any attack on psychology is perceived to be an attack upon the métier of legions of aspiring or current practitioners. (This supposed attack upon métier is also an implicit assault upon the source of one's livelihood, exposing a root love of money in most.)

Finally, Christian's, following the world's suit, have surrendered themselves and their children to psychology theory, in general, and often to psychotropic drugs, in specific. I have had numerous debates with Christians who either prescribe, or are under treatment involving, psychotropic drugs. With stark consistency they believe such drugs to be a miracle cure, when in reality synthetic drugs cure nothing, only serving to mask the conscience's guilt pangs.[15]

Integrationism: A Cunning Snare[16]

---

[15] For further discussion of the dangers of psychotropic drugs see "The Legalized Drug Cartel" (and subsequent sections) in chapter 8: "What Has Jerusalem To Do With Vienna?: The Case Against Psychology."
[16] While I paint the church in broad brushstrokes, by God's grace some faithful Christians are waking up to the

> "He [Faust] laid the Holy Scriptures behind the door and under the bench, refused to be called Doctor of Theology, but preferred to be styled Doctor of Medicine." (*The Tragical History of Doctor Faust*)

One of the most insidious movements in Christianity is what is termed integrationism, the marriage of psychology and the Bible, two competing religious perspectives. The most glaring problem is that psychology necessarily compromises the truth at every turn, as one cannot wear two sets of worldview lenses at once. When the Bible and psychology are combined the taint of the latter predominates on account of the tendencies of fallen human nature. Thus, when superimposed with psychology, God's lenses no longer resolve the human dilemma and its solution.

Second Samuel 6:6, 7 reads,

> When they came to the threshing floor of Nakon, Uzzah reached out and took hold of the ark of God, because the oxen stumbled. The LORD's anger burned against Uzzah because of his irreverent act; therefore God struck him down, and he died there beside the ark of God.

Pandora
John William Waterhouse, 1896

God had strictly forbidden anyone from touching the ark. Yet, Uzzah disregarded God's command, thinking that his helping-hand was actually obedience. God condemned Uzzah for his transgression, striking him down. God did not want Uzzah's supposed assistance; he wanted his uncompromised obedience.

To an extent, Uzzah's offense serves to reify a similar transgression in integrationism.

---

psychology incursion. I am thankful for the opportunity to partner with sincere brothers and sisters in this effort. May this chapter encourage and equip them to admonish and instruct others.

While those who practice integrationism may doctrinally believe in the sufficiency of Scripture, they function as though the Word is insufficient to meet the demands of the modern scientific world, that Scripture alone cannot adequately counsel believers. In this regard, integrationism seeks to "assist" God's Word by superimposing a humanly-derived anthropology. While this may appear noble, as with Uzzah, it is an irreverent act. Even though God's Word may seem vulnerable in light of the demands of a scientific and psychologized world, it is not. God asks his people not to extend faithless assistance, but to uphold stalwart reliance on what God has revealed, trusting in Scripture's sufficiency to not just answer but to, with glowing alacrity, heal the psyche's deepest ailments.

> Consider the fact that oil and water do not mix. What happens when oil and water come in contact? The water retains its constitution while the oil diffuses into layers of various thicknesses. As light reflects off of those layers, a rainbow of colors is produced. Through the colors which emerge, one knows something of the thickness of each oil layer. Consider the water to be the truth of Christianity and the oil as psychology. When the two come in contact the truth reveals psychology's falsehood, exposing the various hues of its lies. Christianity retains its constitution while psychology is dispersed (like Dagon, the Philistine god, losing his head and hands in the presence of the Ark[17]). However, the sinful heart focuses on the bright shiny colors, reckoning their beauty, all the while forsaking the life-giving water.

Dichotomy versus Trichotomy[18]

At the heart of this question of integrationism is the theological debate between dichotomy and trichotomy. Dichotomists believe that the Bible presents the human being as essentially composed of two parts – body and soul (or spirit). Trichotomists believe that the person is composed of three parts – body, soul, and spirit (soul and spirit as distinct entities). Trichotomists are quick to quote Hebrews 4:12, "For the word of God is living and active. Sharper than any double-edged sword, it penetrates even to dividing soul and spirit, joints and marrow; it judges the thoughts and attitudes of the heart." This verse is usually misinterpreted to assert that there is a conceptual division between soul and spirit, when the Bible does not offer such a division.

The question of dichotomy versus trichotomy would seem to be just another intramural debate of little real consequence except that this issue bears life and death repercussions in Christian praxis. Trichotomists espouse a tripartite structure because they make a distinction between medical needs (body), psychological needs (soul), and spiritual needs (spirit). Dichotomists, on the other hand, hold that there are medical needs (body) and spiritual needs (soul/spirit), but no distinctly psychological

---
[17] 1 Samuel 5:4
[18] For further discussion of the dichotomy and trichotomy concepts see the section "Reductionism" in chapter 8: "What Has Jerusalem To Do With Vienna?: The Case Against Psychology"

needs. (In fact, the dichotomist would spurn any discussion of psychic needs.) Trichotomy is actually a subtly veiled form of syncretism which undermines Christ's work and his church's vitality.

Trichotomy, the basis for integrationism, allows secular psychologies to be woven into the Bible's anthropology under the misguided notion that psychology diagnoses and cures the soul's needs. Dichotomists, however, see psychology as antithetical and destructive, directly competing with the Bible's anthropology. The Bible states that it is both authoritative ("God-breathed") and sufficient ("that the servant of God may be thoroughly equipped"),[19] truth Christians are called to uphold on faith. While the integrationist may see the Bible as authoritative, he does not functionally view it as sufficient. Tragically, as with Balaam's seduction of Israel through the Moabite women,[20] so too, psychology seduces the integrationist into a godless worldview to the detriment of himself and his witness for Christ.

I have found that in this debate the first question to be addressed is Scripture's sufficiency. If that issue is not settled all subsequent discussion invariably yields nothing. Undoubtedly, integrationists see the Bible as utterly sufficient to lead sinners to salvation, but as tacitly insufficient to sanctify those who are saved. In other words, while Scripture accomplishes God's work of justification, it is seen as inadequate to effect the Christian's progressive growth in holiness. This view renders the Bible somewhat Janus-faced. But, of course, it is not; if the Bible is fully capable of providing all that is needed for salvation, it is fully equipped to effect God's plan for sanctification.

In the final analysis, the difference between integrationism and an exclusively biblical model comes down to hermeneutics. The integrationist implicitly holds to an "open" hermeneutic (which he may propositionally deny) with regard to Scripture's ability to address the human condition, while the proper view of Scripture holds to a "closed" hermeneutic, Scripture's utter sufficiency in addressing the full spectrum of humanity's psychic plight.

Integrationism as Unholy Fire

With regard to ancient Israel, God intended that all aspects of worship should be conducted according to his every direction. Each sacrifice, in order to be accepted, was to be in accordance with his strict ordinances. Yet, in Leviticus 10:1, Aaron's sons Nadab and Abihu used unauthorized fire to burn incense in the Tent of Meeting. (The reader would rightly infer that God himself previously sent fire as evidence of his presence, and as the means of consuming a sacrifice.) Aaron's sons neglected the

---

[19] 2 Timothy 3:16, 17
[20] Numbers 25:1, 2

divine ordinance, offering incense with common fire. Thus, God's vengeful flame consumed Aaron's sons.[21] That very fire which, if properly applied by God himself, would have sanctified and consumed their gift, became the instrument of their own destruction when applied through their own hands.

This lends insight to the verse, "The Lord is a consuming fire!"[22] God either sanctifies or destroys;[23] there is no third option, no *modus vivendi*. He either purifies through the outpouring of his Spirit, or consumes with that same Spirit.[24] This may point to why Christians are exhorted not to quench the Spirit,[25] because that Spirit moves forward with power to separate, clarify, and define.

Nadab and Abihu's sanctioned fire could be applied to those who use integrationism to effect the supposed sanctification of God's people. The integrationist's fire is from himself leading to the quenching of the Holy Spirit. Consider Leviticus 10:10 which states, "You must distinguish between the holy and the common, between the unclean and the clean."

> "Their work will be shown for what it is, because the Day will bring it to light. It will be revealed with fire, and the fire will test the quality of each man's work." (1 Corinthians 3:13)

Is there a connection between Aaron's fashioning of the golden calf and the fact that his sons later became drunk and offered unauthorized fire?[26] (There is likely some connection.[27]) In the same way that Nadab and Abihu foolishly entered the Tent of Meeting after becoming drunk,[28] so too, the integrationist is functionally in a "drunken state" with regard to his service for the Lord. Additionally, is there an idolatrous precursor (an analogue to the golden calf) which precipitates this drunken state? There likely is, but this is not easily ascertained.

> Ecclesiastes 3:11 states, "God has set eternity in the hearts of men, yet they cannot fathom what God has done from beginning to end." Integrationists often long for something more than the truth; they crave something better than what has been presented to them.

Integrationism as Akin to Balaam's Error[29]

---

[21] Leviticus 10:2
[22] Deuteronomy 4:24
[23] Isaiah 6:6
[24] The Adam Clarke Commentary
[25] 1 Thessalonians 5:19
[26] Exodus 32:4; Leviticus 10:1
[27] Exodus 20:5
[28] Leviticus 10:9
[29] For additional discussion of Balaam see "The Case Study: Balaam and Balak as Tropes of Satan" in the second book in this series, *What Agreement Is There Between the Temple of God and Idols?: The Accidence of Sin and*

Balaam and the Angel, Gustav Jaeger, 1836

One could think of the integrationist as a co-conspirator with God's enemies, and as such falling into Balaam's error.[30]

Balaam's transgressions:

1. It appears that Balaam was greedy as he was known to offer prophecy for a fee (peddling knowledge of God's will for a profit).[31]

2. God admonished Balaam not to throw in his lot with Balak.[32] However, when Balaam inquired of the Lord a second time (presumably through dreams) the Lord seemed to give Balaam over to his greed, allowing him to follow his lust.[33]

3. An angel opposed Balaam because his path was reckless before the Lord.[34]

4. Balaam usually resorted to sorcery to discern God's will.[35]

5. Balaam continued to associate with those who sought, and eventually achieved,

---

Idolatry, chapter 2: "The World, the Flesh, and the Devil: Assessing the Threat Matrix"
[30] Numbers 22:1 – 24:25
[31] Numbers 22:7
[32] Numbers 22:12
[33] Numbers 22:20
[34] Numbers 22:32
[35] Numbers 24:1

Israel's dereliction.

6. Balaam allied himself with the Moabites, advising Balak on how to seduce the Israelites using Moabite women,[36] eventually leading to idol worship.[37] On the verge of entering the Promised Land, the Israelites were led astray through temptation at the hands of the Moabites. (Incidentally, Balaam continued to associate with the Moabites since Joshua later murdered Balaam as he consorted with the Moabites.[38])

7. Balaam is spoken of in association with the murderer Cain and the rebel Korah. While Balaam could not curse the Israelites, he eventually caused them to curse themselves through sexual immorality and idolatry. (This could be applied to the modern church which curses itself through errant teaching which leads to immorality.)

Jude 1:11-13 warns,

> Woe to them! They have taken the way of Cain; they have rushed for profit into Balaam's error; they have been destroyed in Korah's rebellion. These men are blemishes at your love feasts, eating with you without the slightest qualm – shepherds who feed only themselves. They are clouds without rain, blown along by the wind; autumn trees, without fruit and uprooted – twice dead. They are wild waves of the sea, foaming up their shame; wandering stars, for whom blackest darkness has been reserved forever.

Second Peter 2:15-17 states,

> They have left the straight way and wandered off to follow the way of Balaam son of Beor, who loved the wages of wickedness. But he was rebuked for his wrongdoing by a donkey – a beast without speech – who spoke with a man's voice and restrained the prophet's madness. These men are springs without water and mists driven by a storm. Blackest darkness is reserved for them. For they mouth empty, boastful words and, by appealing to the lustful desires of sinful human nature, they entice people who are just escaping from those who live in error.

Revelation 2:14 states,

> Nevertheless, I have a few things against you: You have people there who hold to the teaching of Balaam, who taught Balak to entice the Israelites to sin by eating food sacrificed to idols and by committing sexual immorality.

---

[36] Numbers 31:16
[37] Numbers 25:1-3
[38] Numbers 31:8

Should the question of integrationism be viewed as little more than an intramural squabble or, in the spirit of Balaam, is the integrationist in league with Satan's intent to enslave the church? Does the integrationist, in seeking relevance in the eyes of the world, tacitly neglect God's Word? Does the integrationist seek the world's favor and acceptance? In what way does Balaam's error serve as a prism through which to view integrationism? The integrationist, like Balaam, cavorts with the world to the dereliction of God's people. While not motivated by Balaam-esque greed *per se*, the integrationist clearly traffics in counsel outside of God's declarative will.

A Tale from the Decameron, John William Waterhouse, 1916

The Call to Purgative Measures

Deuteronomy 13:1–18 lists three enticements to following false gods:

1. The teaching of false prophets
2. The acceptance of family members
3. The chicanery of wicked men who had arisen to lead their townspeople astray

A false prophet was not always revealed through speaking explicit falsehood, but in terms of the worship into which he led others.[39] Therefore, even if a false prophet revealed truth, but that revelation led to idolatrous worship, he was still a false prophet. Incidentally, Deuteronomy 13:6 warns that even the "wife you love or your closest friend" could entice one to false worship. Additionally, when false worship

---

[39] Tremper Longman, "Old Testament History and Theology" class, Westminster Theological Seminary, Philadelphia, Pennsylvania

occurred, one's town, in order to be purged, must be utterly ruined, with all its inhabitants and livestock destroyed and everything within it burned.

One could make the analogy that the church has largely turned to psychology as a false prophet, construing psychology as a truth-teller when in reality it leads to false worship. Today, Scripture has functionally become secondary to secular thought, so that sound doctrine is often rejected in favor of more enticing theories that tickle the ears of those who love the lie.[40]

Additionally, many in the church, on account of the fear of man, would rather maintain the acceptance of family and friends rather than risk rejection for upholding truth. Christian "towns" are overrun with falsehood, but rarely are Christians figuratively willing to put detestable beliefs to death. They easily adopt the forms and institutions of their surrounding culture, bowing to faulty worldviews in the process. Psychology is a false god that Christians often raise up in praise, when it should be cast down in disgust, remembering that, in the face of grave idolatry, God commanded *herem* warfare, the enemy's complete annihilation so that absolutely nothing remained.

Numbers 33:55, 56 states,

> 'But if you do not drive out the inhabitants of the land, those you allow to remain will become barbs in your eyes and thorns in your sides. They will give you trouble in the land where you will live. And then I will do to you what I plan to do to them.'

Sadly, Christianity is largely plagued by the same affliction which harangued God's people millennia ago. The warning that those allowed to remain "will become barbs in your eyes and thorns in your sides" seems prophetic of the way in which psychology has infiltrated and devastated Christian thought and life.

Christians must challenge themselves to:

1. Radically redefine life through the centrality of Christ

2. Reorient their lives around daily repentance and the assimilation of Christ himself as indwelling redeemer

3. Fundamentally recast human behavior and existence as displays of worship – that man principally operates as a worshipping being

---

[40] 2 Timothy 4:3

4. Subscribe to a completely Scripture-infused understanding of their experience, emotions, and inner being, to not just intellectually ascribe to Scripture as authoritative, but to see it as utterly sufficient for all matters pertaining to faith

5. Be intellectually converted, to love the Lord their God with all their *minds* (possibly the most neglected aspect of the love of God) [41]

6. Reassess their involvement with all man-centered institutions, as well as their assumptions about the value and purpose of those institutions

---

[41] Mark 12:30

Section IV

Redemption

- 10 -

THE THIRD-WAY OF SANCTIFICATION:
From Abominable to Indomitable[1]

Echoes from Eden

The movie "Fantastic Voyage" (1966) is about a team of surgeons placed into a submarine which is then miniaturized. Injected into a patient's bloodstream, the team travels to a damaged organ to perform microscopic laser surgery. (This may not be so outlandish as today scientists are exploring the use of miniature robots to perform surgery.) This movie premise serves as a fitting metaphor for the counselor's participation in God's sanctifying work in believers. Sanctification is not a topical balm applied to psychic wounds; it is life-saving surgery performed within the deepest recesses of the soul.

The Christian is simultaneously sinner and saint. He recognizes the sinful nature nascent within himself, while he has concurrently been declared righteous and placed on a path of ever-increasing holiness through Jesus' work within him. In this regard, as one takes a light view of his sin he takes an equally light view of Jesus' death and resurrection. The sin nature lingers (though its days are numbered), indelible yet fading in this life, non-existent in the next. The new nature is rising, faint yet innervating in this life, wholly-consuming in the next.

> During the American Civil War (1861-1865) Union soldiers sang, "As Christ died to make men holy, let us die to make men free."

Without a piercing knowledge of sin, Jesus' payment on the cross seems trite and trivial.[2] Conversely, without Christ's completed work of salvation, the full knowledge of one's sin would become a crushing burden, too great to withstand for even a moment (The disciple Judas' suicide bears this out.[3]). Without the good news of Jesus' death and resurrection, the haunt of sin would cause man to, like Judas, commit suicide under its unrelenting fury. Thus, a double-helix emerges in which one must profoundly understand sin to appreciate the force of the gospel, and one must come under the protection of the gospel to countenance the gravity of his sin.

---

[1] This chapter might traditionally include sections on regeneration, perseverance of the saints, and assurance of salvation. (Incidentally, an alternate subtitle for this chapter might be "From Wrecked to Rectified.")
[2] Some ideas in this paragraph from Andrew Field, "Introduction to Redeemer," p. 5, 6, Westminster Theological Seminary, Philadelphia, Pennsylvania
[3] Matthew 27:5

Sin is beyond one's wildest imagining, too tragic, too elephantine for one to ever comprehend, but at the same time the Christian's salvation is, likewise, too wonderful for him to ever fully-grasp. Thus, without accurate knowledge of sin and Christ, sanctification is not only impossible, but any attempts at change invariably spiral into insanity.

The Raft of the Medusa, Theodore Gericault, 1819

> "'...It is the world that has been pulled over your eyes to blind you from the truth.'
> 'What truth?'
> 'That you're a slave, Neo. Like everyone else, you were born into bondage, kept inside a prison that you cannot smell, taste, or touch, a prison for your mind...'"
> ("The Matrix" (1999))

When one thinks of God's grace through Jesus, he tends to think of receiving something. While, in fact, the Christian does receive incomparable gifts of the Spirit,[4] there is an often forgotten aspect to grace, the fact that the Christian has lost something, is restrained from something, and is separated from something. It is a gift to lose one's life for Christ, to be restrained from oneself, and to be denied the desires of one's sinful heart.[5] As quail being driven in from the sea,[6] often the desires of one's heart are a curse, a detriment, and a loss from which one needs deliverance.

Just as antiseptic stings in cleansing a wound, so too the sanctification process, if it is truly working, involves a measure of pain and suffering. God, out of his supreme love,

---

[4] Galatians 5:22, 23
[5] Galatians 2:20
[6] Numbers 11:31-34

chastens his children, disciplines and punishes them with a gracious rod.[7] In this way, he continually draws them out of wayward idolatry and into communion with himself. While some may see this as the mark of a vindictive and capricious God, those who are wise in Christ know the exact opposite to be true. This is the benevolent hand of a good God who longs to free his people from that which encumbers their hearts, controls their minds, captivates their wills, and misdirects their worship.

To be free from oneself, and what one wants, is an invaluable gift. Only when one fully understands the depth of his sin, does he comprehend God's mercy in removing from his people their sinful pursuits. In Christ, God's law is no longer a feared enemy leading one to despair, but rather a crown of glory under which one has been declared righteous, perfect, and justified on account of Jesus.[8] It is this central truth which galvanizes, emboldens, enables, and ultimately transforms.

> In the same way that sin is *active* rebellion against the person of God, so too, repentance is *active* submission to the person of God. Sin is movement against a person; repentance is movement toward a person.

The Creation-Fall-Redemption Model Revisited[9]

Creation	Fall	Redemption
Design:		
Image and likeness of God[10]	Dust and ashes[11]	Temple of the Holy Spirit[12]
Breath of life[13]	Body of death[14]	New creation[15]
Identity:		
As gods[16]	Slaves to sin;[17] children of wrath[18]	Son of God[19]
Speak to God "in the cool of the day"[20]	Sons of the evil one;[21] children of the devil[22]	Sons of the kingdom[23]

---

[7] Hebrews 12:6; Revelation 3:19
[8] Romans 8:2
[9] For more discussion of creation, fall, and redemption see chapter 5: "Redefining the Pygmalion Effect: Exploring the Image of God in Man"
[10] Genesis 1:26; 1 Corinthians 11:7
[11] Genesis 2:7; Genesis 18:27
[12] 1 Corinthians 3:16
[13] Genesis 2:7
[14] Romans 7:24
[15] 2 Corinthians 5:17
[16] Psalm 82: 6, 7
[17] John 8:34
[18] Ephesians 2:3
[19] Matthew 5:45; Romans 8:14
[20] Genesis 3:8
[21] Matthew 13:38

Naked, no shame[24]	Seeking covering, shameful; whitewashed tomb, beautiful on the outside but inside full of dead men's bones and everything unclean;[25] brood of vipers[26]	Clothed in a white robe[27]
Image-bearer[28]	Sinner[29]	Saint;[30] prophet, priest, king
Capability:		
Powerfully and wonderfully made[31]	Worm;[32] wretch;[33] wretched, pitiful, poor, blind, naked[34]	More than a conqueror[35]
	Weeds[36]	Wheat;[37] good seed;[38] first born and firstfruits[39]
	Blackest darkness reserved for them[40]	Light of the world[41]
Purpose:		
God's workmanship[42]	What is man that you are mindful of him[43]	...Much more valuable than they;[44] good and noble soil;[45] a spectacle to the universe[46]

---

[22] John 8:44
[23] Matthew 13:38
[24] Genesis 2:25
[25] Matthew 23:27
[26] Matthew 12:34
[27] Revelation 6:11
[28] Genesis 1:26
[29] Luke 18:13
[30] Ephesians 3:18
[31] Psalm 139:14
[32] Psalm 22:6
[33] Romans 7:24
[34] Revelation 3:17
[35] Romans 8:37
[36] Matthew 13:25
[37] Matthew 13:25
[38] Matthew 13:38
[39] Romans 8:23; Hebrews 12:23; James 1:18; Revelation 14:4
[40] 2 Peter 2:17
[41] Matthew 5:14
[42] Isaiah 45:9-11
[43] Psalm 8:3, 4; Hebrews 2:6-8
[44] Matthew 6:26
[45] Luke 8:15
[46] 1 Corinthians 4:9

Tend the garden in a covenant of obedience[47]	Worthless servant[48]	Salt of the earth[49]
	Evil[50]	Blameless and holy in his sight[51]
	Goats[52]	Sheep[53]

Possibly the greatest implication of the creation-fall-redemption model is the realization that God actually redeems depraved people. This is the towering glory of the Christian worldview, the heart of its exceptionalism. While the world holds no concept of actual change, the Bible offers a highly-compelling model for change. The Bible's change mechanism actually recasts lives so that tangible progress is observed in both the diminishment of sin and in the growth of godly character. That change mechanism may at times be obscured from view, and may at times be sullied by Satan's lies, but it is present and operative nevertheless.

Resolving the Sin Rorschach[54]

Sin can be subtle, it can be brash.
Sin can be cordial; it can be brazen.
Sin can be refined; it can be garish.
Sin can be charming; it can be boorish.
Sin can speak in alluring half-truths; it can tell bald-face lies.
Sin can appear altruistic; it can be shamelessly self-indulgent.
Sin can appear forbearing; it can be impulsive.
Sin can be blindly tolerant; it can be condemning.
Sin can impress through soaring intellect; it can mouth the blather of an imbecile.
Sin can be patriotic; it can be seditious.
Sin can tower; it can cower.
Sin, in short, is a submission to evil which paradoxically makes one ruthlessly imperialistic.

Sin is, in some sense, a living Rorschach image. It wears a Janus-face, takes on various hues, and dances in and out of shifting shadows. Sin makes that which is black-and-white into shades of grey; it makes that which is grey into black-and-white matters.

---

[47] Genesis 2:15
[48] Matthew 25:30
[49] Matthew 5:13
[50] Matthew 7:11
[51] Colossians 1:22
[52] Matthew 25:33
[53] Matthew 25:33
[54] For further discussion of the topic of sin see the second book in this series, *What Agreement Is There Between the Temple of God and Idols?: The Accidence of Sin and Idolatry*, chapter 4: "Hamartiology: Sin in All its Ignobility"

Morning in the Pine Forest, Ivan Shishkin, 1889[55]

Sin readily metamorphoses itself, shields itself, justifies itself. In this way, sin bears the marks and character of Satan himself, maintaining a death-grip upon Satan's co-conspirator, the fallen human psyche. Human effort and reason are foolish and futile, banal and barren, in dealing with man's most glaring pressing plaguing plight. Only the Holy Spirit can free the sinner from his sin, and unless one understands the depth of his sin, he can never possibly understand his desperate need to be sanctified.

> "Man was born free and everywhere he is in shackles." (Jean-Jacques Rousseau)

Sanctification disambiguates the sin Rorschach through a living breathing motive and process, one which begins with a worship transaction between God and man. This transaction, called "justification," is the legal cancellation of man's criminal conviction before God. Justification is acquired through receiving Jesus' death upon the cross as the payment for one's sin, and thus, "launches a thousand ships" in the mission of heart change. Justification invites, initiates, and discharges the work of the Holy Spirit within the heart so that the Christian is indwelled by the person of God. The Christian is, thus, one in whom another person (God himself) works.[56]

---

[55] As a tangent, this painting, *Morning in the Pine Forest*, by Ivan Shishkin originally did not contain the bears. It featured a splintered tree in the foreground symbolizing man's assault upon the forest and, more broadly, the wanton destruction mankind visits upon nature. Later, the frolicking bears were added using the splintered tree as playground. The painting's message had now been reversed to an optimistic view of nature's ability to rejuvenate itself. This painting's duel messages represent the concept of the Rorschach.

[56] David Powlison, Westminster Theological Seminary, Philadelphia, Pennsylvania

> Without a thorough understanding of sin, sanctification becomes little more than quaint sentimentalism, and Jesus, a distant principle. In fact, without a careful understanding of sin, Jesus becomes merely sanctimonious camouflage to the idolatrous heart.

At the fall, man retained God's image but thoroughly lost His likeness. Upon receiving Jesus as savior, God initiates a progressive rejuvenation of his likeness within the believer. That likeness is incrementally restored as the believer lives in the Holy Spirit, the likeness being his new nature, new citizenship, and new identity.[57] Thus, there are two facets of sanctification; the Christian can be sure he will continue to change because God has already reclaimed him.

> "Therefore, if anyone is in Christ, the new creation has come: The old has gone, the new is here!" (2 Corinthians 5:17)

First Corinthians 4:9 states, "For it seems to me that God has put us apostles on display at the end of the procession, like those condemned to die in the arena. We have been made a spectacle to the whole universe, to angels as well as to human beings." The Christian is a spectacle to the whole universe, one who is destined to bring far greater glory to God than the entire universe in all of its wonder and intricacy ever could. The Lord's work of renewal in believers' hearts is of a greater order of magnitude than even his original work of creation. This means that the Christian is recreated with a superior display of power compared with the very formation of the universe itself.

> "Make no little plans; they have no magic to stir men's blood. Make big plans; aim high in hope and work." (Daniel Burnham)

Sanctification as Purification of the Firstfruits

A Consuming Fire

The entire globe longs to be free from environmental pollution. However, there is a vastly greater, far more insidious, pollution which taints the human existence - sin. God longs to free fallen man from the pollution within his own being; that is the purpose of sanctification.[58]

Consider the following verses:

1. "Then one of the seraphim flew to me with a live coal in his hand, which he had

---

[57] 2 Corinthians 5:17
[58] Titus 3:5

taken with tongs from the altar. With it he touched my mouth and said, 'See, this has touched your lips; your guilt is taken away and your sin atoned for.'" (Isaiah 6:6, 7)

2. "I baptize you with water for repentance. But after me comes one who is more powerful than I, whose sandals I am not worthy to carry. He will baptize you with the Holy Spirit and fire." (Matthew 3:11)

3. "If what has been built survives, the builder will receive a reward. If it is burned up, the builder will suffer loss but yet will be saved—even though only as one escaping through the flames." (1 Corinthians 3:14, 15)

Sanctification involves the application of a purifying fire. For the sinner, this is not always a comfortable process, but it is a liberating one. The Holy Spirit places the believer's heart into a crucible in which through the steady application of spiritual flame, sin's dross is slowly burned away. The purpose of this refining fire is to present the Christian as a purified offering of the firstfruits of the creation, the first and greatest gift to Christ himself.[59] In being progressively purified, the Christian yields an abundant harvest.

> "You did not choose me, but I chose you and appointed you so that you might go and bear fruit—fruit that will last—and so that whatever you ask in my name the Father will give you." (John 15:16)
>
> "For those God foreknew he also predestined to be conformed to the image of his Son, that he might be the firstborn among many brothers and sisters." (Romans 8:29)

The New Testament describes Christians as the "firstfruits" or "firstborn."[60] This concept is tied to the redemption of the firstborn in Numbers 3:45-48. In Numbers the Levites were employed in the service of the tabernacle in lieu of Israel's firstborn. However, Israel's firstborn numbered 22,273, while the Levites numbered 22,000. Moses was tasked with the redemption of the remaining 273, setting a price of five shekels of silver for each. First Peter 1:18, 19, alludes to this event:

> For you know that it was not with perishable things such as silver or gold that you were redeemed from the empty way of life handed down to you from your forefathers, but with the precious blood of Christ, a lamb without blemish or defect.

---

[59] For a more complete handling of this issue see "The Gospel and Suffering" in the third book in this series, *The Days of Reckoning Are at Hand: From Fig Leaf to Olive Branch to Laurel Wreath*, chapter 2: "Suffering: The Kintsugi Objective"

[60] Romans 8:23; Hebrews 12:23; James 1:18; Revelation 14:4

The Christian is the rightful spiritual ancestor of this bloodline of the firstborn.[61] But unlike the Levites who fell short of the requirements for their tabernacle service, the Christian has, on account of Christ, been reckoned fully-compliant with God's requirements.

Sanctification means that God's likeness is gradually restored within the believer. God slowly rebuilds his likeness into the believer by progressively renewing his worship, so that his worship conforms more closely to God's desire. Like methodically bending wood using heat, water, and pressure, so too, God meticulously, persistently, and progressively works through daily change to fashion his people into Christ's image. This progressive sanctification could be thought of in terms of the "already, not yet," the Christian is already redeemed by Christ, but is not yet fully conformed to him. The Christian could be summarized as paradoxically already a new creation in the midst of being renewed (not yet renewed).

> "For God, who said, 'Let light shine out of darkness,' made his light shine in our hearts to give us the light of the knowledge of God's glory displayed in the face of Christ." (2 Corinthians 4:6)

If Jesus died for mankind, why would he not also seek to change mankind into his image?

> Through these he has given us his very great and precious promises, so that through them you may participate in the divine nature, having escaped the corruption in the world caused by evil desires. For this very reason, make every effort to add to your faith goodness; and to goodness, knowledge; and to knowledge, self-control; and to self-control, perseverance; and to perseverance, godliness; and to godliness, mutual affection; and to mutual affection, love. (2 Peter 1:4-7)

The world envies and celebrates the wicked, while persecuting the Christian.[62] Regardless of the extent of that persecution, there is absolutely no comparison between that which the Christian loses as he dies to the world, and that which he gains in Christ. That which the Christian receives in Christ, through redemption and sanctification, is infinitely greater than that which he lost through renouncing his sin. In this sense, God's grace is a completely different "unit of measure" from that by which the sinner lives.[63]

> Ezekiel 18:31 states, "Cast away from you all your transgressions which you have committed, and make yourselves a new heart and a new spirit!" This is a cry for

---

[61] Galatians 4:28, 31
[62] John 15:19
[63] David and Sharon Covington, "Introduction to Biblical Counseling" notes, 2004

> God's mercy, that only God, through his Spirit, can bestow a new heart and a new spirit.

The "Over-Plus" of Christ[64]

Alexander Mosaic (Battle of Issus), 333 BC

Alexander the Great (356–323 BC) was one of the wealthiest and most powerful emperors who ever lived, having conquered much of the Western world. Once, one of his officials asked if Alexander would pay for the official's lavish wedding. Some in the emperor's court were aghast, certain that the official would be executed for his brazen request. Shockingly, Alexander commanded his servants to give the official anything he requested. Alexander was honored because the official recognized his untold wealth and generosity, that nothing was too great for him.[65] This is a fitting introduction to the "over-plus" of Christ.

The over-plus of Christ refers to the fact that far more has been gained for mankind in Christ than was lost in the fall. Jesus' death on the cross did not simply neutralize the various curses upon the creation;[66] his death brought with it an overflow of grace so that what the Christian experiences in Christ is vastly superior to what Adam experienced prelapsarian (before the fall). For example, Hebrews 11:39, 40 reads, "These were all commended for their faith, yet none of them received what had been promised, since God had planned something better for us so that only together with us would they be made perfect."

---

[64] This term from Richard Gaffin, "Introduction to Systematic Theology" class, Westminster Theological Seminary, Philadelphia, Pennsylvania

[65] L. B. Cowman, *Streams in the Desert* (Grand Rapids, Michigan: Zondervan Publishing House, 1997)

[66] Genesis 3:15-19

The over-plus of Christ concerns humanity's complete restoration to its birthright. Thus, the Christian experiences the fullness of humanity in a way that those before Christ never could. While Peter referred to the Christian as an "alien" in this world,[67] and Paul described the Christian as a "new creation,"[68] as well as "a spectacle to the whole universe,"[69] this is not to imply that the Christian is a new species. The Christian is humanity at its apex because he is in Christ, humanity *par excellence*.[70] In Christ, the Christian is brought from wrecked to rectified humanity. Thus, the Christian lives in an "Emancipation Proclamation" of the soul, freed from sin's slavery through executive fiat.

> **Proleptic Indicators of the Over-Plus**
>
> "After Job had prayed for his friends, the Lord restored his fortunes and gave him twice as much as he had before. All his brothers and sisters and everyone who had known him before came and ate with him in his house. They comforted and consoled him over all the trouble the Lord had brought on him, and each one gave him a piece of silver and a gold ring. The Lord blessed the latter part of Job's life more than the former part. He had fourteen thousand sheep, six thousand camels, a thousand yoke of oxen and a thousand donkeys. And he also had seven sons and three daughters." (Job 42:10-13)
>
> "At the same time that my sanity was restored, my honor and splendor were returned to me for the glory of my kingdom. My advisers and nobles sought me out, and I was restored to my throne and became even greater than before." (Daniel 4:36)

Thomas Edison (1847-1931) said, "Restlessness and discontent are the first necessities of progress." While Edison spoke of technological advance, his statement could be applied to the concept of sanctification. The Christian is never comfortable in his sin, never content with his level of holiness. Like giddy crowds surging forward to welcome Charles Lindbergh (1902-1974) at Le Bourget Field, the Christian longs, day by day, to be renewed by Christ, to know Christ more deeply, to be liberated in his innermost being. It is for this that Christ bestows upon the Christian the over-plus of his indwelling presence, a genuine and lasting progress that knows no bounds.

The Sanctification Pentagon[71]

There are five elements to sanctification, each operating in tandem with one another.

---

[67] 1 Peter 2:11
[68] 2 Corinthians 5:17
[69] 1 Corinthians 4:9
[70] John 19:5
[71] The following five categories from David Powlison, Westminster Theological Seminary, Philadelphia, Pennsylvania

In order to experience sanctification as God intended all five components must be present in one's life. There may be situations in which one component is more pronounced than the others. However, God's intention is that all have continual input in one's growth in holiness.

The Sanctification Pentagon

```
                          God as
                          Author        In isolation:
                                        becomes Gnosticism
                          ┌─────────┐
                          │  Union  │
                          │with Christ│
                          └─────────┘
              ↙       ↙        │      ↘         ↘
         Keystone   Vine               Head      Bridegroom
           and      and     vertical    and         and
           Arch    Branches   axis      Body        Bride
                                │
                                ↓
            horizontal axis
   ┌──────────────┐        ┌──────────┐           ┌──────────┐
   │   Trials/    │───────→│Believer's│←──────────│ Church as│
   │Circumstances │        │   Will   │           │ Counselor│
   └──────────────┘        └──────────┘           └──────────┘
                                ↑
   In isolation:           In isolation:           In isolation:
   becomes experientialism becomes self-help       becomes a cult

                           ┌─────────┐
                           │Scripture│   In isolation:
                           └─────────┘
                            Mirror       becomes cognitive therapy
                             Lamp
```

1. God as author of sanctification[72]

Leviticus 24:2, 4 reads, "Command the Israelites to bring you clear oil of pressed olives for the light so that the [*lamp*] may be kept burning continually. The *lamps* on the pure gold lamp stand before the Lord must be tended continually." (Under Mosaic Law, the priests were responsible for ensuring that the lamps were kept burning.) In verse two "lamp" is singular in the original text. However, in verse four the word changes to "lamps" plural. Verse two may be a subtle reference to the Holy Spirit, a single lamp, which gives light to the smaller individual lamps (believers). This draws

---

[72] For additional discussion of the issue of God as author of sanctification see "The Bible's Four Primary Metaphors for Relationship with Jesus" in the third book in this series, *The Days of Reckoning Are at Hand: From Fig Leaf to Olive Branch to Laurel Wreath*, chapter 4: "The Umbilicus of Personal Relationship with Christ"

in Revelation 3, in which God speaks about various churches as lamp stands, and Revelation 4:5 mentions the seven lamps of fire before the throne.

The Creation of Adam, Michelangelo Buonarroti, 1511

Under the new covenant in Christ, the Holy Spirit directly indwells believers to produce inner light. Romans 8:26 reads, "In the same way, the Spirit helps us in our weakness. We do not know what we ought to pray for, but the Spirit himself intercedes for us through wordless groans." The Holy Spirit himself directly counsels believers, authoring the Christian's heart change.

Sanctification is first reliance on God himself for change, basking in his grace, and appropriating his promises. This involves drawing near to God so as to more fully bathe in his glory. Thus, this first component of the sanctification pentagon is the crown and the keystone of the Christian faith, to be indwelled by one's God so as to experience his intimate work of change. In this regard, the Puritans wrote extensively about union with Christ; this union is the Christian's greatest pursuit, the source and objective of his entire life. It is in union with the living Christ that the Christian sees himself as he really is, a wicked wretch desperately in need of change.[73] Christ longs to lavish glorious change on those who are his own.

> The Christian faith is often wrongly thought of as mere propositional knowledge, that which is acquired through reading a book. While the Christian does gain knowledge of all things pertaining to faith through the Bible, this is not the sum-total of his knowledge of his faith. The Christian lives out that which he gains through the Bible in direct relationship with God. In this sense, Christianity is best described as craft knowledge or as an apprenticeship, one which holds propositional and tacit knowledge in tension.

---

[73] Revelation 3:17

> To best understand craft knowledge, consider the way in which one would learn to play tennis. One could read about how to play, but to truly know what tennis is one must actually step onto a court and play. One must feel the weight of the racket, judge the path and speed of the ball, and calculate the angles. Thus, one can only understand tennis through actually playing it. Propositional knowledge (gained through reading) and tacit knowledge (gained through relationship-directed firsthand experience) work in tandem to shape the Christian's faith.[74] Jesus, himself, as Word of God (propositional),[75] nevertheless, learned obedience through what he experienced (tacit).[76]

John 14:6 states, "Jesus answered, 'I am the way and the truth and the life. No one comes to the Father except through me.'" Jesus himself is the truth, not that he just presents or upholds the truth. Jesus, as truth itself, reveals that the truth is a *person*. The Christian does not merely live out principles, hold to a certain standard of morality, or uphold a "religious" system. The Christian is indwelled by a *person*. This person is the director and dynamo for his sanctification. An actual person changes the Christian, so that he is confronted and taught by a person; he is broken and rebuilt by a person. This vertical change (with regard to God) drives horizontal change (with regard to the creation, namely people).

The motif of the mountain in Scripture is an image of God's character – enormous, immovable, impregnable, permanent, and timeless. In Isaiah 2:1, 4:5 (and again in Hebrews 12:18-24) God's holy mountain shifts from Sinai to Zion. So God's earthly dwelling moved from a place of mystery and fear (where Moses received the Ten Commandments), to a place of fruitfulness, joy, fertility, and welcome. If any one of the Israelites so much as touched Mount Sinai he would die.[77] Yet, Mount Zion is a place where the seemingly impossible take place, where swords are beat into plowshares, as God himself dwells with his people.[78] God has relocated his mountain dwelling so as to invite believers to fellowship with himself. Thus, Mount Zion is a prophetic picture of rebirth in Jesus, and as such is God's means of personally effecting sanctification.

> It is fascinating that Ezekiel 28:13-16 speaks about the Garden of Eden as a mountain. This may be a veiled reference to Christ, as John 4:20-24 states:
>
>> 'Our fathers worshiped on this mountain, but you Jews claim that the place where we must worship is in Jerusalem.' Jesus declared, 'Believe me,

---

[74] This insight is from classmate Ronald Cray, Westminster Theological Seminary, Philadelphia, Pennsylvania
[75] John 1:1
[76] Hebrews 5:8
[77] Exodus 19:12
[78] Isaiah 2:4

> woman, a time is coming when you will worship the Father neither on this mountain nor in Jerusalem. You Samaritans worship what you do not know; we worship what we do know, for salvation is from the Jews. Yet a time is coming and has now come when the true worshipers will worship the Father in spirit and truth, for they are the kind of worshipers the Father seeks. God is spirit, and his worshipers must worship in spirit and in truth.'

> **When God as author of sanctification functions in isolation…**
>
> In isolation from the other four components listed below (Scripture, the church, trials, and desiring change) relationship with God can easily fall into mysticism or Gnosticism (a first century heresy which privatized knowledge of God). When one merely focuses on personal knowledge of God, to the exclusion of God's Word and his ordained community, one easily falls into the trap of believing he is privy to secret knowledge. This becomes nothing more than the prideful projection of the self that one then calls communication from God. This danger rises with the emerging church as it seeks direct and private revelation. Additionally, those who practice glossolalia often show a prideful disdain for Scripture, as they see their own supposed communication with the Spirit as primary.

2. Scripture as lamp and mirror in sanctification[79]

Jeremiah 23:29 states, "'Is not my word like fire,' declares the Lord, 'and like a hammer that breaks a rock in pieces?'" Scripture functions as a polarizing set of lenses, a wholly revolutionary view of reality, opening up new questions and previously unconsidered answers.[80] Scripture does not exist in isolation, but introduces the person of God himself. As such, it is through this organic relationship between God and his Word that truth is discerned in a world swirling with falsehood of every conceivable color and stripe. Scripture bears a singular obsession, to reveal Jesus. John 1:1 states, "In the beginning was the Word, and the Word was with God, and the Word was God." Jesus is intimately intertwined with his Word so that the Word makes Jesus manifest to those who study it in faith. Yet, the Christian does not worship the Bible; he worships Jesus Christ.[81]

> "I have hidden your word in my heart that I might not sin against you." (Psalm 119:11)

---

[79] For a more complete handing of the doctrine of Scripture see chapter 3: "The Centrality of Scripture in Counseling"
[80] James 1:22-25
[81] John Bettler, "Marriage and Family Counseling" class, Westminster Theological Seminary, Philadelphia, Pennsylvania

Matthew 13:10-16 states that Jesus spoke in parables in order to both conceal the truth from the ungodly and to reveal it to those who honestly desired it. Parables exist to guard the "secrets of the kingdom of heaven" so that those with saving faith are extended more wisdom, while those without are blinded to the truth. With this intent in mind, the Bible assiduously exposes heart motives in ways that are extrasensory and eminently ethereal. With boundless ambition, Scripture uncovers the drives within people, dismantling the propped up façade of feigned righteousness behind which sinners routinely cower. However, in his grace God never holds up a mirror without providing a lamp. This is his "from-to" mechanism for change. Thus, Scripture never reveals bad news without offering far more persuasive good news.

> "For the word of God is alive and active. Sharper than any double-edged sword, it penetrates even to dividing soul and spirit, joints and marrow; it judges the thoughts and attitudes of the heart." (Hebrews 4:12)

Many study Scripture to interpret their circumstances. The assumption is that circumstance is the constant upon which Scripture (the supposed variable) is brought to bear. In other words, they view their circumstance as a preset movie script being unwound like a ribbon. Circumstance is seen as a cold impassive cosmic edict and Scripture as the variable summoned to interpret that circumstance. Therefore, most see circumstance as primary and Scripture as secondary, the latter existing only to interpret the former.

In actuality, God works in the opposite direction. As one studies Scripture, God engineers circumstance to illuminate the truths of Scripture. Thus, studying Scripture profoundly changes one's circumstances, so that Scripture is the constant, and circumstance the elucidating variable. Scripture does not firstly exist to interpret circumstance; circumstance exists to draw out Scripture.

Union with Christ and knowledge of his Word constitute the vertical axis of the believer's sanctification. This axis is God's direct communication, his lifeline, through Word and indwelling Spirit.

> **When Scripture as lamp and mirror in sanctification functions in isolation...**
>
> In isolation from the other four components (relationship with God, the church, trials, and self-control) Scripture becomes a kind of contorted cognitive therapy. Scripture must never be isolated from faithful relationship with God or Scripture itself becomes God. A growing danger in certain church traditions is that Jesus becomes nothing more than the Word. Thus, Jesus loses his flesh-and-blood personhood so as to be reduced to a compilation of propositional statements.[82]

---

[82] 2 John 1:7

3. Church as community of counselors in the sanctification process[83]

A single Christian mother asked me for advice on choosing a congregation. She said that she was searching for a church in which her four year-old daughter could find playmates. I graciously informed her that, while finding children's playmates is worthwhile, this is not the criterion by which to decide on a church, that God has a far higher objective in mind. I encouraged her to search for a church in which she herself could first be taught, encouraged, and rebuked in her personal relationship with Jesus so as to, in turn, be able to raise her daughter in the fear of the Lord. Her daughter does not need playmates so much as she needs a godly mother growing in wisdom.

Wandering Thoughts
Francis David Millet, d. 1912

In line with this mother's thinking, today most Christians have more of a consumer mentality than a member mentality with regard to church involvement. The church has become another carnival in the Vanity Fair, more akin to Disney World® attraction than suffering servant committed to sanctification within the body. As the church neglects its own growth in sanctification, it easily attracts attendees who merely seek a Currier and Ives® social experience. Jesus died for his church that it might not just call some to salvation, but cultivate disciples who desire the living Jesus raiding and rebuilding hearts.[84] The church's *raison d'etre* is that Christians might gather for worship, and experience the sanctification that derives from vibrant Christ-centered community. The church exists to make Christ known within its members, so as to in turn make him known to the world.

---

[83] For a more complete handling of the doctrine of the church see the third book in this series, *The Days of Reckoning Are at Hand: From Fig Leaf to Olive Branch to Laurel Wreath*, chapter 10: "Counseling and the Church: Syndicating the Vision"
[84] Matthew 28:19

The church is God's intended haven of wise counselors and, as such, is a community marked out for sanctifying work. The church was meant to be a wonderland of variegated interactions replete with relational disappointments and joys, pain and encouragement, all the while life-giving and eternally-focused. The church is God's intended engine for generating a dynamic and vibrant community which does not just propositionally ascent to the risen Christ, but actually experiences the risen Christ and, in turn, counsels by means of the risen Christ. The church should be a place where the Christian can experience the humility of offering apology and the treasure of expressing thanks, as well as the revitalization that comes from receiving forgiveness and thanks.

The life of the church could be considered "the truth on wheels," offering an experience of God through study, service, the wise use of gifts, and growth in love toward God and others. The church should offer a glimmer of heaven, the one place on earth where it is safe to be a Christian, where it is joyful to obey God, where Scripture is the *lingua franca*, and where the purity of Christ's bride is exhibited and celebrated.[85] The church should stand on the bedrock of truth,[86] delivering that truth with winsome love.

> **When the church as community of counselors functions in isolation…**
>
> In isolation from the other four sanctification components the church degenerates into a cult. The church is not firstly a "horizontal" experience but a "vertical" entity directly connected to Christ. When the church becomes merely an earthly organization, divorced from God and his Word, it quickly devolves into every form of degradation and dissipation.

4. Trials as fire-testing for the purpose of sanctification[87]

Genesis 3:16-19 reads,

> 'I will make your pains in childbearing very severe; with painful labor you will give birth to children. Your desire will be for your husband, and he will rule over you.' To Adam he said, 'Because you listened to your wife and ate fruit from the tree about which I commanded you, 'You must not eat from it,' 'Cursed is the ground because of you; through painful toil you will eat food from it all the days of your life. It will produce thorns and thistles for you, and you will eat the plants of the field. By the sweat of your brow you will eat your food until you return to the ground, since from it you were taken; for

---

[85] 2 Corinthians 11:2
[86] Matthew 16:18
[87] For a more complete handling of the issue of suffering see the third book in this series, *The Days of Reckoning Are at Hand: From Fig Leaf to Olive Branch to Laurel Wreath*, chapter 2: "Suffering: The Kintsugi Objective"

dust you are and to dust you will return.'

The curses God visited upon creation were not intended to bring harm but to drive newly-minted rebels to seek deliverance in a good God, to cause those under these curses to cry out for mercy in an evil world of their own making. Thus, the enmity between Satan and the woman's offspring, the curse upon child-bearing, the pronouncement of Eve's desire for Adam, and the curse upon the ground, would mar humanity's every pursuit so as to drive it with desperation into God's arms. The point is that trials, suffering, and pain of many kinds, exist for one reason - to affect salvation and sanctification.

> "Adversity introduces a man to himself."

Having bowed to the Egyptian gods, the Israelites needed to be purged of their abomination. Thus, wandering in the desert for forty years was a means of purification,[88] a period of forced isolation intended to keep the Israelites from idolatrous pollution with other nations. When Israel's Exodus generation had finally died off, Israel would be thoroughly sanctified and the subsequent generation would enter the Promised Land.

> When your people Israel have been defeated by an enemy because they have sinned against you, and when they turn back to you and give praise to your name, praying and making supplication to you in this temple, then hear from heaven and forgive the sin of your people Israel and bring them back to the land you gave to their ancestors.
>
> When the heavens are shut up and there is no rain because your people have sinned against you, and when they pray toward this place and give praise to your name and turn from their sin because you have afflicted them, then hear from heaven and forgive the sin of your servants, your people Israel. Teach them the right way to live, and send rain on the land you gave your people for an inheritance.
>
> When famine or plague comes to the land, or blight or mildew, locusts or grasshoppers, or when an enemy besieges them in any of their cities, whatever disaster or disease may come, and when a prayer or plea is made by anyone among your people Israel—being aware of the afflictions of their own hearts, and spreading out their hands toward this temple— then hear from heaven, your dwelling place. Forgive and act; deal with everyone according to all they do, since you know their hearts (for you alone know every human heart), so that they will fear you all the time they live in the land you gave our

---
[88] Numbers 32:13

ancestors. (1 Kings 8:33-40)

The Christian experiences peace within his heart, with his circumstances, and with like-minded Christians, but not with the surrounding world. The greater the world's open hostility to God, the greater the faithful Christian's conflict with the world. In the midst of reigning peace with God, the Christian, thus, often ekes out a contorted and knotted existence within the world.[89] One might label this the "peace-conflict paradox," modeled after John 16:33, "'I have told you these things, so that in me you may have *peace*. In this world you will have *trouble*. But take heart! I have overcome the world.'" The paradox arises in that the Christian experiences both increased peace (in Christ) and increased conflict (with the world) as he draws near to God. The chasm between that peace and conflict magnifies as the Christian grows in sanctification.

Aeneas Flees Burning Troy, Frederico Barocci, 1598

> "Not only so, but we also glory in our sufferings, because we know that suffering produces perseverance; perseverance, character; and character, hope. And hope does not put us to shame, because God's love has been poured out into our hearts through the Holy Spirit, who has been given to us." (Romans 5:3-5)

It would appear that for the Christian there tends to be peace in non-essential matters and conflict in essential ones. While for the non-Christian there is conflict in non-essential matters and peace in essential ones. In other words, the world is in

---

[89] Matthew 8:20 offers some sense of this.

agreement with itself on essential matters (its ideology of existence and purpose), so there is no need for conflict. But in trivial matters the world is often in deadly conflict with itself. However, for the Christian the poles are reversed.

Many Christian ministries tout Jesus' ability to "change lives." (I, too, often use this term.) However, when, in certain contexts, I hear this expression I feel a twinge of discomfort. What is generally meant by this is that Jesus has the ability to change unsavory *situations*. While that is certainly true, there is nestled within this a subtle twist and perversion. Jesus is not firstly concerned with delivering one from his situation;[90] he is concerned with confronting the foolish heart in the middle of that situation. So the situation exists that the heart would be changed, and the situation persists until that work is done. Thus, put most accurately, Jesus changes hearts (*nouthetic* core) so that in the course of that motivational change, life situations invariably change. The priority and thrust of Jesus' work is always in the heart; the dictates of situation are always secondary to that.

> "Talents are best nurtured in solitude; character is best formed in the stormy billows of the world." (Johann Goethe)

Thus, from the Bible's perspective suffering exposes the heart to reveal its contents, what it loves, what it desires, and what it calls home. Suffering is God's megaphone that this world is not one's intended home.[91] (Suffering draws the Christian to focus on his eternal reward, a time when suffering will be alleviated, and warns the non-Christian of his impending doom, a time when suffering will never end.) If one seeks to merely alleviate suffering, without first gaining some understanding of God's purposes, he will have missed the purpose for which that suffering existed. In this sense, pragmatic approaches to suffering invariably ensure that it will arise again. Put simply, the Christian often spins his wheels because he will not ask God for change in the context of circumstance, instead demanding that the very circumstance itself change.

> "Endure hardship as discipline; God is treating you as his children. For what children are not disciplined by their father?" (Hebrews 12:7)
>
> "In all this you greatly rejoice, though now for a little while you may have had to suffer grief in all kinds of trials. These have come so that the proven genuineness of your faith—of greater worth than gold, which perishes even though refined by fire—may result in praise, glory and honor when Jesus Christ is revealed." (1 Peter 1:6, 7)

---

[90] Psalm 23:4
[91] C. S. Lewis, *The Problem of Pain* (The Centenary Press, 1940)

The church community and the believer's suffering form a horizontal axis of experience. However, this horizontal axis is driven by the vertical axis (previously mentioned), so that one's earthly relationships and experiences are defined and interpreted through one's intimate relationship with God and his Word.

> **When trials as fire-testing function in isolation…**
>
> When viewed in isolation, trials and suffering, as mere existential experience, soon control one's interpretation of God. An unregenerate gaze at human experience easily becomes the means for denying or wrongly interpreting Scripture. This gaze can take many forms such as the celebration of the tragic hero, a life consumed with self-pity, Freudian views of one's past, or a morbid focus on personal history. When not under the auspices of Scripture, nor viewed in the context of living relationship with God, personal experience easily slips into experientialism, which at its root is bitterness and simmering contempt for God.

5. One seeks his own sanctification

Soul in Bondage
Elihu Vedder, 1892

Consider the classic literary theme of the ascetic who trains tirelessly day and night, focusing his mind and will to overcome a real or supposed foe. This character trains in solitude often unbeknownst to others, mastering his craft, beating his body into submission, until he emerges from his chrysalis ready to challenge the world at large. The idea of one who trains through shear self-determination to resolutely subdue challengers is a fanciful construct of the psyche. This may arise from mankind's wishful and wistful desire to be able to, in theory, overcome his world in his own strength, through his own will, with only his own resources. This desire is really to be one's own god, sufficient unto oneself to overcome evil, as he defines it. The subtext of the conquering ascetic is defiance of a holy God.

The desire to be self-sufficient, launched in hatred of God, lies at the root of sin. The

Bible calls man's best efforts to overcome evil futile and foolish on account of recognizing the sinner's utter inability to exhibit the needed self-discipline to overcome both intrinsic (within the heart) and extrinsic evil.

> "Like a city that is broken into and without walls is a man who has no control over his spirit." (Proverbs 25:28)

While self-control is one of the fruits of the Spirit,[92] often the Christian erroneously views the Bible's concept of self-control as synonymous with the popular psychology concept of self-help. It is crucial to understand that the Bible's "self" words have nothing to do with self-empowerment; they must be interpreted in light of the Christian's intimate union with Christ.

Second Corinthians 10:5b reads, "…and we take captive every thought to make it obedient to Christ." Thus, the Christian is never passive in his change process. He actively seeks to take captive his every thought as an act of obedience to Christ. The Christian cultivates a lifestyle of self-control and exercises self-discipline, not in his own strength, but in the power of the Holy Spirit. The Christian's self-control is in taking deliberate steps to draw close to God (in shunning evil and desiring sanctification). Most importantly, the Christian daily asks God to show him his sin so as to heighten his vigilance in both identifying that sin and in bringing it before God for absolution. The Christian who desires to know his sin, and to be free from it, finds that sin quickly evaporates as the Son's light brings a disinfecting influence on the soul.

> "Search me, God, and know my heart; test me and know my anxious thoughts. See if there is any offensive way in me, and lead me in the way everlasting." (Psalm 139: 23, 24)

Lack of discipline in one area of the Christian's life has a multiplied effect so that that lack shows itself in many areas at once.[93] For example, gluttony (even sporadic episodes) has a carryover effect into all other areas (driving habits, indulgences, work ethic, sexuality, sensitivity to others, etc.). Thus, the Christian's worship has a cascade effect into all areas of his life, so that absolutely no element is immune.

> The human skeleton becomes stronger or weaker based on the way that it is used. Astronauts spending months in space experience a loss of bone mass, so that they must build up their skeletal integrity upon returning to earth. (They also grow by three centimeters in space's near zero-gravity conditions.) An analogy could be made with the soul which losses strength when persisting in unrepentance, yet

---

[92] Galatians 5:23
[93] Edward Welch, Westminster Theological Seminary, Philadelphia, Pennsylvania

> gains a certain nondescript vitality when sanctified. As the soul is sanctified, it is built up, ennobled, and gains confidence in its God.

Sanctification does not result from passivity or quietism. The Christian must honestly ask God to show him his sin, all the while trusting that God can not only reveal one's sin, but has the power to remove it and bring lasting freedom from it. The Christian must actively seek relationship with God, and honestly invite God to change him. It is on this level that the Christian bears a measure of responsibility for his own sanctification. First Corinthians 10:13 states,

> No temptation has overtaken you except what is common to mankind. And God is faithful; he will not let you be tempted beyond what you can bear. But when you are tempted, he will also provide a way out so that you can endure it.

The implication is that one must wisely recognize, and avail himself of, the escape that God offers.

The Christian is called in Ephesians 6:11, 16, and 17 to put on the armor of God, to take up the shield of faith, and to wield the sword of the Spirit. This is hardly a call to cavalier self-confidence, but exactly the opposite, a daring trust in the God within the armor. The Christian finds assurance in knowing that in the midst of battle, the God of the universe goes before him, with him, and most importantly, in him.

> "Repent, therefore, and return that your sins may be wiped away, in order that times of refreshing may come from the presence of the Lord." (Acts 3:19)

As a side note, in this discussion of seeking one's own sanctification, there are two extremes to avoid: morbid introspection and ignorant activism. Morbid introspection overly analyzes the self without the Holy Spirit's guidance. Without God himself directing the introspection, one can easily develop a hypersensitive conscience paralyzed by every supposed transgression. The biblical counselor directs this person to study himself only through the lens of Scripture, and for the purpose of God's sanctifying work. This person is encouraged to move forward with God's change process, not to remain fixated on sin.

> Consider that the self-righteous obey God to make God indebted to them, while the righteous obey God because they recognize their indebtedness to him.[94] The wise counselor sifts out the two, discerning the self-righteousness and calling them to repentance, identifying the righteous and seeking to magnify their faith.

---

[94] Andrew Field, "Introduction to Redeemer," p. 5, 6, Westminster Theological Seminary, Philadelphia, Pennsylvania

Ignorant activism, on the other hand, resists introspection. One is so engaged in "doing" that he refuses to consider the trajectory of his life. The biblical counselor petitions this person to consider the intentions of his heart, to weigh motives in light of Scripture.

> Place your ear next to your heart and listen hard. (adapted from Anne Sexton)

Portrait of Adele Bloch-Bauer I
Gustav Klimt, 1907

In summary, the Bible's concepts of self-control and self-discipline are not camouflaged self-pride. They involve a deliberate decision to seek God, to draw close to God, to submit to God, to rest in God, to desire God's sanctifying work, and to cooperate in that work through abiding in the Spirit. Cognizant of the evil that lives within himself, one should ask God to save him from himself, to silence the voices of rebellion and hatred that reside within his heart. The wise Christian is leery of his own intentions and earnestly seeks God's purifying daily presence. That is the nature of the Bible's teaching about self-control.

> "How many biblical counselors does it take to change a light bulb? Only one, but the light bulb has to really want to change." (John Bettler)

When one seeks his own sanctification in isolation...

In isolation the desire for change can easily assume a posture of moralistic self-help, a just-try-harder strategy which finally curses mankind with a mock-form of sanctification. Like attempts to just run faster up the down-escalator, moralism sets one up for failure as he can never be "fit enough" to overcome sin's "downward" motion. Moralism may assume a form of godliness but foolishly denies the

> intractable power of sin within the unregenerate heart.[95]

The sanctification pentagon, detailed above, more accurately functions as a five-stranded helix. Each strand, organically related to the others, is inextricably tied one to another. In aggregate, these five components advance the full-extent of God's work in the believer's life, working out the totality of the gospel. As the gospel is made manifest, comprehensive radical worship rehabilitation can take hold. Thus, it is in the completed pentagon that the Christian experiences plenary renewal in Christ.

> "The difference between sin and sanctification is not a large one but divides on a razor's edge." (John Murray)

In Sanctification Who Speaks, Who Decides?

The following is a corporate guideline for how management decisions are made:

1. With a new employee: the manager speaks, the manager decides
2. With an experienced employee: the manager speaks, "we" decide
3. With a seasoned employee: the employee speaks, "we" decide
4. With a veteran employee: the employee speaks, the employee decides

The theory is that as an employee grows in competence he should more actively participate in the decisions pertaining to him, increasingly navigating his own responsibilities.

How might this guideline be redefined to accommodate the Christian's growth in sanctification?

1. With the new Christian (the young, simple, naïve): God speaks, God decides in the context of inviting relationship with himself[96]

2. With the growing Christian: God speaks, God offers ever-expanding opportunity to apply newly-minted wisdom through exercising spiritual gifts[97]

3. With the highly-sanctified Christian: God speaks, God calls on the Christian to assume greater displays of self-sacrificial faith, and to adopt sharper refinement in his doctrine[98]

---

[95] 2 Timothy 3:5
[96] This first stage might be most similar to the approach used in the book of Proverbs.
[97] Romans 12:6
[98] Titus 1:9

4. With the disciple in Christ: God speaks, God "binds and loosens" in accordance with the disciple's wisdom[99]

In the Christian's growth in sanctification, regardless of his degree of faith, the starting point is always the eternal God who speaks. This speaking comes through God's Word, and is in the context of relationship. The Christian, no matter how wise, never stops listening to God's voice as he engages in ever-expanding participation in God's work in and through him.[100]

> The alarm clock was invented in 1787 but only rang at 4:00 a.m. It would take decades for an alarm clock to be invested with greater capabilities. The same can be said for the believer's sanctification. It starts out as a "4:00 a.m. alarm clock" but slowly gains a broader range of responses.

Case Study: The Refusal to Rest

> "Very well then, with foreign lips and strange tongues
>   God will speak to this people,
> to whom he said,
>   'This is the resting place, let the weary rest';
> and, 'This is the place of repose'—
>   but they would not listen.
> So then, the word of the LORD to them will become:
>   Do this, do that,
>   a rule for this, a rule for that;
>   a little here, a little there—
> so that as they go they will fall backward;
>   they will be injured and snared and captured." (Isaiah 28:11-13)

As I ran along a hot dusty road, I saw a crippled young man in a wheelchair with a small dog harnessed to the front like a sledge dog. The dog strained and pulled with all of its might so that its ribcage heaved as it threw its weight forward. This man and his dog daily endured their travels in scorching heat.

By God's grace, the man soon received an electric cart which would now transport him and his dog effortlessly. The man piloted his cart along the country roads with his dog tethered to the side. The dog could easily jump into the cart and enjoy the ride. However, I noticed a perplexing situation. The dog refused to sit in the cart but, instead, continued his habit of pulling. It ran alongside the cart straining with all its might, just as before, even though its efforts were neither desired nor profitable. The

---

[99] Matthew 18:18; John 20:23
[100] John 10:27 captures something of this idea.

man often chided his dog, summoning him to jump into the cart to relax. While the dog might rest for a short while, he soon jumped back onto the street to resume his wrenching labor.

> "There are two kinds of men who never amount to much: those who can't do what they're told, and those who can do nothing else." (Cyrus Curtis)

Photo courtesy of Gold Rush Dog Tours, LLC
Mendenhall Glacier, Juneau, Alaska, c. 1900

I noticed that even the dog somehow sensed that his efforts were no longer needed, that the cart, despite his strain, seemed to move on its own. However, the dog seemed to crave being needed; he wanted to ensure that he was important and worthy of praise. He continued to slavishly earn his master's favor rather than rest in a gift.

So much about this story appears to be directly applicable to the Christian's self-understanding. Those in Christ need no longer pull the weight of their own lives. They can rest in the "electrifying" power of the Holy Spirit to remove the burden of sin and to effect holiness. However, the Christian, often out of self-pride, wants to believe that he is needed, that God's Spirit is not sufficient to affect lasting change, and that his effort somehow adds to God's. John 15:7 states, "If you remain in me and my words remain in you, ask whatever you wish, and it will be done for you." This is the nature of the Christian life, remaining in Christ, and letting his words remain in one's heart. In this way, the Christian is shaped to desire that which God desires, and to seek that which God seeks.

> "Given enough time, even water cuts through stone."

The Christian's job is not to keep pulling as when he was a slave to this world, but rather to draw near to the "cart," jump in, remain in, and understand what it means to be led and transported by God's Spirit. This is the import of Christian self-control and self-discipline, a desire to draw near to God, taking steps to "plug into" his Spirit, and letting that Spirit propel him. However, the Christian often, wanting to be needed, wanting to feel important, and wanting to be worthy of praise, forsakes fellowship with God to pull in his own strength. This is moralism, an insidious enemy of the gospel. With trenchant stubbornness, this Christian takes pride in his own self-defined and self-directed efforts, supposing that he is making progress when he is not. Finally, such stiff-necked determination only results in exhaustion, frustration, and the mere illusion of progress, as he foolishly lives anachronistically.

> Self-directed change could be likened to Zeno's (c. 490–430 BC) classic dichotomy paradox which states that as one approaches a finite point, moving half the distance each time, he never reaches that point. In other words, as one repeatedly moves half of the distance to his destination he never reaches that destination, and, in fact, motion itself is a mere illusion. This perfectly encapsulates the nature of idolatrous self-control; it gives the illusion of progress, but in actuality there is none. Changing in one's own strength is a proposition of infinite proportions, as one would need to traverse that which is infinite in extent.

One of the most crucial issues to understand about sin is its recalcitrance. Sin has extraordinary tensile strength, making it unimaginably resilient and resistant to change.[101] Sin feels like an indomitable force within the psyche, like a highly-sophisticated war machine bent on global domination.[102] It may at times duck in and out of shifting shadows, play dead, or crouch behind a cloak of invisibility, but sin is an incomparable, if often unadorned, puissance. This is the crux of the issue with regard to sanctification. Sanctification is God's siege works amassed to bring down the citadel of sin, to breach its stronghold, to out-maneuver its guerilla tactics, and, in the process, to intenerate the heart to desire God alone.

The Third-Way of Sanctification[103]

> "The world hates change, yet it is the only thing that has brought progress." (Charles Kettering)

---

[101] Jeremiah 18:12 offers a similar concept.
[102] For further discussion of this topic see "Worship Recidivism" in the second book in this series, *What Agreement Is There Between the Temple of God and Idols?: The Accidence of Sin and Idolatry*, chapter 8: "The Search for Eldorado Ends: Repenting of Idols of the Heart"
[103] This term "the third-way" borrowed from David Powlison, Westminster Theological Seminary, Philadelphia, Pennsylvania

The Peril of Moralism[104]

According to Greek mythology, Icarus and his father Daedalus sought to escape from the island of Crete where they were held captive. Daedalus, a skilled craftsman, constructed wings of wax for both he and his son. Before departing, however, Daedalus cautioned Icarus not to fly too close to the sun. But Icarus, intoxicated with his newfound freedom, did not heed the warning. His wings melted; he plummeted to the sea, and was lost. This is an allegory of the brazen human quest for greatness, mankind's aspiration to become a soaring god. Whenever mankind arrogates himself he finds perilous destruction, as all of his attempts at autonomy fail time and again.

Daedalus and Icarus
Domenico Piola, c. 1670

Self-centeredness causes one to fixate on utterly self-directed motives. Moralism, a man-centered and man-defined system of conduct, makes one able to oscillate from overtly self-directed behavior to more socially acceptable (yet equally self-serving) behavior. While moralism operates horizontally, person-to-person, it is, in fact, self-centered in that it is without regard to God (even while it offers some limited value in the form of physical discipline[105]). Self-centeredness makes a person one-dimensional (completely self-absorbed); moralism makes him two-dimensional (morally aware to some degree). The Holy Spirit makes a believer three-dimensional

---

[104] For further discussion of this topic see "Drawing Back the Veil on Moralism" in the second book in this series, *What Agreement Is There Between the Temple of God and Idols?: The Accidence of Sin and Idolatry*, chapter 4: "Hamartiology: Sin in All Its Ignobility"; additionally see the discussion of *metanoia* in the section "Diagnosis: 'Tree Diagrams'" in the third book in this series, *The Days of Reckoning Are at Hand: From Fig Leaf to Olive Branch to Laurel Wreath*, chapter 8: "Diagnosis: Vanishing Secrets"
[105] 1 Timothy 4:8

(renewed and regenerate to recognize that which God recognizes).

The Third-Way of Sanctification

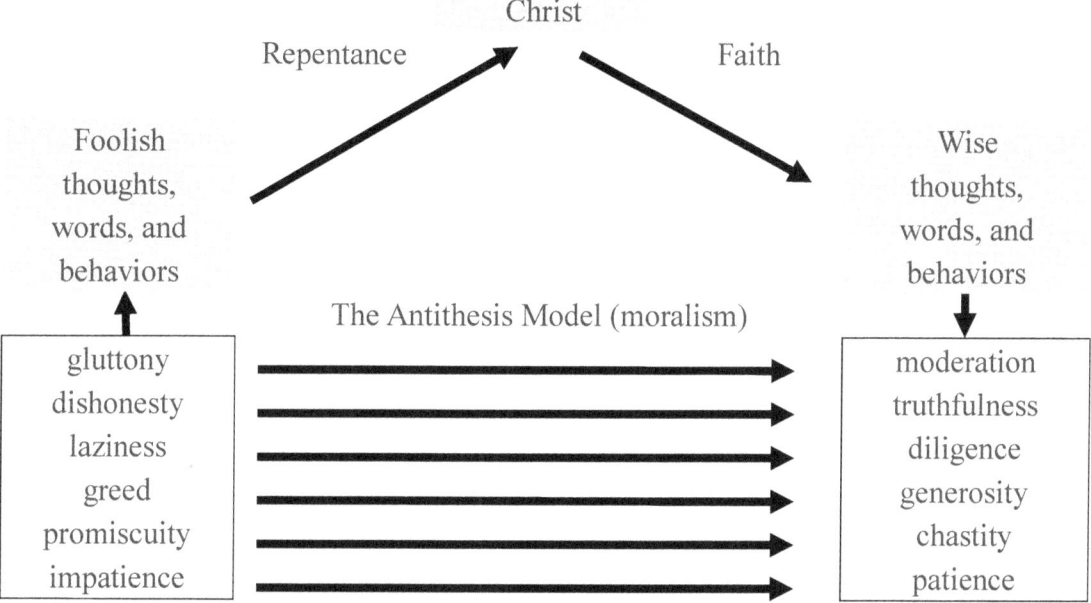

The antithesis model is moralism meaning that foolish thoughts, words, and behaviors are replaced on a horizontal scale with wise thoughts, words, and behaviors. This movement is based in arrogance, the notion that one could correct his errant behavior through the assertion of self-will. Moralism, in effect, commands the sinful heart to, "Stop it!" in the assumption that the heart can and will turn from evil in its own strength. Moralism may identify certain drawbacks in gluttony, dishonesty, laziness, greed, promiscuity, and impatience. In response, it simply directs mankind to adopt the right behavior: moderation, truthfulness, diligence, generosity, chastity, and patience.

However, moralism never works as it simply seeks to replace a humanly-defined negative with another humanly-defined positive. The poles could easily reverse when perceived foolishness suddenly seems like wisdom, and wisdom takes on the appearance of foolishness. Each sinner chisels out his own "Code of Hammurabi," and defines his own "unpardonable sin," but just as soon smashes that code and permits that sin to suit his self-worship agenda.

Oscar Wilde (1854–1900) wrote, "Always forgive your enemies – nothing annoys them so much." Wilde's statement offers a portal into the truth behind moralism. While forgiving one's enemies is the mark of a sanctified Christian,[106] a way to love one's enemies into the kingdom of God, the unsanctified heart turns such an act into simply another form of revenge. Thus, according to Wilde, one is not to forgive his

---

[106] Matthew 5:44; Luke 23:34

enemy in order to love him, but in order to love oneself. This reveals the hidden curse of moralism; it is actually a sophisticated smokescreen for self-love and self-promotion.

Moralism bends every good act into a self-serving ambition and, in so doing, strips that act of its God-invested life. Therefore, in this example, forgiving one's enemies is intended to showcase the gospel, that each is an impoverished sinner before a holy God; each is called to forgive as a display of God-fearing humility, and in so doing bless one's enemies. However, in the hands of moralism, such an act becomes twisted into a curse upon others, a riffling of the gospel so as to desecrate its power.

Moralism is a formidable enemy of the gospel because it easily dons a Christian mask. But moralism never deals with the root of worship, the soul's stronghold, the heart's covering, the sinner's false security in things that are perishing. Thomas Jefferson (1743–1826) wrote, "Nothing gives one person so great advantage over another as to remain always cool and unruffled under all circumstances." As this statement indicates, moralism is not about serving others; it is about gaining an advantage over others, and about gaining an advantage over God.

I wish I were:

Honest enough to admit my failings
Brilliant enough to accept praise without becoming arrogant
Tall enough to tower over deceit
Rich enough to treasure love
Brave enough to welcome criticism
Compassionate enough to understand human frailty
Wise enough to recognize my mistakes
Humble enough to appreciate greatness in others
Loyal enough to stand by my friends
Human enough to be thoughtful of my neighbor
Righteous enough to stand in the presence of a holy God (adapted from Gordon H. Taggart)

A Christian man spoke of his uncontrollable anger as a child.[107] Once, consumed with rage, he attempted to stab a classmate. The thought that he could have murdered another scared him to the point that he surrendered his life to Christ. Now, as an older man, he states that nothing ever gets him angry, that he will never allow himself to become angry over anything.

---

[107] For further discussion of the issue of anger see the case study, "Anger: Shedding Light on the Heat" in chapter 6: "Man Before the Face of God: The Imperium of the Psyche"; also see the discussion of anger in the third book in this series, *The Days of Reckoning Are at Hand: From Fig Leaf to Olive Branch to Laurel Wreath*, chapter 3: "The Hobgoblin in the Inglenook: Assessing Loneliness"

Is the locus of besetting sin in displaying the emotion, or is it in the heart that gave rise to that emotion? It would appear that this man has made the absolute avoidance of anger into a false form of repentance. He has established for himself a moralistic breakwater, a resolve never to allow himself to feel anger again. This may be a way to pay for his past transgressions through avoiding the *emotion*, rather than resting in Jesus who changes the *heart*, so that emotion can be wielded for his purposes. Avoiding the emotion, allows the heart to go unconfronted. Making the display of the emotion into the sin keeps the heart nestled away in a self-righteous cocoon, so that to never display the emotion is to make the heart look sanctified when it is not.

The Good Samaritan
Vincent Willem van Gogh, 1890

Some assert that one must not allow anger to control oneself, but one must control anger. The concept of controlling one's emotions through one's own willpower, and finally achieving mastery over them, is humanistic philosophy, not the Christian message. Emotions arise through what one worships. They are either the symptom of a worship disorder, or arise from a regenerate heart which uses emotion to God's glory. It is not a question of being controlled by emotion or controlling emotion; it is a question of who rules the wellspring from which emotion arises. The Christian allows Jesus to sanctify his heart so that he willingly cedes control to him. Then, the circumstances in which anger arise are dramatically altered.

Albert Einstein (1879–1955) wrote, "It is easier to denature plutonium than to denature the evil spirit of man." The cunning of humanism is that it purports to be able to elevate humanity to a state of peace and harmony through brotherly love. It seeks to uphold the inherent dignity and worth of the human being, but it has no viable means to fight the evil within the human heart. It seeks to tap into mankind's

> supposed niveous goodness but, since that goodness is non-existent, humanism lacks all power to reshape the human will. Thus, humanism remains a utopian vision incapable of implementing lasting change.
>
> What's more, humanism is a false religion which renders its adherents dangerously vulnerable to atrocities against humanity. Anywhere in the world one sees the installation of a humanistic worldview one sees humanity in shambles and ultimately subject to genocide (of one form or another). The twentieth century, like no time in history, bears the scars of humanism. One is left to wonder what bulwark there is against Hitler's (1889-1945) statement, "I do not see why man should not be just as cruel as nature."

Three-Dimensional Image-Bearers

Ephesians 5:16-18 reads,

> So I say, walk by the Spirit, and you will not gratify the desires of the flesh. For the flesh desires what is contrary to the Spirit, and the Spirit what is contrary to the flesh. They are in conflict with each other, so that you are not to do whatever you want. But if you are led by the Spirit, you are not under the law.

These verses specifically refute the antithesis model in that they emphasize the third-way of sanctification, the Bible's assertion that one cannot, and will not, change through shear willpower. One must invite, and be indwelled by, the Holy Spirit so that foolish thoughts, words, and actions are reckoned on a vertical scale where repentance is implemented before Christ. Repentance at the foot of the cross results in growth in faith so that one is made wise through regeneration. That regeneration then results in a cascade effect of holiness: the right thoughts, words, and actions. Thus, the third-way of sanctification is a continual movement toward, not just a Christian way of thinking, but toward Christ himself - "up" by repentance and "down" by faith.

The third-way of sanctification is based on humility before God, the recognition that one is not able in his own strength to please God, or to experience real change unless done in faith. Thus, the antidote to impatience is not patience; it is holiness; the antidote to greed is not generosity; it is holiness; the antidote to dishonesty is not honesty; it is holiness.

> There is an immense difference between these two statements:
>
> 1. "You love money. Stop it!"

> 2. "You love money. Repent before Jesus Christ, asking him to cause you to worship him as your only treasure."
>
> The first is moralism which, as a vapid belief system lacks all power to effect meaningful change and, thus, results in spiritual death. The second is repentance and faith producing life-giving healing, resulting in an abundant yield. The first "de-personifies" Christianity; the second invites the person of God to enact desired change.

Like achieving *Type III* on the Kardashev scale (being able to utilize, to the fullest extent, the energy resources at one's disposal), the Holy Spirit transforms the believer into a three-dimensional image-bearer. The Holy Spirit changes one's perspective from the horizontal (earthly) to the vertical (before the face of God) allowing one to transcend a narrowly self-directed focus. The Holy Spirit makes one able to rise above the fray of endemic self-worship and self-serving designs, to function with the largess of a regenerate spirit, to be transformed into a "*Type III*" human (one able to fully experience his humanity as image-bearer in God's likeness).

> In AD 258 the Roman prefect demanded that Lawrence of Rome (c. 225-258), the Roman church treasurer, relinquish the church's treasures. Lawrence agreed, yet in an act of defiance, presented to the prefect the poor, the crippled, the blind and the suffering, stating that these were the church's true treasures. One account records him declaring to the prefect, "The Church is truly rich, far richer than your emperor. Behold in these poor persons the treasures which I promised to show you; to which I will add pearls and precious stones, those widows and consecrated virgins, which are the church's crown."[108] Incensed, the prefect had Lawrence roasted upon a great gridiron.
>
> While likely hagiographic, there is something in this vignette which draws out the issue of sanctification. The idea of offering the poor, the crippled, and the blind as the church's treasure may make for a dramatic story, but it is an affront to Jesus' death on the cross. The church's treasure is not in existential or external conditions but in changed hearts, semi-ruined temples raised to new life. The story of Lawrence, which deifies human suffering as a treasure in itself, siphons off attention from Christ's work to renew his people's worship. It is renewed worship of the living God which is the church's treasure.

The singular purpose of all of human life is to praise God through growth in holiness. Until one knows and submits to this, life will be a Gordian knot of frustration and disappointment. When one finally sees the surpassing greatness of change in Christ, he gladly trades each year of his earthly existence for just a little more holiness. In

---

[108] Wikipedia article, "Lawrence of Rome"

light of this reality, how does the wise counselor make change attractive? How does the counselor incentivize growth in holiness? For one struggling with sin, to speak of God's love as a generality may offer some momentary emotional comfort, but this spurs little lasting desire for change. In fact, an abstract concept of God's love tends to have the opposite effect; it tends to breed complacency.[109] On the other hand, drawing out sin, untangling its wicked web, unmasking its horror and guile, exposing its clear and present threat, tends to incentivize desire for holiness and movement toward God for lasting change.

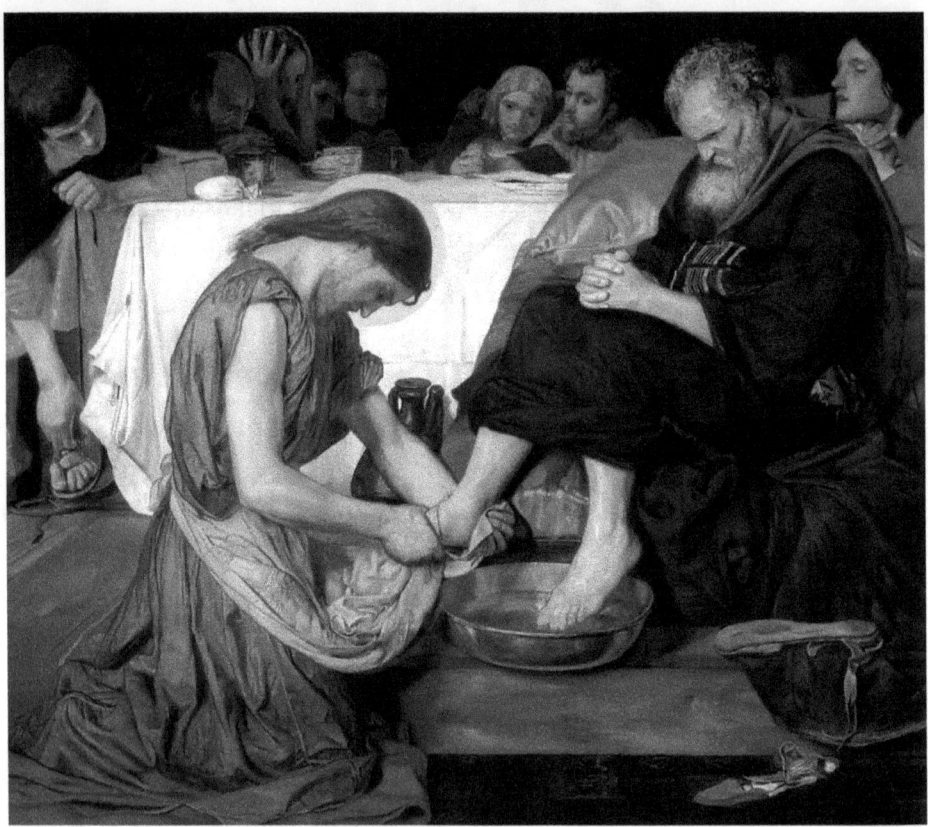

Christ Washing Peter's Feet, Ford Madox Brown, 1856

Excursus: First Corinthians 13:1–12

> Love is patient. Love is kind. It does not envy, it does not boast, it is not proud. It is not rude, it is not self-seeking, it is not easily angered, it keeps no record of wrongs. Love does not delight in evil but rejoices with the truth. It always protects, always trusts, always hopes, always perseveres. (1 Corinthians 13:4-7)

This text is frequently misunderstood because it is taken out of context; it is wrongly "horizontalized," rather than "verticalized." In order to correctly interpret it, one must

---

[109] For development of this point, see "How Does the Christian Rightly Tell Others of God's Love?" in the second book in this series, *What Agreement Is There Between the Temple of God and Idols?: The Accidence of Sin and Idolatry*, chapter 9: "Marauding Visigoths: The Autocratic Self"

appreciate three distinct words for love in the *koine* Greek:

1. ***Philia*** (φιλία) – the love between friends or experienced in marriage. This type of love is grounded in a certain pleasure in the relationship. It may involve a commitment but has a strong emotional component.

2. ***Agapeo*** (αγαπάω) – a love that worships, and offers complete devotion. This love is directed toward God alone, and is based on a conscious decision to love, regardless of feelings.

3. ***Eros*** (ἔρως) – sexual love. This word is not found in the Bible.

Most assume a human relational form of love (*philia*) in this passage, one which makes the expression of love a form of moralism. However, this passage does not speak about *philia* love but, rather, about love that is grounded in the worship of God (*agapeo*), highlighting God's love for the world in sending his one and only Son, Jesus Christ.[110] Therefore, the type of love described does not focus on human relationships, but on the sacrifice and death of Jesus Christ. This is its subtext or context. Therefore, in each instance of the word "love" in 1 Corinthians 13:1-12 one could rightly insert "a love that first worships God…" In other words, it is a love which firstly worships God through Jesus, which results in the actions specified.[111]

Excursus: The Beatitudes

Qualities such as self-denial, self-sacrifice, gentleness, and even kindness are, from an evolutionary point of view, affronts to the natural order. Such qualities detract from the ruthless progress and conquest which humanity must effect in order to advance. Evolution, therefore, makes the bold, the aggressors, and the conquerors into the heroes of its cause. They advance the species through the relentless pursuit of strength, virility, and superiority (as mankind defines those terms). However, the ultimate anti-evolution polemic is Jesus Christ, his teaching and his work of salvation.[112] Jesus' "Sermon on the Mount" presents a seismic shift in humanity's purpose, and in its rightful pursuits.

The Beatitudes

>He [Jesus] said:
>'Blessed are the poor in spirit,

---

[110] John 3:16, 17

[111] For a comprehensive handling of the topic of God's love, see the case study "God's *Sui Generis* Love" found in the third book in this series, *The Days of Reckoning Are at Hand: From Fig Leaf to Olive Branch to Laurel Wreath*, chapter 2: "Suffering: The Kintsugi Objective"

[112] For further discussion of this topic, see the case study "The Ultimate Refutation of Evolution" in chapter 4: "The Gospel as Inception Point: From Immorality to Immortality"

>   for theirs is the kingdom of heaven.
> Blessed are those who mourn,
>   for they will be comforted.
> Blessed are the meek,
>   for they will inherit the earth.
> Blessed are those who hunger and thirst for righteousness,
>   for they will be filled.
> Blessed are the merciful,
>   for they will be shown mercy.
> Blessed are the pure in heart,
>   for they will see God.
> Blessed are the peacemakers,
>   for they will be called children of God.
> Blessed are those who are persecuted because of righteousness,
>   for theirs is the kingdom of heaven.
> Blessed are you when people insult you, persecute you and falsely say all kinds of evil against you because of me. Rejoice and be glad, because great is your reward in heaven, for in the same way they persecuted the prophets who were before you.' (Matthew 5:3-12)

The Beatitudes are typically read through a moralistic lens. This leads to grave misinterpretation which only fosters human pride. The Beatitudes are not encouragement to human effort, or assurance that through one's own attempts he can achieve these statements. They are intended, like the Mosaic Law, to draw out the heart's desperate sinfulness. Jesus' audience should have recognized its abject inner poverty and, thus, should have asked for mercy and forgiveness. The Beatitudes were meant to induce repentance, not self-assurance or false reliance on one's own presumed virtue.

In reality, the Beatitudes were only attainable by one person, Jesus himself, as only Jesus could possibly embody the Beatitudes and live them out. Thus, the Christian seeks to appropriate the Beatitudes through ongoing and abiding relationship with Jesus. In this way, the Christian, as he is more deeply conformed to the vision of the Beatitudes, more fully resembles their author.

> Those who crave power hate the gospel, since any perceived display of weakness is an affront to their ambitions for ascent.

As the Christian is, through ever-deepening relationship with Christ, conformed to the Beatitudes, the range of his sanctification progressively increases. Consider the following examples:

Sinner	**Sanctified**
1. Aggressive	Meek, gentle-hearted, yet assertive for God's purposes
2. Arrogant in his knowledge; needs to assert his superior intellect	Humble, yet not self-deprecating
3. Authoritative[113]	In a position of authority, but not lording it over others
4. Controlling	In control, while resting in God sovereignty
5. Craving affection and acceptance	No need which can be met by people, while not isolated or defiant toward people
6. Insecure, desiring self-esteem	Eternally anchored to Christ[114]
7. Manipulative	Ministering to others
8. Craving respect	No need for respect from others
9. Passive	Patient, while not slipping into passivity or cowardice
10. Seeking to be a hero	Seeking to be a servant; sacrificing quietly and unperceived
11. Rigid; law-giver	Maintains order with flexibility; shows a gracious and charitable demeanor
12. Focused on others' opinions	Serves God without slavish regard for others' opinions,[115] while, at the same time, carefully regarding other's feelings or input
13. Prone either to laziness or workaholism[116]	Hard working, while resting in God for the outcome of one's efforts
14. Regressing farther into sin, delusion, and self-absorption	In the process of being perfected, while never becoming foolishly confident when the occasion for sin is near[117]

A concealed, yet poignant, truth nestled within the Bible's worldview is that every person experiences a continual process of change. The unbeliever is progressively changed into the image of Satan (an incremental state of greater insanity), while the Christian is given a choice to either allow himself to be transformed into the image of Christ or Satan. (The former brings a harvest of peace, while the latter is attended by intense struggle and nagging restiveness.) Each person must experience daily change. The question is, "Into whom will one change?"[118]

---

[113] Matthew 20:25
[114] Hebrews 6:19
[115] Mark 12:14
[116] Matthew 6:32
[117] Colossians 1:28
[118] For additional discussion of this topic, see "If Not Relationship with Christ, Then Relationship with Satan" in the third book in this series, *The Days of Reckoning Are at Hand: From Fig Leaf to Olive Branch to Laurel Wreath*, chapter 4: "The Umbilicus of Personal Relationship with Christ"

Sanctification Cultivates Heart Elasticity

The south-pointing carriage was constructed in China in about the 3rd century A.D. It had a figure mounted on top which, regardless of how many times the carriage turned or how far it traveled, always pointed south. Scientists long believed that the figure was constructed of lodestone which aligned itself with the earth's magnetic field. However, further investigation uncovered that the figure was only wood. The carriage operated by means of precision differentials which maintained its orientation.

Napoleon on His Imperial Throne
Jean Auguste Dominique Ingres, 1806

This metaphor serves as a fitting introduction to the issue of, what I term, "heart elasticity." Regardless of situation, the sanctified heart focuses on a singular objective, glorifying God, being known by God, knowing God, and seeking to be changed more fully into his likeness. Thus, no matter how many times the Christian is "turned," or no matter how far he "travels," his orientation remains precisely upon the polestar of Christ. This focus leads to stunning outcomes with regard to thought, word, and action. Thus, the greater the singular focus on Jesus, the greater the sanctified heart's elasticity, so that it acts and forsakes action, speaks and is silent, all in alignment with that which loves God and others. This is the Christian's hidden paradox, a trenchant worship orientation with regard to Christ which leads to supernatural flexibility of response.

> The Puritans were described as having swallowed a moral gyroscope.

The problem with man-centered attempts at change is that they keep one a slave to a particular "pendulum swing" set of responses. For example, one identifies that he is too passive, so he adopts a counterbalancing aggression. One identifies that he is impatient, so he becomes overly patient to the point of laziness or cowardice. This is the slavery of man-generated attempts at change. However, the third way of sanctification imparts a kind of malleability, a flexibility, to "bob and weave" as God desires. Thus, the sanctified heart knows what is needed in each situation and acts accordingly, not locked into a response pendulum, but operating in a three-dimensional (with-regard-to-God) social and emotional arena.

The antithesis model, as a man-centered means of perceived change, does not allow God to do the needed work of sanctification. Consider one who fears people. In sensing her sin, she may become aggressive, belligerent, or merely independent-minded, in the wrong way and for the wrong purpose. Thus, the antithesis model keeps the sinner trapped in a particular pendulum swing, either cowering fear or towering aggression.[119]

However, the sanctified heart in Christ is given the ability to wisely know when to respond in submission to authority, when to assert a measure of command, when to listen attentively, and when to step forward with words of wisdom. The sanctified heart is placed in a three-dimensional plane of responses so that it wisely knows what is proper in any given circumstance. This is the great hidden treasure of one who is known by Christ and changed by his Spirit. The sanctified heart can assume any needed posture, offer any required counsel, employ any set of words or actions based on the dictates of love of God and neighbor. This elasticity to response is the Christian's resplendence and charm, his wisdom and power, his transcendent ability and polished humility.

The sanctified heart's elasticity arises through the vulcanizing effect of a Christ-centered story with Jesus as hero. Jesus then reinterprets one's personal story so that God no longer plays a side role or the antagonist, but becomes the shining protagonist. In a Christ-centered story, the themes of one's own life's story change:

1. Get becomes give
2. Guard in fear becomes trust in faith
3. Provide for oneself becomes God as refuge and rock
4. Feel good and seek momentary happiness becomes actively seek holiness
5. Meeting personal needs becomes need for Jesus alone
6. The fires of revenge become God-lavished forgiveness[120]

In this way, the heart is alkalized, turning from acerbic defiance to supple submission. This state of submission is an unstoppable force, a quiet strength, that moves seemingly immovable mountains.

"The wolf will live with the lamb, the leopard will lie down with the goat, the calf

---

[119] The concept "towering or cowering" borrowed from David Powlison, Westminster Theological Seminary, Philadelphia, Pennsylvania

[120] Some ideas in this list from David and Sharon Covington's, "Introduction to Biblical Counseling" notes, 2004

> and the lion and the yearling together; and a little child will lead them. The cow will feed with the bear, their young will lie down together, and the lion will eat straw like the ox." (Isaiah 11:6, 7)

Sierra Nevada , Albert Bierstadt, c. 1871

When one walks by the Spirit he views life through a set of lenses that allows him to see the invisible truths of God's will for his creation. Thus, the Christian sees invisible lines of demarcation which God has established in relationships (between people, between mankind and nature, between mankind and spirits, between mankind and God himself) which should not be crossed, and conversely, invisible connections which ought to be established, strengthened, and maintained. These lines are not based on human laws or man-made morality, but rather on ongoing relationship with God, a relationship which renews the vision and enlivens the spirit. Incidentally, those invisible lines have always existed but God's indwelling Spirit is required to refract, polarize, and filter the incoming light so that those connections finally emerge.

The Sanctified Heart's "Patchwork"

Natural growth forests are a patchwork of various type of trees, some evergreen, others deciduous, some softwood, others hardwood. This arrangement functions as an ingenious mechanism for limiting the extent of parasite damage, and in controlling forest fires. For example, pine forests combust easily but, with intermingled slow-burning oak groves, a fire's progress is retarded considerably. Additionally, forest fires are valuable for generating new growth as certain seedpods only open under intense heat. So a measured and controlled fire is paradoxically a necessary means for repopulating the forest.

When foresters repopulate a denuded forest they invariably plant a single tree species (called a monocrop). This leaves the replanted area vulnerable to devastating insect damage, and removes the natural tapestry which serves as a bulwark against rampant fire. Mankind's design efforts, while often well-intentioned, cannot replicate God's.

A certain analogy could be drawn between forest design and the issue of sanctification. Each sinner, when faced with a daunting world, creates a kind of "monocrop" response to his world. He adopts a certain theme such as:

1. I must maintain control.
2. I must cede control.
3. I must be loved.
4. I must be respected.

This monothematic approach brings with it a foolish vulnerability, easily leaving one devastated by tragic events.

One of God's many objectives in sanctification is to repopulate the psyche with a patchwork of themes all in submission to himself. In one context, the Christian is called to rightly submit to authority out of submission to Christ.[121] In another, he is called to lovingly exert authority, also in submission to Christ.[122] At times, he is exhorted to display God's patience and gentleness. At others, he is enlisted to exhibit something of God's righteous wrath.[123] This variation in responses, thus, functions as a kind of vanguard against the ravishing fires of idolatry, and exhibits the full-range of God's character traits. Sanctification, when in effect, begins the slow work of planting this patchwork within the psyche. One can see the hand of the original "forester" at work in those changed by Christ, so that when the "forest fire" of trials comes (as it must to produce new growth), it is not rampant and devastating, but controlled and directed in a heart that is rightly-populated.

As a final note, in his heart "reforestation," God tends to work by means of a sanctification triage, so that the most vital issues of sin and idolatry are addressed first, and so on down the line. As the heart is a labyrinth of sin, God focuses on particular chambers and passageways, one by one in his wise direction. For example, one who experiences an excruciating need for control as well as a fear of man, may find that God focuses one or the other issue first, depending on the pitfalls facing that

---

[121] Romans 13:1
[122] Ephesians 5:23
[123] Acts 16:18; Galatians 2:11

individual. God's objective is total resuscitation, but often that means determining which sin poses the most peril and working progressively. The wise counselor reads God's movement in the counselee's life, helping him to see the triage so as to cooperate with God's work.

The Dynamics of Sanctification: "From Menace into Muse and Muse into Wisdom"[124]

Ancient Greek temples were conceived with both the near and distant viewer in mind, and precisely designed to correct for optical illusions experienced by both. For example, temple columns are wider at the base so that standing next to them they appear perfectly straight. The entire foundation is also convex so that those on distant ships viewed the columns as taller and straighter. This, in a sense, serves as an analogy for sanctification; it concurrently corrects the "near" and "far" distortions of sin, the proximate relationships and the ultimate relationship.

The Consummation, Thomas Cole, 1836

Leviticus 5:15 mentions the sanctuary shekel, a standard weight held in the tabernacle against which the Israelites were to measure everything bought and sold. The sanctuary shekel was God's revealed standard and to deviate from it was an abomination in his sight. This is why Jesus was consumed with zeal as he witnessed the shekel being compromised;[125] God's absolute standard was being transgressed

---

[124] This phrase "from menace into muse and muse into wisdom" from an unknown source
[125] John 2:17

and imperiled. First Corinthians 6:19, 20, states that the believer's body is a temple of the Holy Spirit. This means that each person was designed as a vessel in which God is to be worshipped. Just as Jesus was zealous for the sanctuary shekel's integrity, so too, he is zealous for those who belong to him as a sanctuary in which he lives. With the same jealous rage that he drove out the money changers,[126] Jesus longs to drive out sin in those who are his. This is the nature of Jesus' love for his people, a love that sees, pursues, fights for, fights against, has hate within it, and will not rest until it replicates itself in the believer.

> "…cleansing her by the washing with water through the word, and to present her to himself as a radiant church, without stain or wrinkle or any other blemish, but holy and blameless." (Ephesians 5:26, 27)

For this reason, the Christian life is anything but boring. Rather, it is marked by participation in a cosmic, eternal, and heart-shaping mission. For the Christian, to be in Christ, is to participate in the work of the author of the universe himself, to gain some insight into his ways and movements, tides and seasons, to see life as he sees it. Nothing could ever make the pulse race faster. There is unbridled exhilaration in seeing God work in, and through, one's life, to both witness, and be a participant in, one's own heart change and, likewise, to be used to replicate that change in others.

> "Truly I tell you, if anyone says to this mountain, 'Go, throw yourself into the sea,' and does not doubt in their heart but believes that what they say will happen, it will be done for them." (Mark 11:23) ("Great things are done when men and mountains meet." (William Blake))
>
> "They will pick up snakes with their hands; and when they drink deadly poison, it will not hurt them at all; they will place their hands on sick people, and they will get well." (Mark 16:18)

Yet, most of this sanctification is silent, invisible, and extra-sensory in that it is done without one's direct notice. Like a vapor that migrates through a chamber, so too, sanctification is an incremental creep that may only become apparent on an annual scale.

God's singular objective is to move each Christian toward greater holiness and the elimination of sin. Thus, sanctification could be explained with an asymptotic inverse proportion graph. The x-axis (horizontal) represents sin, the y-axis (vertical), holiness. The Spirit prods and pushes the believer to the left, toward greater holiness. The non-Christian, on the other hand, invariably moves to the right growing more enmeshed with his sin, more complicit with rebellion. The Christian moves up the

---

[126] Matthew 21:12

curve (to the left) as he is sanctified, approaching greater holiness (the y-axis). The non-Christian moves down the curve (to the right) as he continues in his depravity, approaching greater sin (the x-axis).

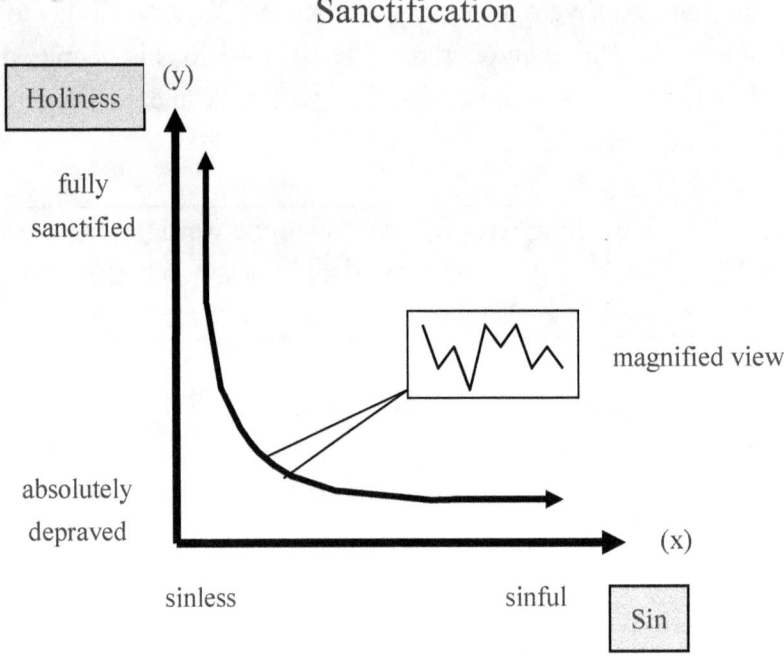

In this life a Christian never reaches perfect holiness, never experiences the complete elimination of sin. That is why the curve is asymptotic. As he draws closer to Christ day by day, the Christian approaches greater holiness, so that he is enabled to resist temptation. However, it is not until heaven that the asymptote reaches the y-axis, that sin is completely and conclusively eliminated. Additionally, while over a lifetime the inverse proportion graph appears to be a smooth curve, if one could magnify it on a daily scale one would see that it is far from smooth (see the "magnified view" above). In actuality, sanctification follows the pattern of a set of saw teeth with varied gullet and rake, jagged and inconsistent.

> If sanctification's actual path were traced visually it might follow that of one playing with a yo-yo while walking upstairs.[127] By this is meant that there are moments of marked progress, as well as regression back into well-worn sin patterns. However, there is a constant "magnetic" pull toward greater holiness so that, over time, the heart is progressively sanctified.
>
> "Therefore we do not lose heart. Though outwardly we are wasting away, yet inwardly we are being renewed day by day." (2 Corinthians 4:16)

---

[127] See Romans 7:15-21; the image of a "yo-yo walking upstairs" from Clair Davis, Westminster Theological Seminary, Philadelphia, Pennsylvania

The slope of the asymptotic curve may not be uniform for all people; some curves may be steeper, others shallower. The steeper the curve, the more submissive one is to Christ, and the more readily one abandons sin. The flatter the curve, the more stiff-necked and resistant one is to God's change process. Some Christians, broken and beaten down by the world, more quickly turn from their sin than others do. Some more readily renounce idols of the heart, while others continue to embrace them as trusted friends. Some humbly cooperate with the work of the Spirit, while others resist that work.[128] Some experience steady growth in holiness, while others show little discernable change. There is always a war within the Christian for the heart's territory, but some love the world and others more readily surrender to the Spirit's advances.

Another key concept is that everyone, whether Christian or not, is necessarily on an asymptotic inverse curve. Each person either moves toward greater holiness or toward more trenchant sin. No one is neutral, immobile, or static. Each is always in motion either toward the left, greater holiness, or toward the right, greater depravity. In this life no Christian ever reaches the y-axis (absolute holiness) and no unbeliever ever reaches the x-axis (absolute depravity). Those axes are reached either in heaven (irretrievable and absolute holiness) or in hell (irretrievable and absolute perdition).

My Wife's Lovers, Carl Kahler, 1891

In light of the asymptotic inverse nature of sanctification, the Christian could be

---

[128] 1 Thessalonians 5:19

likened to the quantum physics thought experiment "Schrodinger's cat" – simultaneously alive and dead.[129] The Christian is alive in Christ and dead to himself.[130] While he has received regeneration through God's Spirit, he has not yet fully availed himself of that gift. It is quite fascinating that, if observed, Schrodinger's cat would appear either alive or dead, but not both. Moment by moment, the Christian makes a decision to dwell in the Spirit, to live in Christ, or to continue in his sin anachronism, to either embrace the reality of his new creation, or to beat a path back to his Byzantine past.

> "May God himself, the God of peace, sanctify you through and through. May your whole spirit, soul and body be kept blameless at the coming of our Lord Jesus Christ. The one who calls you is faithful and he will do it." (1 Thessalonians 5:23, 24)

Augustine of Hippo's (354-430) *Confessions* (398) contains a four-part formulation for sin:[131]

1. In the Garden of Eden, Adam could sin (*posse peccare*).

2. After the fall, mankind can only sin (*non posse non peccare*).

3. Those in Christ can, not sin (have been given the ability not to sin) (*posse non peccare*).

4. Those in heaven will not be able to sin (*non posse peccare*).

In light of Augustine's formulation, the Christian, having been given the Holy Spirit's power to eliminate sin, approaches holiness. However, it is only in heaven that the Christian is completely and finally free from sin, so that sin becomes unimaginable. Thus, only in heaven does one finally reach the y-axis (perfected holiness).

> While clearly one cannot lose his salvation, can one lose his sanctification? Once sanctification is gained, it is a permanent advance in the Christian's life. However, the Christian makes a decision to live in the Spirit or in the flesh so that gains, while not lost, may lie fallow.

As a side note, since the unbeliever can only sin, one expects him to do so (deny Christ in every aspect of his life). However, while one fully expects the unbeliever to sin, one never accepts sin. It is always to be viewed as an aberration, as an abnormality, as an unwelcomed intrusion into the cosmic economy. Thus, sinful

---

[129] Schrodinger's cat is based on the 1935 thought experiment by physicist Erwin Schrodinger (1887–1961).
[130] Galatians 2:20
[131] For a more detailed analysis of sin see the second book in this series, *What Agreement Is There Between the Temple of God and Idols?: The Accidence of Sin and Idolatry*, chapter 4: "Hamartiology: Sin in All its Ignobility"

response to God is never casually overlooked. The counselor maintains an eagle-eyed vision for what freedom from sin, and life in Christ, would mean for each person he encounters.

The Bible's Metaphors for Sanctification[132]

The Bible speaks about sanctification in the following terms:

1. Engaging in warfare

Evil wages war within the sinner, making him a prisoner to sin.[133] Therefore, each is a slave to sin so that good does not dwell within him as an independent motivating force. This means that mankind cannot carry out that which is good in his own strength.[134] Romans 7:23 states, "But I see another law at work in me, waging war against the law of my mind and making me a prisoner of the law of sin at work within me."

A Dash for the Timber, Frederic Remington, 1889

While sin seized the opportunity afforded by the law and brought death,[135] for the Christian, sanctification progressively reverses that state of death. Sanctification is a war waged within the Christian's spirit incrementally freeing him from indwelling sin and evil.

---

[132] The following metaphors could be studied in conjunction with the second book in this series, *What Agreement Is There Between the Temple of God and Idols?: The Accidence of Sin and Idolatry*, chapter 5: "Metaphors for Sin"
[133] Romans 7:21-24
[134] Romans 7:14-20
[135] Romans 7:13

> For though we live in the world, we do not wage war as the world does. The weapons we fight with are not the weapons of the world. On the contrary, they have divine power to demolish strongholds. We demolish arguments and every pretension that sets itself up against the knowledge of God, and we take captive every thought to make it obedient to Christ. And we will be ready to punish every act of disobedience, once your obedience is complete. (2 Corinthians 10:3-6)

Sanctification as warfare invariably involves a measure of intense internal struggle. The Christian is at war with himself as he often reluctantly renounces idols. Rarely is a stronghold of pride or refuge from fear relinquished without a battle. Only the most tenderhearted renounces his will uncontested in the call to greater submission to Christ. The more one loves his sin, the more tenaciously he wages often bitter and exhausting war with his supposed enemy, God himself.[136]

When one earnestly desires to be free from his sin, and longs to abandon worthless idols, there is no longer conflict with God. As the Christian surrenders to God this potentiates rapid, joyful, and energized change. God will eventually have victory in the Christian's heart, but the question is, "Will the Christian cooperate?"

As a side note, the counselor does not change another's heart. Only God, by this Spirit, can do this. The counselor is used by God to facilitate the process, as a mouth-piece and as a tool to affect God's sanctifying work. As one of God's instruments in the war for supremacy of the heart, the counselor often ends up as collateral damage. As he speaks "truth to power" he will at times be the subject of *ad hominem* attack (often vigorous, when the counselor is most effective for God's purpose). What's more, often the tables will be turned so that the counselor, as he is used to draw the counselee to repentance, is labeled the "assailant." The counselor, as the more high-minded party in the counseling equation, overlooks such transgressions, maintaining a forehead like flint,[137] in order to achieve a much greater objective.

God, in his mercy, will wage battle with and against sin until he has accomplished his ultimate goal, the believer's complete purification. So evidence of an internal conflict is a sure sign that God is vigorously at work. A counselor's greatest concern is often when a Christian experiences no internal struggle at all. This is either a sign that the Holy Spirit does not inhabit this person (in which case he is not a Christian) or this person has thoroughly deluded himself into thinking that there is functionally no sin within himself, and therefore no need for change.[138] (There is, however, the remote possibility that the Christian is thoroughly in submission to Christ, in which case the

---

[136] Acts 26:14 alludes to this point.
[137] Ezekiel 3:9
[138] 1 John 1:8

Christian has lain down his arms.)

2. Removing covering

From the moment Adam and Eve fell, they sought covering as self-protection against God's judgment.[139] Sanctification seeks to remove the covering so that Jesus' glory can radiate from the believer's life.

> "But whoever lives by the truth comes into the light, so that it may be seen plainly that what they have done has been done in the sight of God." (John 3:21)

3. Cleaning the inside of the bowl

> "Then the Lord said to him, 'Now then, you Pharisees clean the outside of the cup and dish, but inside you are full of greed and wickedness. You foolish people! Did not the one who made the outside make the inside also?'" (Luke 11:39, 40)

Cup of Mead
Konstantin Makovsky, c. 1880

4. Renewal of the heart and mind

The Christian makes plans for sanctification. He carefully considers, in light of God's Word, each of the various manifestations of sin and evil he is likely to face and prepares his heart on how to respond.[140]

> "Do not conform to the pattern of this world, but be transformed by the renewing of your mind. Then you will be able to test and approve what God's will is—his good, pleasing and perfect will." (Romans 12:2)

5. Continual reevaluation and reassessment of the creation (external and internal)

---

[139] Genesis 3:7
[140] Jay Adams, *How to Overcome Evil* (Presbyterian and Reformed Publishing, 2010) 92, 93.

> "The heavens declare the glory of God; the skies proclaim the work of his hands. Day after day they pour forth speech; night after night they reveal knowledge. They have no speech, they use no words; no sound is heard from them. Yet their voice goes out into all the earth, their words to the ends of the world. In the heavens God has pitched a tent for the sun." (Psalm 19:1-4)

Jesus, as he hung on the cross, said, "Father forgive them, for they do not know what they are doing."[141] In this, Jesus did not excuse his executioners' sin as a mere informational oversight, nor as a cognitive aphasia. Jesus meant that his executioners could not possibly grasp the full-extent of their acts, that in murdering the Son of God they could not countenance all of the unfathomable implications and ramifications. Later Acts 17:30 reads, "In the past God overlooked such ignorance, but now he commands all people everywhere to repent." By "ignorance" Luke does not imply that a lack of knowledge is ever to blame for sin. The motive for sin would not be removed through more effective education, or through exposure to additional information. The Bible never sees sin as simply knowledge deprivation for which man is innocent.

> One of the assumptions behind progressivism or secular humanism is the notion that technology and education can solve every human problem. This is built on the notion that people are essentially good and, therefore, evil is overcome through human advancement. In reality, technology is incapable of eliminating foundational human problems because sin continually negates any supposed improvements. Any technological advance is rendered functionally inert through the machinations of sin.

6. Seeing with new eyes[142]

> "You are judging by appearances. If anyone is confident that they belong to Christ, they should consider again that we belong to Christ just as much as they do." (2 Corinthians 10:7)
>
> "I pray that the eyes of your heart may be enlightened in order that you may know the hope to which he has called you, the riches of his glorious inheritance in his holy people." (Ephesians 1:18)

7. Daily putting off – putting on

Jeremiah 25:5, 6 reads,

---

[141] Luke 23:34
[142] For an excellent treatment of this topic see David Powlison, *Seeing With New Eyes: Counseling and the Human Condition Through the Lens of Scripture* (Presbyterian and Reformed Publishing, 2003)

…Turn now everyone from his evil way and from the evil of your deeds, and dwell on the land which the LORD has given to you and your forefathers forever and ever; and do not go after other gods to serve them and to worship them, and do not provoke me to anger with the work of your hands, and I will do you no harm.

It is fascinating to note the causal connection between worshipping false gods and serving them. Action grows from worship. Thus, God commands putting off false worship, discarding it like an old garment, and putting on true worship, slipping into it like new clothing.

> "You were taught, with regard to your former way of life, to put off your old self, which is being corrupted by its deceitful desires; to be made new in the attitude of your minds; and to put on the new self, created to be like God in true righteousness and holiness." (Ephesians 4:22–24)

The Rod of Aaron Devours the Other Rods, James Jacques Joseph Tissot, c. 1902

8. Turning away from

The Greek for "repentance," *metanoia*, literally means "turning from" sin. The visual image is of one who formerly faced sin, to now turn his back on it.

> "Turn my eyes away from worthless things; preserve my life according to your word." (Psalm 119:37)

9. No longer "turning back to Egypt in their hearts"

> "But our ancestors refused to obey him. Instead, they rejected him and in their hearts turned back to Egypt." (Acts 7:39)

10. Refusal to "make gods who will go before us"

> "They told Aaron, 'Make us gods who will go before us. As for this fellow Moses who led us out of Egypt—we don't know what has happened to him!'" (Acts 7:40)

11. No longer demanding an inheritance

> "The younger one said to his father, 'Father, give me my share of the estate.' So he divided his property between them." (Luke 15:12)

> "…an inheritance that can never perish, spoil or fade. This inheritance is kept in heaven for you," (1 Peter 1:4)

12. Silencing a complaint

> "He says, 'Be still, and know that I am God; I will be exalted among the nations, I will be exalted in the earth.'" (Psalm 46:10)

13. Forgoing revenge[143]

> "Do not take revenge, my dear friends, but leave room for God's wrath, for it is written: 'It is mine to avenge; I will repay,' says the Lord." (Romans 12:19)

14. Stilling a storm

The same evil which produces a storm on the seas produces a storm in the heart of man. Thus, as Jesus demonstrated the power to still sea storms,[144] he likewise, demonstrated his power to still the heart's storms. Consider Hebrews 2:11, 12,

> Both the one who makes men holy and those who are made holy are of the same family. So Jesus is not ashamed to call them brothers. He says,

---

[143] For additional discussion of this topic see "The Transformative Power of Forgiveness" in chapter 4: "The Gospel as Inception Point: From Immorality to Immortality"
[144] Mark 4:39-41

'I will declare your name to my brothers;
In the presence of the congregation I will sing your praises.'

If Jesus will sing one's praises in front of the congregation, then one does not need to sing his own praises. If Jesus will one day honor one, then one does not need to honor himself. Appropriating this knowledge by faith works to still the heart's storms, so that there is a quietude about the Christian. He does not need to be noticed since Jesus promises to notice him.

15. Returning home

> "So he got up and went to his father. But while he was still a long way off, his father saw him and was filled with compassion for him; he ran to his son, threw his arms around him and kissed him." (Luke 15:20)

16. Pulling up the roots of sin

> "The ax is already at the root of the trees, and every tree that does not produce good fruit will be cut down and thrown into the fire." (Luke 3:9)

17. Breaking down the strong holds and cities of refuge (strong hold as defensive position)

> "Cain made love to his wife, and she became pregnant and gave birth to Enoch. Cain was then building a city, and he named it after his son Enoch." (Genesis 4:17)

18. Tearing down the high-places (high-place as offensive position)

> "He rebuilt the high places his father Hezekiah had destroyed; he also erected altars to Baal and made an Asherah pole, as Ahab king of Israel had done. He bowed down to all the starry hosts and worshiped them." (2 Kings 21:3)

19. Continual movement from a position of functional death to life

John 11:14-44 describes the death and resurrection of Lazarus. After Lazarus lay in the tomb for four days, John 11:43b recounts, "Jesus called in a loud voice, 'Lazarus, come out!'" When Jesus cried out to Lazarus, Lazarus' auditory nerves could not receive impulses; they were dead. However, Lazarus responded to Jesus' call and was raised to life because of God's grace.[145] This serves as a metaphor for the Christian's salvation. The Christian is in a state of spiritual death, so that the heart's "auditory

---

[145] Sinclair Ferguson, Westminster Theological Seminary, Philadelphia, Pennsylvania

nerve" cannot receive impulses. Only God's direct intervention can raise a corpse to life, can transform a sinner into a saint.

> "...so that, just as sin reigned in death, so also grace might reign through righteousness to bring eternal life through Jesus Christ our Lord." (Romans 5:21)

20. Producing good fruit

> "Produce fruit in keeping with repentance. And do not begin to say to yourselves, 'We have Abraham as our father.' For I tell you that out of these stones God can raise up children for Abraham." (Luke 3:8)
>
> "I am the vine; you are the branches. If you remain in me and I in you, you will bear much fruit; apart from me you can do nothing." (John 15:5)
>
> "But the fruit of the Spirit is love, joy, peace, forbearance, kindness, goodness, faithfulness, gentleness and self-control. Against such things there is no law." (Galatians 5:22, 23)

Lawn Tennis, Louis Prang, 1887

People almost never attain success through innate talent. Success at nearly any endeavor requires approximately 10,000 hours of practice. For instance, a star basketball player, concert violinist, skilled artist, or renowned surgeon must each invest 10,000 hours of practice before he masters his field. This is true regardless of one's degree of natural talent or intelligence.[146] I raise this issue to point out that, in similar fashion, sanctification requires practice. It is a daily exercise in renouncing sin and drawing close to God. Sanctification is not mastered in this life, but it can become more spontaneous as one actively cultivates worship of Christ. While 10,000 hours of practice may be necessary to excel at tennis, the Christian is called to make every moment of everyday his practice time.[147]

The Sanctification Shell Game

> I have listened attentively,
>   but they do not say what is right.
> None of them repent of their wickedness,
>   saying, 'What have I done?'
> Each pursues their own course
>   like a horse charging into battle.
> Even the stork in the sky
>   knows her appointed seasons,
> and the dove, the swift and the thrush
>   observe the time of their migration.
> But my people do not know
>   the requirements of the LORD.
> 'How can you say, 'We are wise,
>   for we have the law of the LORD,'
> when actually the lying pen of the scribes
>   has handled it falsely?
> The wise will be put to shame;
>   they will be dismayed and trapped.
> Since they have rejected the word of the LORD,
>   what kind of wisdom do they have?
> Therefore I will give their wives to other men
>   and their fields to new owners.
> From the least to the greatest,
>   all are greedy for gain;
> prophets and priests alike,
>   all practice deceit. (Jeremiah 8:6-10)

Tragically, Christians overwhelmingly hijack the concept of sanctification as an excuse for *not* changing. When confronted with sin, some use the concept of

---

[146] Malcolm Gladwell, *Outliers: The Story of Success* (New York: Little, Brown and Company, 2008)
[147] Deuteronomy 6

sanctification as an excuse for why they cannot renounce that sin. In their connivance, they may state that because sanctification is slow and progressive one needs time to renounce his sin fully. The twisted logic is that God has not yet initiated sanctifying work in him; therefore he is still in the grip of his sin until God acts. What this amounts to is falsely substituting the concept of progressive change for the call to immediate repentance.

Such an argument is a crafty means for excusing and shielding sin. For example, I confronted a young Christian man with a longstanding pattern of bald-faced lies and deliberate deception. After first seeking to cover his lies with further lies, he finally admitted his sin. When called to repentance and definitive renunciation of his sin, he stated that God's sanctifying work is slow, so it would take him a long time to turn from his sin. I sensed he was simply grabbing for an excuse to continue in his calumny unopposed. He sought to exploit the nature of sanctification to allow his transgression to continue for his own idolatrous pleasure.

Les Petites Menageres
Henry Jules Jean Geoffroy, d. 1924

Let's be clear. This man's habitual mendacity must end immediately; there is absolutely no excuse for this, or any sin, to continue. It is not his place to determine or gauge the rate of his own sanctification. His responsibility is to immediately turn from sin. (Of course, there will invariably be setbacks and failures in this change process.) This man has co-opted sanctification to suit his purpose, turning it into a covert ally in sin. He has redefined sanctification as a slow turning from his sin, at *his* own pace, rather than as a slow victory over his sin in *God's* power. (In reality, this man has denied his need for repentance altogether.) It is this redefining of sanctification which bears out the distinction between life in the Spirit and death in one's continued love for his sin.

Thus, as this example illustrates, sanctification can function as a double-edged sword. Shanghaiing the sanctification concept as a means to control one's rate of repentance is a cunning form of "playing God." It is a way to remain comfortable in sin, shielded from repentance, and exonerated through a seemingly plausible excuse for one's hardheartedness. The rate of sanctification is not for the Christian to determine; that is God's sole provenance. The Christian's call is to completely renounce sin here and now, and to continue that renunciation in the expectation that God's change can and will be actuated when repentance is genuine.

> How patient should the biblical counselor be concerning the sanctification process? This depends upon the person to whom he is ministering. There should be a tangible sense of progress at some juncture in the counseling process. However, this progress will often be slight, maybe even barely detectable. The counselor must seek God's wisdom in this matter, as there are no definitive scriptural guidelines.

The Allure of Caring Pragmatism:[148] "Solutions Are Not the Answer"[149]

To make a movie character appear to be in a particular location an actor stands in front of a green screen. Using chroma key effects an image is projected onto the screen but not onto the actor. Green surfaces receive the image but other surfaces do not. In this way, an actor can appear to be at a particular location when he is not.

One could think of God's work throughout history, both in aggregate and in specific, as a kind of "chroma key effect" for the heart, illuminating it for proper worship. God does not focus his light on situation; he zeroes-in on the heart. This selectivity and precision is like a kind of specialized projector of history which casts its image only on "heart surfaces," while bypassing others. God, in every event, every moment of every day, projects his image onto the heart.[150]

Biblical counseling, properly focused on changing the heart, thus, avoids the trap of what might be termed "caring pragmatism." Counseling is God's instrument to rescue the sinner from his foolishness and, in this way, is firstly about the restoration of one central relationship, the sinner with God. Biblical counseling is not about changing experiences, but about dealing with the fool in the middle of those experiences.[151] If counseling does not expose the idols of the heart then it tends toward a custodial

---

[148] The concept "caring pragmatism" from David Powlison, Westminster Theological Seminary, Philadelphia, Pennsylvania
[149] Richard Nixon (1913-1994)
[150] In Nathaniel Hawthorne's (1804-1864) short-story, "Ethan Brand" (1852), one night a man commits suicide by throwing himself into a blazing limekiln. In the morning, all that was found was his skeleton with his heart turned to lime. Hawthorne seemed to recognize the centrality and enduring nature of the human heart.
[151] Paul David Tripp, *Instruments in the Redeemer's Hand: People in Need of Change Helping People in Need of Change* (Presbyterian and Reformed Publishing, 2002)

approach, merely seeking to remedy seemingly broken situations. In the process, it inadvertently institutionalizes idols through strengthening the rationale for them.[152] If one gives the idolater better tools for dealing with his world, without confronting motive, he will just use those tools to enhance the effectiveness of his idolatry.

> Chinese philosopher Lin Yu Tang (1895-1976) wrote, "The secret of contentment is knowing how to enjoy what you have, and to be able to lose all desire for things beyond your reach." This is a prime example of the trap of caring pragmatism, simply trying to make life work. The "secret of contentment" is not about losing desire, but about assuming the right desire.

The counselor is not simply trying to make people's lives work for them. Such an objective will invariably prove an enemy to faith. The counselor seeks to help the counselee become more like Jesus, not to merely better imitate Jesus (although that is an aspect of sanctification), and not to simply admire Jesus from afar. Thus, the counselor does not offer sound principles, high morality, a cogent life system, or a set of logical procedures. The counselor does not offer a means for self-protection, rational explanations, or methods for relationship management. The counselor is fundamentally on a search and destroy mission to bring the holy and living God into direct contact with the sinner, that God (working through his Word) and the

The Judgment of Solomon
Henri-Frederic Schopin, 1842

---

[152] Paul David Tripp, *Instruments in the Redeemer's Hand: People in Need of Change Helping People in Need of Change* (Presbyterian and Reformed Publishing, 2002)

sinner (quickened by the Spirit) would personally meet, so that the sinner is brought to ongoing and sincere repentance. God's mission is always to target the heart, either to illuminate its sin and replace it with faith, or to illuminate its faith and expand it. This is God's chroma key effect.

> Anything which allows the unrepentant to find comfort in his sin is from Satan, as is anything which causes the penitent to lose comfort in his faith. The counselor, thus, seeks to avoid fostering a "prosthetic environment" in which debilitated idols are deliberately or inadvertently rehabilitated. The wise counselor seeks to confront, not accommodate, the heart's tyrants.

The Christian is called to do good to oppressors, to pray for those who mistreat him,[153] to entrust himself to the just Judge, to prefer and actively seek the good of others more so than his own good. These require the Christian to come face-to-face with the poverty of his own spirit, and his need for the transforming power of the gospel.[154] The wise biblical counselor does not prop up a "do-able law" for the counselee, a way to be self-righteous and outwardly compliant while never evaluating, confronting, impacting, and seeking to reform his heart. Therefore, the counselor holds out the promise of grace, a certain reassurance in "doing business with God,"[155] a reassurance that God is good as he exposes and purifies the heart. He can be trusted throughout the sanctification process to affect the right outcome.

Consider King Solomon's judgment of the two harlots in 1 Kings 3:16-28. Solomon was eminently wise concerning the heart's deception. He saw through posturing and emotions into motives; he discerned evil intent. Solomon recognized the tides and seasons of human desire, the cadence points of its worship. He rightly identified that people are desperate to overcome their finiteness problem, to devise methods and machinations to cover and prosper their most treasured idols. The wise counselor, therefore, targets that which God himself targets, and forsakes that which God himself forsakes. The counselor poses the right questions and listens with the right ears to discern the rhythms of the heart, its assumptions and loves, its pulsing drives.

But the counselor does not stop there, lest he leave a worship vacuum in his wake. As he uproots falsehood, he replaces it with truth. As he is used to remove idols, he replaces them with covenant commitment in the living God. As he labors to extricate sin, he hammers out newly-minted faith. Thus, counseling always presents the bad news followed by the good news. Mirroring the Bible's own pattern, counseling follows a "from-to" model for change.[156] More pointedly, the Bible is written as

---

[153] Matthew 5:44
[154] David and Sharon Covington, "Introduction to Bible Counseling" notes, 2004
[155] The term "do business with God" from Sharon Covington, Biblical Counselor
[156] This concept from David Powlison, Westminster Theological Seminary, Philadelphia, Pennsylvania

"indicative" followed by "imperative."[157] The indicative states the truth of sin and salvation, idolatry and regeneration, and the believer's new identity in Christ. The imperative is the ensuing action, changed lives working out salvation with "fear and trembling."[158]

To isolate a need, and to then try to meet that need, is to leave the individual untouched. The individual is to be challenged, ambitions are not to be left unchecked, and sin is to be addressed. The fibers of worship, of character, and of motive must be exposed. Therefore, the counselor either works in concert with God's plan of sanctification, or else hinders it. Put another way, the counselor either functions as a champion of the gospel, or as its de facto enemy. There is no neutral ground, no innocent error, and no cursory considerations which exclude the gravity and import of the gospel.

In this regard, it is crucial to note that the Holy Spirit does not directly reveal the answer to personal life questions such as whom to marry, which career to pursue, or how exactly to spend one's money. The Holy Spirit's work is always to prompt growth in holiness.[159] The Holy Spirit leads one in paths of righteousness so as to offer answers on issues of obedience, holiness, and God's larger objective to be glorified within the heart.[160] In the course of growth in holiness, one may receive wise counsel on marriage, career, finance, and a host of other matters. But these are secondary to heart transformation in the midst of those life events. Sanctification never occurs through merely addressing situation.

Consider Jesus' exchange with the Samaritan woman in John 4:15. In dealing with Jesus, she sought a change of situation, a way to avoid daily drawing water from the well. She desired relief from her circumstance. Jesus did not address her circumstance because he knew that was not her problem. He put the focus squarely upon her sinful heart.

> 'I have no husband,' she replied. Jesus said to her, 'You are right when you say you have no husband. The fact is, you have had five husbands, and the man you now have is not your husband. What you have just said is quite true.' (John 4:17, 18)

The Samaritan woman sought to conceal her heart, but Jesus exposed its intentions placing them squarely before her. John 4:10 states, "Jesus answered her, 'If you knew the gift of God and who it is that asks you for a drink, you would have asked him and he would have given you living water.'"

---

[157] This idea from David Covington, Biblical Counselor
[158] Philippians 2:12
[159] Romans 8:14; Galatians 5:18
[160] Jay Adams, *How to Overcome Evil* (Presbyterian and Reformed Publishing, 2010) 99.

Extracting Sanctification's Treasure

First to discover the Americas, the Spanish only sought quick pecuniary gain from the land's fabled gold and silver deposits. The British, however, faced with overpopulation, had the vision to colonize the Americas, to establish permanent settlements which would develop the land. Jamestown, while a British settlement, followed the pattern set by the Spanish; the town's inhabitants squandered their time clamoring for gold rather than planting fields. Consequently, as winter set in, most perished from starvation.[161]

This serves as a fitting metaphor for the way in which a biblical counselor operates. He does not focus on the quick fix but rather on a lifetime "colonized" by Christ. The counselor who hunts for a "golden" answer to the counselee's problems does nothing more than hold forth worthless pyrite. However, the counselor who sees into worship matters strikes into a "pay-dirt" of blessing.

> 'I bathed you with water and washed the blood from you and put ointments on you. I clothed you with embroidered dress and put leather sandals on you. I dressed you in fine linen and covered you with costly garments. I adorned you with jewelry: I put bracelets on your arms and a necklace around your neck, and I put a ring in your nose, earrings on your ears and a beautiful crown on your head. So you were adorned with gold and silver; your clothes were of fine linen and costly fabric and embroidered cloth. Your food was fine flour, honey and olive oil. You became very beautiful and rose to be a queen. And your fame spread among the nations on account of your beauty, because the splendor I had given you made your beauty perfect,' declares the sovereign Lord. (Ezekiel 16: 9-14)

Remember, in 1 Samuel 17:45-47, David ventured forth to fight Goliath. David entered into battle on account of a passion for God's honor. He did not consider his slight stature or lack of armor, but charged himself with upholding and exalting the name of his God.[162] David saw rank defiance and knew it must end. It is with this same passion for God's honor that the wise counselor enters into the lives of God's people. The counselor longs to dignify God's name in hearts he claims as his own.

---

[161] Peter Marshall and David Manuel, *The Light and the Glory: God's Plan for America: 1492-1793* (Revell Publishing, 2009)

[162] It is likely that a measure of selfish ambition also attended David's service as, in 1 Samuel 17:26, he first asked what would be done for the one who killed the Philistine.

Epilogue

Fra Hardanger, Hans Gude, 1847

Revelations Are Nothing Without Revolutions[1]

> "Do not seek to follow in the footsteps of the wise; seek what they sought." (Matsuo Basho)

People talk a great deal about change of one kind or another. They speak about being a better citizen, a kinder parent, a more loving spouse, or being more considerate of others. They speak about the need for civility, to show more gratitude, to care for the environment, or to conserve resources. This talk of improvement seems like an exercise that society must go through every so often, a kind of periodic self-conscious corporate guilt, a moment of faux-humility in admitting collective failings. However, invariably there is rarely any meaningful change. All of these good intentions routinely lead nowhere as society seems to degenerate year after year, generation after generation.

The bad news concerning the extent, depth, and devastation of indwelling sin is far worse than can ever be imagined. Each Christian, if he is honest with himself and God, recognizes that his inner condition lies in shambles, beset by marauding idols which

---

[1] The phrase, "Revelations are nothing without revolutions" from Greg Gutfeld's commentary "Small Government is Back" on Fox News, June 6, 2013.

ravage his heart and mind. He knows that daily he must burn and pulverize the legion golden calves which stampede through his heart. One must admit that, through protracted negligence, he rarely deals forthrightly with God, choosing rather to allow idols of his own making to stand unassayed, unopposed, and untoppled. This is why each is a desperate sinner critically in need of ongoing lifelong rehabilitation.

Where is hope for change? Only the gospel of Jesus Christ can truly change people, change what they worship, change what they love, change what they desire, so that they desire relationship with God, and submit to him in obedience. When Jesus personally enters into a life, it is progressively transformed so that prior empty promises of change are replaced with that which is hope-filled and permanent.

It is time to rebuild God's temple and, with that, to enter into a new reality, a shining epoch. There is tremendous joy in being searched and changed by God.[2] God longs to rebuild entire persons, to reclaim every aspect of human existence. In the same way that mankind is totally depraved, so too, in Christ he is totally redeemed (even more so, utterly and irretrievably redeemed). God longs to reclaim not just one's soul for eternity (justification), but one's heart, mind, emotions, body, will, purpose, and relationships (sanctification). There is no aspect of one's life that God does not long to ravish and rebuild in Christ. In working through this book, my hope is that this ravishing and rebuilding process has either begun for the first time, or has accelerated in you.

Romans 8:32 states, "He who did not spare his own Son, but gave him up for us all--how will he not also, along with him, graciously give us all things?" The Christian's life, as it harbors indwelling sin, is a pathetic contradiction. However, as the Christian continually renounces sin he steps into a hidden universe of "all things," one that comes to fruition in, and through, him. The Christian is daily being transformed by the renewing of his mind,[3] which renders the Christian an intensifying incarnation of Christ's character and likeness. Desire to know, and be known by, Christ. Desire that he would personally change you. Ask for the ancient paths.[4]

---

[2] Psalm 139:23
[3] Romans 12:2
[4] Jeremiah 6:16

- Appendix -

A Sanctification Plan

The Purpose of Sanctification

*L*ove the Lord your God with all your heart, and with all your soul, and with all your mind, and with all your strength. The second is this: 'Love your neighbor as yourself.' There is no commandment greater than these. (Mark 12:30, 31)

A Sample of Idolatry and Sin Patterns to be Addressed

God loves the sinner but hates his indwelling sin.[1] His objective is to free the Christian from the sin that still harangues him.[2]

Idolatry or Sin Pattern	Scripture to Consider
1. Hatred of God for not giving you what you want	Genesis 4:5–7 Psalm 2:1, 2 Ephesians 4:30, 31 Revelation 2:4
2. Hatred of your parents for their sins against you	Matthew 5:44; 6:14, 15; 7:1-5; 18:21-35 Mark 7:9-23 Luke 15:28-31
3. Apathy toward God's Word	John 5:38 Revelation 2:14; 3:16-19
4. A prayer life which makes demands of God	Ecclesiastes 5:2 Matthew 6:7
5. Hypocrisy in your service to the church	Philippians 1:15-17 Jude 8, 16
6. Fasting, suffering, and self-denial as another form of demand directed toward God	Matthew 6:16-18
7. Blame-shifting - excusing yourself for your own sin	Genesis 3:12, 13 Exodus 21:34
8. Seeking easy grace which merely makes you comfortable in your sin	Hebrews 10:26-31 Titus 2:11-14
9. Repenting of thoughts, words, or emotions, but not repenting of your idolatry	Judges 2:10–23 Luke 6:43–45

---

[1] Leviticus 26:30; 2 Corinthians 10:6
[2] 1 Corinthians 10:13; Galatians 5:1

	1 John 5:21
10. Constant focus on yourself, expecting others to serve you	Esther 1:15-18 Ezekiel 28:17
11. Seeking covering from anyone who might see you as you really are	Genesis 3:9, 10
12. "The spoiled brat syndrome" – lack of gratitude, lack of discipline, acting childishly, cultivating a complaining spirit	1 Corinthians 3:1, 2 1 Corinthians 10: 6–11 Jude 15, 16
13. Manipulating others for your own supposed need of self-esteem and self-confidence	2 Samuel 12:1-14
14. Drawing attention to yourself	Philippians 3:18, 19
15. Wanting others to meet your "needs"; seeking the praise of men	2 Samuel 15:4–10
16. Punishing those who do not meet your needs	2 Samuel 13:15 Hosea 6:6 Matthew 18:21-35
17. Hurtful words directed at others – especially when you are in emotional pain	Acts 13:45 James 3:2–12
18. Gossip – engaging in slander, destroying others' reputations, all under the guise of simply providing "factual information"	Isaiah 6:5
19. Raising up people as idols, and then tearing them down in hatred	Revelation 17:4, 16
20. Seeking out supposed counselors who are merely rallied allies in your sin – those who just assist you in your hatred of God	2 Timothy 4:3, 4
21. Pride in yourself, in your culture, or in your service to God	Luke 18:9–14 John 5:39, 40
22. Competition with others	1 Corinthians 3:3-9
23. Contempt for authority	Judges 21:25 Proverbs 5:12 2 Timothy 3:2
24. Hypersensitivity to perceived injustices	
25. Making your own pleasure, and personal plans for the future, your highest goal	Exodus 32:1–10 Haggai 1:2–5 Luke 14:25-34

At any moment you should know the sin that God is working on in you. You should be able to name that sin and explain your progress in repenting of it.

Qualities of a Wise and Faithful Christian

> "'Everything is permissible' – but not everything is beneficial. 'Everything is permissible' – but not everything is constructive." (1 Corinthians 10:23)

How Lisa Loved the King (Two), Edmund Blair Leighton, 1890

The Christian life is one of…	Scripture to Consider
1. Abiding in Christ	John 15:7 1 Corinthians 6:9–11
2. Moment by moment repentance	Matthew 12:36, 37 Ephesians 5:3
3. Daily Bible study and growth in understanding	Psalm 45:1 Proverbs 2:1–5
4. Daily and fervent prayer	Luke 18:1 Romans 8:26, 27 Ephesians 6:18
5. Simplicity – having few possessions, few activities, and little focus on oneself	Matthew 10: 9, 10 1 Timothy 6:7, 8
6. Humility – putting others before oneself, being willing to associate with those of low position, being willing to do the worst jobs and to sacrifice one's dreams for others	Isaiah 57:15 Micah 6:8 Philippians 2:3
7. A quiet spirit – teaching, serving, giving without being noticed; not drawing attention to oneself but drawing attention to Jesus	2 Timothy 3:10–11 1 Peter 3:4, 5
8. Purity	Job 31:1 Psalm 101:3 Romans 12:1

	1 Corinthians 4:4
	Ephesians 5:3
9. Joy in all circumstances – never complaining about anything	2 Corinthians 6:4–10 James 1:2, 3
10. Fearing nothing but God alone	Psalm 118:6 Proverbs 1:7
11. Enduring persecution and trials	Matthew 5:38–40 2 Timothy 3:12
12. Preparing oneself for battle with the spiritual forces of evil	Ephesians 6:10-18
13. Selfless regard for others – making oneself decrease so that Jesus can increase	John 3:30
14. Generosity	Matthew 5:42
15. Selflessly helping others to grow and repent	Ephesians 4:29 Philippians 2:4
16. Extending forgiveness and a demonstration of God's grace, recognizing that one is a sinner saved by grace	Luke 6:38 Ephesians 2:3, 8, 9
17. Seeing with new eyes - reinterpreting one's past through God's perspective	Romans 8:28 Hebrews 12:11
18. Recognizing that nothing in one's life exists for personal happiness	Romans 11:36 1 Corinthians 6:19, 20
19. Recognizing that time is precious - not making oneself "busy" but making oneself wise in the use of time	1 Corinthians 10:24 Ephesians 5:15, 16 Revelation 3:11
20. Working with passion and intention, while recognizing that one's work is for God and used by him for his glory	Ephesians 4:28 Colossians 3:23, 24
21. Pursuing a life goal which God has set	1 Corinthians 3:11–15 Hebrews 12:1-3

A Sanctification Plan[3]

1. Begin each day with quiet prayer.[4] This should be alone.

Prayer	Scripture
1. Praise and glorify God	Psalm 47
2. Thank the Father for Jesus and the salvation he wrought	Hebrews 12:2

---

[3] 1 Chronicles 22:15–19
[4] Matthew 6:6–13; for additional discussion of prayer see the case study "Prayer as Life-Blood of Relationship with Jesus" in the third book in this series, *The Days of Reckoning Are at Hand: From Fig Leaf to Olive Branch to Laurel Wreath*, chapter 4: "The Umbilicus of Personal Relationship with Christ"

3. Renew your faith in the gospel	Romans 1:16, 17
4. Ask for God's help in your daily repentance	John 14:14 Hebrews 7:23-28
5. Repent of anything that is not from him.	Psalm 51:10
a. Repent of any needs that you feel you must have met by people.	1 Corinthians 4:3
b. Repent of the fear of man.	Proverbs 29:25
c. Repent of pride.	Proverbs 16:18
d. Repent of living your life in your own way for your own glory.	Luke 18:18–30
e. Repent of every recognized source of idolatry.	Matthew 18:8, 9
6. Ask Jesus to be close to you, your source of wisdom, help, and love.	Psalm 46:1-3
7. Ask Jesus to change you, to bring down your self-protective fortress, to break your spirit, to invade your heart. Ask him to raze your strongholds, to take captive every thought, to put to death the old man and to prosper the new man.	2 Corinthians 10:5 Philippians 1:4-6
8. Praise God that there is hope for change, that he can accomplish anything in any life.	Galatians 1:13–16

Socrates Seeking Alcibiades in the House of Aspasia, Jean-Léon Gérôme, 1861

Sometime during the day:

1. Bible study[5]

    a. Work through the Bible in an organized manner. Take careful notes on what you are learning. Write down questions. Organize the information in a way that can help with your daily repentance. (If you organize what you are learning and put it into practice, it will take root in the heart.)

    b. Continually ask God to help you understand what you are learning. Ask him to make it come alive, to bring healing, to teach others truth. Ask him to make his Word live inside of you.

2. Serving others

    a. Serving others means putting aside your own will (forgetting yourself), and doing that which often only God will recognize.

    b. God must show you each day how to take up your cross and follow him, without regard for yourself.[6]

    c. Find a way to serve those who are of no benefit to you.[7] This is an act of self-sacrifice. It is a way to stop focusing on your "needs." This can involve serving others in ways they may never see, and for which they may never thank you.

3. Time to meet with other Christians[8]

    a. This is an opportunity to spend time with Christian friends each day (or non-Christian friends for the purpose of evangelism).[9]

    b. Your interaction with others should never be purely for your own personal pleasure. (People are not in your life for your personal happiness. They are placed there by God for his purpose of changing them and you, so that together you would glorify him.[10])

    c. Every interaction should be about advancing God's purpose in that person's life. This means that you have a vision and objective in each interaction.[11]

---

[5] Psalm 119:11
[6] Matthew 16:24
[7] Matthew 5:46–48
[8] Hebrews 10:25
[9] Matthew 5:13–16; 2 Timothy 4:2-5
[10] Acts 4:32, 33
[11] Proverbs 29:18

d. You are called to help each person move toward a specific God-directed goal. You are helping others change in Christ.[12]

The Reading Lesson
Knut Ekvall, d. 1912

e. You are asked to help others apply the gospel in new situations, to see their lives through the lens of the gospel.[13]

f. You are helping others to more deeply repent and experience grace in a way that was previously not possible. You are to model repentance and rich displays of grace,[14] continually expressing a spirit of gratitude toward God, and asking for forgiveness with each failure.[15]

4. Any study/interaction/activity/prayer that advances the following is valuable:

   a. Daily repentance with regard to faulty worship, not just for words, actions, or thoughts. Your repentance must be on the deepest level, reforming your worship.

   b. Daily growth in discipline

   c. Serving others in a way that denies yourself[16]

   d. Helping others to repent and experience grace

   e. Building relationships that advance God's purpose both in your life and in

---

[12] 2 Timothy 4:6
[13] 1 Corinthians 2:15, 16
[14] Isaiah 61:1
[15] 1 Thessalonians 5:18
[16] 2 Timothy 4:6

others' lives, while avoiding relationships that will implicitly deny that purpose.

    f. Anyone who keeps you accountable.
        i. Ask one or more friends to confront you with your faithlessness or neglect of God's Word (if they, in fact, see that).
        ii. A true friend will not allow you to rest in your sin.
        iii. A true friend encourages repentance and spurs you on to remain disciplined, focused, and growing in Christ.

> "When a dove associates with crows, its feathers remain white but its heart grows black." (German proverb)

5. In dealing with your parents:

    a. Pray before each interaction.[17] Ask God for very specific help in the situation you will face. Ask for wisdom to see your own sinfulness in the interaction, to love your parents in ways that you may not have expressed before, and to seek opportunities to help your parents change through teaching and even respectful confrontation.

    b. Before you talk to your parents remember your heavenly Father's goodness, protection, and love. This is the character of your true father.[18] Remember all his blessings and kindness to you. Be filled with the love of your true father – God the Father.

    c. Recount all the good your earthly parents have done for you.[19] They provided for you, taught you, and long to see you prosper. They sacrificed their time, money, and effort to raise you. They disciplined you. They forsook their own pleasures to serve you. They cried for you on many occasions. They planned for your future. They long for deeper relationship with you. Even "bad" parents have done many of these things. Rehearse your parents' goodness to you as a way to see more of your heavenly Father's goodness to you. God the Father allowed your earthly parents to do all of this to bless you. Even if your parents did all of these things for idolatrous reasons, they still did them. They still blessed you in more ways than you can imagine.

    d. Stop focusing your attention on what your parents are not, have not done, or have failed in. Focus your attention on your need to help your parents change, that they would know God, and repent of their transgressions against you and

---

[17] Psalm 46:1
[18] Matthew 6:32–34
[19] Matthew 7:9–11

others. (This will only come as you yourself first change, know God, and repent.)

e. Remember that your daily sin against God is infinitely greater than any sin your parents have committed against you.[20] You may help them to see their sin, while not condemning them (that is solely God's provenance). When you condemn and hate anyone you only "trample on the cross" and manifest the judgment that you rightly deserve, but Jesus took upon himself.[21]

7. Sunday

   a. Sunday should be completely set aside for worship, rest, and enjoying relationships.[22] Just be with God and rejoice in him.

   b. Do not work on Sunday.[23] Do not let the day become "busy."[24]

   c. Let Sunday be a day to celebrate the victories you experienced in your daily repentance. Let God be the focus of your praise, especially as it relates to your heart change.[25]

---

[20] Matthew 18:24-30
[21] Hebrews 10:29
[22] Genesis 2:3
[23] Exodus 20:8–11
[24] Isaiah 58:13, 14
[25] 1 Corinthians 15:57

The Author

James Venezia studied physics at Haverford College and later divinity and apologetics at Westminster Theological Seminary. He currently serves as a college instructor and pastor.

Please direct comments or questions concerning this series to jamesvenezia@yahoo.com.

The Christian Exceptionalism in Counseling Series™

The first book in the series, *Ask for the Ancient Paths,* is an introduction to biblical counseling.

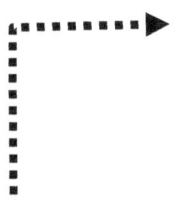

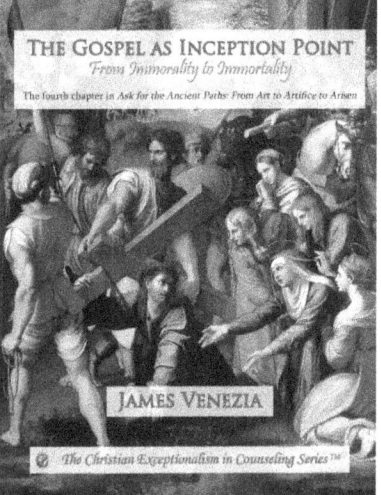

Chapter four (here shown in booklet form) offers a comprehensive exposition of the gospel.

Chapter eight presents a biblical response to psychology.

Chapter ten examines the concept of sanctification.

The second book, *What Agreement Is There Between the Temple of God and Idols?*, is an in-depth study of sin and idolatry.

Chapter two introduces the triple concept - the world, the flesh, and the devil.

Chapter six introduces the issue of idolatry.

Chapter nine investigates the modern construal of the self.

The third book, *The Days of Reckoning Are at Hand,* focuses on application of the biblical counseling paradigm.

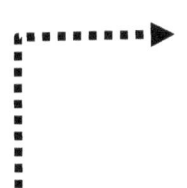

Chapter two analyzes suffering from a biblical perspective.

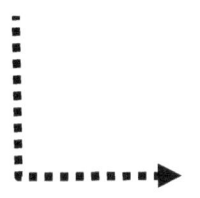

Chapter four argues for living relationship with Jesus himself, the life-blood of the Christian faith.

Chapter three considers the issue of loneliness.

A Summary of *The Christian Exceptionalism in Counseling Series*™

Textbook	Textbook Chapter in Booklet Form[1]
ASK FOR THE ANCIENT PATHS *From Art to Artifice to Arisen*	**THE GOSPEL AS INCEPTION POINT** *From Immorality to Immortality* (chapter 4)
	WHAT HAS JERUSALEM TO DO WITH VIENNA? *The Case Against Psychology* (chapter 8)
	THE THIRD-WAY OF SANCTIFICATION *From Abominable to Indomitable* (chapter 10)
WHAT AGREEMENT IS THERE BETWEEN THE TEMPLE OF GOD AND IDOLS? *The Accidence of Sin and Idolatry*	**UNCOVERING IDOLS OF THE HEART** *Make Us Gods to Go Before Us* (chapter 6)
	MARAUDING VISIGOTHS *The Autocratic Self* (chapter 9)
THE DAYS OF RECKONING ARE AT HAND *From Fig Leaf to Olive Branch to Laurel Wreath*	**SUFFERING** *The Kintsugi Objective* (chapter 2)
	THE HOBGOBLIN IN THE INGLENOOK *Assessing Loneliness* (chapter 3)
	THE UMBILICUS OF PERSONAL RELATIONSHIP WITH CHRIST (chapter 4)

All materials in *The Christian Exceptionalism in Counseling Series*™ available for sale through the CreateSpace eStore and Amazon.com bookseller

---

[1] Please note that each booklet is an exact reprinting of its respective chapter in the textbook.

Also by the Author

*The Lord Kept Vigil That Night:
An Exposition of the Parable of the Lost
Son*

*Rescue Us from the Present Evil Age: Array
of Hope*

*Hurl All Our Iniquities
into the Depths of the Sea*

www.ingramcontent.com/pod-product-compliance
Lightning Source LLC
Chambersburg PA
CBHW080527170426
43195CB00016B/2495